ARTIFICIAL NEURAL NETWORKS TECHNOLOGY

AF674907

MUNESH CHANDRA TRIVEDI
Asst. Professor (IT)
Institute of Management Studies,
Ghaziabad (NCR)

KHANNA BOOK PUBLISHING CO. (P) LTD.
Publisher of Engineering and Computer Books
4C/4344, Ansari Road, Darya Ganj, New Delhi-110002
Phone : 011-23244447-48 **Mobile:** +91-9910909320
E-mail : contact@khannabooks.com
Website : www.khannabooks.com

Dear Readers,

To prevent the piracy, this book is secured with HIGH SECURITY HOLOGRAM on the front title cover. In case you don't find the hologram on the front cover title, please write us to at *contact@khannabooks.com* or whatsapp us at +91-99109 09320 and avail special gift voucher for yourself.

Specimen of Hologram on front Cover title:

Enlargement Of Overlay

Moreover, there is a SPECIAL DISCOUNT COUPON for you with EVERY HOLOGRAM.

How to avail this SPECIAL DISCOUNT:

Step 1: Scratch the hologram
Step 2: Under the scratch area, your "coupon code" is available
Step 3: Logon to *www.khannabooks.com*
Step 4: Use your "coupon code" in the shopping cart and get your copy at a special discount
Step 5: Enjoy your reading!

Thanks,
Khanna Publishing House

Price: ₹ 550.00

ARTIFICIAL NEURAL NETWORKS TECHNOLOGY

Munesh Chandra Trivedi

Copyright © Khanna Book Publishing Co. (P) Ltd.

This book is sold subject to the condition that it shall not, by way of trade or otherwise, be lent, resold, hired out, or otherwise circulated without the publisher's prior consent in any form of binding or cover other than that in which it is published and without a similar condition including this condition being imposed on the subsequent purchaser and without limiting the rights under copyright reserved above, no part of this publication may be reproduced, stored in or introduced into retrieval system, or transmitted any form or by any means (electronic, mechanical, photocopying, recording or otherwise), without the prior written permission of both the copyright owner and the above mentioned publisher of this book.

ISBN: 978-81-90744-85-0

Edition: 2025

Published by:

Khanna Book Publishing Co. (P) Ltd.
4C/4344, Ansari Road, Darya Ganj, New Delhi-110 002
Phone: 011-23244447-48 **Mobile:** +91-9910909320
E-mail: contact@khannabooks.com

Printed in Bharat.

Dedicated to My Parents
&
My wife Alpana

PREFACE

Neural network is a subject that is an integral component of the ubiquitous soft computing paradigm. An in depth understanding and appreciations of the field requires some background knowledge of the neuroscience, mathematics and computer programming. This is a difficult task. The " Artificial Neural Network Technology" aims to achieve a balanced of these areas. Artificial Neural Network Technology is the discipline that attempts to provide methods to handle this complexity and enable us to produce reliable real time systems with maximum productivity.

This book is for students who have not had previous training in Artificial Neural Network Technology, and is suitable for a one-semester course. This book is for students who have not had previous training in Neural Network, and is suitable for a one-semester course. This book covers Gujrat Technical University Gandhi Nagar, Rajasthan Technical University Kota, J.R.N. Rajasthan Vidhyapeeth University, Udaipur, M.P.Technical & U.P. Technical University Lucknow, and B.Tech. & M.C.A.syllabus. This is also useful for a project based introducing course in software engineering in which both the students and the instructor can follow the chapters in the order given both in the lectures as well as in the project.

This is also useful for a project based introducing course in Artificial Neural Network Technology in which both the students and the instructor can follow the chapters in the order given both in the lectures as well as in the project.

ACKNOWLEDGEMENT

At the various stages in the writing of this book, a number of people have given invaluable comments on the manuscript. In this regard, I owe a debt of gratitude to Prof B.S. Garg Chancellor, Prof Lokesh Bhatt Vice-Chancellor J.R.N. Rajasthan Vidhyapeeth University, Udaipur & Dr. R.K. Bharadwaj, Director I.M.S. Ghaziabad.

I am also grateful to the Dr. Ashok Patel Director M.C.A. Programme North Gujrat University Patan, Dr. Sanjay Sah Director M.C.A. Programme Kadi M.C.A. College, Kadi, Dr. Neeraj Bharadwaj Director M.C.A. Programme M.D.S University Ajmer and Mr. Tarun Shrimali J.R.N. Rajasthan Vidhyapeeth University, Udaipur for his encouragement at the very outset of this project. An excellent Support in writing this book was received from Dr. S.S. Sarangedevot, Director (Computer Science & IT) J.R.N. Rajasthan Vidhyapeeth University, Udaipur.

Just as one does not thank himself, expressing gratitude to one's wife in public is not a Hindu custom. For the wife is considered a part of the husband, and her co-authorship is Tacitly assumed in any book her husband writer? There is little doubt that without Alpana's help this book would not have been possible.

Munesh Chandra Trivedi

Table of Contents

Chapter No. 1

Introduction And Purpose

A Neural Network is a computing paradigm that is loosely modeled after critical structures of the brain. It consists of interconnected processing elements called neurons that work together to produce an output *function. The output of a neural network relies on the cooperation* of the individual neurons within the network to operate. Processing of information by neural networks is often done in parallel rather than in series (or sequentially). Since it relies on its member neurons collectively to perform its function, a unique property of a neural network is that it can still perform its overall function even if some of the neurons are not functioning. That is, they are very robust to error or failure (i.e., fault tolerant).

Neural Network is sometimes used to refer to a branch of computational science that uses neural networks as models to either simulate or analyze complex phenomena and/or study the principles of operation of neural networks analytically. It addresses problems similar to artificial intelligence (AI) except that AI uses traditional computational algorithms to solve problems whereas neural networks use 'networks of agents' (software or hardware entities linked together) as the computational architecture to solve problems. Well-designed neural networks are trainable systems that can often "learn" to solve complex problems from a set of exemplars and generalize the "acquired knowledge" to solve unforeseen problems, i.e., they are self-adaptive systems.

Traditionally, a Neural Network is used to refer to a network of biological neurons. In modern usage, the term is often used to refer to artificial neural networks, which are composed of artificial neurons. Thus the term 'Neural Network' has two distinct connotations:

1. Biological Neural Networks are made up of real biological neurons that are connected or functionally-related in the

peripheral nervous system or the central nervous system. In the field of neuroscience, they are often identified as groups of neurons that perform a specific physiological function in laboratory analysis.

2. Artificial neural networks are made up of interconnecting artificial neurons (usually simplified neurons) designed to model (or mimic) some properties of biological neural networks. Artificial neural networks can be used to model the modes of operation of biological neural networks, whereas cognitive models are theoretical models that mimic cognitive brain functions without necessarily using neural networks while artificial intelligence are well-crafted algorithms that solve specific intelligent problems (such as chess playing, pattern recognition, etc.) without using neural network as the computational architecture.

1.1 Definition

Inspired by the structure of the brain, a Neural Network consists of a set of highly interconnected entities, called nodes or units. Each unit is designed to mimic its biological counterpart, the neuron. Each accepts a weighted set of inputs and responds with an output. Figure 1presents a picture of one unit in a neural network.

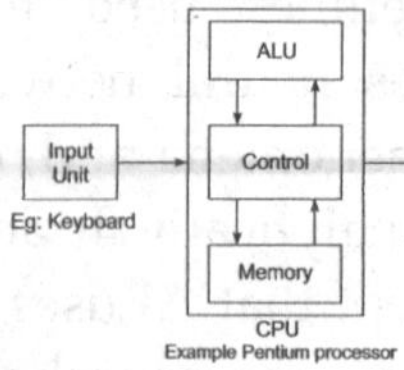

Figure. 1. A single unit in a neural network.

Let X = (x1, x2, ..., xn), where the xi are real numbers, represent the set of inputs presented to the unit U. Each input has an associated weight that represents the strength of that particular connection. Let W = (w1,w2,..., wn), with wi real, represent the weight vector corresponding to the input vector X. Applied to U, these weighted inputs produce a net sum at U given by

S = SUM(wi*xi) = W.V.

The state of a unit U is represented by a numerical value A, the activation value of U. An activation function f determines the new activation value of a unit from the net sum to the unit and the current activation value. In the simplest case, f is a function of only the net sum, so A = f(S). The output at unit U is in turn a function of A, usually taken to be just A.

A neural network is composed of such units and weighted unidirectional connections between them. In some neural nets, the number of units may be in the thousands. The output of one unit typically becomes an input for another. There may also be units with external inputs and/or outputs. Figure 2 shows one example of a possible neural network structure.

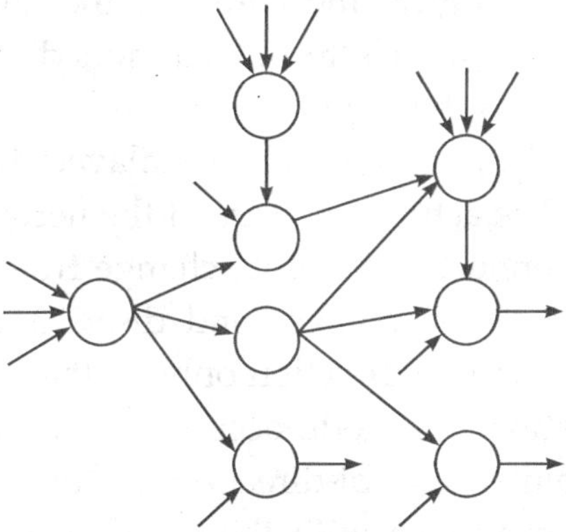

Figure 2. An example of a neural network structure.

For a simple linear network, the activation function is a linear function, so that

$f(cS) = cf(S)$,

$f(S1 + S2) = f(S1) + f(S2)$.

Another common form for an activation function is a threshold function, thc activation value is 1 if the net sum S is greater than a given constant T, and is 0 otherwise.

History of the Neural Network Analogy

The concept of neural networks started in the late-1800s as an effort to describe how the human mind performed. These ideas started being applied to computational models with the Perceptron.

In early 1950s Friedrich Hayek was one of the first to posit the idea of spontaneous order in the brain arising out of decentralized networks of simple units (neurons). In the late 1940s, Donald Hebb made one of the first hypotheses for a mechanism of neural plasticity (i.e. learning), Hebbian learning. Hebbian learning is considered be a 'typical' unsupervised learning rule and it (and variants of it) was an early model for long term potentiation.

The Perceptron is essentially a linear classifier for classifying data specified by parameters and an output function f = w'x + b. Its parameters are adapted with an ad-hoc rule similar to stochastic steepest gradient descent. Because the inner product is linear operator in the input space, the Perceptron can only perfectly classify a set of data for which different classes are linearly separable in the input space, while it often fails completely for non-separable data. While the development of the algorithm initially generated some enthusiasm, partly because of its apparent relation to biological mechanisms, the later discovery of this inadequacy caused such models to be abandoned until the introduction of non-linear models into the field.

The Cognitron (1975) was an early multilayered neural network with a training algorithm. The actual structure of the network and the methods used to set the interconnection weights change from one neural strategy to another, each with its advantages and disadvantages. Networks can propagate information in one direction only, or they can bounce back and forth until self-activation at a node occurs and the network settles on a final state. The ability for bi-directional flow of inputs between neurons/nodes was produced with the Hopfield's network (1982), and specialization of these node layers for specific purposes was introduced through the first hybrid network.

The backpropagation network was probably the main reason behind the repopularisation of neural networks after the publication of "Learning Internal Representations by Error Propagation" in 1986. The original network utilised multiple layers of weight-sum units of the type f = g(w'x + b), where g was a sigmoid function or logistic function such as used in logistic regression. Training was done by a form of stochastic steepest gradient descent. The employment of the chain rule of differentiation in deriving the appropriate parameter updates results in an algorithm that seems to 'backpropagate errors', hence the nomenclature. However it is essentially a form of gradient descent. Determining the optimal parameters in a model of this type is not trivial, and steepest gradient descent methods cannot be relied upon to give the solution without a good starting point. In recent times, networks with the same architecture as the backpropagation network are referred to as Multi-Layer Perceptrons. This name does not impose any limitations on the type of algorithm used for learning.

The backpropagation network generated much enthusiasm at the time and there was much controversy about whether such learning could be implemented in the brain or not, partly because a mechanism for reverse signalling was not obvious at the time, but most importantly because there was no plausible source for the 'teaching' or 'target' signal.

In more recent times, neuroscientists have successfully made some associations between reinforcement learning and the dopamine system of reward. However, the role of this and other neuromodulators is still under active investigation.

Neural networks and neuroscience

Theoretical and computational neuroscience is the field concerned with the theoretical analysis and computational modeling of biological neural systems. Since neural systems are intimately related to cognitive processes and behaviour, the field is closely related to cognitive and behavioural modeling.

The aim of the field is to create models of biological neural systems in order to understand how biological systems work. To gain this understanding, neuroscientists strive to make a link between observed biological processes (data), biologically plausible mechanisms for neural processing and learning (biological neural network models) and theory (statistical learning theory and information theory).

Types of models

Many models are used in the field, each defined at a different level of abstraction and trying to model different aspects of neural systems. They range from models of the short-term behaviour of individual neurons, through models of how the dynamics of neural circuitry arise from interactions between individual neurons, to models of how behaviour can arise from abstract neural modules that represent complete subsystems. These include models of the long-term and short-term plasticity of neural systems and its relation to learning and memory, from the individual neuron to the system level.

The brain, neural networks and computers

While historically the brain has been viewed as a type of computer, and vice-versa, this is true only in the loosest sense. Computers do not provide us with accurate hardware for describing the brain (even though it is possible to describe a logical process as a computer program, or to simulate a brain using a computer) as they do not possess the parallel processing architectures that have been described in the brain. Even when speaking of multiprocessor computers, the functions are not nearly as distributed as in the brain.

Neural networks, as used in artificial intelligence, have traditionally been viewed as simplified models of neural processing in the brain, even though the relation between this model and brain biological architecture is very much debated. To answer this question, Marr has proposed various levels of analysis which provide us with a plausible answer for the role of neural networks in the understanding of human cognitive functioning.

The question of what is the degree of complexity and the properties that individual neural elements should have in order to reproduce something resembling animal intelligence is a subject of current research in theoretical neuroscience.

Historically computers evolved from Von Neumann architecture, based on sequential processing and execution of explicit instructions. On the other hand origins of neural networks are based on efforts to model information processing in biological systems, which are primarily based on parallel processing as well as implicit instructions based on recognition of patterns of 'sensory' input from external sources. In other words, rather than sequential processing and execution, at their very heart, neural networks are complex statistic processors.

Neural networks and Artificial intelligence

An artificial neural network (ANN), also called a simulated neural network (SNN) or commonly just neural network (NN) is an interconnected group of artificial neurons that uses a mathematical or computational model for information processing based on a connectionist approach to computation. In most cases an ANN is an adaptive system that changes its structure based on external or internal information that flows through the network.

In more practical terms neural networks are non-linear statistical data modeling tools. They can be used to model complex relationships between inputs and outputs or to find patterns in data.

1.2 Single-Layer Linear Networks

A single-layer neural network consists of a set of units organized in a layer. Each unit Ui receives a weighted input xj with weight wji. Figure 3 shows a single-layer linear model with m inputs and n outputs.

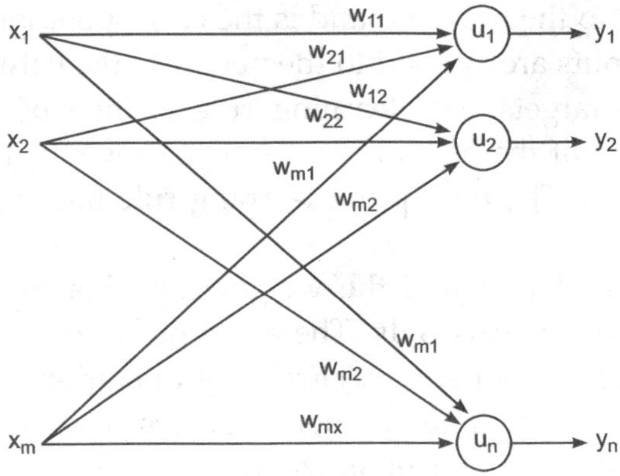

Figure 3. A single-layer linear model.

Let X = (x1, x2, ... ,xm) be the input vector and let the activation function f be simply, so that the activation value is just the net sum to a unit. The m x n weight matrix is

$$W = \begin{pmatrix} w11 & w12 & w1n \\ w21 & 22 & w2n \\ \vdots & & \\ wy & wmz & wwx \end{pmatrix}$$

Thus the coutput y_t at unit U_t is

$$yk = (w1k, w2k, \dots, wmx) \begin{pmatrix} x1 \\ x2 \\ \vdots \\ x_m \end{pmatrix}$$

so the output vector $\overline{Y} = (y1, y2, \dots, yn)^T$ is given by

$$\overline{Y}_{n \times 1} = W_{n \times x}^T \overline{X}_{m \times 1}$$

so the output vector Y = (y1, y2, ... , yn)'I' is given by

Y = WT*X

1.3 Learning Rules

A learning rule is defined as a procedure for modifying the weights and biases of a network. (This procedure can also be referred to as a training algorithm.) The learning rule is applied to train the network to perform some particular task. Learning rules in this toolbox fall into two broad categories: supervised learning, and unsupervised learning.

In supervised learning, the learning rule is provided with a set of examples (the training set) of proper network behavior

* $\{p_1, t_1\}, \{p_2, t_2\}, \dots, \{p_Q, t_Q\}$

where is an input to the network, and is the corresponding correct (target) output. As the inputs are applied to the network, the network outputs are compared to the targets. The learning rule is then used to adjust the weights and biases of the network in order to move the network outputs closer to the targets. The perceptron learning rule falls in this supervised learning category.

In unsupervised learning, the weights and biases are modified in response to network inputs only. There are no target outputs available. Most of these algorithms perform clustering operations. They categorize the input patterns into a finite number of classes. This is especially useful in such applications as vector quantization.

A simple linear network, with its fixed weights, is limited in the range of output vectors it can associate with input vectors. For example, consider the set of input vectors (xl,x2), where each xi is either 0 or 1. No simple linear network can produce outputs as shown in Table 1, for which the output is the boolean exclusive-or (XOR) of the inputs. Implementing the XOR function is a classic problem in neural networks, as it is a sub problem of other more complicated problems.

Table 1.
Inputs and outputs for a neural net that implements the boolean exclusive-or (XOR) function.

x_1	x_2	**output** y
0	0	0
0	1	1
1	0	1
1	1	0

Hence, in addition to the network topology, an important component of most neural networks is a learning rule. A learning rule allows the network to adjust its connection weights in order to associate given input vectors with corresponding output vectors. During training periods, the input vectors are repeatedly presented, and the weights are adjusted according to the learning rule, until the network learns the desired associations, i.e., until Y = WT*X. It is this ability to learn that is one of the most attractive features of neural networks.

A single-layer model usually uses either the Hebb rule or the delta rule.

In the Hebb rule, the change dij in the weights is calculated as follows.

Let X = (x1,...,xm), Y = (y1,...yn) be the input and output vectors that we wish to associate. In each training iteration, the weights are adjusted by

dwij = e*xi*yj,

where e is a constant called the learning rate, usually taken to be the reciprocal of the number of training vectors presented. During the training period, a number of such iterations can be made, letting the (X,Y) pairs vary over the associations to be learned. A network using the Hebb rule is guaranteed to be able to learn associations for which the set of input vectors are orthogonal .A disadvantage of the Hebb rule is that if the input vectors are not mutually orthogonal, interference may occur and the network may not be able to learn the associations.

The delta rule was developed to address the deficiencies of the Hebb rule. Under the delta rule, the change in weight is

Dwij = r*xi*(tj - yj),

Where r- is the learning rate,

Tj - is the target output, and

Yj- is the actual output at unit Uj.

The delta rule changes the weight vector in a way that minimizes the error, the difference between the target output and the actual output. It can be shown mathematically that the delta rule provides a very efficient way to modify the initial weight vector toward the optimal one i.e. the one that corresponds to minimum error. It is possible for a network to learn more associations with the delta rule than with the Hebb rule. McClelland and Rumelhart et al. prove that a network using the delta rule can learn associations whenever the inputs are linearly independent.

1.4. Threshold Networks

A perceptron is a single-layer network with a activation function given by

f(S) = {1 if S T

{0 Otherwise

Where T is some constant. Because it uses a threshold function, such a network is called a threshold network.

But even though it uses a nonlinear activation function, the perceptron still cannot implement the XOR function. That is, a perceptron is not capable of responding with an output of 1 whenever it is presented with input vectors (0,1) or (1,0), and responding with output 0 otherwise.

The impossibility proof is easy. There would have to be a weight vector T = (w1lXwl2) for which the scalar product net sum

S = W*X = w11*x1 + w21*x2

Leads to an output of 1 for input (0,1) or (1,0), and 0 otherwise (see Table 2).

Table 2.
Inputs, net sum, and desired output for a perceptron that implements the Boolean exclusive or (XOR) function.

x_1	x_2	S	output
0	0	0	0
0	1	w_1	1
1	0	w_2	1
1	1	$w_1 + w_2$	0

Now, the line with equation w11*x1 + w21*x2 = T divides the x1x2-plane into two regions, as illustrated in Figure 4.

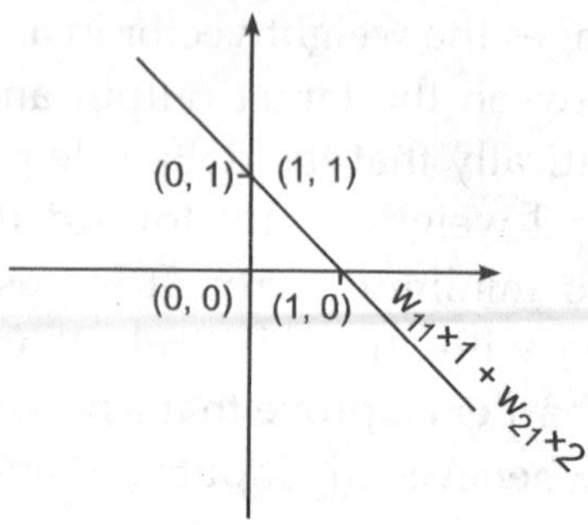

Figure 4. The graph of $w + w = T$

Input vectors that produce a net sum S greater than T lie on one side of the line, while those with net sum less than T lie on the other side. For the network to represent the XOR function, the inputs (1,1) and (0,0), with sums (wl+W2) and 0, must produce outputs on one side, while the inputs (1,0) and (0,1), with sums wl and w2, must produce outputs on the other side. But if wl T and w2 T, then w1+w2 T; and similarly for . So a perceptron cannot represent the XOR function.

In fact, there are many other functions that cannot be represented by a single-layer network with fixed weights. While such limitations were the cause of a temporary decline of interest in the perceptron and in neural networks in general, the perceptron laid foundations for much of the later work in neural networks. The limitations of single-layer networks can, in fact, be overcome by adding more layers.

1.5 Multilayer Networks

A multilayer network has two or more layers of units, with the output from one layer serving as input to the next. The layers with no external output connections are referred to as hidden layers (Figure 5).

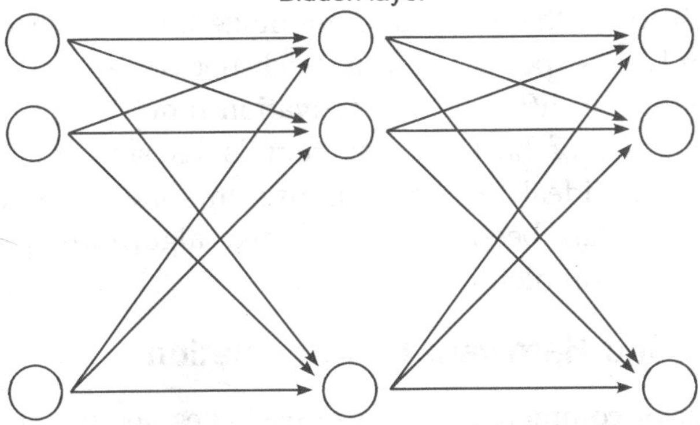

Figure 5. A Multilayer Networks

However, any multilayer system with fixed weights that has a linear activation function is equivalent to a single-layer linear system. for example, the case of a two-layer linear system. The input vector to the first layer is X, the output Y = W1*X of the first layer is given as input to the second layer, and the second layer produces output Z = W2*Y. Hence Z = W2*(W1*X) = (W2*W1)*X.

Consequently, the system is equivalent to a single-layer network with weight matrix W = W2*W1. By induction, a linear system with any number n of layers is equivalent to a single-layer linear system whose weight matrix is the product of the n intermediate weight matrices.

On the other hand, a multilayer system that is not linear can provide more computational capability than a single-layer system. For instance, the problems encountered by the perceptron can be overcome with the addition of hidden layers.Multilayer networks have proven to be very powerful. In fact, any boolean function can be implemented by such a network.

1.6 Multilayer Networks with Learning

No learning algorithm had been available for multilayer networks until Rumelhart, Hinton, and Williams introduced the back propagation training algorithm, also referred to as the generalized delta rule. At the output layer, the output vector is compared to the expected output. If the difference is zero, no changes are made to the weights of the connections. If the difference is not zero, the error is calculated from the delta rule and is propagated back through the network. The idea, similar to that of the delta rule, is to adjust the weights to minimize the difference between the real output and the expected output. Such networks can learn arbitrary associations by using differentiable activation functions.

One drawback of back propagation is its slow rate of learning, making it less than ideal for real-time use. In spite of some drawbacks, back propagation has been a widely used algorithm, particularly in pattern recognition problems.

1.7 Software and Hardware Implementation

A number of commercial software packages are available, including some for microcomputers. Many programs feature a neural-network development system that supports several different neural types, to allow the user to build, train, and test networks for different applications.

The training of a neural network through software simulation demands intensive mathematical computation, often leading to excessive training times on ordinary general-purpose processors. A neural network accelerator board, such as the NeuroBoard developed to support the NeuroShell package, can provide high-speed performance. NeuroBoard's speed is up to 100 times that of a 20 MHz 30386 chip with a math co-processor. Another alternative is a chip that implements neural networks in hardware; both analog and digital implementations are available. These chips, however, do not have the capabilities of on-chip learning. In both cases, the chip is interfaced with a software simulation package, based on back propagation, which is used for training and adjustment of weights; the adjusted weights are then transferred to the chip.

1.8 Applications of neural networks

Neural networks have been applied to a wide variety of different areas including speech synthesis, pattern recognition, diagnostic problems, medical illnesses, robotic control and computer vision.

Character Recognition - The idea of character recognition has become very important as handheld devices like the Palm Pilot are becoming increasingly popular. Neural networks can be used to recognize handwritten characters.

Image Compression - Neural networks can receive and process vast amounts of information at once, making them useful in image compression. With the Internet explosion and more sites using more images on their sites, using neural networks for image compression is worth a look.

Stock Market Prediction - The day-to-day business of the stock market is extremely complicated. Many factors weigh in whether a given stock will go up or down on any given day. Since neural networks can examine a lot of information quickly and sort it all out, they can be used to predict stock prices.

Traveling Salesman's Problem - Interestingly enough, neural networks can solve the traveling salesman problem, but only to a certain degree of approximation.

Medicine, Electronic Nose, Security, and Loan Applications - These are some applications that are in their proof-of-concept stage, with the acception of a neural network that will decide whether or not to grant a loan, something that has already been used more successfully than many humans.

Miscellaneous Applications - These are some very interesting (albeit at times a little absurd) applications of neural networks.

Application of Feed-forward networks - character recognition:-

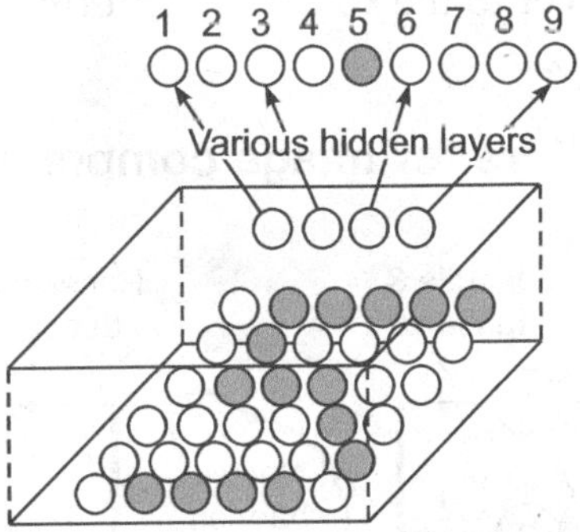

Fig. 6 : A feed-forward network for character recognition

The idea of using feedforward networks to recognize handwritten characters is rather straightforward. As in most supervised training, the bitmap pattern of the handwritten character is treated as an input, with the correct letter or digit as the desired output. Normally such programs require the user to train the network by providing the program with their handwritten patterns.

Neural Networks and Image Compression

Because neural networks can accept a vast array of input at once, and process it quickly, they are useful in image compression.

Bottleneck-type Neural Net Architecture for Image Compression

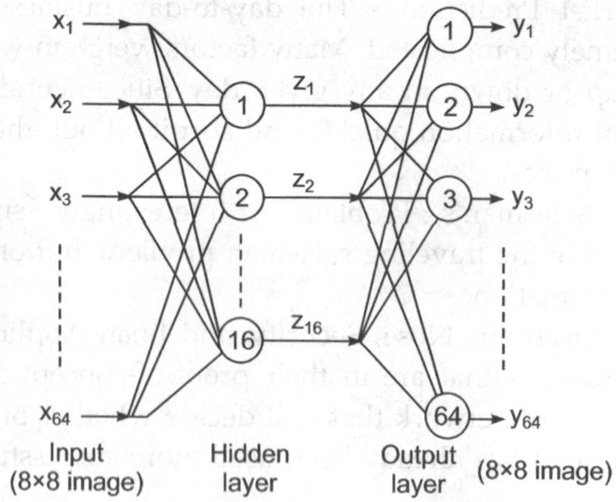

Here is a neural net architecture suitable for solving the image compression problem. This type of structure is referred to as a bottleneck type network, and consists of an input layer and an output layer of equal sizes, with an intermediate layer of smaller size in-between. The ratio of the size of the input layer to the size of the intermediate layer is - of course - the compression ratio.

Bottleneck architecture for image compression over a network or over time

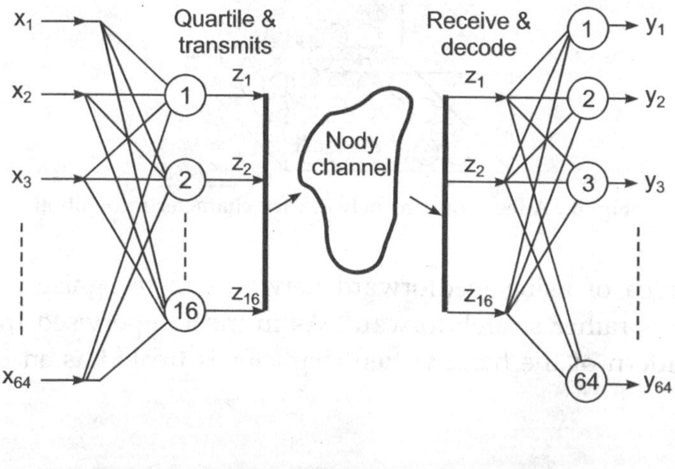

This is the same image compression scheme, but implemented over a network. The transmitter encodes and then transmits the output of the hidden layer, and the receiver receives and decodes the 16 hidden outputs to generate 64 outputs.

This is the same image compression scheme, but implemented over a network. The transmitter encodes and then transmits the output of the hidden layer, and the receiver receives and decodes the 16 hidden outputs to generate 64 outputs.

Pixels, which consist of 8 bits, are fed into each input node, and the hope is that the same pixels will be outputted after the compression has occurred. That is, we want the network to perform the identity function.

Actually, even though the bottleneck takes us from 64 nodes down to 16 nodes, no real compression has occurred. The 64 original inputs are 8-bit pixel values. The outputs of the hidden layer are, however, decimal values between -1 and 1. These decimal values can require a possibly infinite number of bits.

Quantization for Image Compression

We do not need to be able to represent every possible decimal value, but instead can clump the possible values into, say, 3-bit units. 8 possible binary codes can be formed: 000, 001, 010, 011, 100, 101, 110, 111, and each of these codes represents a range of values for a hidden unit output. For example, when a hidden value is between -1.0 and -.75, the code 000 is transmitted.

Hence, the image is compressed from 64 pixels * 8 bits each = 512 bits to 16 hidden values * 3 bits each = 48 bits : the compressed image is about 1/10th the size of the original!

However, this encoding scheme is not lossless; the original image cannot be retrieved because information is lost in the process of quantizing. Nonetheless, it can produce quite good results, as shown (though, of course, this image has been turned into a jpeg as well, so the actual results of the original compressopm cannot be seen. However, the contrast between the two images (or the lack of contrast, as is the goal of compression!) should be sufficient for this brief discussion.

ORIGINAL **RECONSTRUCTED IMAGE**

Original Reconstructed Image

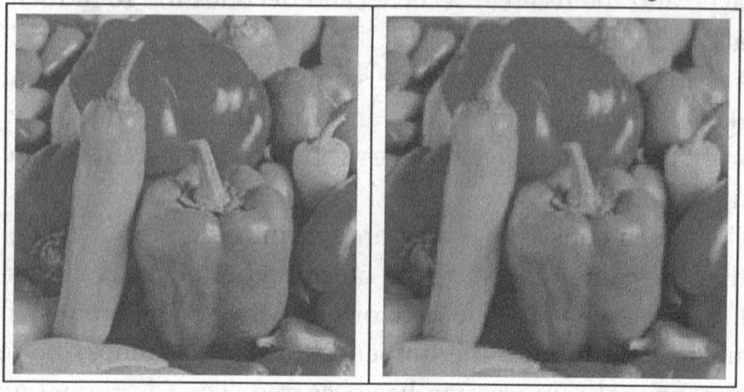

How does a network learn to do this?

The goal of these data compression networks is to re-create the input itself. Hence, the input is used as its own output for training purposes. The input is produced from the 256x256 training image by extracting small 8x8 chunks of the image chosen at a uniformly random location in the image. This data is presented over and over, and the weights adjusted, until the network reproduces the image relatively faithfully. You can see this randomization of the 8x8 chunks in the top row of the applet. The randomization helps ensure generalization of the network so that it will work on other images as well.

Once training is complete, image re-construction is demonstrated in the recall phase. In this case, we still present the neural net with 8x8 chunks of the image, but now instead of randomly selecting the location of each chunk, we select the chunks in sequence from left to right and from top to bottom. For each such 8x8 chunk, the output the network can be computed and displayed on the screen to visually observe the performance of neural net image compression.

We can test how well the network has generalized the data by testing image compression on other pictures, such as the one on the bottom. And we can continue to train the network if the output is not of high enough quality.

Neural networks and financial prediction

Neural networks have been touted as all-powerful tools in stock-market prediction. Companies such as MJ Futures claim amazing 199.2% returns over a 2-year period using their neural network prediction methods. They also claim great ease of use; as technical editor John Sweeney said in a 1995 issue of "Technical Analysis of Stocks and Commodities.

These may be exaggerated claims, and, indeed, neural networks may be easy to use once the network is set up, but the setup and training of the network requires skill, experience, and patience. It's not all hype, though neural networks have shown success at prediction of market trends.

The idea of stock market prediction is not new, of course. Business people often attempt to anticipate the market by interpreting external parameters, such as economic indicators, public opinion, and current political climate. The question is, though, if neural networks can discover trends in data that humans might not notice, and successfully use these trends in their predictions. Good results have been achieved by Dean Barr and Walter Loick at LBS Capital Management using a relatively simple neural network with just 6 financial indicators as inputs. These inputs include the ADX, which indicates the average directional movement over the previous 18 days, the current value of the S&P 500, and the net change in the S&P 500 value from five days prior.

This is a simple back-propagation network of three layers, and it is trained and tested on a high volume of historical market data. The challenge here is not in the network architecture itself, but instead in the choice of variables and the information used for training. Even better results have been achieved with a back-propagated neural network with 2 hidden layers and many more than 6 variables.

Additional Neural Network Applications in the financial world:

- Currency prediction
- Futures prediction
- Bond ratings
- Business failure prediction
- Debt risk assessment
- Credit approval
- Bank theft
- Bank failure

The Traveling salesman's problem:

Definition: Given a number of cities on a plane, find the shortest path through which one can visit all of the cities.

In contrast to using recursion to try all the different possibilities, we are going to approximate the solution using a Kohonen SOM, which organizes itself like a elastic rubber band. The basic idea of this solution is to start out with a elastic net in a random orientation:

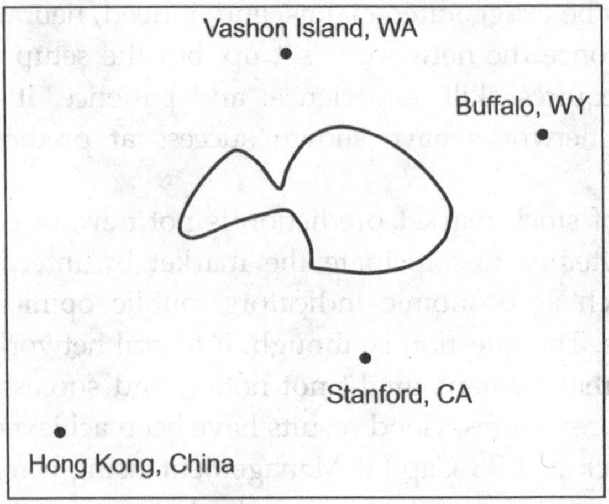

Fig. 7 A random ring

The algorithm is to choose a random city each time, and pull the point on the net that is closest to the city towards the city:

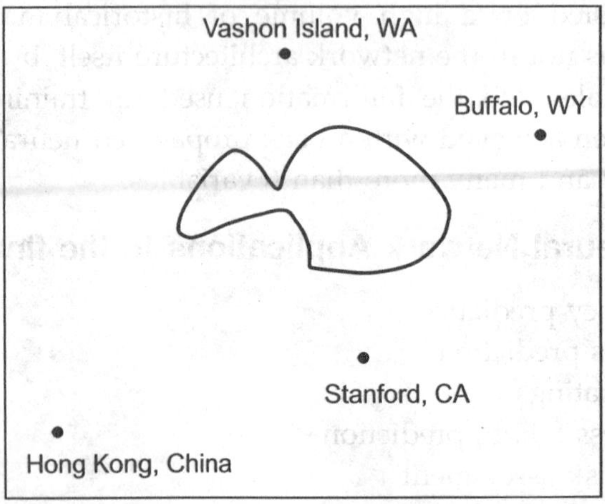

Fig. 8 A point pulled towards Vashon Island brings the net closer to the city

Since the net is elastic, each pull changes the shape of the net. After many pulls for different cities, the net eventually converges into a ring around the cities. Given the elastic property of the ring, the length of the ring tends to be minimized. This is how the TSP can be approximated.

The details:

As in simple competitive networks, the weight vectors of the networks are randomly assigned at the beginning in SOM's. Another similarity is that SOM also identifies the winner (the perceptron whose weight vector is closest to the input vector) every time an input vector is presented. The only difference is that while in simple competitive networks only the winner learns, in SOM's all nodes learn, but the rate of learning varies inversely with the node's physical distance from the winner.

The Kohonen SOM used in solving the TSP has the following structure:

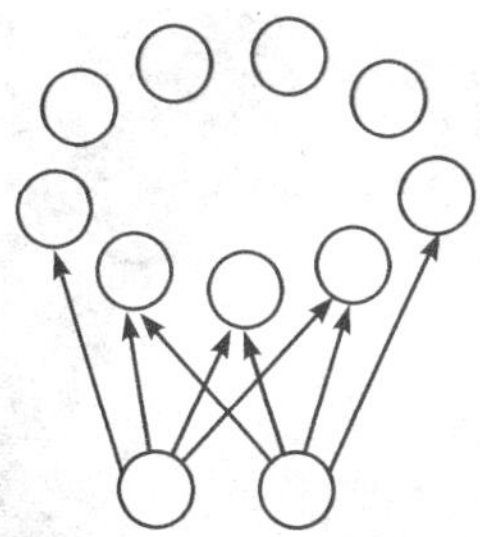

Fig. 9 A Kohonen net with a ring-shaped top layer

Recall the elastic rubber-band model mentioned above, such a ring shaped map simulates a rubber band if we consider the weight vectors as points on a plane. We can join these points together according to the position of their respective perceptron in the ring of the top layer of the network.

Suppose the coordinates of a city (x, y) is presented as the input vector of the network, the network will identify the weight vector closest to the city and move it and its neighbors closer to the city. In this manner, the weight vectors behave as points on a rubber band and each "learning" is analogous to pulling the closest point of the band towards a city. The rule that the amount of learning varies inversely with the physical distance between the node and the winner is what leads to the elastic property of the rubber band.

Applications of neural networks Medicine

One of the areas that has gained attention is in cardiopulmonary diagnostics. The ways neural networks work in this area or other areas of medical diagnosis is by the comparison of many different models. A patient may have regular checkups in a particular area, increasing the possibility of detecting a disease or dysfunction.

The data may include heart rate, blood pressure, breathing rate, etc. to different models. The models may include variations for age, sex, and level of physical activity. Each individual's physiological data is compared to previous physiological data and/or data of the various generic models. The deviations from the norm are compared to the known causes of deviations for each medical condition. The neural network can learn by studying the different conditions and models, merging them to form a complete conceptual picture, and then diagnose a patient's condition based upon the models.

Electronic Noses

An actual electronic "nose"

The idea of a chemical nose may seem a bit absurd, but it has several real-world applications. The electronic nose is composed of a chemical sensing system (such as a spectrometer) and an artificial neural network, which recognizes certain patterns of chemicals. An odor is passed over the chemical sensor array, these chemicals are then translated into a format that the computer can understand, and the artificial neural network identifies the chemical. A list at the Pacific Northwest Laboratory has several different applications in the environment, medical, and food industries.

Environment: identification of toxic wastes, analysis of fuel mixtures, detection of oil leaks, identification of household odors, monitoring air quality, monitoring factory emission, and testing ground water for odors.

Medical: The idea of using these in the medical field is to examine odors from the body to identify and diagnose problems. Odors in the breath, infected wounds, and body fluids all can indicate problems. Artificial neural networks have even been used to detect tuberculosis.

Food: The food industry is perhaps the biggest practical market for electronic noses, assisting or replacing entirely humans. Inspection of food, grading quality of food, fish inspection, fermentation control, checking mayonnaise for rancidity, automated flavor control, monitoring cheese ripening, verifying if orange juice is natural, beverage container inspection, and grading whiskey.

Security: One program that has already been started is the CATCH program. CATCH, an acronyms for Computer Aided Tracking and Characterization of Homicides. It learns about an existing crime, the location of the crime, and the particular characteristics of the offense. The program is subdivided into different tools, each of which place an emphasis on a certain characteristic or group of characteristics. This allows the user to remove certain characteristics, which humans determine are unrelated.

Loans and credit cards: Loan granting is one area in which neural networks can aid humans, as it is an area not based on a predetermined and pre-weighted criteria, but answers are instead nebulous. Banks want to make as much money as they can, and one-way to do this is to lower the failure rate by using neural networks to decide whether the bank should approve the loan. Neural networks are particularly useful in this area since no process will guarantee 100% accuracy. Even 85-90% accuracy would be an improvement over the methods humans use.

In fact, in some banks, the failure rate of loans approved using neural networks is lower than that of some of their best traditional methods. Some credit card companies are now beginning to use neural networks in deciding whether to grant an application. The process works by analyzing past failures and making current decisions based upon past experience. Nonetheless, this creates its own problems. For example, the bank or credit company must justify their decision to the applicant. The reason "my neural network computer recommended against it" simply isn't enough for people to accept. The process of explaining how the network learned and on what characteristics the neural network made its decision is difficult. As we alluded to earlier in the history of neural networks, self-modifying code is very difficult to debug and thus difficult to trace. Recording the steps it went through isn't enough, as it might be using conventional computing, because even the individual steps the neural network went through have to be analyzed by human beings, or possibly the network itself, to determine that a particular piece of data was crucial in the decision-making process.

Neural networks have been shown to be particularly useful in solving problems where traditional artificial intelligence techniques involving symbolic methods have failed or proved inefficient. Such networks have shown promise in problems involving low-level tasks that are computationally intensive, including vision, speech recognition, and many other problems that fall under the category of pattern recognition. Neural networks, with their massive parallelism, can provide the computing power needed for these problems. A major shortcoming of neural networks lies in the long training times that they require, particularly when many layers are used. Hardware advances should diminish these limitations, and neural-network-based systems will become greater complements to conventional computing systems.

Researchers at Ford Motor Company are developing a neural-network system that diagnoses engine malfunctions. While an experienced technician can analyze engine malfunction given a set of data, it is extremely complicated to design a rule-based expert system to do the same diagnosis. Marko et al. [1990] trained a neural net to diagnose engine malfunction, given a number of different faulty states of an engine such as open plug, broken manifold, etc. The trained network had a high rate of correct diagnoses. Neural nets have also been used in the banking industry, for example, in the evaluation of credit card applications.

Most neural network applications, however, have been concentrated in the area of pattern recognition, where traditional algorithmic approaches have been ineffective. Such nets have been used for classifying a given input into one of a number of categories and have demonstrated success, even with noisy input, when compared to other more conventional techniques.

Since the 1970s, work has been done on monitoring the Space Shuttle Main Engine (SSME), involving the development of an Integrated Diagnostic System (IDS). The IDS is a hierarchical multilevel system, which integrates various fault detection algorithms to provide a monitoring system that works for all stages of operation of the SSME. Three fault-detection algorithms have been used, depending on the SSME sensor data. These employ statistical methods that have a high computational complexity and a low degree of reliability, particularly in the presence of noise. Systems based on neural networks offer promise for a fast and reliable real-time system to help overcome these difficulties, This work involves the development of a fault diagnostic system for the SSME that is based on three-layer back propagation networks. Neural networks in this application allow for better performance and for the diagnosis to be accomplished in real time. Furthermore, because of the parallel structure of neural networks, better performance is realized by parallel algorithms running on parallel architectures.

At Boeing Aircraft Company, researchers have been developing a neural network to identify aircraft parts that have already been designed and manufactured, in efforts to help them with the production of new part s. Given a new design, the system attempts to identify a previously designed part that resembles the new one. If one is found, it may be able to be modified to conform to the new specifications, thus saving time and money in the manufacturing process.

Neural networks have also been used in biomedical research, which often involves the analysis and classification of an experiment's outcomes. Traditional techniques include the linear discriminant function and the analysis of covariance. The outcome of the experiment is in some cases dependent on a number of variables, with the dependence usually a nonlinear function that is not known. Neural networks can in many cases, manage such problems.

1.9 Summary

- A neural network is a computing paradigm that is loosely modeled after cortical structures of the brain. It consists of interconnected processing elements called neurons that work together to produce an output function.
- Neural network is sometimes used to refer to a branch of computational science that uses neural networks as models to either simulate or analyze complex phenomena and/or study the principles of operation of neural networks analytically. It addresses problems similar to artificial intelligence (AI) except that AI uses traditional computational algorithms to solve problems whereas neural networks use 'networks of agents'.
- Biological neural networks are made up of real biological neurons that are connected or functionally-related in the peripheral nervous system or the central nervous system. In the field of neuroscience, they are often identified as groups of neurons that perform a specific physiological function in laboratory analysis.
- Artificial neural networks are made up of interconnecting artificial neurons (usually simplified neurons) designed to model (or mimic) some properties of biological neural networks.
- Artificial neural networks can be used to model the modes of operation of biological neural networks, whereas cognitive models are theoretical models that mimic cognitive brain functions without necessarily using neural networks while artificial intelligence are

well-crafted algorithms that solve specific intelligent problems (such as chess playing, pattern recognition, etc.) without using neural network as the computational architecture.

- The backpropagation network was probably the main reason behind the repopularisation of neural networks after the publication of "Learning Internal Representations by Error Propagation" in 1986.
- The backpropagation network generated much enthusiasm at the time and there was much controversy about whether such learning could be implemented in the brain or not, partly because a mechanism for reverse signalling was not obvious at the time, but most importantly because there was no plausible source for the 'teaching' or 'target' signal.
- Theoretical and computational neuroscience is the field concerned with the theoretical analysis and computational modeling of biological neural systems. Since neural systems are intimately related to cognitive processes and behaviour, the field is closely related to cognitive and behavioural modeling.
- An artificial neural network (ANN), also called a simulated neural network (SNN) or commonly just neural network (NN) is an interconnected group of artificial neurons that uses a mathematical or computational model for information processing based on a connectionist approach to computation.
- A learning rule is defined as a procedure for modifying the weights and biases of a network. (This procedure can also be referred to as a training algorithm.) The learning rule is applied to train the network to perform some particular task. Learning rules in this toolbox fall into two broad categories: supervised learning, and unsupervised learning.
- In supervised learning, the learning rule is provided with a set of examples (the training set) of proper network behavior.
- In unsupervised learning, the weights and biases are modified in response to network inputs only. There are no target outputs available. Most of these algorithms perform clustering operations. They categorize the input patterns into a finite number of classes. This is especially useful in such applications as vector quantization.
- A perceptron is a single-layer network with a activation function.
- A multilayer network has two or more layers of units, with the output from one layer serving as input to the next. The layers with

no external output connections are referred to as hidden layers.

- The training of a neural network through software simulation demands intensive mathematical computation, often leading to excessive training times on ordinary general-purpose processors.

1.10 Review Question

1. The network of figure 1, is:

(a) a single layer feed-forward neural network
(b) an autoassociative neural network
(c) a multiple layer neural network

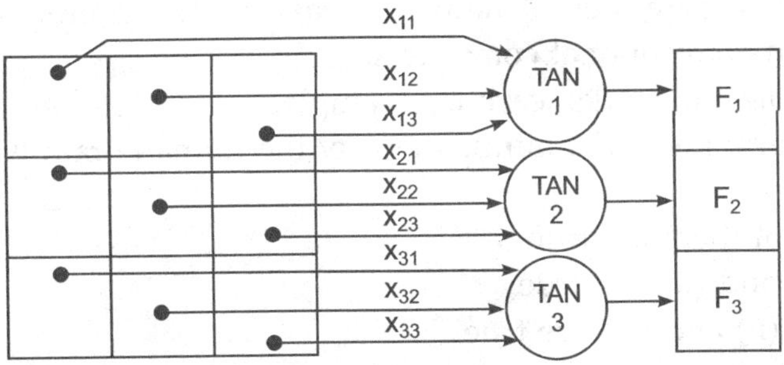

Figure 1

2. A 3-input neuron is trained to output a zero when the input is 110 and a one when the input is 111. After generalisation, the output will be zero when and only when the input is:

(a) 000 or 110 or 011 or 101
(b) 010 or 100 or 110 or 101
(c) 000 or 010 or 110 or 100

3. A perceptron is:

(a) a single layer feed-forward neural network with preprocessing
(b) an autoassociative neural network
(c) a double layer autoassociative neural network

4. An autoassociative network is:

(a) a neural network that contains no loops
(b) a neural network that contains feedback

(c) a neural network that has only one loop

5. A 4-input neuron has weights 1, 2, 3 and 4. The transfer function is linear with the constant of proportionality being equal to 2. The inputs are 4, 10, 5 and 20 respectively. The output will be:

(a) 238
(b) 76
(c) 119

6. Which of the following is true?

(i) On average, neural networks have higher computational rates than conventional computers.
(ii) Neural networks learn by example.
(iii) Neural networks mimic the way the human brain works.

(a) all of them are true
(b) (ii) and (iii) are true
(c) (i), (ii) and (iii) are true

7. Which of the following is true for neural networks?

(i) The training time depends on the size of the network.
(ii) Neural networks can be simulated on a conventional computer.
(iii) Artificial neurons are identical in operation to biological ones.
(a) all of them are true.
(b) (ii) is true.
(c) (i) and (ii) are true.

8. What are the advantages of neural networks over conventional computers?

(i) They have the ability to learn by example
(ii) They are more fault tolerant
(iii) They are more suited for real time operation due to their high 'computational' rates
(a) (i) and (ii) are true
(b) (i) and (iii) are true
(c) all of them are true

9. Which of the following is true?

Single layer associative neural networks do not have the ability to:
(i) perform pattern recognition
(ii) find the parity of a picture
(iii) determine whether two or more shapes in a picture are connented or not
 (a) (ii) and (iii) are true
 (b) (ii) is true
 (c) all of them are true

10. The network shown in Figure 1 is trained to recognize the characters H and T as shown below:

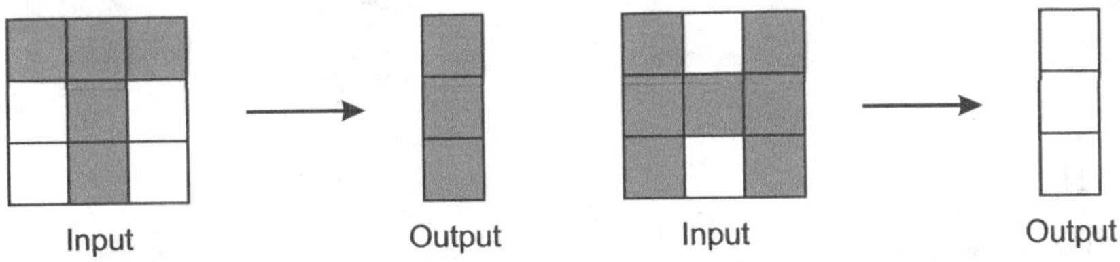

If the following pattern was given

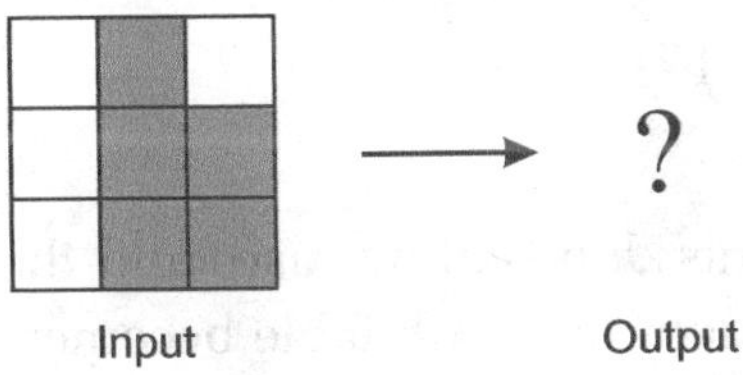

What would be the output of the network?

(a) 

(b) 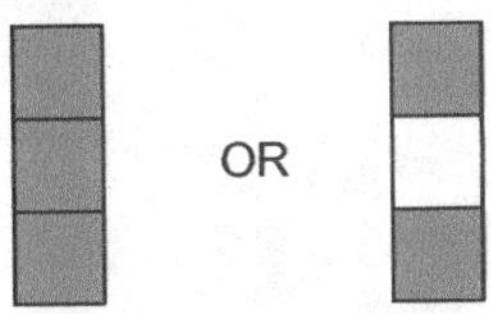

(c) 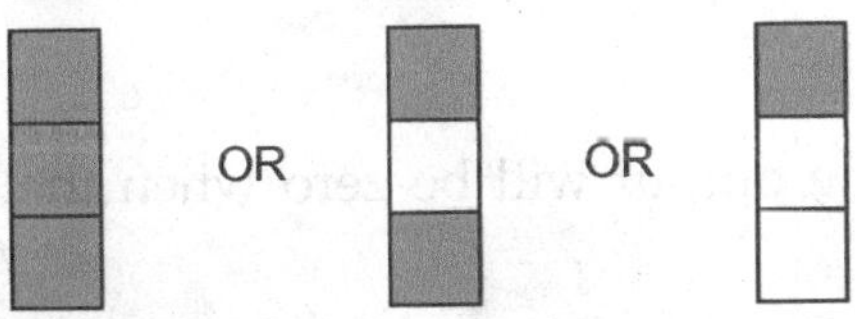

Answers:

1. The answer is (a).

The network of figure 1, is a single layer feed-forward neural network because there is only one neuron between any input and output. The network is not autoassociative i.e. doesn't have feedback because there are no loops in it.

2. The answer is (c).

The truth table before generalisation is:

Inputs	Output
000	$
001	$
010	$
011	$
100	$
101	$
110	0
111	1

where $ represents don't know cases and the output is random.

After generalisation, the truth table becomes:

Inputs	Output
000	0
001	1
010	0
011	1
100	0
101	1
110	0
111	1

Therefore, the output will be zero when the input is 000 or 010 or 110 or 100

3. The answer is (a).

The perceptron is a single layer feed-forward neural network. It is not an autoassociative network because it has no feedback and is not a multiple layer neural network because the preprocessing stage is not made of neurons.

4. The answer is (b).

An autoassociative network is equivalnet to a neural network that conatins feedback. The number of feedback paths(loops) does not have to be one.

5. The answer is (b).

The output is found by multipling the weights with their respective inputs, summing the results and multipling with the trasfer function. Therefore:

Output = 2 * (1*4 + 2*10 + 3*5 + 4*20) = 238

6. The answer is (a)

Neural networks have higher computational rates than conventional computers because a lot of the operation is done in parallel.

Note: that is not the case when the neural network is simulated on a computer. The idea behind neural nets is based on the way the human brain works. Neural nets cannot be programmed, they cam only learn by examples.

7. The answer is (c).

The training time depends on the size of the network; the number of neuron is greater and therefore the number of possible 'states' is increased. Neural networks can be simulated on a conventional computer but the main advantage of neural networks - parallel execution - is lost. Artificial neurons are not identical in operation to the biological ones. We don't know yet what the real neurons do in detail.

8. The answer is (c).

Neural networks learn by example.

They are more fault tolerant because they are always able to respond and small changes in input do not normally cause a change in output.

Because of their parallel architecture, high computational rates are achived.

9. The answer is (a).

Pattern recognition is what single layer neural networks are best at but they don't have the ability to find the parity of a picture or to determine whether two shapes are connected or not.

10. The answer is (b).

The top square of the output is black because the top pattern differs in two squares from a T and in 3 squares from an H.

The middle square is not defined because the middle row of the input defers the same amount from both T and H(differs in 1). Therefore, the output can be either black or white.

The bottom square is black because it differs from a T and in 2 from an H.

Chapter No. 2

What is Artificial Neural Networks?

An Artificial Neural Network (ANN) or commonly just neural network (NN) is an interconnected group of artificial neurons that uses a mathematical model or computational model for information processing based on a connectionist approach to computation. In most cases an Artificial Neural Network is an adaptive system that changes its structure based on external or internal information that flows through the network.In more practical terms neural networks are non-linear statistical data modeling tools. They can be used to model complex relationships between inputs and outputs or to find patterns in data.

Employing artificial neural networks

Perhaps the greatest advantage of Artificial Neural Networks is their ability to be used as an arbitrary function approximation mechanism which 'learns' from observed data. However, using them is not so straightforward and a relatively good understanding of the underlying theory is essential.

- **Choice of model:** This will depend on the data representation and the application. Overly complex models tend to lead problems with learning.
- **Learning algorithm:** There are numerous tradeoffs between learning algorithms. Almost any algorithm will work well with the correct hyperparameters for training on a particular fixed dataset. However selecting and tuning an algorithm for training on unseen data requires a significant amount of experimentation.
- **Robustness:** If the model, cost function and learning algorithm are selected appropriately the resulting Artificial Neural Network can be extremely robust.

With the correct implementation Artificial NeuralNetworks can be used naturally in online learning and large dataset applications. Their simple implementation and the existence of mostly local dependencies exhibited in the structure allows for fast, parallel implementations in hardware.

Applications

The utility of artificial neural network models lies in the fact that they can be used to infer a function from observations. This is particularly useful in applications where the complexity of the data or task makes the design of such a function by hand impractical.

Real life applications

The tasks to which artificial neural networks are applied tend to fall within the following broad categories:

- Function approximation, or regression analysis, including time series prediction and modeling.
- Classification, including pattern and sequence recognition, novelty detection and sequential decision making.
- Data processing, including filtering, clustering, blind source separation and compression.

Application areas include system identification and control (vehicle control, process control), game-playing and decision making (backgammon, chess, racing), pattern recognition (radar systems, face identification, object recognition and more), sequence recognition (gesture, speech, handwritten text recognition), medical diagnosis, financial applications, data mining (or knowledge discovery in databases, "KDD"), visualization and e-mail spam filtering.

2.1 Analogy to the Human Brain

The exact workings of the human brain are still a mystery. Some aspects of this amazing processor are known. In particular, the most basic element of the human brain is a specific type of cell, which, unlike the rest of the body, doesn't appear to regenerate. Because this type of cell is the only part of the body that is not slowly replaced, it is assumed that these cells are what provide us with our abilities to remember, think, and apply previous experiences to our every action. These cells, all 100 billion of them, are known as neurons. Each of these neurons can connect with up to 200,000 other neurons, although 1,000 to 10,000 are typical.

The power of the human mind comes from the sheer numbers of

these basic components and the multiple connections between them. It also comes from genetic programming and learning.

The individual neurons are complicated. They have a myriad of parts, sub-systems, and control mechanisms. They convey information via a host of electrochemical pathways. There are over one hundred different classes of neurons, depending on the classification method used. Together these neurons and their connections form a process, which is not binary, not stable, and not synchronous. In short, it is nothing like the currently available electronic computers, or even artificial neural networks.

These artificial neural networks try to replicate only the most basic elements of this complicated, versatile, and powerful organism. They do it in a primitive way. But for the software engineer who is trying to solve problems, neural computing was never about replicating human brains. It is about machines and a new way to solve problems.

2.2 Biological & Artificial Neurons and How They Work

The fundamental processing element of a neural network is a neuron. This building block of human awareness encompasses a few general capabilities. Basically, a biological neuron receives inputs from other sources, combines them in some way, performs a generally nonlinear operation on the result, and then outputs the final result. Figure 2.2.1 shows the relationship of these four parts.

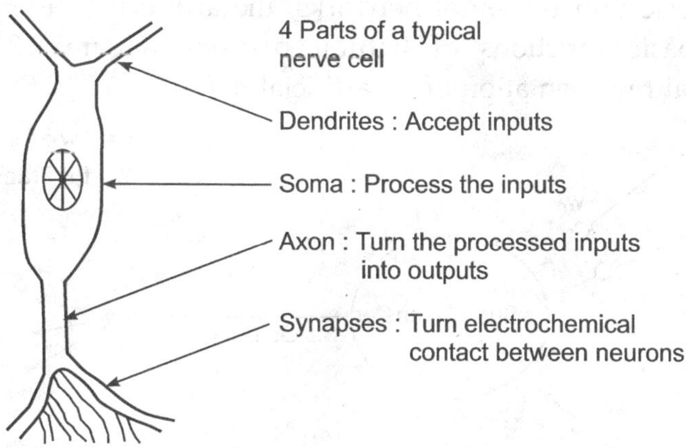

Figure 2.2.1 A Simple Neuron.

Within humans there are many variations on this basic type of neuron, further complicating man's attempts at electrically replicating the process of thinking. Yet, all natural neurons have the same four basic components. These components are known by their biological names -

dendrites, soma, axon, and synapses. Dendrites are hair-like extensions of the soma, which act like input channels. These input channels receive their input through the synapses of other neurons. The soma then processes these incoming signals over time. The soma then turns that processed value into an output, which is sent out to other neurons through the axon and the synapses.

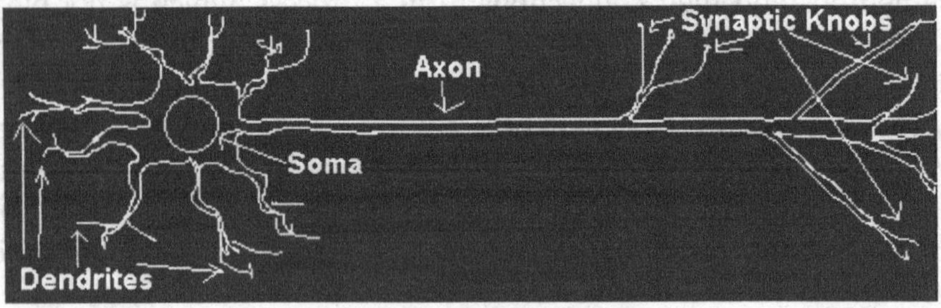

Figure 2.2.2 working of Biological Neurons

Biological neurons are structurally more complex than simple neurons. They are significantly more complex than the existing artificial neurons that are built into today's artificial neural networks. As biology provides a better understanding of neurons, and as technology advances, network designers can continue to improve their systems by building upon man's understanding of the biological brain.

The basic unit of neural networks, the artificial neurons, simulates the four basic functions of natural neurons. Figure 2.2.3 shows a fundamental representation of an artificial neuron.

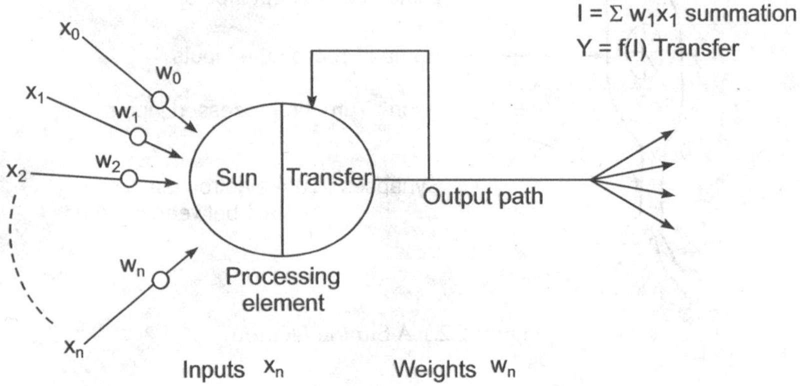

Figure 2.2.3 A Basic Artificial Neuron.

In Figure 2.2.3, various inputs to the network are represented by the mathematical symbol, x (n). Each of these inputs is multiplied by a connection weight. These weights are represented by w (n). In the simplest case, these products are simply summed, fed through a transfer function to generate a result, and then output. This process lends itself to physical implementation on a large scale in a small package. This electronic implementation is still possible with other network structures, which utilize different summing functions as well as different transfer functions.

Some applications require "black and white," or binary, answers. These applications include the recognition of text, the identification of speech, and the image deciphering of scenes. These applications are required to turn real-world inputs into discrete values. These potential values are limited to some known set, like the ASCII characters or the most common 50,000 English words. Because of this limitation of output options, these applications don't always utilize networks composed of neurons that simply sum up, and thereby smooth, inputs. These networks may utilize the binary properties of ORing and ANDing of inputs. These functions, and many others, can be built into the summation and transfer functions of a network.

Other networks work on problems where the resolutions are not just one of several known values. These networks need to be capable of an infinite number of responses. Applications of this type include the "intelligence" behind robotic movements. This "intelligence" processes inputs and then creates outputs, which actually cause some device to move. That movement can span an infinite number of very precise motions. These networks do indeed want to smooth their inputs which, due to limitations of sensors, comes in non-continuous bursts, say thirty times a second. To do that, they might accept these inputs, sum that data, and then produce an output by, for example, applying a hyperbolic tangent as a transfer function. In this manner, output values from the network are continuous and satisfy more real world interfaces.

Other applications might simply sum and compare to a threshold, thereby producing one of two possible outputs, a zero or a one. Other functions scale the outputs to match the application, such as the values minus one and one. Some functions even integrate the input data over time, creating time-dependent networks.

Artificial neuron

An artificial neuron (also called a "node" or "Nv neuron" or "Binary neuron" or "McCulloch-Pitts neuron") is an abstraction of biological neurons and the basic unit in an artificial neural network. The Artificial

Neuron receives one or more inputs (representing the one or more dendrites) and sum them to produce an output (synapse). Usually the sums of each node are weighted, and the sum is passed through a non-linear function known as an activation or transfer function. The canonical form of transfer functions is the sigmoid, but they may also take the form of other non-linear functions, piecewise linear functions, or step functions. Generally, transfer functions are monotonically increasing

Basic structure

For a given artificial neuron, let there be m inputs with signals x1 through xm and weights w1 through wm.

The output of neuron k is:

$$y_k = \varphi\left(\sum_{j=0}^{m} w_{kj}\, x_j\right)$$

Where φ (Phi) is the transfer function.

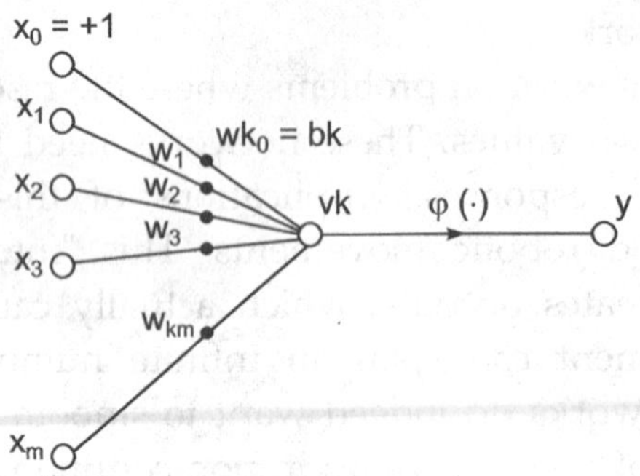

The output propagates to the next layer (through a weighted synapse) or finally exits the system as part or all of the output.

History

The original artificial neuron is the Threshold Logic Unit first proposed by Warren McCulloch and Walter Pitts in 1943. As a transfer function, it employs a threshold or step function taking on the values 1 or 0 only.

Types of transfer functions

The transfer function of a neuron is chosen to have a number of properties which either enhance or simplify the network containing the neuron. Crucially, for instance, any multi-layer perceptron using a linear transfer function has an equivalent single-layer network; a non-linear function is therefore necessary to gain the advantages of a multi-layer network.

Below, u refers in all cases to the weighted sum of all the inputs to the neuron, i.e. for n inputs,

$$u = \sum_{i=1}^{n} w_i x_i$$

where w is a vector of synaptic weights and x is a vector of inputs.

Step function

The output y of this transfer function is binary, depending on whether the input meets a specified threshold, ?. The "signal" is sent, i.e. the output is set to one, if the activation meets the threshold.

$$y = \begin{cases} 1 \text{ if } u \geq \theta \\ 1 \text{ if } u < \theta \end{cases}$$

Linear combination

The output unit y is a linearly weighted sum of its outputs plus a bias term, similar to ? above, which is independent of the inputs.

$$y = (u + b)$$

Networks based on this formulation are known as perceptrons. Typically the above transfer function in its pure form would only be useful in a regression setting. For a binary classification setting, the sign of the output denotes the class predicted; in this case it is more sensible (and more convenient in the context of the learning algorithm) to consider positive outputs to be 1 and negative outputs to be 0, thus reducing the transfer function to that of the step function above, where ? = - b.

Sigmoid

A fairly simple non-linear function, the sigmoid also has an easily calculated derivative, which is used when calculating the weight updates in the network. It thus makes the network more easily manipulable mathematically, and was attractive to early computer scientists who needed to minimise the computational load of their simulations.

Criticism

The Artificial neuron is generally criticized for not having a correct biophysical mapping. Although it does capture the numerous incoming dendrites, it fails to provide multiple output synapses. This helps speed up computation, but at the loss of biophysical accuracy.

Biological Neurons and memory: -

Recent research into brain functions has failed to find any trace of specific locations for specific memories. It appears that memories are somehow stored throughout the whole of the cerebral cortex frontal area or at least throughout a sizeable portion of it. Thus damage to a part of the memory area does not necessarily result in a loss of memory. The brain also appears to have a very large memory capacity that in the case of the majority of people never gets completely filled up, although there may be some exceptions to this: for example, people who are said to be in their second childhood. The memory function and its retrieval system could be considered quite baffling especially when people try to build models of it using current computer and data processing philosophies.

This discussion departs from the conventional serial storage memory concept and borrows from the rapidly growing field of laser holography to present a model for memory processes. There are several points within the discussion where the reader is left to his own imagination and background to conceive of the particular mechanism that may be operating. The underlying purpose thus, is to present a framework on which to build a viable theory regarding the human memory.

In laser holography one of the techniques of recording graphic information is theoretically and to a limited degree almost practically, capable of storing an infinite or at least a very large number of different pictures, all within the same photographic emulsion.

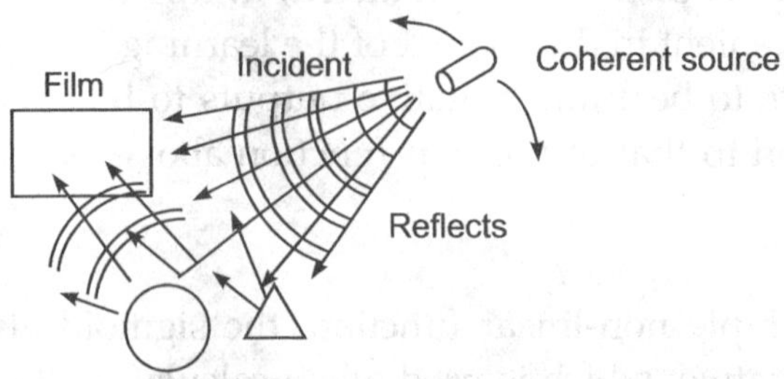

The coherent source illuminates a scene to be recorded. Part of the coherent light travels directly to the photographic emulsion and is called the incident or reference energy. Light reflected/refracted from the objects also impinges on the emulsion. The two forms of energy, incident and reflected, interfere with one another within the emulsion and create a hologram or an interference pattern. Other scenes may also be recorded on the same emulsion without degrading each other, by moving the coherent source to different locations.

After a sufficient number of interference patterns are registered on the emulsion it can be processed chemically to produce a "playback" device. By placing the developed emulsion back into its original holder, each scene previously recorded, can be re-created by illuminating the emulsion with a coherent source positioned at the same locations as were used in exposing the film. Some emulsions have recorded up to 100 scenes in this fashion and the limiting number is a matter of technological expertise and materials. The viewer of the reconstructed scene has to place himself at the proper location to view the series of pictures.

The next most, or equally, fascinating aspect of this whole process is that the emulsion can be cut in half or quarters or even smaller pieces and the whole scene can still be reconstructed from the fractional part being used. True, there will be an overall degradation in the quality of the smaller version reproductions and the viewer will have to restrict his viewing angle due to the smaller size of the film, but the entire scene, as visible from the particular viewing angle will be reproduced.

A means of providing rapid flashback can be had by programming the coherent light source to jump from position to position in sequence. Movies could even be made by a rapid fire recording technique where the light source would move in short increments and flashing at each stop.

Now comes the biological hologram. Let us hypothesize a coherent source of biological (electrical) impulses within the brain stem that could illuminate the bodily projection areas of the cerebral cortex and the frontal "memory" area. Lets discuss the visual portion of memory first, but keep in mind that the other sensory areas can be (and must be) included once the concept is clearly grasped.

Let the frontal cortex be a holographic medium for bio-electrical interference patterns. Suppose a visual pattern is registered in the occipital area (rear) of the brain. This will be represented by varying levels of electrical activity as a function of the light levels impinging on the retina.

Now, somewhere down in the brain stem, let there be an irritated neuron that is firing a train of nerve impulses to its surrounding neighbors, which in turn fire off secondary impulses. After successive repetitions of this process by other neurons in the stem mass a repetitive wave front will be generated and will be propagated throughout the entire cerebral cortex via nerve bundles that radiate away from the brain stem. (These radiating fibers could possibly be from the thalmus region or perhaps the reticular formation).

These bio-electrical pulse trains that make up the repetitive wave fronts have a parallel to the coherent wave fronts or waves of the laser. When the wave fronts impinge on the visual projection area, secondary wave fronts will be generated that will travel to the frontal memory area via fiber bundles that traverse the brain fore and aft. The intensity of the secondary wave front from any portion of the visual projection area will be a function (function undefined) of the state of electrical activity at that point.

When the secondary wave front (which has the same frequency or repetition rate as the primary) reaches the frontal area, interference will occur between primary and secondary waves, and the overall interference pattern will recorded electrochemically in the frontal area. Once a given number of impulses are generated by the originating neuron in the brain stem, it will taper off (probably due to exhaustion) and one of its neighbors will go into spasm, and carry on the process -- but with the noticeable and important difference that the waves are now originating from a new source location.

This parallels moving the laser source as in laser holography, and allows subsequent impressions to be recorded in the same medium. Probably at birth, or somewhere back there, the process starts with a given neuron firing off and the subsequent locations of the wave front source being a logical function of the brain's construction, in that region. The active source neuron pattern might be a spiral chain or some such arrangement.

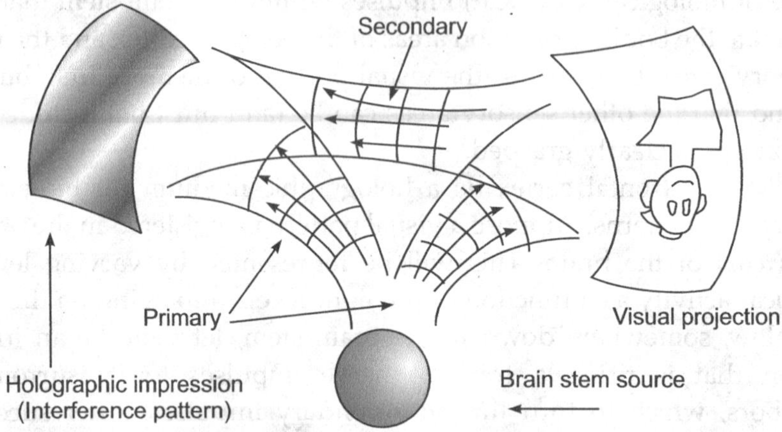

To recall any given memory, the control aspect of the brain would turn off (or reduce) activity from the "here and now" wave front source in the stem, and by some slight of hand arrange for the neuron in the stem that is associated with a given event to start firing. The control would also have to inhibit or stop paying attention to the visual image coming from the retinas. As in laser holography the biological wave front, that is called up, will illuminate the frontal area and the visual projection area (or perhaps the personal area of the conscious mind, which might be separate from which is associated with retinal images and produce a "readout," which is visual in nature, based on the stored interference pattern in the frontal area.

The construction of the stem mechanism (or wherever the pulse generator function is) would be such that whenever a memory is being reviewed, the original series of neurons would fire off in the same sequence, thus permitting "running the record" until the proper scene is recreated. The "A HA!" function could be wired in to keep the playback gain low until the desired info is found.

A person's ability to recall a given event would be related to his control function regarding turning on the correct neuron, to evoke the desired memory. Malfunctions, or dead cells, (natural or otherwise) in the brainstem might make portions, or all, of certain memories unavailable for voluntary recalls.

It seems that there must be a finite limit to the number of impressions that can be stored using this model, because there would be a finite number of "source" locations within the stem. If a person lives longer than his supply of new source locations, or centers for the bio-electrical wave fronts, his brain stem may in fact reset itself to "zero" and presto, the individual is in his second childhood. True, he could do some recording over the original memories, but his recording mechanism, at current age will probably not be as good as when new, so the individual would live a double life, his childhood memories being superimposed on his present world impressions. His behavior and responses would most likely be directed toward the stronger of the tug-of-war contestants for his attention.

2.3 Electronic Implementation of Artificial Neurons

In currently available software packages these artificial neurons are called "processing elements" and have many more capabilities than the simple artificial neuron described above. Those capabilities will be discussed later in this report. Figure 2.2.9 is a more detailed schematic of this still simplistic artificial neuron.

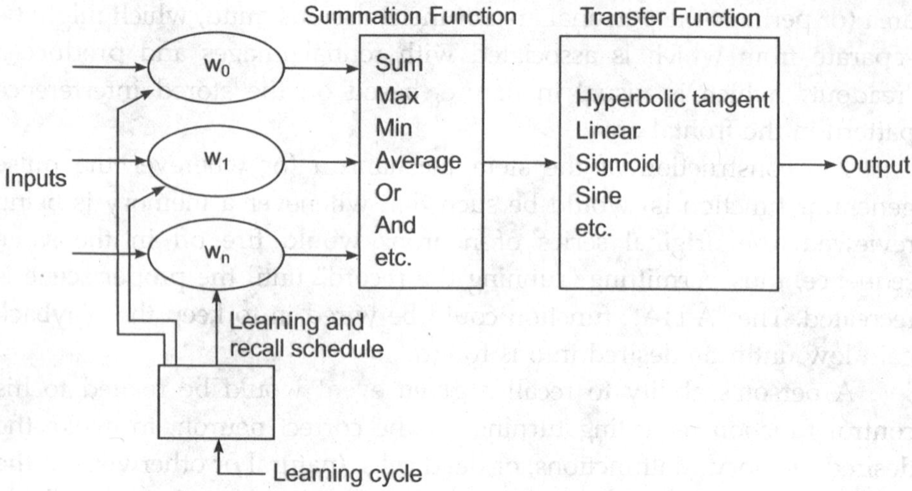

Figure 2.3.1 A Model of a "Processing Element".

In Figure 2.2.1, inputs enter into the processing element from the upper left. The first step is for each of these inputs to be multiplied by their respective weighting factor (w (n)). Then these modified inputs are fed into the summing function, which usually just sums these products. Many different types of operations can be selected. These operations could produce a number of different values, which are then propagated forward; values such as the average, the largest, the smallest, the ORed values, the ANDed values, etc. Furthermore, most commercial development products allow software engineers to create their own summing functions via routines coded in a higher-level language (C is commonly supported). Sometimes the summing function is further complicated by the addition of an activation function which enables the summing function to operate in a time sensitive way.

Either way, the output of the summing function is then sent into a transfer function. This function then turns this number into a real output via some algorithm. It is this algorithm that takes the input and turns it into a zero or a one, a minus one or a one, or some other number. The transfer functions that are commonly supported are sigmoid, sine, hyperbolic tangent, etc. This transfer function also can scale the output or control its value via thresholds. The result of the transfer function is usually the direct output of the processing element. An example of how a transfer function works is shown in Figure 2.3.2.

This sigmoid transfer function takes the value from the summation function, called sum in the Figure 2.3.2, and turns it into a value between zero and one.

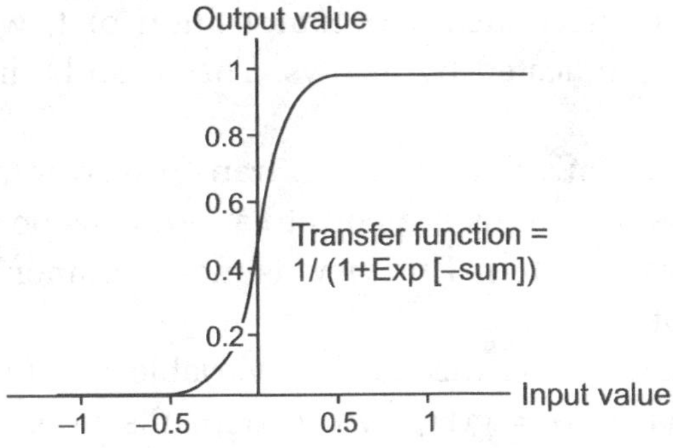

Figure 2.3.2 Sigmoid Transfer Function

Finally, the processing element is ready to output the result of its transfer function. This output is then input into other processing elements, or to an outside connection, as dictated by the structure of the network.

All artificial neural networks are constructed from this basic building block - the processing element or the artificial neuron. It is variety and the fundamental differences in these building blocks, which partially cause the implementing of neural networks to be an "art."

The network in artificial neural network

The word network in the term 'artificial neural network' arises because the function f(x) is defined as a composition of other functions gi(x), which can further be defined as a composition of other functions. This can be conveniently represented as a network structure, with arrows depicting the dependencies between variables.

$$f(x) = K \sum_i wigi(x)$$

A widely used type of composition is the nonlinear weighted sum. where, where K is some predefined function, such as the hyperbolic tangent. It will be convenient for the following to refer to a collection of functions gi as simply a vector

$$q = (q1 , q2 , \ldots , qn)$$

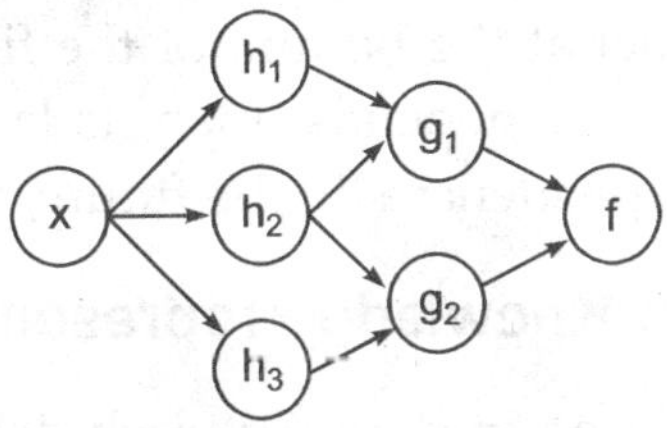

ANN dependency graph

This figure depicts such a decomposition of f, with dependencies between variables indicated by arrows. These can be interpreted in two ways.

i) Functional view: the input x is transformed into a 3-dimensional vector h, which is then transformed into a 2-dimensional vector g, which is finally transformed into f. This view is most commonly encountered in the context of optimization.

ii)Probabilistic view: the random variable F = f(G) depends upon the random variable G = g(H), which depends upon H = h(X), which depends upon the random variable X. This view is most commonly encountered in the context of graphical models.

These two views are largely equivalent. In either case, for this particular network architecture, the components of individual layers are independent of each other (e.g., the components of g are independent of each other given their input h). This naturally enables a degree of parallelism in the implementation.

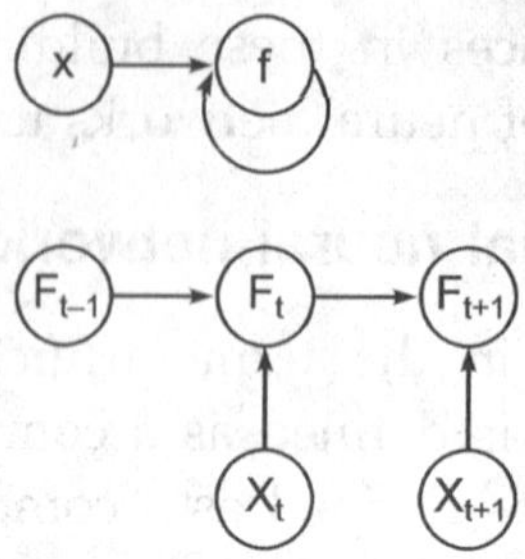

Fig. Recurrent ANN dependency graph

Networks such as the previous one are commonly called feedforward, because their graph is a directed acyclic graph. Networks with cycles are commonly called recurrent. Such networks are commonly depicted in the manner shown at the top of the figure above, where f is shown as being dependent upon itself. However, there is an implied temporal dependence which is not shown. What this actually means in practice is that the value of f at some point in time t depends upon the values of f at zero or at one or more other points in time.

The graphical model at the bottom of the figure illustrates the case: the value of f at time t only depends upon its last value. Models such as these, which have no dependencies in the future, are called causal models.

2.4 Model of Neuron Knowledge representation

Many models are used in the field, each defined at a different level of abstraction and trying to model different aspects of neural systems.

They range from models of the short-term behaviour of individual neurons, through models of how the dynamics of neural circuitry arise from interactions between individual neurons, to models of how behaviour can arise from abstract neural modules that represent complete subsystems. These include models of the long-term and short-term plasticity of neural systems and its relation to learning and memory, from the individual neuron to the system level.

Neural network models in artificial intelligence are usually referred to as artificial neural networks (ANNs); these are essentially simple mathematical models defining a function . Each type of Artificial Neural Network model corresponds to a class of such functions.

Neuron Model

Simple Neuron

A neuron with a single scalar input and no bias appears on the left below.

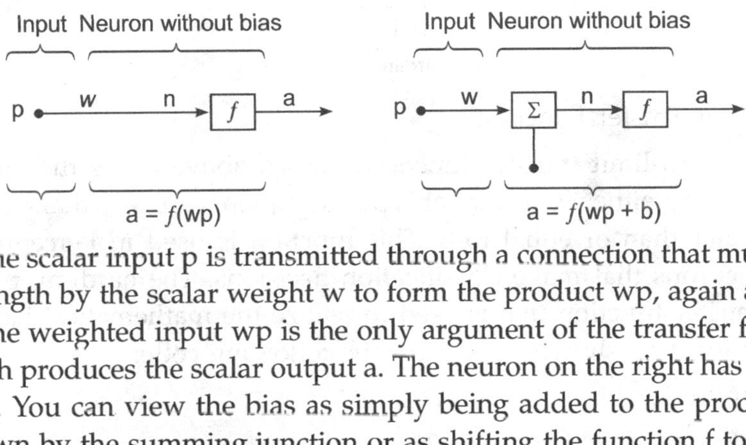

The scalar input p is transmitted through a connection that multiplies its strength by the scalar weight w to form the product wp, again a scalar. Here the weighted input wp is the only argument of the transfer function f, which produces the scalar output a. The neuron on the right has a scalar bias, b. You can view the bias as simply being added to the product wp as shown by the summing junction or as shifting the function f to the left by an amount b. The bias is much like a weight, except that it has a constant input of 1.

The transfer function net input n, again a scalar, is the sum of the weighted input wp and the bias b. This sum is the argument of the transfer function f. (Radial Basis Networks, discusses a different way to form the net input n.) Here f is a transfer function, typically a step function or a sigmoid function, that takes the argument n and produces the output a. Examples of various transfer functions are in Transfer Functions.

Note: w and b are both adjustable scalar parameters of the neuron. The central idea of neural networks is that such parameters can be adjusted so that the network exhibits some desired or interesting behavior. Thus, you can train the network to do a particular job by adjusting the weight or bias parameters, or perhaps the network itself will adjust these parameters to achieve some desired end. The bias b is an adjustable (scalar) parameter of the neuron. It is not an input. However, the constant 1 that drives the bias is an input and must be treated as such when you consider the linear dependence of input vectors in Linear Filters.

Transfer Functions

Many transfer functions are used. Three of the most commonly used functions are shown below.

1) Hard Limit Transfer Functions

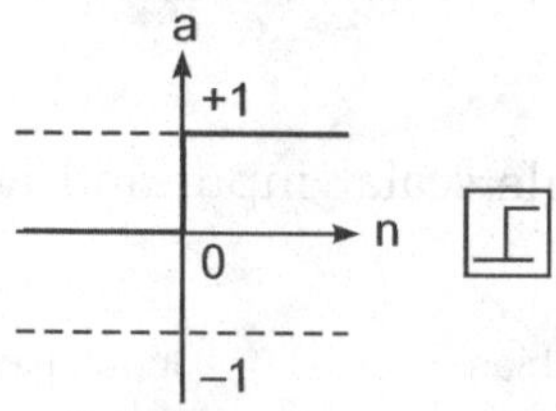

a = hardlim (n)

Hard Limit Trnsfer Function

The hard-limit transfer function shown above limits the output of the neuron to either 0, if the net input argument n is less than 0, or 1, if n is greater than or equal to 0. This function is used in Perceptrons, to create neurons that make classification decisions. The hardlim, is a hard limit transfer function that is used to realize the mathematical hard-limit transfer function shown above. Try the following code:

- N = -5:0.1:5;
- Plot (n, hardlim (n),'c+:');
-

It produces a plot of the function hardlim over the range -5 to +5.

2) Linear transfer function: -

The linear transfer function is shown below.

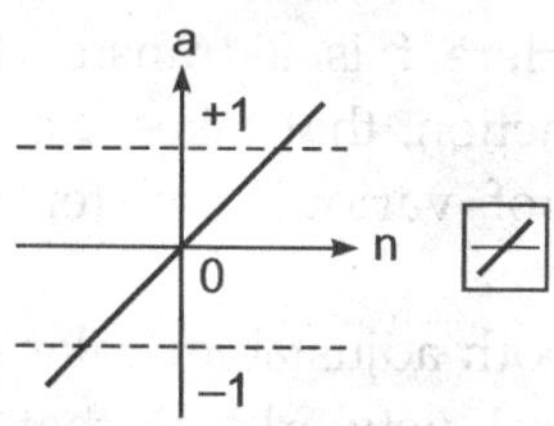

a = purelin (n)

Linear Transfer Function

Neurons of this type are used as linear approximations in Linear Filters.

3) Sigmoid transfer function: -

The sigmoid transfer function shown below takes the input, which can have any value between plus and minus infinity, and squashes the output into the range 0 to 1.

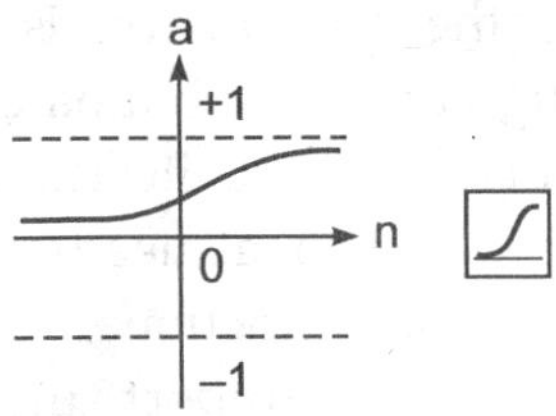

a = logsig (n)

This transfer function is commonly used in back propagation networks, in part because it is differentiable.The symbol in the square to the right of each transfer function graph shown above represents the associated transfer function. These icons replace the general f in the boxes of network diagrams to show the particular transfer function being used.

Network Architectures

Network architecture is an abstraction level of an overall system, in which the goals of a user action are representable as functional architectural properties. For example, a hypermedia application must be concerned with the location of information pages, performing requests, and rendering data streams. This is in contrast to a networking abstraction, where the goal is to move bits from one location to another without regard to why those bits are being moved. It is only at the application level that we can evaluate design trade-offs based on the number of interactions per user action, the location of application state, the effective throughput of all data streams (as opposed to the potential throughput of a single data stream), the extent of communication being performed per user action, etc.

Architecture is the realization of an architectural design and not the design itself. Architecture can be evaluated by its run-time characteristics, but we would obviously prefer an evaluation mechanism that could be applied to the candidate architectural designs before having to implement all of them. Unfortunately, architectural designs are notoriously hard to evaluate and compare in an objective manner. Like most artifacts of creative design, architectures are normally presented as a completed work, as if the design simply sprung fully formed from the architect's mind. In order to evaluate an architectural design, we need to examine the design rationale behind the constraints it places on a system, and compare the properties derived from those constraints to the target application's objectives.

The first level of evaluation is set by the application's functional requirements. For example, it makes no sense to evaluate the design of process control architecture against the requirements of a distributed hypermedia system, since the comparison is moot if the architecture would not function. Although this will eliminate some candidates, in most cases there will remain many other architectural designs that are capable of meeting the application's functional needs. The remainder differs by their relative emphasis on the non-functional requirements--the degree to which each architecture would support the various non-functional architectural properties that have been identified as necessary for the system. Since properties are created by the application of architectural constraints, it is possible to evaluate and compare different architectural designs by identifying the constraints within each architecture, evaluating the set of properties induced by each constraint, and comparing the cumulative properties of the design to those properties required of the application.

Network architecture can be described either a single layer neurons or multiple layers neurons.

Single Layer Neurons

A one-layer network with R input elements and S neurons follow.

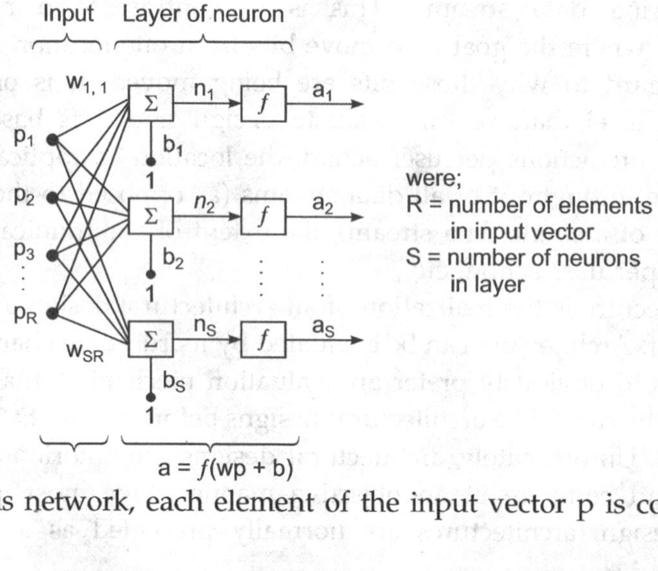

In this network, each element of the input vector p is connected to each neuron input through the weight matrix W. The ith neuron has a summer that gathers its weighted inputs and bias to form its own scalar output n(i). The various n(i) taken together form an S-element net input vector n. Finally, the neuron layer outputs form a column vector a. The expression for a is shown at the bottom of the figure.

It is common for the number of inputs to a layer to be different from the number of neurons (i.e., R is not necessarily equal to S). A layer is not constrained to have the number of its inputs equal to the number of its neurons. A single (composite) layer of neurons having different transfer functions is created, simply by putting two of the networks shown earlier in parallel. Both networks would have the same inputs, and each network would create some of the outputs.

The input vector elements enter the network through the weight matrix W.

$$W = \begin{bmatrix} w1,1 & w1,2 & \cdots & w1,R \\ w2,1 & w2,2 & \cdots & w2,R \\ & & & \\ ws,1 & ws,2 & \cdots & ws,R \end{bmatrix}$$

•

The row indices on the elements of matrix W indicate the destination neuron of the weight, and the column indices indicate which source is the input for that weight. Thus, the indices in w1,2 say that the strength of the signal from the second input element to the first (and only) neuron is w1,2. The S neuron R input one-layer network also can be drawn in abbreviated notation.

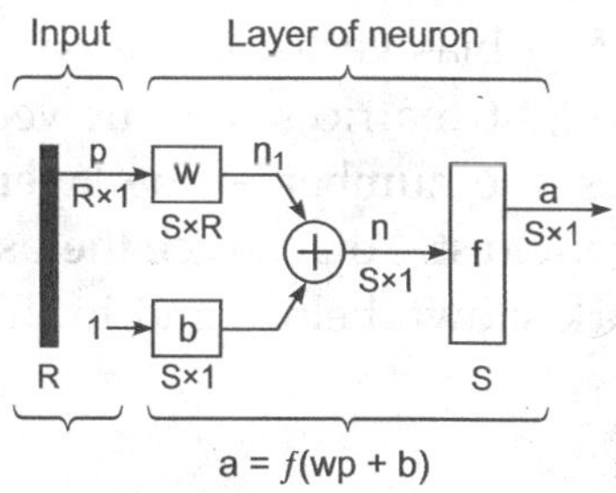

were;
R = number of elements in input vector
S = number of neurons in layer 1

Here p is an R length input vector, W is an SxR matrix, and a and b are S length vectors. As defined previously, the neuron layer includes the weight matrix, the multiplication operations, the bias vector b, the summer, and the transfer function boxes.

Inputs and Layers

To describe networks having multiple layers, the notation must be extended. Specifically, it needs to make a distinction between weight matrices that are connected to inputs and weight matrices that are connected between layers. It also needs to identify the source and destination for the weight matrices. The weight matrices connected to inputs known as input weights and weight matrices coming from layer known as outputs layer weights. Further, superscripts are used to identify the source (second index) and the destination (first index) for the various weights and other elements of the network. The one-layer multiple input network shown earlier is redrawn in abbreviated form below.

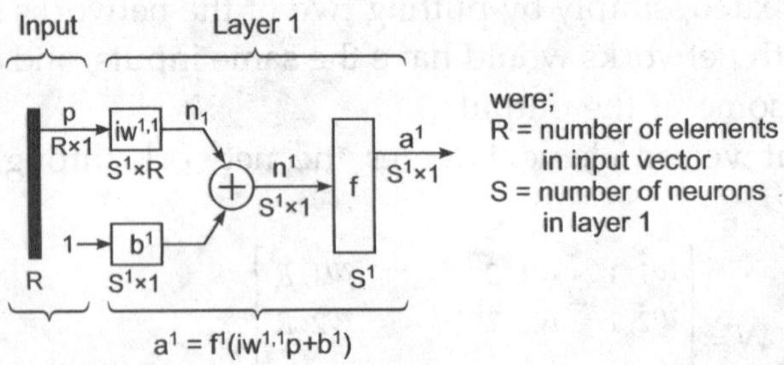

The weight matrix connected to the input vector p is labeled as an input weight matrix (IW1,1) having a source 1 (second index) and a destination 1 (first index). Elements of layer 1, such as its bias, net input, and output have a superscript 1 to say that they are associated with the first layer.

Multiple Layers of Neurons

Multiple Layers of Neurons uses layer weight (LW) matrices as well as input weight (IW) matrices. In this a network can have several layers. Each layer has a weight matrix W, a bias vector b, and an output vector a. To distinguish between the weight matrices, output vectors, etc., for each of these layers in the figures, the number of the layer is appended as a superscript to the variable of interest. You can see the use of this layer notation in the three-layer network shown below, and in the equations at the bottom of the figure.

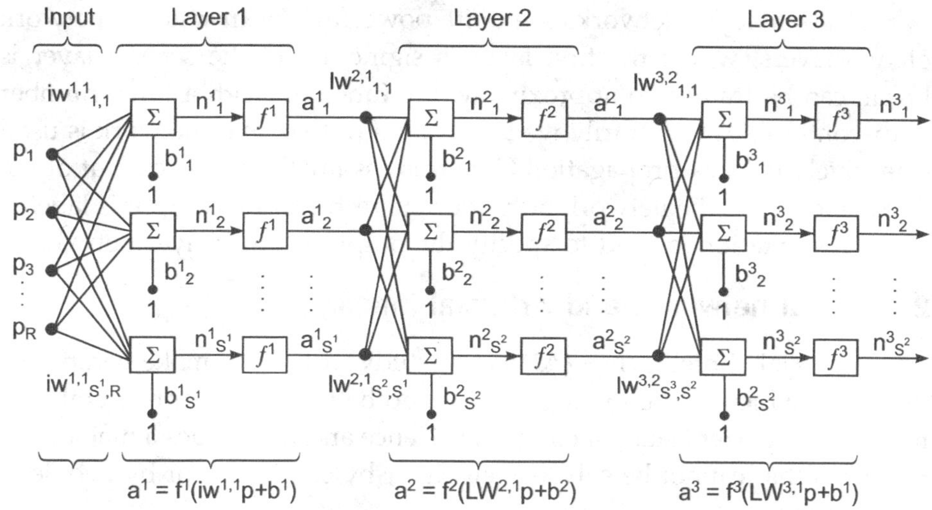

$$a^3 = f^3(LW^{3,2}f^2(LW^{2,1}f^1(IW^{1,1}p+b^3)+b^2)+b^1)$$

The network shown above has R1 inputs, S1 neurons in the first layer, S2 neurons in the second layer, etc. It is common for different layers to have different numbers of neurons. A constant input 1 is fed to the bias for each neuron. The outputs of each intermediate layer are the inputs to the following layer. Thus layer 2 can be analyzed as a one-layer network with S1 inputs, S2 neurons, and an S2xS1 weight matrix W2. The input to layer 2 is a1; the output is a2. Now that all the vectors and matrices of layer 2 have been identified, it can be treated as a single-layer network on its own. This approach can be taken with any layer of the network.

The layers of a multilayer network play different roles. A layer that produces the network output is called an output layer. All other layers are called hidden layers. The three-layer network shown earlier has one output layer (layer 3) and two hidden layers (layer 1 and layer 2). Some authors refer to the inputs as a fourth layer.The same three-layer network can also be drawn using abbreviated notation.

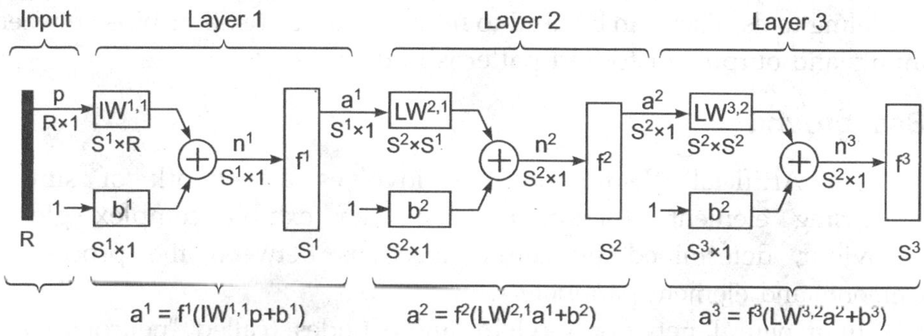

$$a^3 = f^3(LW^{3,2}f^2(LW^{2,1}f^1(IW^{1,1}p+b^1)+b^2)+b^3 = y$$

Multiple-layer networks are quite powerful. For instance, a network of two layers, where the first layer is sigmoid and the second layer is linear, can be trained to approximate any function (with a finite number of discontinuities) arbitrarily well. This kind of two-layer network is used extensively in Back propagation.Here it is assumed that the output of the third layer, a3, is the network output of interest, and this output is labeled as y. This notation is used to specify the output of multilayer networks.

2.5 Neural networks and Artificial intelligence

Artificial Iintelligence (AI) is the study of how to make computers do things which at the moment people do better. This is ephemeral as it refers to the current state of computer science and it excludes a major area, problems that cannot be solved well either by computers or by people at the moment.

Alternative

Artificial Intelligence is the branch of computer science that is concerned with the automation of intelligent behaviour. A I is based upon the principles of computer science namely data structures used in knowledge representation, the algorithms needed to apply that knowledge and the languages and programming techniques used in their implementation.

An artificial neural network (ANN), also called a simulated neural network (SNN) or commonly just neural network (NN) is an interconnected group of artificial neurons that uses a mathematical or computational model for information processing based on a connectionist approach to computation. In most cases an ANN is an adaptive system that changes its structure based on external or internal information that flows through the network.

In more practical terms neural networks are non-linear statistical data modeling tools. They can be used to model complex relationships between inputs and outputs or to find patterns in data.

Background

An Artificial Neural network involves a network of simple processing elements (neurons) which can exhibit complex global behaviour, determined by the connections between the processing elements and element parameters.

In a neural network model, simple nodes (called "neurons") are connected together to form a network of nodes - hence the term "neural network".In modern software implementations of artificial neural networks the approach inspired by biology has more or less been abandoned for a more practical approach based on statistics and signal processing. In some of these systems neural networks, or parts of neural networks (such as artificial neurons) are used as components in larger systems that combine both adaptive and non-adaptive elements.

Applications

The utility of artificial neural network models lies in the fact that they can be used to infer a function from observations. This is particularly useful in applications where the complexity of the data or task makes the design of such a function by hand impractical.

Real life applications

The tasks to which artificial neural networks are applied tend to fall within the following broad categories:

- Function approximation, or regression analysis, including time series prediction and modelling.
- Classification, including pattern and sequence recognition, novelty detection and sequential decision making.
- Data processing, including filtering, clustering, blind source separation and compression.

Application areas include system identification and control (vehicle control, process control), game-playing and decision making (backgammon, chess, racing), pattern recognition (radar systems, face identification, object recognition and more), sequence recognition (gesture, speech, handwritten text recognition), medical diagnosis, financial applications, data mining (or knowledge discovery in databases, "KDD"), visualisation and e-mail spam filtering.

Neural Network Applications

Control Systems, describes three practical neural network control system applications, including neural network model predictive control, model reference adaptive control, and a feedback linearization controller. Other neural network applications are

Business Applications

The 1988 DARPA Neural Network Study lists various neural network applications, beginning in about 1984 with the adaptive channel equalizer. This device, which is an outstanding commercial success, is a single-neuron network used in long-distance telephone systems to stabilize voice signals. The DARPA report goes on to list other commercial applications, including a small word recognizer, a process monitor, a sonar classifier, and a risk analysis system. Neural networks have been applied in many other fields.

Aerospace

- High-performance aircraft autopilot, flight path simulation, aircraft control systems, autopilot enhancements, aircraft component simulation, aircraft component fault detection

Automotive

- Automobile automatic guidance system, warranty activity analysis

Banking

- Check and other document reading, credit application evaluation

Credit Card Activity Checking

- Spot unusual credit card activity that might possibly be associated with loss of a credit card

Defense

- Weapon steering, target tracking, object discrimination, facial recognition, new kinds of sensors, sonar, radar and image signal processing including data compression, feature extraction and noise suppression, signal/image identification

Electronics

- Code sequence prediction, integrated circuit chip layout, process control, chip failure analysis, machine vision, voice synthesis, nonlinear modeling

Entertainment

- Animation, special effects, market forecasting

Financial

- Real estate appraisal, loan advising, mortgage screening, corporate bond rating, credit-line use analysis, portfolio trading program, corporate financial analysis, currency price prediction

Industrial

- Neural networks are being trained to predict the output gases of furnaces and other industrial processes. They then replace complex and costly equipment used for this purpose in the past.

Insurance

- Policy application evaluation, product optimization

Manufacturing

- Manufacturing process control, product design and analysis, process and machine diagnosis, real-time particle identification, visual quality inspection systems, beer testing, welding quality analysis, paper quality prediction, computer-chip quality analysis, analysis of grinding operations, chemical product design analysis, machine maintenance analysis, project bidding, planning and management, dynamic modeling of chemical process system

Medical

- Breast cancer cell analysis, EEG and ECG analysis, prosthesis design, optimization of transplant times, hospital expense reduction, hospital quality improvement, emergency-room test advisement

Oil and Gas

- Exploration

Robotics

- Trajectory control, forklift robot, manipulator controllers, vision systems

Speech

- Speech recognition, speech compression, vowel classification, text-to-speech synthesis

Securities

- Market analysis, automatic bond rating, stock trading advisory systems

Telecommunications

- Image and data compression, automated information services, real-time translation of spoken language, customer payment processing systems

Transportation

- Truck brake diagnosis systems, vehicle scheduling, routing systems

2.7 Basic Approach of the working of ANN

A neural network can learn, and therefore can be trained to find solutions, recognize patterns, classify data, and forecast future events. The behavior of a neural network is defined by the way its individual computing elements are connected and by the strength of those connections, or weights. The weights are automatically adjusted by training the network according to a specified learning rule until it performs the desired task correctly.

The Neural Network Toolbox GUIs make it easy to work with neural networks. The Neural Network Fitting Tool is a wizard that leads you through the process of fitting data using neural networks. You can use the tool to import large and complex data sets, quickly create and train networks, and evaluate network performance.

A second GUI gives you greater ability to customize the network architecture and learning algorithms. Simple graphical representations enable you to visualize and understand network architecture.

2.8 Artificial Network Operations

The other part of the "art" of using neural networks revolve around the myriad of ways these individual neurons can be clustered together. This clustering occurs in the human mind in such a way that information can be processed in a dynamic, interactive, and self-organizing way. Biologically, neural networks are constructed in a three-dimensional world from microscopic components. These neurons seem capable of nearly unrestricted interconnections. That is not true of any proposed, or existing, man-made network. Integrated circuits, using current technology, are two-dimensional devices with a limited number of layers for interconnection. This physical reality restrains the types, and scope, of artificial neural networks that can be implemented in silicon.

Currently, neural networks are the simple clustering of the primitive artificial neurons. This clustering occurs by creating layers, which are then connected to one another. How these layers connect is the other part of the "art" of engineering networks to resolve real world problems.

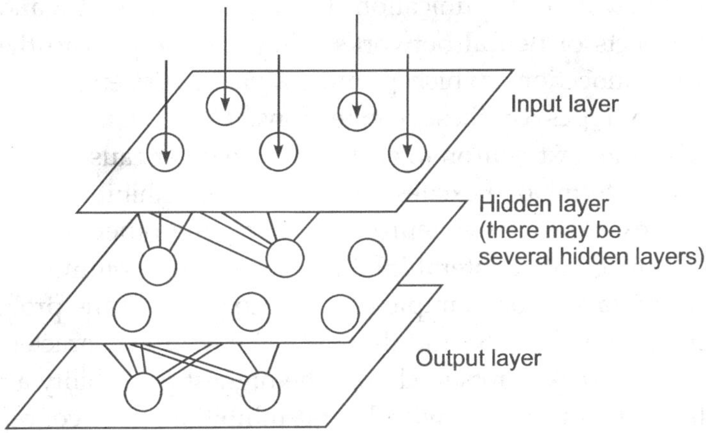

Figure 2.8.1 A Simple Neural Network Diagram.

Basically, all artificial neural networks have a similar structure or topology as shown in Figure 2.8.1. In that structure some of the neurons interfaces to the real world to receive its inputs. Other neurons provide the real world with the network's outputs. This output might be the particular character that the network thinks that it has scanned or the particular image it thinks is being viewed. All the rest of the neurons are hidden from view.

But a neural network is more than a bunch of neurons. It is the grouping of these neurons into layers, the connections between these layers, and the summation and transfer functions that comprises a functioning neural network. The general terms used to describe these characteristics are common to all networks.

Although there are useful networks, which contain only one layer, or even one element, most applications require networks that contain at least the three normal types of layers - input, hidden, and output. The layer of input neurons receives the data either from input files or directly from electronic sensors in real-time applications. The output layer sends information directly to the outside world, to a secondary computer process, or to other devices such as a mechanical control system. Between these two layers can be many hidden layers. These internal layers contain many of the neurons in various interconnected structures. The inputs and outputs of each of these hidden neurons simply go to other neurons.

In most networks each neuron in a hidden layer receives the signals from all of the neurons in a layer above it, typically an input layer. After a neuron performs its function it passes its output to all of the neurons in the layer below it, providing a feed forward path to the output.

These lines of communication from one neuron to another are important aspects of neural networks. They are the glue to the system. They are the connections, which provide a variable strength to an input. There are two types of these connections. One causes the summing mechanism of the next neuron to add while the other causes it to subtract. In more human terms one excites while the other inhibits.

Some networks want a neuron to inhibit the other neurons in the same layer. This is called lateral inhibition. The most common use of this is in the output layer. For example in text recognition if the probability of a character being a "P" is .85 and the probability of the character being an "F" is .65, the network wants to choose the highest probability and inhibit all the others. It can do that with lateral inhibition. This concept is also called competition.

Another type of connection is feedback. This is where the output of one-layer routes backs to a previous layer. An example of this is shown in Figure 2.8.2.

Figure 2.8.2 Simple Network with Feedback and Competition.

The way that the neurons are connected to each other has a significant impaction the operation of the network. In the larger, more professional software development packages the user is allowed to add, delete, and control these connections at will. By "tweaking" parameters these connections can be made to either excite or inhibit.

2.9 Detailed Description of Neural Network Components and How They Work

Now that there is a general understanding of artificial neural networks, it is appropriate to explore them in greater detail. But before jumping into the various networks, a more complete understanding of the inner workings of a neural network is needed. As stated earlier, artificial neural networks are a large class of parallel processing architectures, which are useful in specific types of complex problems. These architectures should not be confused with common parallel processing configurations, which apply many sequential processing units to standard computing topologies. Instead, neural networks are radically different than conventional Von Neumann computers in that they crudely mimic the fundamental properties of man's brain.

Artificial neural networks are loosely based on biology. Current research into the brain's physiology has unlocked only a limited understanding of how neurons work or even what constitutes intelligence in general. Researchers are working in both the biological and engineering fields to further decipher the key mechanisms for how man learns and reacts to everyday experiences. Improved knowledge in neural processing helps create better, more succinct artificial networks. It also creates a cornucopia of new, and ever evolving, architectures. Kunihiko Fukushima, a senior research scientist in Japan, describes the give and take of building a neural network model; "We try to follow physiological evidence as faithfully as possible. For parts not yet clear, however, we construct a hypothesis and build a model that follows that hypothesis. We then analyze or simulate the behavior of the model and compare it with that of the brain. If we find any discrepancy in the behavior between the model and the brain, we change the initial hypothesis and modify the model. We repeat this procedure until the model behaves in the same way as the brain." This common process has created thousands of network topologies.

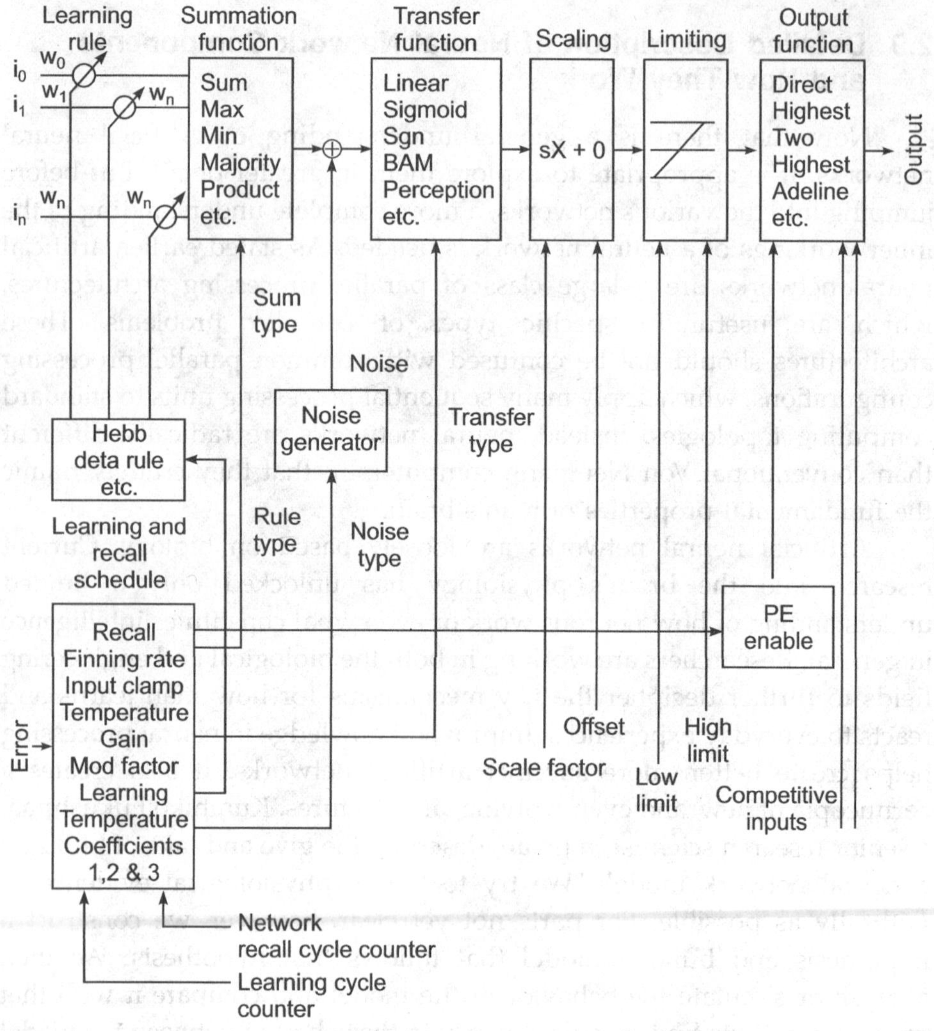

Figure 2.9.1 Processing Element.

Neural computing is about machines, not brains. It is the process of trying to build processing systems that draw upon the highly successful designs naturally occurring in biology. This linkage with biology is the reason that there is a common architectural thread throughout today's artificial neural networks. Figure 2.9.1 shows a model of an artificial neuron, or processing element, which embodies a wide variety of network architectures.

This figure is adapted from Neural Ware's simulation model used in Neural Works Profession II/Plus. Neural Ware sells a artificial neural network design and development software package. Their processing element model shows that networks designed for prediction can be very similar to networks designed for classification or any other network category. Prediction, classification and other network categories will be discussed later. The point here is that all artificial neural processing elements have common components.

2.10 Major Components of an Artificial Neuron

This section describes the seven major components, which make up an artificial neuron. These components are valid whether the neuron is used for input, output, or is in one of the hidden layers.

Component 1. Weighting Factors: A neuron usually receives many simultaneous inputs. Each input has its own relative weight, which gives the input the impact that it needs on the processing element's summation function. These weights perform the same type of function, as do the varying synaptic strengths of biological neurons. In both cases, some inputs are made more important than others so that they have a greater effect on the processing element as they combine to produce a neural response.

Weights are adaptive coefficients within the network that determine the intensity of the input signal as registered by the artificial neuron. They are a measure of an input's connection strength. These strengths can be modified in response to various training sets and according to a network's specific topology or through its learning rules.

Component 2. Summation Function: The first step in a processing element's operation is to compute the weighted sum of all of the inputs. Mathematically, the inputs and the corresponding weights are vectors which can be represented as (i1, i2 . . . in) and (w1, w2 . . . wn). The total input signal is the dot, or inner, product of these two vectors. This simplistic summation function is found by multiplying each component of the i vector by the corresponding component of the w vector and then adding up all the products. Input1 = i1 * w1, input2 = i2 * w2, etc., are added as input1 + input2 + . . . + input n. The result is a single number, not a multi-element vector.

Geometrically, the inner product of two vectors can be considered a measure of their similarity. If the vectors point in the same direction, the inner product is maximum; if the vectors point in opposite direction (180 degrees out of phase), their inner product is minimum.

The summation function can be more complex than just the simple input and weight sum of products. The input and weighting coefficients can be combined in many different ways before passing on to the transfer function. In addition to a simple product summing, the summation function can select the minimum, maximum, majority, product, or several normalizing algorithms. The specific algorithm for combining neural inputs is determined by the chosen network architecture and paradigm.

Some summation functions have an additional process applied to the result before it is passed on to the transfer function. This process is sometimes called the activation function. The purpose of utilizing an activation function is to allow the summation output to vary with respect to time. Activation functions currently are pretty much confined to research. Most of the current network implementations use an "identity" activation function, which is equivalent to not having one. Additionally, such a function is likely to be a component of the network as a whole rather than of each individual processing element component.

Component 3. Transfer Function: The result of the summation function, almost always the weighted sum, is transformed to a working output through an algorithmic process known as the transfer function. In the transfer function the summation total can be compared with some threshold to determine the neural output. If the sum is greater than the threshold value, the processing element generates a signal. If the sum of the input and weight products is less than the threshold, no signal (or some inhibitory signal) is generated. Both types of response are significant.

The threshold, or transfer function, is generally non-linear. Linear (straight-line) functions are limited because the output is simply proportional to the input. Linear functions are not very useful. That was the problem in the earliest network models as noted in Minsky and Papert's book Perceptrons.

The transfer function could be something as simple as depending upon whether the result of the summation function is positive or negative. The network could output zero and one, one and minus one, or other numeric combinations. The transfer function would then be a "hard limiter" or step function. See Figure 4.1.1 for sample transfer functions.

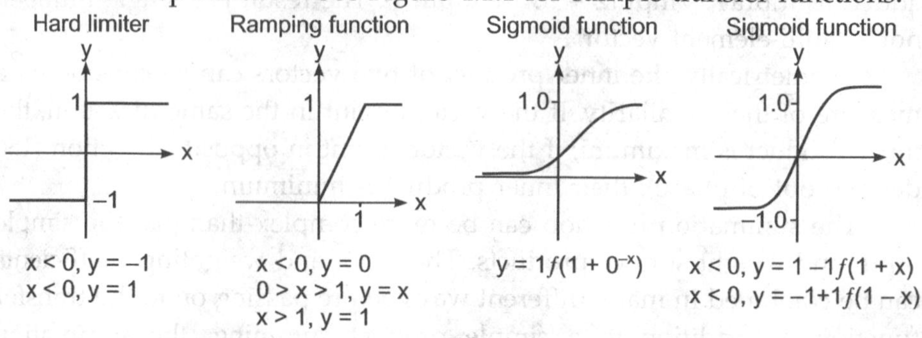

Figure 4.1.1 Sample Transfer Functions.

Another type of transfer function, the threshold or ramping function, could mirror the input within a given range and still act as a hard limiter outside that range. It is a linear function that has been clipped to minimum and maximum values, making it non-linear. Yet another option would be a sigmoid or S-shaped curve. That curve approaches a minimum and maximum value at the asymptotes. It is common for this curve to be called a sigmoid when it ranges between 0 and 1, and a hyperbolic tangent when it ranges between -1 and 1. Mathematically, the exciting feature of these curves is that both the function and its derivatives are continuous. This option works fairly well and is often the transfer function of choice. Other transfer functions are dedicated to specific network architectures and will be discussed later.

Prior to applying the transfer function, uniformly distributed random noise may be added. The source and amount of this noise is determined by the learning mode of a given network paradigm. This noise is normally referred to as "temperature" of the artificial neurons. The name, temperature, is derived from the physical phenomenon that as people become too hot or cold their ability to think is affected. Electronically, this process is simulated by adding noise. Indeed, by adding different levels of noise to the summation result, more brain-like transfer functions are realized. To more closely mimic nature's characteristics, some experimenters are using a gaussian noise source. Gaussian noise is similar to uniformly distributed noise except that the distribution of random numbers within the temperature range is along a bell curve. The use of temperature is an ongoing research area and is not being applied to many engineering applications.

NASA just announced a network topology, which uses what it calls a temperature coefficient in a new feed-forward, back-propagation learning function. But this temperature coefficient is a global term, which is applied to the gain of the transfer function. It should not be confused with the more common term, temperature, which is simple noise being added to individual neurons. In contrast, the global temperature coefficient allows the transfer function to have a learning variable much like the synaptic input weights. This concept is claimed to create a network, which has a significantly faster (by several order of magnitudes) learning rate and provides more accurate results than other feed forward, back-propagation networks.

Component 4. Scaling and Limiting: After the processing element's transfer function, the result can pass through additional processes, which scale and limit. This scaling simply multiplies a scale factor times the transfer value, and then adds an offset. Limiting is the mechanism which insures that the scaled result does not exceed an upper or lower bound. This limiting is in addition to the hard limits that the original transfer function may have performed.

This type of scaling and limiting is mainly used in topologies to test biological neuron models, such as James Anderson's brain-state-in-the-box.

Component 5. Output Function (Competition): Each processing element is allowed one output signal, which it may output to hundreds of other neurons. This is just like the biological neuron, where there are many inputs and only one output action. Normally, the output is directly equivalent to the transfer function's result. Some network topologies, however, modify the transfer result to incorporate competition among neighboring processing elements. Neurons are allowed to compete with each other, inhibiting processing elements unless they have great strength. Competition can occur at one or both of two levels. First, competition determines which artificial neuron will be active, or provides an output. Second, competitive inputs help determine which processing element will participate in the learning or adaptation process.

Component 6. Error Function and Back-Propagated Value: In most learning networks the difference between the current output and the desired output is calculated. This raw error is then transformed by the error function to match particular network architecture. The most basic architectures use this error directly, but some square the error while retaining its sign, some cube the error, other paradigms modify the raw error to fit their specific purposes. The artificial neuron's error is then typically propagated into the learning function of another processing element. This error term is sometimes called the current error.

The current error is typically propagated backwards to a previous layer. Yet, this back-propagated value can be either the current error, the current error scaled in some manner (often by the derivative of the transfer function), or some other desired output depending on the network type. Normally, this back-propagated value, after being scaled by the learning function, is multiplied against each of the incoming connection weights to modify them before the next learning cycle.

Component 7. Learning Function: The purpose of the learning function is to modify the variable connection weights on the inputs of each processing element according to some neural based algorithm. This process of changing the weights of the input connections to achieve some desired result can also be called the adaption function, as well as the learning mode. There are two types of learning: supervised and unsupervised. Supervised learning requires a teacher. The teacher may be a training set of data or an observer who grades the performance of the network results. Either way, having a teacher is learning by reinforcement. When there is no external teacher, the system must organize itself by some internal criteria designed into the network. This is learning by doing.

2.11 Training an Artificial Neural Network

Once a network has been structured for a particular application, that network is ready to be trained. To start this process the initial weights are chosen randomly. Then, the training, or learning, begins.

There are two approaches to training - supervised and unsupervised. Supervised training involves a mechanism of providing the network with the desired output either by manually "grading" the network's performance or by providing the desired outputs with the inputs. Unsupervised training is where the network has to make sense of the inputs without outside help.

The vast bulk of networks utilize supervised training. Unsupervised training is used to perform some initial characterization on inputs. However, in the full-blown sense of being truly self-learning, it is still just a shining promise that is not fully understood, does not completely work, and thus is relegated to the lab.

2.11.1 Supervised Training.

In supervised training, both the inputs and the outputs are provided. The network then processes the inputs and compares its resulting outputs against the desired outputs. Errors are then propagated back through the system, causing the system to adjust the weights, which control the network. This process occurs over and over as the weights are continually tweaked. The set of data, which enables the training, is called the "training set." During the training of a network the same set of data is processed many times as the connection weights are ever refined.

The current commercial network development packages provide tools to monitor how well an artificial neural network is converging on the ability to predict the right answer. These tools allow the training process to go on for days; stopping only when the system reaches some statistically desired point, or accuracy. However, some networks never learn. This could be because the input data does not contain the specific information from which the desired output is derived. Networks also don't converge if there is not enough data to enable complete learning. Ideally, there should be enough data so that part of the data can be held back as a test. Many layered networks with multiple nodes are capable of memorizing data. To monitor the network to determine if the system is simply memorizing its data in some no significant way, supervised training needs to hold back a set of data to be used to test the system after it has undergone its training.

Note: memorization is avoided by not having too many processing elements.

If a network simply can't solve the problem, the designer then has to review the input and outputs, the number of layers, the number of elements per layer, the connections between the layers, the summation, transfer, and training functions, and even the initial weights themselves. Those changes required to create a successful network constitute a process wherein the "art" of neural networking occurs. Another part of the designer's creativity governs the rules of training. There are many laws (algorithms) used to implement the adaptive feedback required to adjust the weights during training. The most common technique is backward-error propagation, more commonly known as back-propagation.

Training involves a "feel," and conscious analysis, to insure that the network is not over trained. Initially, an artificial neural network configures itself with the general statistical trends of the data. Later, it continues to "learn" about other aspects of the data, which may be spurious from a general viewpoint. When finally the system has been correctly trained, and no further learning is needed, the weights can, if desired, be "frozen." In some systems this finalized network is then turned into hardware so that it can be fast. Other systems don't lock themselves in but continue to learn while in production use.

2.11.2 Unsupervised, or Adaptive Training.

The other type of training is called unsupervised training. In unsupervised training, the network is provided with inputs but not with desired outputs. The system itself must then decide what features it will use to group the input data. This is often referred to as self-organization or adaption.

At the present time, unsupervised learning is not well understood. This adaption to the environment is the promise, which would enable science fiction types of robots to continually learn on their own as they encounter new situations and new environments. Life is filled with situations where exact training sets do not exist. Some of these situations involve military action where new combat techniques and new weapons might be encountered. Because of this unexpected aspect to life and the human desire to be prepared, there continues to be research into, and hope for, this field. Yet, at the present time, the vast bulk of neural network work is in systems with supervised learning. Supervised learning is achieving results.

One of the leading researchers into unsupervised learning is Tuevo Kohonen, an electrical engineer at the Helsinki University of Technology. He has developed a self-organizing network, sometimes called an auto-associator, that learns without the benefit of knowing the right answer. It is an unusual looking network in that it contains one single layer with many connections. The weights for those connections have to be initialized and the inputs have to be normalized. The neurons are set up to compete in a winner-take-all fashion.

Kohonen continues his research into networks that are structured differently than standard, feed forward, back-propagation approaches. Kohonen's work deals with the grouping of neurons into fields. Neurons within a field are "topologically ordered." Topology is a branch of mathematics that studies how to map from one space to another without changing the geometric configuration. The three-dimensional groupings often found in mammalian brains are an example of topological ordering.

Kohonen has pointed out that the lack of topology in neural network models make today's neural networks just simple abstractions of the real neural networks within the brain. As this research continues, more powerful self-learning networks may become possible. But currently, this field remains one that is still in the laboratory.

2.12 Learning an Artificial Neural Network

Neural network software is used to simulate, research, develop and apply artificial neural networks, biological neural networks and in some cases a wider array of adaptive systems.

Learning paradigms

There are three major learning paradigms, each corresponding to a particular abstract learning task. These are supervised learning, unsupervised learning and reinforcement learning. Usually any given type of network architecture can be employed in any of those tasks.

2.12.1 Learning Laws.

Many learning laws are in common use. Most of these laws are some sorts of variation of the best-known and oldest learning law, Hebb's Rule. Research into different learning functions continues as new ideas routinely show up in trade publications. Some researchers have the modeling of biological learning as their main objective. Others are experimenting with adaptations of their perceptions of how nature handles learning. Either way, man's understanding of how neural processing actually works is very limited. Learning is certainly more complex than the simplifications represented by the learning laws currently developed. A few of the major laws are presented as examples.

Hebb's Rule: The first, and undoubtedly the best known, learning rule was introduced by Donald Hebb. The description appeared in his book The Organization of Behavior in 1949. His basic rule is: If a neuron receives an input from another neuron, and if both are highly active (mathematically have the same sign), the weight between the neurons should be strengthened.

Hopfield Law: It is similar to Hebb's rule with the exception that it specifies the magnitude of the strengthening or weakening. It states, "if the desired output and the input are both active or both inactive, increment the connection weight by the learning rate, otherwise decrement the weight by the learning rate."

The Delta Rule: This rule is a further variation of Hebb's Rule. It is one of the most commonly used. This rule is based on the simple idea of continuously modifying the strengths of the input connections to reduce the difference (the delta) between the desired output value and the actual output of a processing element. This rule changes the synaptic weights in the way that minimizes the mean squared error of the network. This rule is also referred to as the Widrow-Hoff Learning Rule and the Least Mean Square (LMS) Learning Rule.

The way that the Delta Rule works is that the delta error in the output layer is transformed by the derivative of the transfer function and is then used in the previous neural layer to adjust input connection weights. In other words, this error is back propagated into previous layers one layer at a time. The process of back-propagating the network errors continues until the first layer is reached. The network type called Feed forward, Back-propagation derives its name from this method of computing the error term.

When using the delta rule, it is important to ensure that the input data set is well randomized. Well-ordered or structured presentation of the training set can lead to a network, which cannot converge to the desired accuracy. If that happens, then the network is incapable of learning the problem.

The Gradient Descent Rule: This rule is similar to the Delta Rule in that the derivative of the transfer function is still used to modify the delta error before it is applied to the connection weights. Here, however, an additional proportional constant tied to the learning rate is appended to the final modifying factor acting upon the weight. This rule is commonly used, even though it converges to a point of stability very slowly.

It has been shown that different learning rates for different layers of network help the learning process converge faster. In these tests, the learning rates for those layers close to the output were set lower than those layers near the input. This is especially important for applications where the input data is not derived from a strong underlying model.

Kohonen's Learning Law: This procedure, developed by Teuvo Kohonen, was inspired by learning in biological systems. In this procedure, the processing elements compete for the opportunity to learn, or update their weights. The processing element with the largest output is declared the winner and has the capability of inhibiting its competitors as well as exciting its neighbors. Only the winner is permitted an output, and only the winner plus its neighbors are allowed to adjust their connection weights.

Further, the size of the neighborhood can vary during the training period. The usual paradigm is to start with a larger definition of the neighborhood, and narrow in as the training process proceeds. Because the winning element is defined as the one that has the closest match to the input pattern, Kohonen networks model the distribution of the inputs. This is good for statistical or topological modeling of the data and is sometimes referred to as self-organizing maps or self-organizing topologies.

2.12.2 Supervised learning

In supervised learning, we are given a set of example pairs and the aim is to find a function f in the allowed class of functions that matches the examples. In other words, we wish to infer the mapping implied by the data and the cost function is related to the mismatch between our mapping and the data and it implicitly contains prior knowledge about the problem domain.

A commonly used cost is the mean-squared error which tries to minimise the average error between the network's output, f(x), and the target value y over all the example pairs. When one tries to minimise this cost using gradient descent for the class of neural networks called Multi-Layer Perceptrons, one obtains the well-known backpropagation algorithm for training neural networks.

Tasks that fall within the paradigm of supervised learning are pattern recognition (also known as classification) and regression (also known as function approximation). The supervised learning paradigm is also applicable to sequential data (e.g., for speech and gesture recognition).

2.12.3 Unsupervised learning

In unsupervised learning we are given some data x, and the cost function to be minimised can be any function of the data x and the network's output, f. The cost function is determined by the task formulation. Most applications fall within the domain of estimation problems such as statistical modelling, compression, filtering, blind source separation and clustering.

As a trivial example, consider the model f(x) = a, where a is a constant and the cost C = (E[x] - f(x))2. Minimising this cost will give us a value of a that is equal to the mean of the data. The cost function can be much more complicated. Its form depends on the application: For example in compression it could be related to the mutual information between x and y. In statistical modelling, it could be related to the posterior probability of the model given the data.

Tasks that fall within the paradigm of unsupervised learning are in general estimation problems; the applications include clustering, the estimation of statistical distributions, compression and filtering.

2.12.4 Reinforcement learning

In reinforcement learning, data x is usually not given, but generated by an agent's interactions with the environment. At each point in time t, the agent performs an action yt and the environment generates an observation xt and an instantaneous cost ct, according to some (usually unknown) dynamics. The aim is to discover a policy for selecting actions that minimises some measure of a long-term cost, i.e. the expected cumulative cost. The environment's dynamics and the long-term cost for each policy are usually unknown, but can be estimated. ANNs are frequently used in reinforcement learning as part of the overall algorithm. Tasks that fall within the paradigm of reinforcement learning are control problems, games and other sequential decision making tasks.

2.12.5 Learning algorithms

There are numerous algorithms available for training neural network models; most of them can be viewed as a straightforward application of optimization theory and statistical estimation. This is done by simply taking the derivative of the cost function with respect to the network parameters and then changing those parameters in a gradient-related direction.

Evolutionary computation methods, simulated annealing, expectation maximization and non-parametric methods are among other commonly used methods for training neural networks. Recent developments in this field also saw the use of Particle Swarm Optimizations and other Swarm Intelligence techniques used in the training of neural networks, in this case fitness would be defined as the accuracy of the neural network.

2.13 Generalization of Artificial Neural Network

In applications where the goal is to create a system that generalises well in unseen examples, the problem of overtraining has emerged. This arises in overcomplex or overspecified systems when the capacity of the network significantly exceeds the needed free parameters. There are two schools of thought for avoiding this problem: The first is to use cross-validation and similar techniques to check for the presence of overtraining and optimally select hyperparameters such as to minimise the generalisation error. The second is to use some form of regularisation. This is a concept that emerges naturally in a probabilistic (Bayesian) framework, where the regularisation can be performed by putting a larger prior probability over simpler models; but also in statistical learning theory, where the goal is to minimise over two quantities: the 'empirical risk' and the 'structural risk', which roughly correspond to the error over the training set and the predicted error in unseen data due to overfitting.

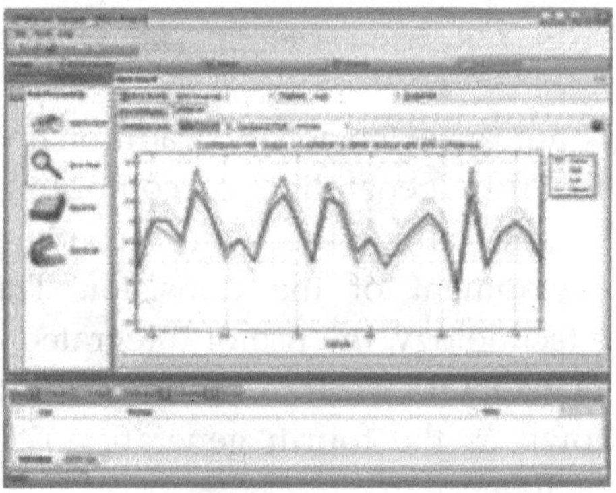

Confidence analysis of a neural network

Supervised neural networks that use an MSE cost function can use formal statistical methods to determine the confidence of the trained model. The MSE on a validation set can be used as an estimate for variance. This value can then be used to calculate the confidence interval of the output of the network, assuming a normal distribution. A confidence analysis made this way is statistically valid as long as the output probability distribution stays the same and the network is not modified.

By assigning a softmax activation function on the output layer of the neural network (or a softmax component in a component-based neural network) for categorical target variables, the outputs can be interpreted as posterior probabilities. This is very useful in classification as it gives a certainty measure on classifications.

The softmax activation function : $y_1 = \frac{e^{x_i}}{\sum_{j=1}^{c} e^{x_j}}$

2.14 How Neural Networks Differ from Traditional Computing and Expert Systems

Neural networks offer a different way to analyze data, and to recognize patterns within that data, than traditional computing methods. However, they are not a solution for all computing problems. Traditional computing methods work well for problems that can be well characterized. Balancing checkbooks, keeping ledgers, and keeping tabs of inventory are well defined and do not require the special characteristics of neural networks. Table 2.14.1 identifies the basic differences between the two computing approaches.

Traditional computers are ideal for many applications. They can process data, track inventories, network results, and protect equipment. These applications do not need the special characteristics of neural networks.

Expert systems are an extension of traditional computing and are sometimes called the fifth generation of computing. (First generation computing used switches and wires. The second generation occurred because of the development of the transistor. The third generation involved solid-state technology, the use of integrated circuits, and higher level languages like COBOL, Fortran, and "C". End-user tools, "code generators," are known as the fourth generation.) The fifth generation involves artificial intelligence.

CHARACTERISTICS	TRADITIONAL COMPUTING (including Expert Systems)	ARTIFICIAL NEURAL NETWORKS
Processing style	Sequential	Parallel
Functions	Logically (left brained) via Rules Concepts	Gestault (right brained)

	Calculations	via Images Pictures Controls
Learning Method Applications	By rules (didactically) Accounting word processing math inventory digital communications	By example (Socratic ally) Sensor processing speech recognition pattern recognition text recognition

Table 2.14.1 Comparison of Computing Approaches.

Typically, an expert system consists of two parts, an inference engine and a knowledge base. The inference engine is generic. It handles the user interface, external files, *program access, and scheduling*. The knowledge base contains the information that is specific to a particular problem. This knowledge base allows an expert to define the rules, which govern a process. This expert does not have to understand traditional programming. That person simply has to understand both what he wants a computer to do and how the mechanism of the expert system shell works. It is this shell, part of the inference engine, that actually tells the computer how to implement the expert's desires. This implementation occurs by the expert system generating the computer's programming itself; it does that through "programming" of its own. This programming is needed to establish the rules for a particular application. This method of establishing rules is also complex and does require a detail-oriented person.

Efforts to make expert systems general have run into a number of problems. As the complexity of the system increases, the system simply demands too much computing resources and becomes too slow. Expert systems have been found to be feasible only when narrowly confined.

Artificial neural networks offer a completely different approach to problem solving and they are sometimes called the sixth generation of computing. They try to provide a tool that both programs itself and learns on its own. Neural networks are structured to provide the capability to solve problems without the benefits of an expert and without the need of programming. They can seek patterns in data that no one knows are there.

A comparison of artificial intelligence's expert systems and neural networks is contained in Table 2.14.2.

Characteristics	Von Neumann Architecture Used for Expert Systems	Artificial Neural Networks
Processors	VLSI (traditional processors)	Artificial Neural Networks; variety of technologies; hardware development is on going
Processing Approach	Separate	The same
Processing Approach	Processes problem rule at a one time; sequential	Multiple, simultaneously
Connections	Externally programmable	Dynamically self programming
Self learning	Only algorithmic parameters modified	Continuously adaptable
Fault tolerance	None without special processors	Significant in the very nature of the interconnected neurons
Neurobiology in design	None	Moderate
Programming	Through a rule based complicated	Self-programming; but network must be set up properly
Ability to be fast	Requires big processors	Requires multiple custom-built chips

Table 2.14.2 Comparisons of Expert Systems and Neural Networks.

Expert systems have enjoyed significant successes. However, artificial intelligence has encountered problems in areas such as vision, continuous speech recognition and synthesis, and machine learning. Artificial intelligence also is hostage to the speed of the processor that it runs on. Ultimately, it is restricted to the theoretical limit of a single processor. Artificial intelligence is also burdened by the fact that experts don't always speak in rules.

Yet, despite the advantages of neural networks over both expert systems and more traditional computing in these specific areas, neural nets are not complete solutions. They offer a capability that is not ironclad, such as a debugged accounting system. They learn, and as such, they do continue to make "mistakes." Furthermore, even when a network has been developed, there is no way to ensure that the network is the optimal network.

Neural systems do exact their own demands. They do require their implementer to meet a number of conditions. These conditions include:

- A data set, which includes the information, which can characterize the problem.
- An adequately sized data set to both train and test the network.
- An understanding of the basic nature of the problem to be solved so that basic first-cut decision on creating the network can be made. These decisions include the activization and transfer functions, and the learning methods.
- An understanding of the development tools.
- Adequate processing powers (some applications demand real-time processing that exceeds what is available in the standard, sequential processing hardware. The development of hardware is the key to the future of neural networks).

Once these conditions are met, neural networks offer the opportunity of solving problems in an arena where traditional processors lack both the processing power and a step-by-step methodology. A number of very complicated problems cannot be solved in the traditional computing environments. For example, speech is something that all people can easily parse and understand. A person can understand a southern drawl, a Bronx accent, and the slurred words of a baby. Without the massively paralleled processing power of a neural network, this process is virtually impossible for a computer. Image recognition is another task that a human can easily do but which stymies even the biggest of computers. A person can recognize a plane as it turns, flies overhead, and disappears into a dot. A traditional computer might try to compare the changing images to a number of very different stored patterns.

This new way of computing requires skills beyond traditional computing. It is a natural evolution. Initially, computing was only hardware and engineers made it work. Then, there were software specialists - programmers, systems engineers, data base specialists, and designers. Now, there are also neural architects. This new professional needs to be skilled different than his predecessors of the past. For instance, he will need to know statistics in order to choose and evaluate training and testing situations. This skill of making neural networks work is one that will stress the logical thinking of current software engineers.

In summary, neural networks offer a unique way to solve some problems while making their own demands. The biggest demand is that the process is not simply logic. It involves an empirical skill, an intuitive feel as to how a network might be created.

2.15 History of Neural Networks

The study of the human brain is thousands of years old. With the advent of modern electronics, it was only natural to try to harness this thinking process. The first step toward artificial neural networks came in 1943 when Warren McCulloch, a neuro-physiologist, and a young mathematician, Walter Pitts, wrote a paper on how neurons might work. They modeled a simple neural network with electrical circuits.

Reinforcing this concept of neurons and how they work was a book written by Donald Hebb. The Organization of Behavior was written in 1949. It pointed out that neural pathways are strengthened each time that they are used. As computers advanced into their infancy of the 1950s, it became possible to begin to model the rudiments of these theories concerning human thought. Nathaniel Rochester from the IBM research laboratories led the first effort to simulate a neural network. That first attempt failed. But later attempts were successful. It was during this time that traditional computing began to flower and, as it did, the emphasis in computing left the neural research in the background.

Yet, throughout this time, advocates of "thinking machines" continued to argue their cases. In 1956 the Dartmouth Summer Research Project on Artificial Intelligence provided a boost to both artificial intelligence and neural networks. One of the outcomes of this process was to stimulate research in both the intelligent side, AI, as it is known throughout the industry, and in the much lower level neural processing part of the brain.

In the years following the Dartmouth Project, John von Neumann suggested imitating simple neuron functions by using telegraph relays or vacuum tubes. Also, Frank Rosenblatt, a neuro-biologist of Cornell, began work on the Perceptron. He was intrigued with the operation of the eye of a fly. Much of the processing which tells a fly to flee is done in its eye. The Perceptron, which resulted from this research, was built in hardware and is the oldest neural network still in use today. A single-layer perceptron was found to be useful in classifying a continuous-valued set of inputs into one of two classes. The perceptron computes a weighted sum of the inputs, subtracts a threshold, and passes one of two possible values out as the result. Unfortunately, the perceptron is limited and was proven as such during the "disillusioned years" in Marvin Minsky and Seymour Papert's 1969 book Perceptrons.

In 1959, Bernard Widrow and Marcian Hoff of Stanford developed models they called ADALINE and MADALINE. These models were named for their use of Multiple Adaptive Linear Elements. MADALINE was the first neural network to be applied to a real world problem. It is an adaptive filter, which eliminates echoes on phone lines. This neural network is still in commercial use.

Unfortunately, these earlier successes caused people to exaggerate the potential of neural networks, particularly in light of the limitation in the electronics then available. This excessive hype, which flowed out of the academic and technical worlds, infected the general literature of the time. Disappointment set in, as promises were unfilled. Also, a fear set in as writers began to ponder what effect "thinking machines" would have on man. Asimov's series on robots revealed the effects on man's morals and values when machines where capable of doing all of mankind's work. Other writers created more sinister computers, such as HAL from the movie 2001.

These fears, combined with unfulfilled, outrageous claims, caused respected voices to critique the neural network research. The result was to halt much of the funding. This period of stunted growth lasted through 1981. In 1982 several events caused a renewed interest. John Hopfield of Caltech presented a paper to the national Academy of Sciences. Hopfield's approach was not to simply model brains but to create useful devices. With clarity and mathematical analysis, he showed how such networks could work and what they could do. Yet, Hopfield's biggest asset was his charisma. He was articulate, likeable, and a champion of a dormant technology.

At the same time, another event occurred. A conference was held in Kyoto, Japan. This conference was the US-Japan Joint Conference on Cooperative/Competitive Neural Networks. Japan subsequently announced their Fifth Generation effort. US periodicals picked up that story, generating a worry that the US could be left behind. Soon funding was flowing once again. By 1985 the American Institute of Physics began what has become an annual meeting - Neural Networks for Computing. By 1987, the Institute of Electrical and Electronic Engineer's (IEEE) first International Conference on Neural Networks drew more than 1,800 attendees. By 1989 at the Neural Networks for Defense meeting Bernard Widrow told his audience that they were engaged in World War IV,

"World War III never happened," where the battlefields are world trade and manufacturing. The 1990 US Department of Defense Small Business Innovation Research Program named 16 topics, which specifically targeted neural networks with an additional 13 mentioning the possible use of neural networks.

Today, neural networks discussions are occurring everywhere. Their promise seems very bright, as nature itself is the proof that this kind of thing works. Yet, its future, indeed the very key to the whole technology, lies in hardware development. Currently most neural network development is simply proving that the principal works. This research is developing neural networks that, due to processing limitations, take weeks to learn.

To take these prototypes out of the lab and put them into use requires specialized chips. Companies are working on three types of neuro chips - digital, analog, and optical. Some companies are working on creating a "silicon compiler" to generate a neural network Application Specific Integrated Circuit (ASIC). These ASICs and neuron-like digital chips appear to be the wave of the near future. Ultimately, optical chips look very promising. Yet, it may be years before optical chips see the light of day in commercial applications.

2.16 Summary

- Artificial Neural Networks are relatively crude electronic models based on the neural structure of the brain.
- The power of the human mind comes from the sheer numbers of these basic components and the multiple connections between them. It also comes from genetic programming and learning.
- The individual neurons are complicated. They have a myriad of parts, sub-systems, and control mechanisms. They convey information via a host of electrochemical pathways. There are over one hundred different classes of neurons, depending on the classification method used.
- The fundamental processing element of a neural network is a neuron. This building block of human awareness encompasses a few general capabilities. Basically, a biological neuron receives inputs from other sources, combines them in some way, performs a generally nonlinear operation on the result, and then outputs the final result.
- Many models are used in the field, each defined at a different level of abstraction and trying to model different aspects of neural systems. They range from models of the short-term

behaviour of individual neurons, through models of how the dynamics of neural circuitry arise from interactions between individual neurons, to models of how behaviour can arise from abstract neural modules that represent complete subsystems.

- An artificial neural network (ANN), also called a simulated neural network (SNN) or commonly just neural network (NN) is an interconnected group of artificial neurons that uses a mathematical or computational model for information processing based on a connectionist approach to computation.
- An artificial neural network involves a network of simple processing elements (neurons) which can exhibit complex global behaviour, determined by the connections between the processing elements and element parameters.
- The utility of artificial neural network models lies in the fact that they can be used to infer a function from observations. This is particularly useful in applications where the complexity of the data or task makes the design of such a function by hand impractical.
- Network architecture is an abstraction level of an overall system, in which the goals of a user action are representable as functional architectural properties. For example, a hypermedia application must be concerned with the location of information pages, performing requests, and rendering data streams.
- In most networks each neuron in a hidden layer receives the signals from all of the neurons in a layer above it, typically an input layer. After a neuron performs its function it passes its output to all of the neurons in the layer below it, providing a feed forward path to the output.
- In supervised training, both the inputs and the outputs are provided. The network then processes the inputs and compares its resulting outputs against the desired outputs. Errors are then propagated back through the system, causing the system to adjust the weights, which control the network.
- In unsupervised training, the network is provided with inputs but not with desired outputs. The system itself must then decide what features it will use to group the input data. This is often referred to as self-organization or adaption.
- A simple recurrent network (SRN) is a variation on the multi-layer perceptron, sometimes called an "Elman network" due to its invention by Jeff Elman. A three-layer network is used, with the addition of a set of "context units" in the input layer.

- Neural computing is about machines, not brains. It is the process of trying to build processing systems that draw upon the highly successful designs naturally occurring in biology.
- Weights are adaptive coefficients within the network that determine the intensity of the input signal as registered by the artificial neuron. They are a measure of an input's connection strength.
- The summation function can be more complex than just the simple input and weight sum of products. The input and weighting coefficients can be combined in many different ways before passing on to the transfer function.
- The transfer function could be something as simple as depending upon whether the result of the summation function is positive or negative. The network could output zero and one, one and minus one, or other numeric combinations.
- The rate at which Artificial Neural Networks learn depends upon several controllable factors. In selecting the approach there are many trade-offs to consider. Obviously, a slower rate means a lot more time is spent in accomplishing the off-line learning to produce an adequately trained system.
- Many learning laws are in common use. Most of these laws are some sort of variation of the best known and oldest learning law, Hebb's Rule. Research into different learning functions continues as new ideas routinely show up in trade publications. Some researchers have the modeling of biological learning as their main objective.

2.17 Review Questions

1. Discuss Biological &Artificial Neurons and How They Work.
2. Discuss the Electronic Implementation of Artificial Neurons.
3. Discuss the training procedure of a neural network and discuss the two types of neural networking training.
4. Discuss the model of knowledge representation of a neural network/
5. Discuss the working of a artificial neural network and explain the back propagations neural network.
6. How Neural Networks Differ from Traditional Computing and Expert Systems
7. Explain the History of Neural Networks.

8. Explain the Generalization of Artificial Neural Network.
9. Discuss Detailed Description of Neural Network Components and How They Work.
10. Discuss the Major Components of an Artificial Neuron.
11. Discuss the Teaching an Artificial Neural Network.

Chapter No. 3

Application of Artificial Neural Network Classification

3.1 Clustering : -

Clustering can be considered the most important unsupervised learning problem; so, as every other problem of this kind, it deals with finding a structure in a collection of unlabeled data. A loose definition of clustering could be "the process of organizing objects into groups whose members are similar in some way". A cluster is therefore a collection of objects, which are "similar" between them and are "dissimilar" to the objects belonging to other clusters.

Data clustering is a common technique for statistical data analysis, which is used in many fields, including machine learning, data mining, pattern recognition, image analysis and bioinformatics. Clustering is the classification of similar objects into different groups, or more precisely, the partitioning of a data set into subsets (clusters), so that the data in each subset (ideally) share some common trait - often proximity according to some defined distance measure.Machine learning typically regards data clustering as a form of unsupervised learning.

Besides the term data clustering (or just clustering), there are a number of terms with similar meanings, including cluster analysis, automatic classification, numerical taxonomy, botryology and typological analysis.

We can show this with a simple graphical example:

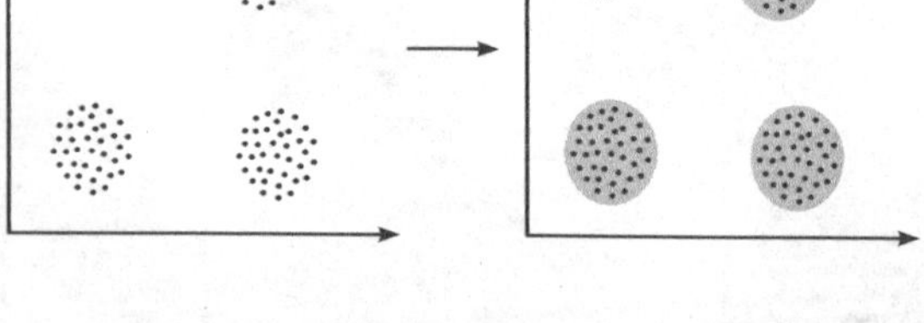

In this case we easily identify the 4 clusters into which the data can be divided; the similarity criterion is distance: two or more objects belong to the same cluster if they are "close" according to a given distance (in this case geometrical distance). This is called distance-based clustering.

Another kind of clustering is conceptual clustering: two or more objects belong to the same cluster if this one defines a concept common to all that objects. In other words, objects are grouped according to their fit to descriptive concepts, not according to simple similarity measures.

3.2 Types of clustering

Data clustering algorithms can be hierarchical or partitional. Hierarchical algorithms find successive clusters using previously established clusters, whereas partitional algorithms determine all clusters at once. Hierarchical algorithms can be agglomerative ("bottom-up") or divisive ("top-down"). Agglomerative algorithms begin with each element as a separate cluster and merge them into successively larger clusters. Divisive algorithms begin with the whole set and proceed to divide it into successively smaller clusters.

Two-way clustering, co-clustering or bi-clustering are the names for clusterings where not only the objects are clustered but also the features of the objects, i.e., if the data is represented in a data matrix, the row and columns are clustered simultaneously. Another important distinction is whether the clustering uses symmetric or asymmetric distances. A property of Euclidean space is that distances are symmetric (the distance from object A to B is the same as the distance from B to A). In other applications (e.g., sequence-alignment methods, see Prinzie & Van den Poel (2006)), this is not the case.

3.2.1 Hierarchical clustering

Distance measure

A key step in a hierarchical clustering is to select a distance measure. A simple measure is manhattan distance, equal to the sum of absolute differences for each variable. The name comes from the fact that in a two-variable case, the variables can be plotted on a grid that can be compared to city streets, and the distance between two points is the number of blocks a person would walk.

A more common measure is Euclidean distance, computed by finding the square of the distance between each variable, summing the squares, and finding the square root of that sum. In the two-variable case, the distance is analogous to finding the length of the hypotenuse in a triangle; that is, it is the distance as the crow flies. A review of cluster analysis in health psychology research found that the most common distance measure in published studies in that research area is the Euclidean distance or the squared Euclidean distance.

Creating clusters

Given a distance measure, elements can be combined. Hierarchical clustering builds (agglomerative), or breaks up (divisive), a hierarchy of clusters. The traditional representation of this hierarchy is a tree data structure (called a dendrogram), with individual elements at one end and a single cluster with every element at the other. Agglomerative algorithms begin at the top of the tree, whereas divisive algorithms begin at the bottom. (In the figure, the arrows indicate an agglomerative clustering.)

Cutting the tree at a given height will give a clustering at a selected precision. In the following example, cutting after the second row will yield clusters {a} {b c} {d e} {f}. Cutting after the third row will yield clusters {a} {b c} {d e f}, which is a coarser clustering, with a fewer number of larger clusters.

3.2.2 Agglomerative hierarchical clustering

For example, suppose this data is to be clustered. Where euclidean distance is the distance metric.

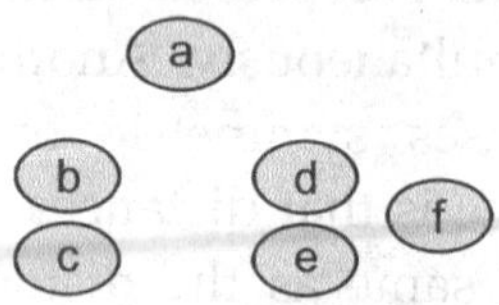

Raw data

The hierarchical clustering dendrogram would be as such:

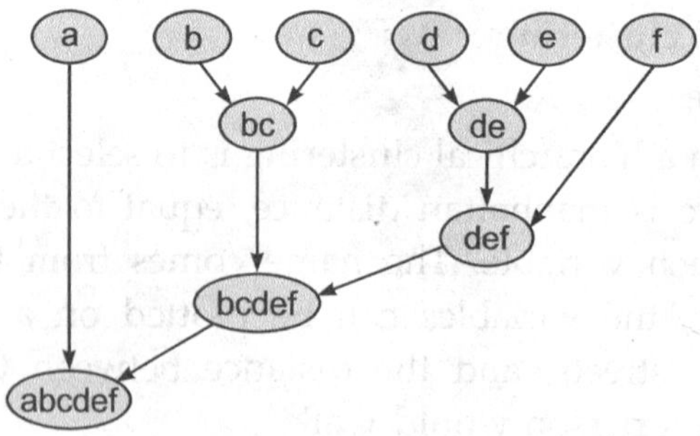

Traditional representation

This method builds the hierarchy from the individual elements by progressively merging clusters. Again, we have six elements {a} {b} {c} {d} {e} and {f}. The first step is to determine which elements to merge in a cluster. Usually, we want to take the two closest elements, therefore we must define a distance d(element1,element2) between elements. One can also construct a distance matrix at this stage.

Suppose we have merged the two closest elements b and c, we now have the following clusters {a}, {b, c}, {d}, {e} and {f}, and want to merge them further. But to do that, we need to take the distance between {a} and {b c}, and therefore define the distance between two clusters. Usually the distance between two clusters and is one of the following:

- The maximum distance between elements of each cluster (also called complete linkage clustering):

  $\max \{d(x, y) : x \in A, y \in B\}$

- The minimum distance between elements of each cluster (also called single linkage clustering):

  $\min \{d(x, y) : x \in A, y \in B\}$

- The mean distance between elements of each cluster (also called average linkage clustering):

  $$\frac{1}{\text{card }(A)\text{ card }(B)} \sum_{x \in A} \sum_{y \in B} d(x, y)$$

- The sum of all intra-cluster variance
- The increase in variance for the cluster being merged
- The probability that candidate clusters spawn from the same distribution function (V-linkage)

Each agglomeration occurs at a greater distance between clusters than the previous agglomeration, and one can decide to stop clustering either when the clusters are too far apart to be merged (distance criterion) or when there is a sufficiently small number of clusters (number criterion).

Another variation (typically) of the agglomerative clustering approach is called conceptual clustering.

3.2.3 Partitional clustering(K-means clustering)

The K-means algorithm assigns each point to the cluster whose center (also called centroid) is nearest. The center is the average of all the points in the cluster - that is, its coordinates are the arithmetic mean for each dimension separately over all the points in the cluster.

Example: The data set has three dimensions and the cluster has two points: X = (x1, x2, x3) and Y = (y1, y2, y3). Then the centroid Z becomes Z = (z1, z2, z3), where z1 = (x1 + y1)/2 and z2 = (x2 + y2)/2 and z3 = (x3 + y3)/2.

The algorithm is as follows-

- Choose the number of clusters, k.

- Randomly generate k clusters and determine the cluster centers, or directly generate k seed points as cluster centers.
- Assign each point to the nearest cluster center.
- Recompute the new cluster centers.
- Repeat until some convergence criterion is met (usually that the assignment hasn't changed).

The main advantages of this algorithm are its simplicity and speed which allows it to run on large datasets. Its disadvantage is that it does not yield the same result with each run, since the resulting clusters depend on the initial random assignments. It maximizes inter-cluster (or minimizes intra-cluster) variance, but does not ensure that the result has a global minimum of variance.

Quality Threshold Clustering Algorithms

QT (Quality Threshold) Clustering is an alternative method of partitioning data, invented for gene clustering. It requires more computing power than k-means, but does not require specifying the number of clusters a priori, and always returns the same result when run several times.

The algorithm is:

- The user chooses a maximum diameter for clusters.
- Build a candidate cluster for each point by including the closest point, the next closest, and so on, until the diameter of the cluster surpasses the threshold.
- Save the candidate cluster with the most points as the first true cluster, and remove all points in the cluster from further consideration.
- Recurse with the reduced set of points.

The distance between a point and a group of points is computed using complete linkage, i.e. as the maximum distance from the point to any member of the group.

3.2.4 Fuzzy c-means clustering

In fuzzy clustering, each point has a degree of belonging to clusters, as in fuzzy logic, rather than belonging completely to just one cluster. Thus, points on the edge of a cluster, may be in the cluster to a lesser degree than points in the center of cluster. For each point x we have a coefficient giving the degree of being in the kth cluster uk(x). Usually, the sum of those coefficients is defined to be 1, so that uk(x) denotes a probability of belonging to a certain cluster:

$$\forall \sum_{k=1}^{num\ clusters} u_k(x) = 1.$$

With fuzzy c-means, the centroid of a cluster is the mean of all points, weighted by their degree of belonging to the cluster:

$$center_k = \frac{\Sigma_x u_k(x)^m x}{\Sigma_x u_k(x)^m}.$$

The degree of belonging is related to the inverse of the distance to the cluster

$$u_k(T) = \frac{1}{d(center_k, x)},$$

then the coefficients are normalized and fuzzyfied with a real parameter m 1 so that their sum is 1. So

$$u_k(x) = \frac{1}{\Sigma_j \left(\frac{d'(center_k, x)}{d(center_j, x)} \right)^{1/(m-1)}},$$

For m equal to 2, this is equivalent to normalising the coefficient linearly to make their sum 1. When m is close to 1, then cluster center closest to the point is given much more weight than the others, and the algorithm is similar to k-means.

The fuzzy c-means algorithm is very similar to the k-means algorithm:

- Choose a number of clusters.
- Assign randomly to each point coefficients for being in the clusters.
- Repeat until the algorithm has converged (that is, the coefficients' change between two iterations is no more than e, the given sensitivity threshold) :
  - o Compute the centroid for each cluster, using the formula above.
  - o For each point, compute its coefficients of being in the clusters, using the formula above.

The algorithm minimizes intra-cluster variance as well, but has the same problems as k-means, the minimum is a local minimum, and the results depend on the initial choice of weights.

3.2.5 Graph-theoretic methods

Formal concept analysis is a technique for generating clusters of objects and attributes, given a bipartite graph representing the relations between the objects and attributes. Other methods for generating overlapping clusters (a cover rather than a partition) are discussed by Jardine and Sibson (1968) and Cole and Wishart (1970).

Elbow criterion

The elbow criterion is a common rule of thumb to determine what number of clusters should be chosen, for example for k-means and agglomerative hierarchical clustering. It should also be noted that the initial assignment of cluster seeds has bearing on the final model performance. Thus, it is appropriate to re-run the cluster analysis multiple times.

The elbow criterion says that you should choose a number of clusters so that adding another cluster doesn't add sufficient information. More precisely, if you graph the percentage of variance explained by the clusters against the number of clusters, the first clusters will add much information (explain a lot of variance), but at some point the marginal gain will drop, giving an angle in the graph (the elbow). This elbow can not always be unambigiously identified. On the following graph, the elbow is indicated by the red circle. The number of clusters chosen should therefore be 4.

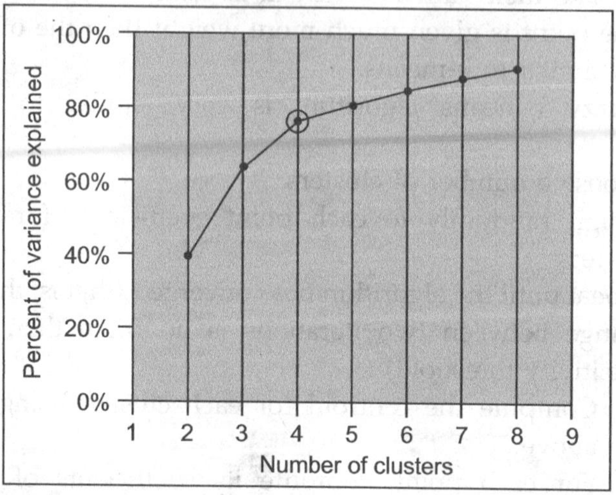

3.2.6 Spectral clustering

Given a set of data points A, the similarity matrix may be defined as a matrix S where Sij represents a measure of the similarity between points . Spectral clustering techniques make use of the spectrum of the similarity matrix of the data to cluster the points. Sometimes such techniques are also used to perform dimensionality reduction for clustering in fewer dimensions.

One such technique is the Shi-Malik algorithm, commonly used for image segmentation. It partitions points into two sets (S1,S2) based on the eigenvector v corresponding to the second-smallest eigenvalue of the Laplacian matrix

$$L = I - D^{-1/2} SD^{-1/2}$$

of S, where D is the diagonal matrix

$$ADii = \sum_j Sij.$$

This partitioning may be done in various ways, such as by taking the median m of the components in v, and placing all points whose component in v is greater than m in S1, and the rest in S2. The algorithm can be used for hierarchical clustering, by repeatedly partitioning the subsets in this fashion.

A related algorithm is the Meila-Shi algorithm, which takes the eigenvectors corresponding to the k largest eigenvalues of the matrix P = SD - 1 for some k, and then invokes another (e.g. k-means) to cluster points by their respective k components in these eigenvectors.

3.3 Applications of Clustering

3.3.1 Biology

In biology clustering has many applications

- In the fields of plant and animal ecology, clustering is used to describe and to make spatial and temporal comparisons of communities (assemblages) of organisms in heterogeneous environments; it is also used in plant systematics to generate artificial phylogenies or clusters of organisms (individuals) at the species, genus or higher level that share a number of attributes
- In computational biology and bioinformatics:
    - o In transcriptomics, clustering is used to build groups of genes with related expression patterns. Often such groups contain functionally related proteins, such as enzymes for a specific pathway, or genes that are co-regulated. High throughput experiments using expressed sequence tags (ESTs) or DNA microarrays can be a powerful tool for genome annotation, a general aspect of genomics.
    - o In sequence analysis, clustering is used to group homologous sequences into gene families. This is a very important concept in bioinformatics, and evolutionary biology in general. See evolution by gene duplication.

3.3.2 Market research

Cluster analysis is widely used in market research when working with multivariate data from surveys and test panels. Market researchers use cluster analysis to partition the general population of consumers into market segments and to better understand the relationships between different groups of consumers/potential customers.

- Segmenting the market and determining target markets
- Product positioning
- New product development
- Selecting test markets

Other applications

Social network analysis: In the study of social networks, clustering may be used to recognize communities within large groups of people.

Image segmentation: Clustering can be used to divide a digital image into distinct regions for border detection or object recognition.

Data mining: Many data mining applications involve partitioning data items into related subsets; the marketing applications discussed above represent some examples. Another common application is the division of documents, such as World Wide Web pages, into genres.

Slippy map optimisation: Flickr's map of photos and other map sites use clustering to reduce the number of markers on a map. This makes it both faster and reduces the amount of visual clutter.

3.4 The Goals of Clustering

The goal of clustering is to determine the intrinsic grouping in a set of unlabeled data. But how to decide what constitutes a good clustering? It can be shown that there is no absolute "best" criterion, which would be independent of the final aim of the clustering. Consequently, it is the user, which must supply this criterion, in such a way that the result of the clustering will suit their needs.

For instance, we could be interested in finding representatives for homogeneous groups (data reduction), in finding "natural clusters" and describe their unknown properties ("natural" data types), in finding useful and suitable groupings ("useful" data classes) or in finding unusual data objects (outlier detection).

Possible Applications

Clustering algorithms can be applied in many fields, for instance:

- Marketing: finding groups of customers with similar behavior

given a large database of customer data containing their properties and past buying records;
- Biology: classification of plants and animals given their features;
- Libraries: book ordering;
- Insurance: identifying groups of motor insurance policy holders with a high average claim cost; identifying frauds;
- City-planning: identifying groups of houses according to their house type, value and geographical location;
- Earthquake studies: clustering observed earthquake epicenters to identify dangerous zones;
- WWW: document classification; clustering weblog data to discover groups of similar access patterns.

Requirements

The main requirements that a clustering algorithm should satisfy are:
- Scalability;
- Dealing with different types of attributes;
- Discovering clusters with arbitrary shape;
- Minimal requirements for domain knowledge to determine input parameters;
- Ability to deal with noise and outliers;
- Insensitivity to order of input records;
- High dimensionality;
- Interpretability and usability.

Problems

There are a number of problems with clustering. Among them:
- Current clustering techniques do not address all the requirements adequately (and concurrently);
- Dealing with large number of dimensions and large number of data items can be problematic because of time complexity;
- The effectiveness of the method depends on the definition of "distance" (for distance-based clustering);
- If an obvious distance measure doesn't exist we must "define" it, which is not always easy, especially in multi-dimensional spaces;
- The result of the clustering algorithm (that in many cases can be arbitrary itself) can be interpreted in different ways.

3.5 Clustering Algorithms

Clustering algorithms may be classified as listed below :

- Exclusive Clustering
- Overlapping Clustering
- Hierarchical Clustering
- Probabilistic Clustering

In the first case data are grouped in an exclusive way, so that if a certain datum belongs to a definite cluster then it could not be included in another cluster. A simple example of that is shown in the figure below, where the separation of points is achieved by a straight line on a bi-dimensional plane.

On the contrary the second type, the overlapping clustering, uses fuzzy sets to cluster data, so that each point may belong to two or more clusters with different degrees of membership. In this case, data will be associated to an appropriate membership value.

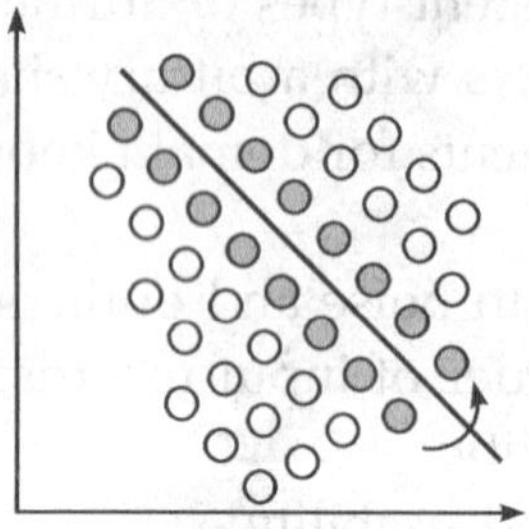

Instead, a hierarchical clustering algorithm is based on the union between the two nearest clusters. The beginning condition is realized by setting every datum as a cluster. After a few iterations it reaches the final clusters wanted.Finally, the last kind of clustering uses a completely probabilistic approach.

The four types clustering algorithms are:

- K-means
- Fuzzy C-means
- Hierarchical clustering
- Mixture of Gaussians

Each of these algorithms belongs to one of the clustering types listed above. So that, K-means is an exclusive clustering algorithm, Fuzzy C-means is an overlapping clustering algorithm, Hierarchical clustering is obvious and lastly Mixture of Gaussian is a probabilistic clustering algorithm.

Distance Measure

An important component of a clustering algorithm is the distance measure between data points. If the components of the data instance vectors are all in the same physical units then it is possible that the simple Euclidean distance metric is sufficient to successfully group similar data instances. However, even in this case the Euclidean distance can sometimes be misleading. Figure shown below illustrates this with an example of the width and height measurements of an object. Despite both measurements being taken in the same physical units, an informed decision has to be made as to the relative scaling. As the figure shows, different scalings can lead to different clusterings.

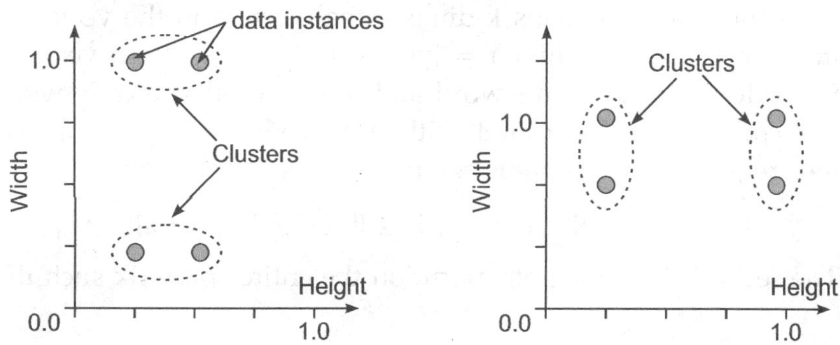

before scaling after scaling

Notice however that this is not only a graphic issue: the problem arises from the mathematical formula used to combine the distances between the single components of the data feature vectors into a unique distance measure that can be used for clustering purposes: different formulas leads to different clusterings.

Again, domain knowledge must be used to guide the formulation of a suitable distance measure for each particular application.

Minkowski Metric

For higher dimensional data, a popular measure is the Minkowski metric,

where d is the dimensionality of the data. The Euclidean distance is a special case where p=2, while Manhattan metric has p=1. However, there are no general theoretical guidelines for selecting a measure for any given application.

It is often the case that the components of the data feature vectors are not immediately comparable. It can be that the components are not continuous variables, like length, but nominal categories, such as the days of the week. In these cases again, domain knowledge must be used to formulate an appropriate measure.

3.6 Vector Quantization

Vector quantization is used in many applications such as image and voice compression, voice recognition (in general statistical pattern recognition), and surprisingly enough in volume rendering.

What is VQ?

A vector quantizer maps k-dimensional vectors in the vector space Rk into a finite set of vectors Y = {yi: i = 1, 2, ..., N}. Each vector yi is called a code vector or a codeword and the set of all the code words is called a codebook. Associated with each codeword, yi, is a nearest neighbor region called Voronoi region, and it is defined by:

$$V_1 = \{x \in R^k : \| x - y_i \| \leq \| x - y_j \| \quad \text{, for all } j \neq i\}$$

The set of Voronoi regions partition the entire space Rk such that:

$$\bigcup_{i=1}^{N} V_1 = R^k$$

$$\bigcap_{i=1}^{N} V_1 = \phi$$

For all $i \neq j$

As an example we take vectors in the two-dimensional case without loss of generality. Figure 1 shows some vectors in space. Associated with each cluster of vectors is a representative codeword. Each codeword resides in its own Voronoi region. These regions are separated with imaginary lines in figure 1 for illustration. Given an input vector, the codeword that is chosen to represent it is the one in the same Voronoi region.

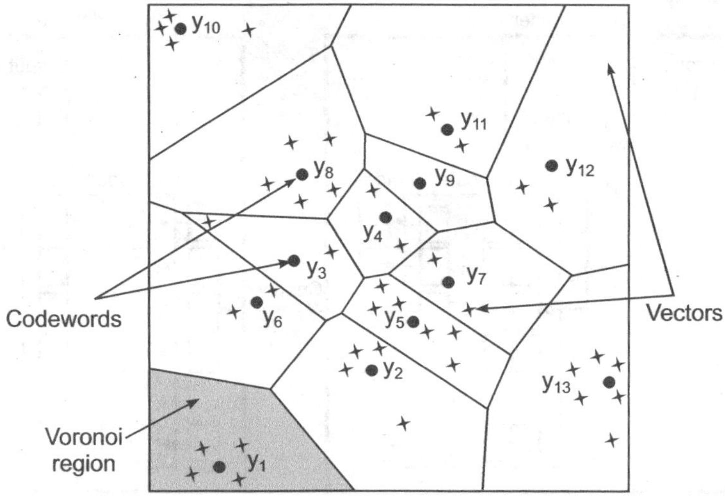

Figure 1: Code words in 2-dimensional space. Input vectors are marked with an x, code words are marked with red circles, and the Voronoi regions are separated with boundary lines.

The representative codeword is determined to be the closest in Euclidean distance from the input vector. The Euclidean distance is defined by:

$$d\,(x, y_i) = \sqrt{\sum_{j=1}^{k} (x_j - y_y)^2}$$

where xj is the jth component of the input vector, and yij is the jth is component of the codeword yi.

3.6.1 How does VQ work in compression?

A vector quantizer is composed of two operations. The first is the encoder, and the second is the decoder. The encoder takes an input vector and outputs the index of the codeword that offers the lowest distortion. In this case the lowest distortion is found by evaluating the Euclidean distance between the input vector and each codeword in the codebook. Once the closest codeword is found, the index of that codeword is sent through a channel (the channel could be a computer storage, communications channel, and so on). When the encoder receives the index of the codeword, it replaces the index with the associated codeword. Figure 2 shows a block diagram of the operation of the encoder and decoder.

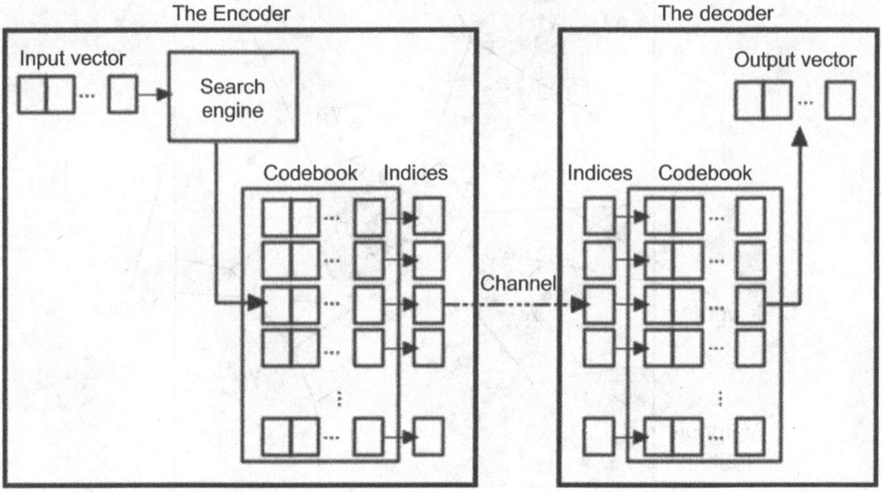

Figure 2: The Encoder and decoder in a vector quantizer. Given an input vector, the closest codeword is found and the index of the codeword is sent through the channel. The decoder receives the index of the codeword, and outputs the codeword.

3.6.2 How is the Codebook designed?

Designing a codebook that best represents the set of input vectors is NP-hard. That means that it requires an exhaustive search for the best possible code words in space, and the search increases exponentially as the number of code words increases. We therefore resort to sub optimal codebook design schemes, and the first one that comes to mind is the simplest. It is named LBG for Linde-Buzo-Gray, the authors of this idea. This algorithm is similar to the k-means algorithm.

The algorithm

1. Determine the number of code words, N, or the size of the codebook.
2. Select N code words at random, and let that be the initial codebook. The initial code words can be randomly chosen from the set of input vectors.
3. Using the Euclidean distance measure, clusterize, the vectors around each codeword. This is done by taking each input vector and finding the Euclidean distance between it and each codeword. The input vector belongs to the cluster of the codeword that yields the minimum distance.
4. Compute the new set of code words. This is done by obtaining

the average of each cluster. Add the component of each vector and divide by the number of vectors in the cluster.

$$y_i = \frac{1}{m} \sum_{j=1}^{m} x_y$$

Where i is the component of each vector (x, y, z, ... directions), m is the number of vectors in the cluster.

5. Repeat steps 3 and 4 until the either the code words don't change or the change in the code words is small.

This algorithm is by far the most popular, and that is due to its simplicity. Although it is locally optimal, yet it is very slow. The reason it is slow is because for each iteration, determining each cluster requires that each input vector be compared with all the code words in the codebook. There are many other methods to designing the codebook, methods such as Pair wise Nearest Neighbor (PNN), Simulated Annealing, Maximum Descent (MD), and Frequency-Sensitive Competitive Learning (FSCL), etc.

3.6.3 How does the search engine work?

Although VQ offers more compression for the same distortion rate as scalar quantization and PCM, yet is not as widely implemented. This due to two things.

1) The first is the time it takes to generate the codebook.
2) The second is the speed of the search.

Many algorithms have be proposed to increase the speed of the search. Some of them reduce the math used to determine the codeword that offers the minimum distortion, other algorithms preprocess the code words and exploit underlying structure.

The simplest search method, which is also the slowest, is full search. In full search an input vector is compared with every codeword in the codebook. If there were M input vectors, N codewords, and each vector is in k dimensions, then the number of multiplies becomes kMN, the number of additions and subtractions become MN((k - 1) + k) = MN(2k-1), and the number of comparisons becomes MN(k - 1). This makes full search an expensive method.

3.6.4 What is the measure of performance VQ?

How does one rate the performance of a compressed image or sound using VQ? There is no good way to measure the performance of VQ. This is because the distortion that VQ incurs will be evaluated by us humans and that is a subjective measure. We can always resort to good old Mean Squared Error (MSE) and Peak Signal to Noise Ratio (PSNR).

MSE is defined as follows:

$$MSE = \frac{1}{M} \sum_{i=1}^{M} (\bar{x}_i - x_i)^2$$

Where M is the number of elements in the signal, or image. For example, if we wanted to find the MSE between the reconstructed and the original image, then we would take the difference between the two images pixel-by-pixel, square the results, and average the results.

The PSNR is defined as follows:

$$PSNR = 10\log_{10}\left(\frac{(2^n - 1)^2}{MSE}\right)$$

Where n is the number of bits per symbol. As an example, if we want to find the PSNR between two 256 gray level images, then we set n to 8 bits.

3.7 Pattern recognition: -

An important application of neural networks is pattern recognition. Pattern recognition can be implemented by using a feed-forward (figure 3.7.1) neural network that has been trained accordingly. During training, the network is trained to associate outputs with input patterns. When the network is used, it identifies the input pattern and tries to output the associated output pattern. The power of neural networks comes to life when a pattern that has no output associated with it, is given as an input. In this case, the network gives the output that corresponds to a taught input pattern that is least different from the given pattern.

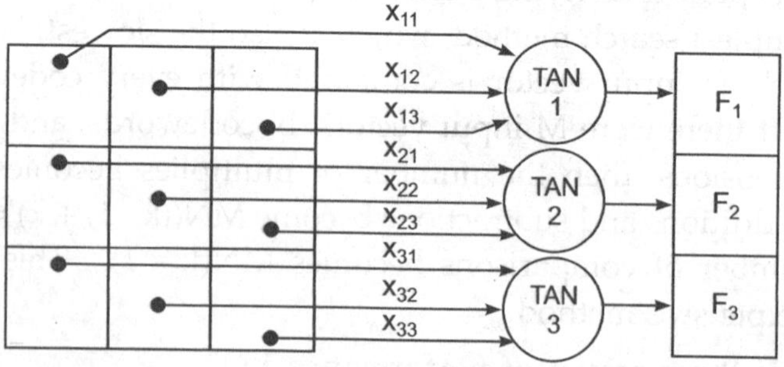

Figure 3.7.1.

For example:

The network of figure 3.7.1 is trained to recognise the patterns T and H. The associated patterns are all black and all white respectively as shown below.

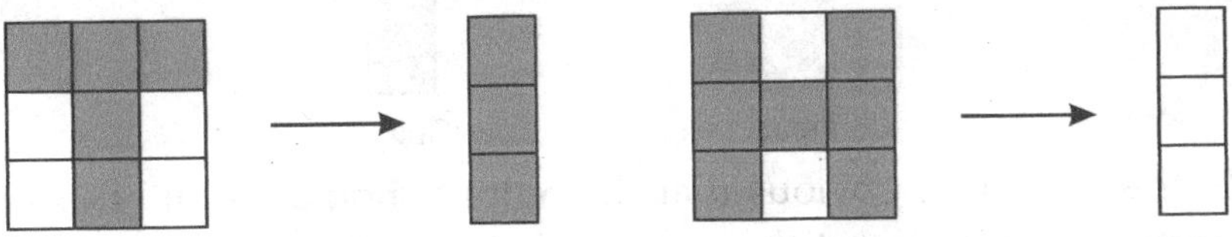

If we represent black squares with 0 and white squares with 1 then the truth tables for the 3 neurones after generalisation are;

X11:		0	0	0	0	1	1	1	1
X12:		0	0	1	1	0	0	1	1
X13:		0	1	0	1	0	1	0	1
OUT:		0	0	1	1	0	0	1	1

Top neuron

X12:		0	0	0	0	1	1	1	1
X22:		0	0	1	1	0	0	1	1
X23:		0	1	0	1	0	1	0	1
OUT:		1	0/1	1	0/1	0/1	0	0/1	0

Middle neuron

X21:		0	0	0	0	1	1	1	1
X22:		0	0	1	1	0	0	1	1
X23:		0	1	0	1	0	1	0	1
OUT:		1	0	1	1	0	0	1	0

Bottom neuron

From the tables it can be seen the following associations can be extracted:

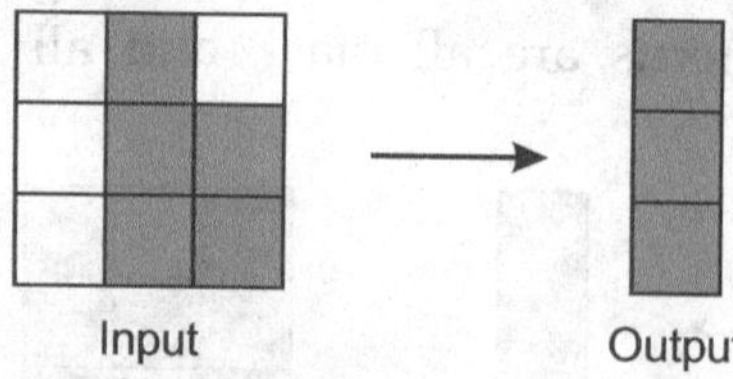

In this case, it is obvious that the output should be all blacks since the input pattern is almost the same as the 'T' pattern.

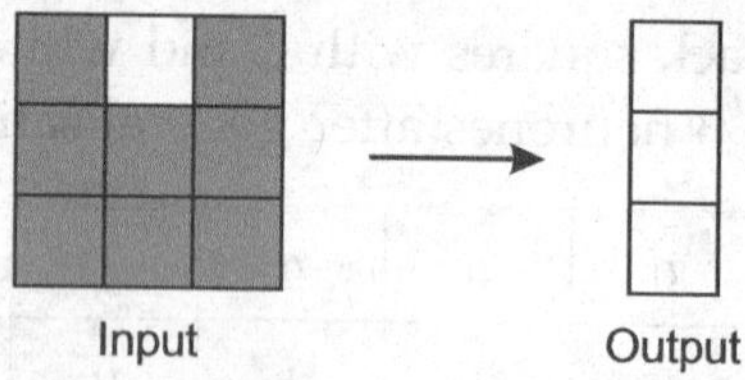

Here also, it is obvious that the output should be all whites since the input pattern is almost the same as the 'H' pattern.

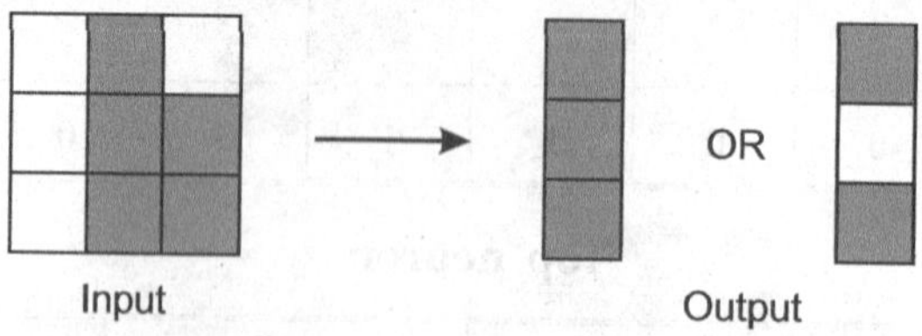

Here, the top row is 2 errors away from the a T and 3 from an H. So the top output is black. The middle row is 1 error away from both T and H so the output is random. The bottom row is 1 error away from T and 2 away from H. Therefore the output is black. The total output of the network is still in favour of the T shape.

3.8 Function approximation: -

The need for function approximations arises in many branches of applied mathematics, and computer science in particular. In general, a function approximation problem asks us to select a function among a well-defined class that closely matches ("approximates") a target function in a task-specific way.

One can distinguish two major classes of function approximation problems: First, for known target functions approximation theory is the branch of numerical analysis that investigates how certain known functions (for example, special functions) can be approximated by a specific class of functions (for example, polynomials or rational functions) that often have desirable properties (inexpensive computation, continuity, integral and limit values, etc.).

Second, the target function, call it g, may be unknown; instead of an explicit formula, only a set of points of the form (x, g(x)) is provided. Depending on the structure of the domain and codomain of g, several techniques for approximating g may be applicable. For example, if g is an operation on the real numbers, techniques of interpolation, extrapolation, regression analysis, and curve fitting can be used. If the codomain of g is a finite set, one is dealing with a classification problem instead.

To some extent the different problems (regression, classification) have received a unified treatment in statistical learning theory, where they are viewed as supervised learning problems.

3.9 Generalization and Function Approximation

We have so far assumed that our estimates of value functions are represented as a table with one entry for each state or for each state-action pair. This is a particularly clear and instructive case, but of course it is limited to tasks with small numbers of states and actions. The problem is not just the memory needed for large tables, but the time and data needed to accurately fill them. In other words, the key issue is that of generalization. How can experience with a limited subset of the state space be usefully generalized to produce a good approximation over a much larger subset?

This is a severe problem. In many tasks to which we would like to apply reinforcement learning, most states encountered will never have been experienced exactly before. This will almost always be the case when the state or action spaces include continuous variables or large number of sensors, such as a visual image. The only way to learn anything at all on these tasks is to generalize from previously experienced states to ones that have never been seen.

Fortunately, generalization from examples has already been extensively studied, and we do not need to invent totally new methods for use in reinforcement learning. To a large extent we need only combine reinforcement learning methods with existing generalization methods. The kind of generalization we require is often called function approximation because it takes examples from a desired function (e.g., a value function) and attempts to generalize from them to construct an approximation of the entire function. "Function approximation is an instance of supervised learning, the primary topic studied in machine learning, artificial neural networks, pattern recognition, and statistical curve fitting".

3.10 Value Prediction with Function Approximation

As usual, we begin with the prediction problem, that of estimating the state-value function from experience generated using policy . The novelty in this chapter is that the approximate value function at time t, , is represented not as a table, but as a parameterized functional form with parameter vector . This means that the value function depends totally on , varying from time step to time step only as varies. For example, might be the function computed by an artificial neural network, with the vector of connection weights. By adjusting the weights, any of a wide range of different functions can be implemented by the network. Or might be the function computed by a decision tree, where is all the parameters defining the split points and leaf values of the tree. Typically, the number of parameters (the number of components of) is much less than the number of states, and changing one parameter changes the estimated value of many states. Consequently, when a single state is backed up, the change generalizes from that state to affect the values of many other states.

All of the prediction methods covered in this book have been described as backups, that is, as updates to an estimated value function that shift its value at particular states toward a "backed-up value" for that state. Let us refer to an individual backup by the notation , where s is the state backed up and v is the backed-up value that s's estimated value is shifted toward. For example, the DP backup for value prediction is , the Monte Carlo backup is , the TD(0) backup is , and the general TD() backup is . In the DP case, an arbitrary state s is backed up, whereas in the the other cases the state, , encountered in (possibly simulated) experience is backed up.

It is natural to interpret each backup as specifying an example of the desired input-output behavior of the estimated value function. In a sense, the backup means that the estimated value for state s should be more like v. Up to now, the actual update implementing the backup has been trivial: the table entry for s's estimated value has simply been shifted a fraction of the way towards v. Now we permit arbitrarily complex and sophisticated function approximation methods to implement the backup. The normal inputs to these methods are examples of the desired input-output behavior of the function they are trying to approximate. We use these methods for value prediction simply by passing to them the of each backup as a training example. The approximate function they produce we then interpret as an estimated value function.

Viewing each backup as a conventional training example in this way enables us to use any of a wide range of existing function approximation methods for value prediction. In principle, we can use any method for supervised learning from examples, including artificial neural networks, decision trees, and various kinds of multivariate regression. However, not all function-approximation methods are equally well suited for use in reinforcement learning. The most sophisticated neural-network and statistical methods all assume a static training set over which multiple passes are made. In reinforcement learning, however, it is important that learning be able to occur online, while interacting with the environment or with a model of the environment. To do this requires methods that are able to learn efficiently from incrementally-acquired data. In addition, reinforcement learning generally requires function approximators able to handle nonstationary target functions (functions that change over time). For example, in GPI (Generalized Policy Iteration) control methods we often seek to learn while changes. Even if the policy remains the same, the target values of training examples are nonstationary if they are generated by bootstrapping methods (DP and TD). Methods that cannot easily handle such nonstationarity are less suitable for reinforcement learning.

What performance measures are appropriate for evaluating function-approximation methods? Most supervised-learning methods seek to minimize the mean squared error over some distribution, P, of the inputs. In our value-prediction problem, the inputs are states and the target function is the true value function , so the mean squared error (MSE) for an approximation , using parameter , is

$$\text{MSE}(\bar{\theta}_t) = \sum_{s \in S} P(s) \left(V^{\pi}(s)\right)^2 , \tag{8.1}$$

where P is a distribution weighting the errors of different states. This distribution is important because it is usually not possible to reduce the error to zero at all states. After all, there are generally far more states than there are components to . The flexibility of the function approximator is thus a scarce resource. Better approximation at some states can be gained generally only at the expense of worse approximation at other states. The distribution, P, specifies how these tradeoffs should be made.

The distribution P is also usually the distribution from which the states in the training examples are drawn, and thus the distribution of states at which backups are done. If we wish to minimize error over a certain distribution of states, then it makes sense to train the function approximator with examples from that same distribution. For example, if you want a uniform level of error over the entire state set, then it makes sense to train with backups distributed uniformly over the entire state set, such as in the exhaustive sweeps of some DP methods. Henceforth, let us assume that the distribution of states at which backups are done and the distribution that weights errors, P, are the same.

A distribution of particular interest is the one describing the frequency with which states are encountered while the agent is interacting with the environment and selecting actions according to , the policy whose value function we are approximating. We call this the on-policy distribution, in part because it is the distribution of backups in on-policy control methods. Minimizing error over the on-policy distribution focuses function-approximation resources on the states that actually occur while following the policy, ignoring those that never occur. The on-policy distribution is also the one for which it is easiest to get training examples using Monte Carlo or TD methods. These methods generate backups from sample experience using the policy . Because a backup is generated for each state encountered in the experience, the training examples available are naturally distributed according to the on-policy distribution. Stronger convergence results are available for the on-policy distribution than for other distributions, as we discuss later.

It is not completely clear that we should care about minimizing the MSE. Our goal in value prediction is potentially different because our ultimate purpose is to use the predictions to aid in finding a better policy. The best predictions for that purpose are not necessarily the best for minimizing MSE. However, it is not yet clear what a more useful alternative goal for value prediction might be. For now, we continue to focus on MSE.

An ideal goal in terms of MSE would be to find a global optimum, a parameter vector for which for all possible . Reaching this goal is sometimes possible for simple function approximators such as linear ones, but is rarely possible for complex function approximators such as artificial neural networks and decision trees. Short of this, complex function approximators may seek to converge instead to a local optimum, a parameter for which for all in some neighborhood of . Although this guarantee is only slightly reassuring, it is typically the best that can be said for nonlinear function approximators. For many cases of interest in reinforcement learning, convergence to an optimum, or even true convergence, does not occur. Nevertheless, a MSE that is within a small bound of an optimum may still be achieved with some methods. Others may in fact diverge, with their MSE approaching infinity in the limit.

In this section we have outlined a framework for combining a wide range of reinforcement learning methods for value prediction with a wide range of function-approximation methods, using the backups of the former to generate training examples for the latter. We have also outlined a range of MSE performance measures to which these methods may aspire. The range of possible methods is far too large to cover all, and anyway there is too little known about most of them to make a reliable evaluation or recommendation. Of necessity, we consider only a few possibilities. In the rest of this chapter we focus on function-approximation methods based on gradient principles, and on linear gradient-descent methods in particular.

3.11 Control with Function Approximation

We now extend value-prediction methods using function approximation to control methods, following the pattern of GPI. First we extend the the state-value prediction methods to action-value prediction methods, then we combine them with policy-improvement and action-selection techniques. As usual, the problem of ensuring exploration is solved by pursuing either an on-policy or an off-policy approach.

The extension to action-value prediction is straightforward. In this case it is the action-value function, $Q_t \approx Q^{\pi}$, that is represented as a parameterized functional form with parameter vector $\overline{\theta}_t$. Whereas before we considered training examples of the form $s_t \rightarrow v_t$, now we consider examples of the form $s_t : a_t \rightarrow v_t$. The example output, v_t, can be any approximation of $Q^{\pi}(s_t ; a_t)$, including the usual backed-up values such as the full Monte-Carlo return, R_i, or the 1-step Sarsa-style return, $r_{t+1} + Q_t(s_{t+1} ; a_{t+1})$. The general gradient-descent update for action-value prediction is

$$\overline{\theta}_{t+1} = \overline{\theta}_t + \alpha\,(v_t - Q_t(s_t, a_t))\,\nabla_{\overline{\theta}_t} Q_t(s_t, a_t)$$

For example, the backward view of the action-value method analogous to TD(λ) is

$$\overline{\theta}_{t+1} = \overline{\theta}_t + \alpha\,\delta_t\,\overline{e}_t$$

where

$$\delta_t = t_{t+1} + \gamma Q_t(s_{t+1}, a_{t+1}) - Q_t(s_t, a_t),$$

and

$$\overline{e}_t = \gamma\lambda\overline{e}_{t-1} + \nabla_{\theta_t} Q_t(s_t; a_t)$$

with $\overline{e}_0 = \overline{0}$. We call this method gradient-descent Sarsa() , particularly when it is elaborated to form a full control method. For a constant policy, this method converges in the same way that TD() does, with the same kind of error bound (8.9).

To form control methods, we need to couple such action-value prediction methods with techniques for policy improvement and action selection. Suitable techniques applicable to continuous actions, or to actions from large discrete sets, are a topic of ongoing research with as yet no clear resolution. On the other hand, if the action set is discrete and not too large, then we can use the techniques already developed in previous chapters. That is, for each possible action, a, available in the current state, , we can compute and then find the greedy action . Policy improvement is done by changing the estimation policy to the greedy policy (in off-policy methods) or to a soft approximation of the greedy policy such as the -greedy policy (in on-policy methods). Actions are selected according to this same policy in on-policy methods, or by an arbitrary policy in off-policy methods.

Initialize θ arbitrarily and $\overline{e} = \overline{0}$

Repeat (for each episode):

$s \leftarrow$ intial state episode

For all $a \in A(s)$:

$F_a \leftarrow$ set of features present in s, a

$Q_a \leftarrow \Sigma_{i \in F_a} \theta(i)$

$a \leftarrow$ arg max $_aQ_a$

$a \leftarrow$ a random action $\in A(s)$

With probability e:

Repeat (for each step of episode):

$\overline{e} \leftarrow \gamma\lambda\overline{e}$

For all $a \neq a$: (optional block for replacing traces)

For all $i \in F_a$:

$e(i) \leftarrow 0$

For all $i \in F_a$:

$e(i) \leftarrow e(i) + 1$ (accumulating traces)

or $e(i) \leftarrow 1$ (replacing traces)

Take action a, observe reward, r, and next state,

$\delta \leftarrow r - Q_a$

For all $a \in A(s)$:

$F_a \leftarrow$ set of features present in s' , a

$Q_a \leftarrow \Sigma_{i \in F_a} \theta\,(t)$

$a' \leftarrow \arg\max_a Q_a$

$a' \leftarrow$ a random action $\in A(s)$

With probability :

$\delta \leftarrow \delta + \gamma Q_{a'}$

$\bar{\theta} \leftarrow \bar{\theta} + \alpha\,\delta\,\bar{e}$

$a \leftarrow a'$

until is terminal

Figure 3.11.1: Linear, gradient-descent Sarsa() with binary features and -greedy policy. Updates for both accumulating and replacing traces are specified, including the option (when using replacing traces) of clearing the traces of non-selected actions.

Initialize $\bar{\theta}$ arbitrarily and $\bar{e} = \bar{0}$
Repeat (for each episode):

$s \leftarrow$ initial state of episode

For all $a \in A(s)$:

$F_a \leftarrow$ set of features present in s, a

$Q_a \leftarrow \Sigma_{i \in F_a} \theta\,(i)$

Repeat (for each step of episode):
With probability $1 - e$:

$a \leftarrow \arg\max_a Q_a$

$\bar{e} \leftarrow \gamma \lambda \bar{e}$

else

$a \leftarrow$ a random action $\in A(s)$

$\bar{e} \leftarrow 0$

For all $i \in F_a\; e(i) \leftarrow e\,(i) + 1$:

Take action a, observe reward, r, and next state, s'

$\delta \leftarrow r - Q_a$

For all $a \in A(s)$:

$F_a \leftarrow$ set of features present in s', a

$Q_a \leftarrow \Sigma_{i \in F_a} \theta(i)$

$a' \leftarrow \arg\max_a Q_a$

$\delta \leftarrow \delta + \gamma Q_a$

$\theta \leftarrow \theta + \alpha \delta \overline{e}$

until s' is terminal

Figure 3.11.2 : A linear, gradient-descent version of Watkins's Q() with binary features, -greedy policy, and accumulating traces.

Figures 3.11.1 and 3.11.2 show examples of on-policy (Sarsa()) and off-policy (Watkins's Q()) control methods using function approximation. Both methods use linear, gradient-descent function approximation with binary features, such as in tile coding and Kanerva coding. Both methods use an -greedy policy for action selection, and the Sarsa method uses it for GPI as well. Both compute the sets of present features, , corresponding to the current state and all possible actions, a. If the value function for each action is a separate linear function of the same features (a common case), then the indices of all the may be the same except for an offset, simplifying the computation significantly.

All the methods we have discussed above have used accumulating eligibility traces. Although replacing traces are known to have advantages in tabular methods, they do not directly extend to the use of function approximation. Recall that the idea of replacing traces is to reset a state's trace to 1 each time it is visited instead of incrementing it by 1. But with function approximation there is no single trace corresponding to a state, just a trace for each component of , each of which corresponds to many states. One approach that seems to work well for linear, gradient-descent function approximation with binary features is to treat the features as if they were states for the purposes of replacing traces. That is, each time a state is encountered that has feature i, the trace for feature i is set to 1 rather than being incremented by 1 as it would be with accumulating traces.

When working with state-action traces, it may also be useful to clear (set to zero) the traces of all non-selected actions in the states encountered. This idea can also be extended to the case of linear function approximation with binary features. For each state encountered, we first clear the traces of all features for the state and the actions not selected, then we set to 1 the traces of the features for the state and the action that was selected. As we noted for the tabular case, this may or may not be the best way to proceed when using replacing traces. A procedural specification of both kinds of traces, including the optional clearing for non-selected actions, is given for the Sarsa algorithm in Figure 3.11.1.

Example 3.11.1. The Mountain-Car Task. Consider the task of driving an underpowered car up a steep mountain road, as suggested by the diagram in the upper left of Figure 3.11.3. The difficulty is that gravity is stronger than the car's engine, and even at full throttle it cannot accelerate up the steep slope. The only solution is to first move away from the goal and up the opposite slope on the left. Then, by applying full throttle the car can build up enough inertia to carry it up the steep slope even though it is slowing down the whole way. This is a simple example of a continuous control task where things have to get worse in a sense (farther from the goal) before they can get better. Many control methodologies have great difficulties with tasks of this kind unless explicitly aided by a human designer.

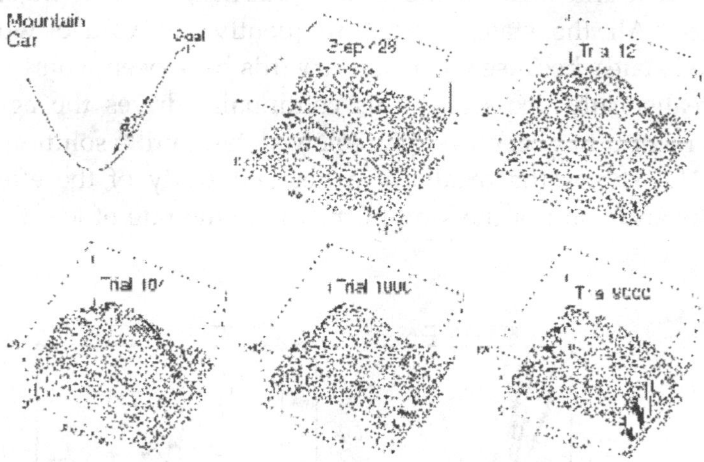

Figure 3.11.3 : The mountain-car task (upper left panel) and the cost-to-go function ($-\max_a Q_t(s; a)$) learned during one run.

The reward in this problem is -1 on all time steps until the car has moved past its goal position at the top of the mountain, which ends the episode. There are three possible actions: full throttle forward (+1), full throttle reverse (-1), and zero throttle (0). The car moves according to a simplified physics. It's position, x_t, and velocity, x_t, are given by

$$x_{t+1} = bound\ [x_t + x_{t+1}]$$

$$x_{t+1} = bound\ [x_t + 0.001\ a_t + -0.0025 \cos(3x_t)]$$

where the bound operation enforces $-1.2 \leq x_{t+1} \leq 0.5$ and $-0.07 \leq x_{t+1} \leq 0.07$. When x_{t+1} reached the left bound, then was reset to zero. When it reached right bound, then the goal was reached and the episode was terminated. Each episode started from a random position and velocity uniformly chosen from these ranges. To convert the two continuous state variables to binary features, we used grid-tilings. We used ten 9×9 tilings, each offset by a random fraction of a tile width.

The Sarsa algorithm in Figure 3.11.1 (using replace traces and the optional clearing) readily solved this task, learning a near optimal policy within 100 episodes. Figure 3.11.3 shows the negative of the value function (the cost-to-go function) learned on one run, using the parameters $\lambda = 9, e = 0$, and $a = .05\ (\frac{0.1}{m})$. The initial action values were all zero, which was optimistic (all true values are negative in this task), causing extensive exploration to occur even though the exploration parameter, , was 0. This can be seen in the middle-top panel of the figure, labeled "Step 428." At this time not even one episode has been completed, but the car has oscillated back and forth in the valley, following circular trajectories in state space. All the states visited frequently are valued worse than unexplored states, because the actual rewards have been worse than what was (unrealistically) expected. This continually drives the agent away from wherever it has been to explore new states, until a solution is found. Figure 3.11.4 shows the results of a detailed study of the effect of the parameters and , and of the kind of traces, on the rate of learning on this task.

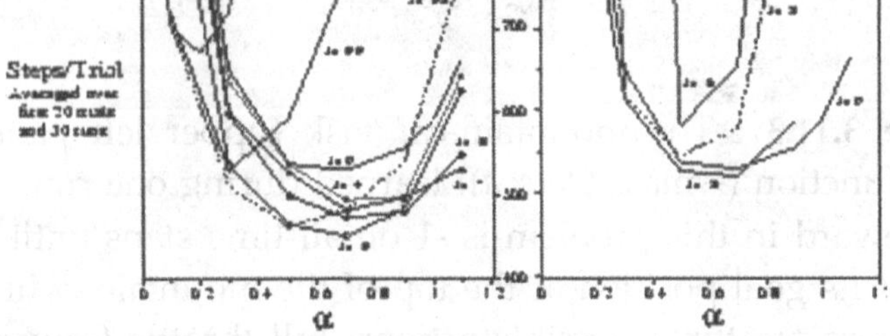

Figure 3.11.4 : The effect of α, λ, and the kind of traces on early performance on the Mountain-Car task.

3.12 Forecasting, control, optimization:

3.13 Summary

- Clustering can be considered the most important unsupervised learning problem; so, as every other problem of this kind, it deals with finding a structure in a collection of unlabeled data.
- lustering could be "the process of organizing objects into groups whose members are similar in some way". A cluster is therefore a collection of objects, which are "similar" between them and are "dissimilar" to the objects belonging to other clusters.
- Two-way clustering, co-clustering or bi-clustering are the names for clusterings where not only the objects are clustered but also the features of the objects, i.e., if the data is represented in a data matrix, the row and columns are clustered simultaneously.
- A distance measure is manhattan distance, equal to the sum of absolute differences for each variable. The name comes from the fact that in a two-variable case, the variables can be plotted on a grid that can be compared to city streets, and the distance between two points is the number of blocks a person would walk.
- The K-means algorithm assigns each point to the cluster whose center (also called centroid) is nearest. The center is the average of all the points in the cluster - that is, its coordinates are the arithmetic mean for each dimension separately over all the points in the cluster.
- QT (Quality Threshold) Clustering is an alternative method of partitioning data, invented for gene clustering. It requires more computing power than k-means, but does not require specifying the number of clusters a priori, and always returns the same result when run several times.
- The distance between a point and a group of points is computed using complete linkage, i.e. as the maximum distance from the point to any member of the group.
- In fuzzy clustering, each point has a degree of belonging to clusters, as in fuzzy logic, rather than belonging completely to just one cluster. Thus, points on the edge of a cluster, may be in the cluster to a lesser degree than points in the center of cluster.
- Formal concept analysis is a technique for generating clusters of objects and attributes, given a bipartite graph representing the relations between the objects and attributes. Other methods for

generating overlapping clusters (a cover rather than a partition) are discussed by Jardine and Sibson (1968) and Cole and Wishart (1970).

- The elbow criterion is a common rule of thumb to determine what number of clusters should be chosen, for example for k-means and agglomerative hierarchical clustering.
- The goal of clustering is to determine the intrinsic grouping in a set of unlabeled data. But how to decide what constitutes a good clustering? It can be shown that there is no absolute "best" criterion, which would be independent of the final aim of the clustering. Consequently, it is the user, which must supply this criterion, in such a way that the result of the clustering will suit their needs.
- Vector quantization is used in many applications such as image and voice compression, voice recognition (in general statistical pattern recognition), and surprisingly enough in volume rendering.

3.14 Review Questions

1. Explain the principles of clustering and algorithms.
2. Discuss the types of clustering in detailed.
3. Describe the quality threshold clustering algorithms.
4. Explain the Elbow criterion.
5. Discuss the applications of clustering.
6. Explain vector quantisation and how the codebook is designed.
7. Write short notes on :

   (i) Pattern recognition (ii) Function approximation

   (iii) Value prediction.

—•—•—•—•—•—

Chapter No. 4
Supervised learning

4.1 Supervised learning

Supervised learning is a machine learning technique for creating a function from training data. The training data consist of pairs of input objects (typically vectors), and desired outputs. The output of the function can be a continuous value (called regression), or can predict a class label of the input object (called classification). The task of the supervised learner is to predict the value of the function for any valid input object after having seen number of training examples (i.e. pairs of input and target output). To achieve this, the learner has to generalize from the presented data to unseen situations in a "reasonable" way.

In supervised learning, we are given a set of example pairs and the aim is to find a function f in the allowed class of functions that matches the examples. In other words, we wish to infer the mapping implied by the data and the cost function is related to the mismatch between our mapping and the data and it implicitly contains prior knowledge about the problem domain.

A commonly used cost is the mean-squared error which tries to minimise the average error between the network's output, f(x), and the target value y over all the example pairs. When one tries to minimise this cost using gradient descent for the class of neural networks called Multi-Layer Perceptrons, one obtains the well-known backpropagation algorithm for training neural networks. Tasks that fall within the paradigm of supervised learning are pattern recognition (also known as classification) and regression (also known as function approximation). The supervised learning paradigm is also applicable to sequential data (e.g., for speech and gesture recognition).

4.1.1 Overview

Supervised learning can generate models of two types. Most

commonly, supervised learning generates a global model that maps input objects to desired outputs. In some cases, however, the map is implemented as a set of local models (such as in case-based reasoning or the nearest neighbor algorithm).

In order to solve a given problem of supervised learning (e.g. learning to recognize handwriting) one has to consider various steps:

1. Determine the type of training examples. Before doing anything else, the engineer should decide what kind of data is to be used as an example. For instance, this might be a single handwritten character, an entire handwritten word, or an entire line of handwriting.
2. Gathering a training set. The training set needs to be characteristic of the real-world use of the function. Thus, a set of input objects is gathered and corresponding outputs are also gathered, either from human experts or from measurements.
3. Determine the input feature representation of the learned function. The accuracy of the learned function depends strongly on how the input object is represented. Typically, the input object is transformed into a feature vector, which contains a number of features that are descriptive of the object. The number of features should not be too large, because of the curse of dimensionality; but should be large enough to accurately predict the output.
4. Determine the structure of the learned function and corresponding learning algorithm. For example, the engineer may choose to use artificial neural networks or decision trees.
5. Complete the design. The engineer then runs the learning algorithm on the gathered training set. Parameters of the learning algorithm may be adjusted by optimizing performance on a subset (called a validation set) of the training set, or via cross-validation. After parameter adjustment and learning, the performance of the algorithm may be measured on a test set that is separate from the training set.

4.1.2 Empirical risk minimization

The goal of supervised learning of a global model is to find a function g, given a set of points of the form (x, g(x)). It is assumed that the set of points for which the behavior of g is known is an i.i.d. sample drawn according to an unknown probability distribution p of a larger, possibly infinite, population. Furthermore, one assumes the existence of a task-specific loss function L of type

$$L: Y \times Y \rightarrow R^{+}$$

where Y is the co-domain of g and L maps into the nonnegative real numbers (further restrictions may be placed on L). The quantity L(z, y) is the loss incurred by predicting z as the value of g at a given point when the true value is y.

The risk associated with a function f is then defined as the expectation of the loss function, as follows:

$$R(f) = \sum_i L(f(x_i), g(x_i))\, p(x_i)$$

if the probability distribution p is discrete (the analogous continuous case employs a definite integral and a probability density function).

The goal is now to find a function f* among a fixed subclass of functions for which the risk R(f*) is minimal.

However, since the behavior of g is generally only known for a finite sequence of points (x1, y1), ..., (xn, yn), one can only approximate the true risk, for example with the *empirical risk:*

$$R_n(f) = \frac{1}{n} \sum_{i=1}^{n} L(f(x_i), y_i)$$

Selecting the function f* that minimizes the empirical risk is known as the principle of empirical risk minimization. Statistical learning theory investigates under what conditions empirical risk minimization is admissible and how good the approximations can be expected to be.

4.1.3 Single- layer networks

The earliest kind of neural network is a single-layer perceptron network, which consists of a single layer of output nodes; the inputs are fed directly to the outputs via a series of weights. In this way it can be considered the simplest kind of feed-forward network. The sum of the products of the weights and the inputs is calculated in each node, and if the value is above some threshold (typically 0) the neuron fires and takes the activated value (typically 1); otherwise it takes the deactivated value (typically -1). Neurons with this kind of activation function are also called McCulloch-Pitts neurons or threshold neurons. In the literature the term perceptron often refers to networks consisting of just one of these units. They were described by Warren McCulloch and Walter Pitts in the 1940s.

A perceptron can be created using any values for the activated and deactivated states as long as the threshold value lies between the two. Most perceptrons have outputs of 1 or -1 with a threshold of 0 and there is some evidence that such networks can be trained more quickly than networks created from nodes with different activation and deactivation values.

Perceptrons can be trained by a simple learning algorithm that is usually called the delta rule. It calculates the errors between calculated output and sample output data, and uses this to create an adjustment to the weights, thus implementing a form of gradient descent.

Single-unit perceptrons are only capable of learning linearly separable patterns; in 1969 in a famous monograph entitled Perceptrons Marvin Minsky and Seymour Papert showed that it was impossible for a single-layer perceptron network to learn an XOR function. They conjectured (incorrectly) that a similar result would hold for a multi-layer perceptron network. Although a single threshold unit is quite limited in its computational power, it has been shown that networks of parallel threshold units can approximate any continuous function from a compact interval of the real numbers into the interval .A single-layer neural network can compute a continuous output instead of a step function. A common choice is the so-called logistic function:

$$\frac{1}{1+e^{-x}}$$

With this choice, the single-layer network is identical to the logistic regression model, widely used in statistical modelling. The logistic function is also known as the sigmoid function. It has a continuous derivative, which allows it to be used in backpropagation.

4.1.4 Perception-linear separability

Perception, in psychology, mental organization and interpretation of sensory information. The Gestalt psychologists studied extensively the ways in which people organize and select from the vast array of stimuli that are presented to them, concentrating particularly on visual stimuli. Perception is influenced by a variety of factors, including the intensity and physical dimensions of the stimulus; such activities of the sense organs as effects of preceding stimulation; the subject's past experience; attention factors such as readiness to respond to a stimulus; and motivation and emotional state of the subject. Stimulus elements in visual organization form perceived patterns according to their nearness to each other, their similarity, the tendency for the subject to perceive complete figures, and the ability of the subject to distinguish important figures from background. Perceptual constancy is the tendency of a subject to interpret one object in the same manner, regardless of such variations as distance, angle of sight, or brightness. Through selective attention, the subject focuses on a limited number of stimuli, and ignores those that are considered less important. Depth perception, considered to be innate in most animals, is produced by a variety of visual cues indicating perspective, and by a slight disparity in the images of an object on the two retinas. An absolute threshold is the minimal physical intensity of a stimulus that a subject can normally perceive, whereas a difference threshold is the minimal amount of change in a stimulus that can be consciously detected by the subject. Recent studies have shown that stimuli are actually perceived in the brain, while sensory organs merely gather the signals.

The concept of linearity can be extended to linear operators. Important examples of linear operators include the derivative considered as a differential operator, and many constructed from it, such as del and the Laplacian. When a differential equation can be expressed in linear form, it is particularly easy to solve by breaking the equation up into smaller pieces, solving each of those pieces, and adding the solutions up.

Note: Nonlinear equations and functions are of interest to physicists and mathematicians because they are hard to solve and give rise to interesting phenomena such as chaos.Linear algebra is the branch of mathematics concerned with the study of vectors, vector spaces (or linear spaces), linear transformations, and systems of linear equations

4.1.5 Limitations of Multi Layer Network Architecture

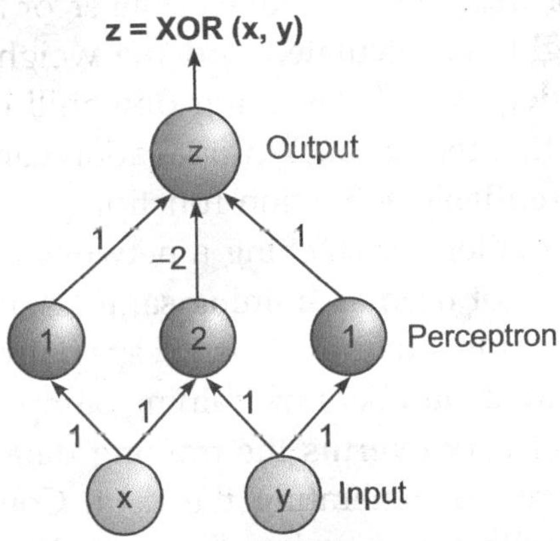

A two-layer neural network capable of calculating XOR. The numbers within the neurons represent each neuron's explicit threshold (which can be factored out so that all neurons have the same threshold, usually 1). The numbers that annotate arrows represent the weight of the inputs. This net assumes that if the threshold is not reached, zero (not -1) is output. Note that the bottom layer of inputs is not always considered a real neural network layer

This class of networks consists of multiple layers of computational units, usually interconnected in a feed-forward way. Each neuron in one layer has directed connections to the neurons of the subsequent layer. In many applications the units of these networks apply a sigmoid function as an activation function.

The universal approximation theorem for neural networks states that every continuous function that maps intervals of real numbers to some output interval of real numbers can be approximated arbitrarily closely by a multi-layer perceptron with just one hidden layer. This result holds only for restricted classes of activation functions, e.g. for the sigmoidal functions.

Multi-layer networks use a variety of learning techniques, the most popular being back-propagation. Here the output values are compared with the correct answer to compute the value of some predefined error-function. By various techniques the error is then fed back through the network. Using this information, the algorithm adjusts the weights of each connection in order to reduce the value of the error function by some small amount. After repeating this process for a sufficiently large number of training cycles the network will usually converge to some state where the error of the calculations is small. In this case one says that the network has learned a certain target function. To adjust weights properly one applies a general method for non-linear optimization task that is called gradient descent. For this, the derivative of the error function with respect to the network weights is calculated and the weights are then changed such that the error decreases (thus going downhill on the surface of the error function). For this reason back-propagation can only be applied on networks with differentiable activation functions.

In general the problem of teaching a network to perform well, even on samples that were not used as training samples, is a quite subtle issue that requires additional techniques. This is especially important for cases where only very limited numbers of training samples are available. The danger is that the network overfits the training data and fails to capture the true statistical process generating the data. Computational learning theory is concerned with training classifiers on a limited amount of data. In the context of neural networks a simple heuristic, called early stopping, often ensures that the network will generalize well to examples not in the training set.

Other typical problems of the back-propagation algorithm are the speed of convergence and the possibility of ending up in a local minimum of the error function. Today there are practical solutions that make back-propagation in multi-layer perceptrons the solution of choice for many machine learning tasks.

4.1.6 back propagation algorithm (BPA) and other training algorithms

The Back propagation Algorithm

1. Propagates inputs forward in the usual way, i.e.
   - All outputs are computed using sigmoid threshold of the inner product of the corresponding weight and input vectors.
   - All outputs at stage n are connected to all the inputs at stage n+1
2. Propagates the errors backwards by apportioning them to each unit according to the amount of this error the unit is responsible for. We now derive the stochastic Back propagation algorithm for the general case. The derivation is simple, but unfortunately the book-keeping is a little messy.

- $\overline{x}_j$ = input vector for unit j (xji = ith input to the jth unit)
- $\overrightarrow{w_j}$ = weight vector for unit j (wji = weight on xji)
- $z_j = \overrightarrow{w_j} \cdot \overrightarrow{x_j}$, The weighted sum of inputs for unit j
- oj = output of unit j $(O_j = \sigma(z_j))$
- tj = target for unit j
- Downstream (j) = set of units whose immediate inputs include the output of j
- Outputs = set of output units in the final layer

Since we update after each training example, we can simplify the notation somewhat by imagining that the training set consists of exactly one example and so the error can simply be denoted by E.

We want to calculate $\frac{\partial E}{\partial w_{ji}}$ for each input weight wji for each output unit j. Note first that since zj is a function of wji regardless of where in the network unit j is located,

$$\frac{\partial E}{\partial w_{ji}} = \frac{\partial E}{\partial z_j} \cdot \frac{\partial z_j}{\partial w_{ji}}$$

$$= \frac{\partial E}{\partial z_j} x_{ji}$$

Furthermore, $\frac{\partial E}{\partial z_j}$ is the same regardless of which input weight of unit j we are trying to update. So we denote this quantity by ∂_j.

Consider the case when $e \in$ Outputs. We know

$$E = \frac{1}{2} \sum_{k \in Outputs} (t_k - \sigma(z_k))^2$$

Since the outputs of all units $k \neq j$ are independent of wji, we can drop the summation and consider just the contribution to E by j.

$$\delta_j = \frac{\partial E}{\partial z_j} = \frac{\partial}{\partial z_j} \frac{1}{2} (t_j - o_j)^2$$

$$= -(t_j - o_j) \frac{\partial o_j}{\partial z_j}$$

$$= -(t_j - o_j) \frac{\partial}{\partial z_j} \sigma(z_j)$$

$$= -(t_j - o_j)(1 - \sigma(z_j))\, \sigma(z_j)$$

$$= -(t_j - o_j)(1 - o_j)\, o_j$$

Thus

$$\Delta w_{ji} = -\eta \frac{\partial E}{\partial w_{ij}} = \eta \delta_j x_{ji} \qquad (17)$$

Now consider the case when j is a hidden unit. Like before, we make the following two important observations.

1. For each unit k downstream from j, zk is a function of zj
2. The contribution to error by all units $l \neq j$ in the same layer as j is independent of wji

We want to calculate $\frac{\partial E}{\partial w_{ji}}$ for each input weight wji for each hidden unit j. Note that wji influences just zj which influences oj which influences $z_k\ \forall\, k \in$ Downstream (J) each of which influence E. So we can write

$$\frac{\partial E}{\partial w_{ji}} = \sum_{k \in Doenstream\,(j)} \frac{\partial E}{\partial z_k} \cdot \frac{\partial z_k}{\partial o_j} \cdot \frac{\partial o_j}{\partial z_j} \cdot \frac{\partial z_j}{\partial w_{ji}}$$

$$= \sum_{k \in Downstream\,(j)} \frac{\partial E}{\partial z_k} \cdot \frac{\partial z_k}{\partial o_j} \cdot \frac{\partial o_j}{\partial z_j} \cdot x_{ji}$$

Again note that all the terms except x_{ji} in the above product are the same regardless of which input weight of unit j we are trying to update. Like before, we denote this common quantity by δ_j. Also note that $\frac{\partial E}{\partial z_k} = \delta_k$, $\frac{\partial z_k}{\partial o_j} = w_{kj}$ and $\frac{\partial o_j}{\partial z_j} = O_j (1 - O_j)$. Substituting,

$$\delta_j = \sum_{k \in Downstream\,(j)} \frac{\partial E}{\partial z_k} \cdot \frac{\partial z_k}{\partial o_j} \cdot \frac{\partial o_j}{\partial z_j}$$

$$= \sum_{k \in Downstream\,(j)} \partial_k w_{kj} O_j (1 - O_j)$$

Thus,

$$\delta_k = O_j (1 - O_j) \sum_{k \in Downstream (j)} \delta_k w_{kj} \quad (18)$$

We are now in a position to state the Backpropagation algorithm formally.

Formal statement of the algorithm:

Each training example is of the form $(\vec{x}, \vec{t})$ where $\vec{x}$ is the input vector and $\vec{t}$ is the target vector. η is the learning rate (e.g., .05). n_i , n_h and n_o are the number of input, hidden and output nodes respectively. Input from unit i to unit j is denoted xji and its weight is denoted by wji.

- Create a feed-forward network with ni inputs, nh hidden units, and no output units.
- Initialize all the weights to small random values (e.g., between -.05 and .05)
- Until termination condition is met, Do
    - o For each training example $(\vec{x}, \vec{t})$, Do

1. Input the instance $\vec{x}$ and compute the output ou of every unit.
2. For each output unit k, calculate

$$\delta_k = O_k (1 - O_k) (t_k - O_k)$$

3. For each hidden unit h, calculate

$$\delta_h = O_h (1 - O_h) \sum_{k \in Downstream (j)} w_{kh} \delta_k$$

4. Update each network weight wji as follows :

$$w_{ji} \leftarrow w_{ji} + \Delta w_{ji}$$

where $\Delta w_{ji} = \eta \delta_j x_j i$

4.1.7 Applications of Adaptive Multi-Layer Network Architecture

Multi-layer networks use a variety of learning techniques, the most popular being back-propagation. Here the output values are compared with the correct answer to compute the value of some predefined error-function. By various techniques the error is then fed back through the network. Using this information, the algorithm adjusts the weights of each connection in order to reduce the value of the error function by some small amount. After repeating this process for a sufficiently large number of training cycles the network will usually converge to some state where the error of the calculations is small. In this case one says that the network has learned a certain target function. To adjust weights properly one applies a general method for non-linear optimization task that is called gradient descent. For this, the derivative of the error function with respect to the network weights is calculated and the weights are then changed such that the error decreases (thus going downhill on the surface of the error function). For this reason back-propagation can only be applied on networks with differentiable activation functions.

In general the problem of teaching a network to perform well, even on samples that were not used as training samples, is a quite subtle issue that requires additional techniques. This is especially important for cases where only very limited numbers of training samples are available. The danger is that the network overfits the training data and fails to capture the true statistical process generating the data. Computational learning theory is concerned with training classifiers on a limited amount of data. In the context of neural networks a simple heuristic, called early stopping, often ensures that the network will generalize well to examples not in the training set.

Other typical problems of the back-propagation algorithm are the speed of convergence and the possibility of ending up in a local minimum of the error function. Today there are practical solutions that make back-propagation in multi-layer perceptrons the solution of choice for many machine learning tasks.

4.2 Recurrent Network

Contrary to feedforward networks, recurrent neural networks (RNs) are models with bi-directional data flow. While a feedforward network propagates data linearly from input to output, RNs also propagate data from later processing stages to earlier stages.

Consider the following two networks :

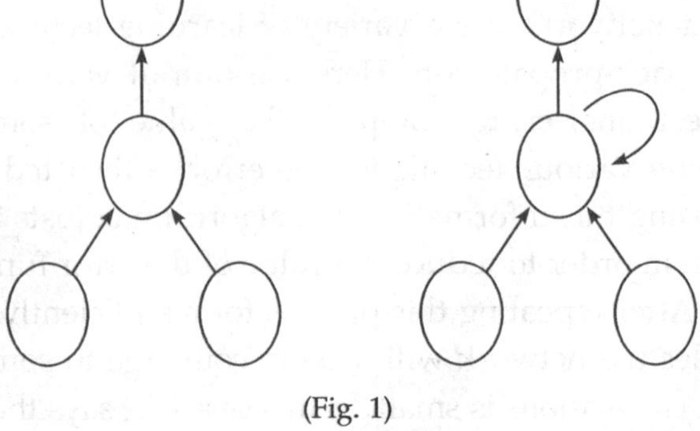

(Fig. 1)

The network on the left is a simple feed forward network of the kind we have already met. The right hand network has an additional connection from the hidden unit to itself. What difference could this seemingly small change to the network make?

Each time a pattern is presented, the unit computes its activation just as in a feed forward network. However its net input now contains a term which reflects the state of the network (the hidden unit activation) before the pattern was seen. When we present subsequent patterns, the hidden and output units' states will be a function of everything the network has seen so far.

4.2.1 Network topology

Once we allow feedback connections, our network topology becomes very free: we can connect any unit to any other, even to itself. Two of our basic requirements for computing activations and errors in the network are now violated. When computing activations, we required that before computing yi, we had to know the activations of all units in the posterior set of nodes, Pi. For computing errors, we required that before computing δ_j, we had to know the errors of all units in its anterior set of nodes, Ai.

For an arbitrary unit in a recurrent network, we now define its activation at time t as :

$$y_i(t) = f_i(\text{net}_i(t-1))$$

At each time step, therefore, activation propagates forward through one layer of connections only. Once some level of activation is present in the network, it will continue to flow around the units, even in the absence of any new input whatsoever. We can now present the network with a time series of inputs, and require that it produce an output based on this series. These networks can be used to model many new kinds of problems, however, these nets also present us with many new difficult issues in training.

Before we address the new issues in training and operation of recurrent neural networks, let us first look at some sample tasks which have been attempted (or solved) by such networks.

- **Learning formal grammars**

Given a set of strings S, each composed of a series of symbols, identify the strings which belong to a language L. A simple example: L = {an,bn} is the language composed of strings of any number of a's, followed by the same number of b's. Strings belonging to the language include aaabbb, ab, aaaaaabbbbbb. Strings not belonging to the language include aabbb, abb, etc. A common benchmark is the language defined by the reber grammar. Strings which belong to a language L are said to be grammatical and are ungrammatical otherwise.

- **Speech recognition**

In some of the best speech recognition systems built so far, speech is first presented as a series of spectral slices to a recurrent network. Each output of the network represents the probability of a specific phone (speech sound, e.g. /i/, /p/, etc), given both present and recent input. The probabilities are then interpreted by a Hidden Markov Model which tries to recognize the whole utterance.

- **Music composition**

A recurrent network can be trained by presenting it with the notes of a musical score. It's task is to predict the next note. Obviously this is impossible to do perfectly, but the network learns that some notes are more likely to occur in one context than another. Training, for example, on a lot of music by J. S. Bach, we can then seed the network with a musical phrase, let it predict the next note, feed this back in as input, and repeat, generating new music. Music generated in this fashion typically sounds fairly convincing at a very local scale, i.e. within a short phrase. At a larger scale, however, the compositions wander randomly from key to key, and no global coherence arises. This is an interesting area for further work.

4.2.2 The Simple Recurrent Network

One way to meet these requirements is illustrated below in a network known variously as an Elman network (after Jeff Elman, the originator), or as a Simple Recurrent Network. At each time step, a copy of the hidden layer units is made to a copy layer. Processing is done as follows:

1. Copy inputs for time t to the input units
2. Compute hidden unit activations using net input from input units and from copy layer
3. Compute output unit activations as usual
4. Copy new hidden unit activations to copy layer

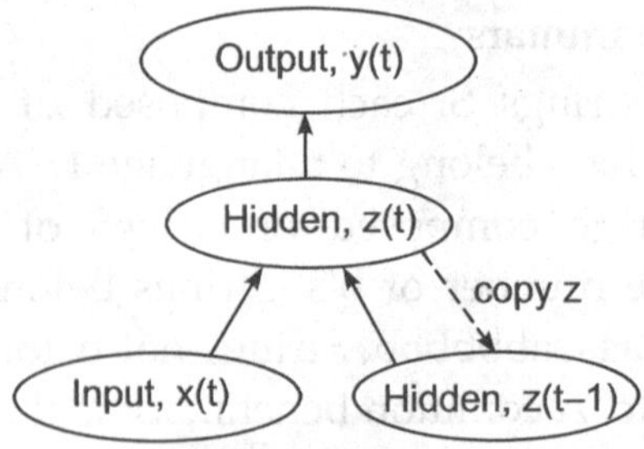

In computing the activation, we have eliminated cycles, and so our requirement that the activations of all posterior nodes be known is met. Likewise, in computing errors, all trainable weights are feed forward only, so we can apply the standard backpropagation algorithm as before. The weights from the copy layer to the hidden layer play a special role in error computation. The error signal they receive comes from the hidden units, and so depends on the error at the hidden units at time t. The activations in the hidden units, however, are just the activation of the hidden units at time t-1. Thus, in training, we are considering a gradient of an error function which is determined by the activations at the present and the previous time steps.

A generalization of this approach is to copy the input and hidden unit activations for a number of previous timesteps. The more context (copy layers) we maintain, the more history we are explicitly including in our gradient computation. This approach has become known as Back Propagation Through Time. It can be seen as an approximation to the ideal of computing a gradient which takes into consideration not just the most recent inputs, but all inputs seen so far by the network. The figure below illustrates one version of the process:

The inputs and hidden unit activations at the last three time steps are stored. The solid arrows show how each set of activations is determined from the input and hidden unit activations on the previous time step. A backward pass, illustrated by the dashed arrows, is performed to determine separate values of delta (the error of a unit with respect to its net input) for each unit and each time step separately. Because each earlier layer is a copy of the layer one level up, we introduce the new constraint that the weights at each level be identical. Then the partial derivative of the negative error with respect to wi,j is simply the sum of the partials calculated for the copy of wi,j between each two layers.

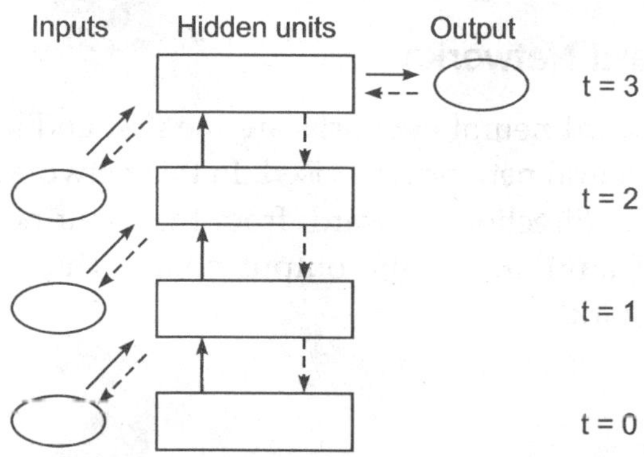

Elman networks and their generalization, Back Propagation Through Time, both seek to approximate the computation of a gradient based on all past inputs, while retaining the standard back prop algorithm. BPTT has been used in a number of applications. The main task is to to produce a particular output sequences in response to specific input sequences. The downside of BPTT is that it requires a large amount of storage, computation, and training examples in order to work well.

4.2.3 Simple recurrent network

A simple recurrent network (SRN) is a variation on the multi-layer perceptron, sometimes called an "Elman network" due to its invention by Jeff Elman. A three-layer network is used, with the addition of a set of "context units" in the input layer. There are connections from the middle (hidden) layer to these context units fixed with a weight of one. At each time step, the input is propagated in a standard feed-forward fashion, and then a learning rule (usually back-propagation) is applied. The fixed back connections result in the context units always maintaining a copy of the previous values of the hidden units (since they propagate over the connections before the learning rule is applied). Thus the network can maintain a sort of state, allowing it to perform such tasks as sequence-prediction that are beyond the power of a standard multi-layer perceptron.

In a fully recurrent network, every neuron receives inputs from every other neuron in the network. These networks are not arranged in layers. Usually only a subset of the neurons receive external inputs in addition to the inputs from all the other neurons, and another disjunct subset of neurons report their output externally as well as sending it to all the neurons. These distinctive inputs and outputs perform the function of the input and output layers of a feed-forward or simple recurrent network, and also join all the other neurons in the recurrent processing.

4.3 Feed-forward Networks

The feedforward neural networks are the first and arguably simplest type of artificial neural networks devised. In this network, the information moves in only one direction, forward, from the input nodes, through the hidden nodes (if any) and to the output nodes. There are no cycles or loops in the network.

Feed-Forward networks :

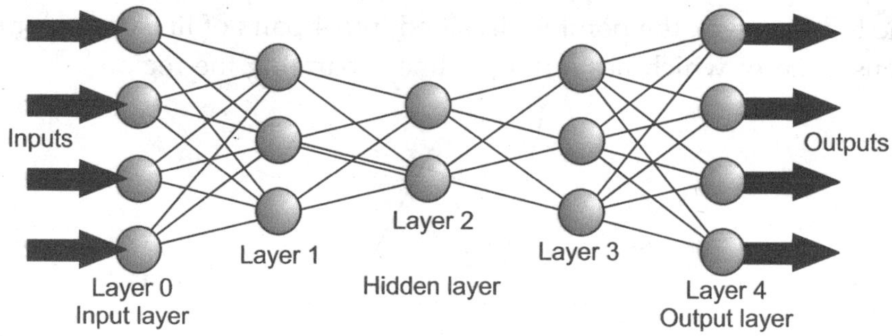

Fig: A Feed -Forward Network

Feed-forward networks have the following characteristics:

1) Perceptrons are arranged in layers, with the first layer taking in inputs and the last layer producing outputs. The middle layers have no connection with the external world, and hence are called hidden layers.
2) Each perceptron in one layer is connected to every perceptron on the next layer. Hence information is constantly "fed forward" from one layer to the next. And this explains why these networks are called feed-forward networks.
3) There is no connection among perceptrons in the same layer.

4.3.1 What's so cool about feed-forward networks?

Recall that a single perceptron can classify points into two regions that are linearly separable. Now let us extend the discussion into the separation of points into two regions that are not linearly separable. Consider the following network:

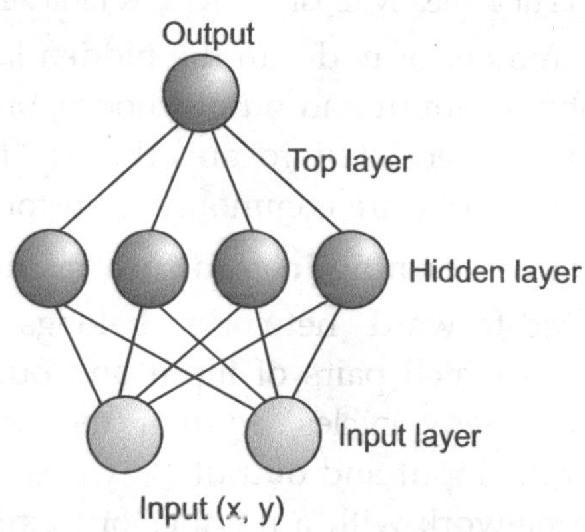

Fig.2: A feed-forward network with one hidden layer

The same (x, y) is fed into the network through the perceptrons in the input layer. With four perceptrons that are independent of each other in the hidden layer, the point is classified into 4 pairs of linearly separable regions, each of which has a unique line separating the region.

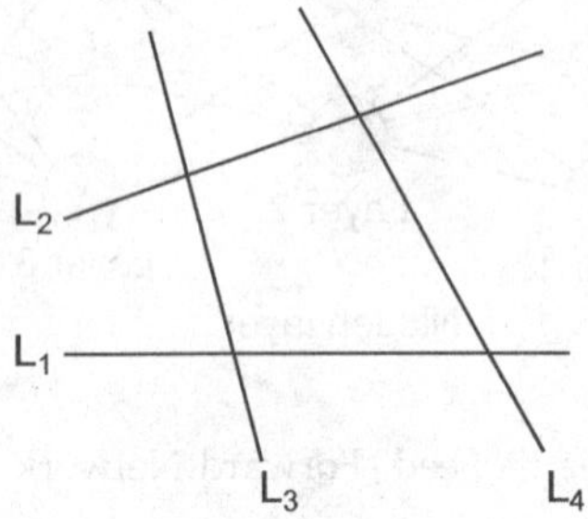

Fig.3: 4 lines each dividing the plane into 2 linearly separable regions

The top perceptron performs logical operations on the outputs of the hidden layers so that the whole network classifies input points in 2 regions that might not be linearly separable. For instance, using the AND operator on these four outputs, one gets the intersection of the 4 regions that forms the center region.

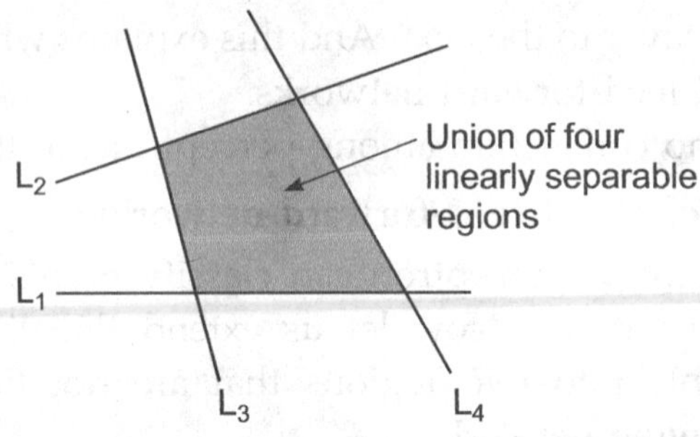

Fig. 4 : Intersection of 4 linearly separable regions forms the center region

By varying the number of nodes in the hidden layer, the number of layers, and the number of input and output nodes, one can classification of points in arbitrary dimension into an arbitrary number of groups. Hence feed-forward networks are commonly used for classification.

4.3.2 Back propagation -- learning in feed-forward networks:

Learning in feed-forward networks belongs to the realm of supervised learning, in which pairs of input and output values are fed into the network for many cycles, so that the network 'learns' the relationship between the input and output.

We provide the network with a number of training samples, which consists of an input vector its desired output o and I. For instance, in the classification problem, suppose we have points (1, 2) and (1, 3) belonging to group 0, points (2, 3) and (3, 4) belonging to group 1, (5, 6) and (6, 7) belonging to group 2, then for a feed-forward network with 2 input nodes and 2 output nodes, the training set would be:

{ i = (1, 2) , o =(0, 0)
i = (1, 3) , o = (0, 0)
i = (2, 3) , o = (1, 0)
i = (3, 4) , o = (1, 0)
i = (5, 6) , o = (0, 1)
i = (6, 7) , o = (0, 1) }

The basic rule for choosing the number of output nodes depends on the number of different regions. It is advisable to use a unary notation to represent the different regions, i.e. for each output only one node can have value 1. Hence the number of output nodes = number of different regions -1. In back propagation learning, every time an input vector of a training sample is presented, the output vector o is compared to the desired value d. The comparison is done by calculating the squared difference of the two :

$$\mathbf{Err = (d - o)^2}$$

The value of Err tells us how far away we are from the desired value for a particular input. The goal of backpropagation is to minimize the sum of Err for all the training samples, so that the network behaves in the most "desirable" way.

$$\textbf{Minimize } \Sigma\, \mathbf{Err = (d - o)^2}$$

We can express Err in terms of the input vector (i), the weight vectors (w), and the threshold function of the perceptions. Using a continuous function (instead of the step function) as the threshold function, we can express the gradient of Err with respect to the w in terms of w and i.

Given the fact that decreasing the value of w in the direction of the gradient leads to the most rapid decrease in Err, we update the weight vectors every time a sample is presented using the following formula:

$$\mathbf{w_{new} = w_{old} - n \frac{\partial\, Err}{\partial\, w}}$$ where n is the learning rate (a small number ~ 0.1)

Using this algorithm, the weight vectors are modified so that the value of Err for a particular input sample decreases a little bit every time the sample is presented. When all the samples are presented in turns for many cycles, the sum of Err gradually decreases to a minimum value, which is our goal as mentioned above.

Feed forward neural networks (FF networks) are the most popular and most widely used models in many practical applications. They are known by many different names, such as "multi-layer perceptions."

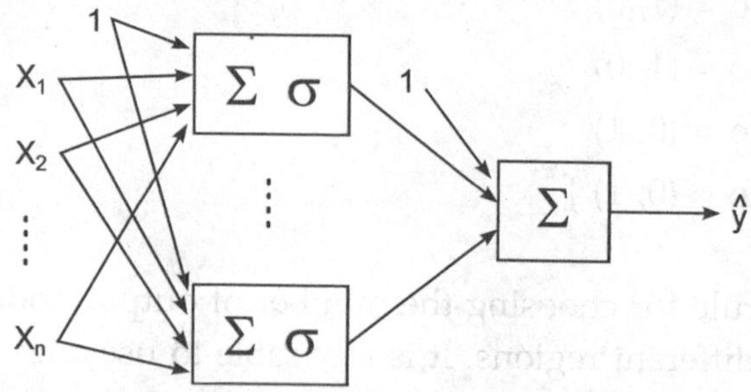

Figure 2.5 illustrates a one-hidden-layer FF network with inputs

Mathematically the functionality of a hidden neuron is described by

$$\sigma\left(\sum_{j=1}^{n} w_j x_j + b_j\right)$$

where the weights $\{w_j, b_j\}$ are symbolized with the arrows feeding into the neuron.

The network output is formed by another weighted summation of the outputs of the neurons in the hidden layer. This summation on the output is called the output layer. In Figure 2.5 there is only one output in the output layer since it is a single-output problem. Generally, the number of output neurons equals the number of outputs of the approximation problem.

The neurons in the hidden layer of the network in Figure 2.5 are similar in structure to those of the perceptron, with the exception that their activation functions can be any differential function. The output of this network is given by

$$Y(\theta) = g(\theta, x) = \sum_{i=1}^{nh} w_1^2 \, \sigma \, \alpha\left(\sum_{j=1}^{n} w_{1,j}^1 x_j + b_{j,i}^1\right) + b^2 \qquad (8)$$

Where n is the number of inputs and nh is the number of neurons in the hidden layer. The variables { } are the parameters of the network model that are represented collectively by the parameter vector . In general, the neural network model will be represented by the compact notation g(,x) whenever the exact structure of the neural network is not necessary in the context of a discussion.

Note that the size of the input and output layers are defined by the number of inputs and outputs of the network and, therefore, only the number of hidden neurons has to be specified when the network is defined. The network in Figure 2.5 is sometimes referred to as a three-layer network, counting input, hidden, and output layers. However, since no processing takes place in the input layer, it is also sometimes called a two-layer network. To avoid confusion this network is called a one-hidden-layer FF network throughout this documentation.

In training the network, its parameters are adjusted incrementally until the training data satisfy the desired mapping as well as possible; that is, until matches the desired output y as closely as possible up to a maximum number of iterations.

The nonlinear activation function in the neuron is usually chosen to be a smooth step function. The default is the standard sigmoid

$$\text{Sigmoid}\,[x] = \frac{1}{1+e^{-x}}$$

that looks like this.

<<NueralNetworks.

In [1] : = Plot [Sigmoid [x], {x, – 8, 9}]

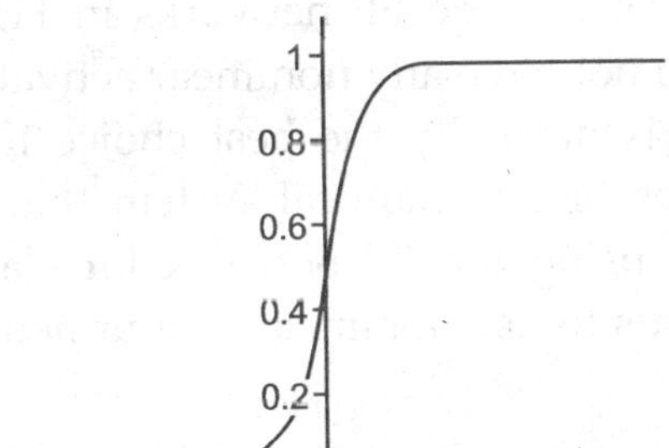

The FF network in Figure 2.5 is just one possible architecture of an FF network. You can modify the architecture in various ways by changing the options. For example, you can change the activation function to any differentiable function you want.

4.4 Multilayer Networks

The package supports FF neural networks with any number of hidden layers and any number of neurons (hidden neurons) in each layer. In Figure 2.6 a multi-output FF network with two hidden layers is shown.

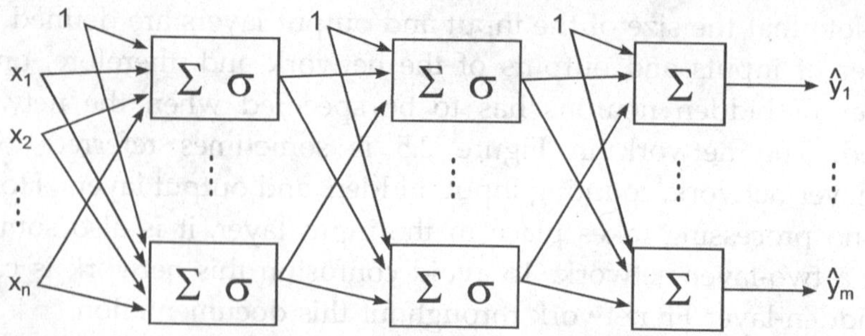

Figure 2.6. A multi-output feedforward network with two hidden layers.

The number of layers and the number of hidden neurons in each hidden layer are user design parameters. The general rule is to choose these design parameters so that the best possible model with as few parameters as possible is obtained. This is, of course, not a very useful rule, and in practice you have to experiment with different designs and compare the results, to find the most suitable neural network model for the problem at hand.

For many practical applications, one or two hidden layers will suffice. The recommendation is to start with a linear model; that is, neural networks with no hidden layers, and then go over to networks with one hidden layer but with no more than five to ten neurons. As a last step you should try two hidden layers.

The output neurons in the FF networks in Figures 2.5 and 2.6 are linear; that is, they do not have any nonlinear activation function after the weighted sum. This is normally the best choice if you have a general function, a time series or a dynamical system that you want to model. However, if you are using the FF network for classification, then it is generally advantageous to use nonlinear output neurons. You can do this by using the option

4.5 Radial basis function (RBF)

A radial basis function (RBF) is a real-valued function whose value depends only on the distance from the origin. They are used in function approximation, time series prediction, and control. In artificial neural networks radial basis functions are utilized as activation functions.

Radial Basis Functions are powerful techniques for interpolation in multidimensional space. A RBF is a function which has built into a distance criterion with respect to a centre. Radial basis functions have been applied in the area of neural networks where they may be used as a replacement for the sigmoidal hidden layer transfer characteristic in multi-layer perceptrons. RBF networks have 2 layers of processing : In the first, input is mapped onto each RBF in the 'hidden' layer. The RBF chosen is usually a Gaussian. In regression problems the output layer is then a linear combination of hidden layer values representing mean predicted output. The interpretation of this output layer value is the same as a regression model in statistics. In classification problems the output layer is typically a sigmoid function of a linear combination of hidden layer values, representing a posterior probability. Performance in both cases is often improved by shrinkage techniques, known as ridge regression in classical statistics and known to correspond to a prior belief in small parameter values (and therefore smooth output functions) in a Bayesian framework.

RBF networks have the advantage of not suffering from local minima in the same way as multi-layer perceptrons. This is because the only parameters that are adjusted in the learning process are the linear mapping from hidden layer to output layer. Linearity ensures that the error surface is quadratic and therefore has a single easily found minimum. In regression problems this can be found in one matrix operation. In classification problems the fixed non-linearity introduced by the sigmoid output function is most efficiently dealt with using iterated reweighted least squares.

RBF networks have the disadvantage of requiring good coverage of the input space by radial basis functions. RBF centres are determined with reference to the distribution of the input data, but without reference to the prediction task. As a result, representational resources may be wasted on areas of the input space that are irrelevant to the learning task. A common solution is to associate each data point with its own centre, although this can make the linear system to be solved in the final layer rather large, and requires shrinkage techniques to avoid overfitting.

Associating each input data with an RBF leads naturally to kernel methods such as Support Vector Machines and Gaussian Processes (the RBF is the kernel function). All three approaches use a non-linear kernel function to project the input data into a space where the learning problem can be solved using a linear model. Like Gaussian Processes, and unlike SVMs, RBF networks are typically trained in a Maximum Likelihood framework by maximizing the probability (minimizing the error) of the data under the model. SVMs take a different approach to avoiding overfitting by maximizing instead a margin. RBF networks are outperformed in most classification applications by SVMs. In regression applications they can be competitive when the dimensionality of the input space is relatively small.

4.5.1 RBF types

Types of the RBF include:

- Gaussian: $\rho(r) = \exp\,(-\beta r^2)$ for some $\beta > 0$
- Multiquadratic : $\rho\,(r) = \sqrt{r^2 + \beta^2}$ for some $\beta > 0$

4.5.2 Interpolation problem

The interpolation problem solved by RBF's is the development of an analytic approximation for the input/output mappings described by a deterministic, noisy, or stochastic data stream

$$\{[x\,(t), y\,(t)] : [R^n\,, R]\}_{t=1}^{\infty}$$

where

$x\,(t)$ is the input vector at time t,

$y\,(t)$ is the output at time t, and

n is the dimension of the input space.

In the deterministic case the data is drawn from the set

$$\{[x\,(t), y\,(t) = f\,(x\,(t))]\}_{t=1}^{\infty}$$

In the noisy case data is drawn from the set

$$\{[x\,(t), y\,(t) = f\,(x\,(t)) + \in(t)]\}_{t=1}^{\infty}$$

where $\varepsilon(t)$ is a partially known random process.

In the stochastic case, data is drawn from the joint probability distribution

$$P\,(x \wedge y).$$

4.5.3 Architecture

RBF networks typically have 3 layers, the input layer, the hidden layer with the RBF non-linearity and a linear output layer. The most popular choice for the non-linearity is the Gaussian. RBF networks have the advantage of not being locked into local minima as do the MLP networks.

RBF architectures come in two forms, normalized and unnormalized. The forms can be expanded into a superposition of local linear models

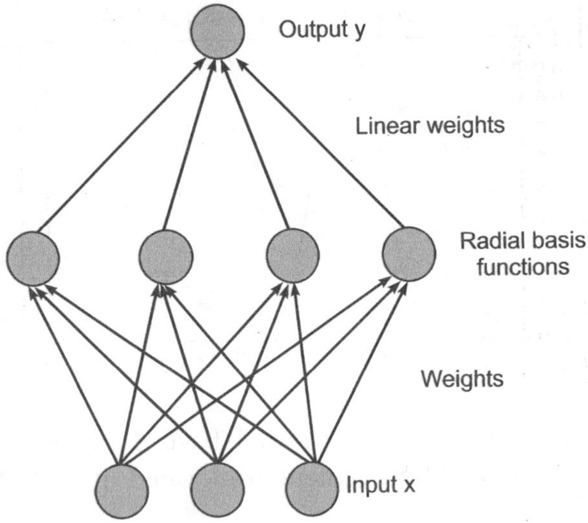

Figure 1: Architecture of a radial basis function network. An input vector x is used as input to several radial basis functions, each with different parameters. The output of the network is a linear combination of the outputs from radial basis functions.

4.5.3.1 Unnormalized radial basis function

The unnormalized radial basis function architecture, $\varphi : R^n \to R$, is

$$\varphi(X)' \stackrel{def}{=} \sum_{i=1}^{N} a_i \rho(\| x - c_i \|)$$

where φ is the approximation to the data, $\rho(\|x - c_i\|)$, known as a "radial basis function," is a local function of the distance $\|x - c_i\|$ between the input vector and a "basis function center"

$$c_i \ (i = 1, N),$$

and

$$a_i \ (i = 1, N)$$

are weights to be determined by data. Typically the distance is taken to be the Euclidean distance and the basis function is taken to be Gaussian

$$\rho(\|x - c_i\|) \ \alpha \ \exp[-\beta \ \|x - c_i\|^2].$$

- The weights a_i, c_i, and β are determined in a manner that optimizes the fit between and the data.

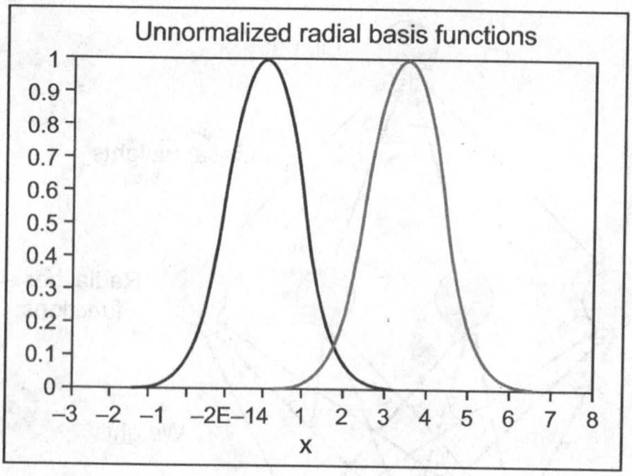

Figure 2: Two unnormalized radial basis functions in one input dimension. The basis function centers are located at c1 = 0.75 and c2 = 3.25.

4.5.3.2 Normalized radial basis function

The normalized RBF architecture is

$$\varphi(x) \overset{def}{=} \frac{\sum_{i=1}^{N} a_i \rho(\| x - c_i \|)}{\sum_{i=1}^{N} \rho(\| x - c_i \|)} = \sum_{i=1}^{N} a_i u(\| x - c_i \|)$$

where

$$u(\| x - c_i \|) \overset{def}{=} \frac{\rho(\| x - c_i \|)}{\sum_{i=1}^{N} \rho(\| x - c_i \|)}$$

- is known as a "normalized radial basis function."

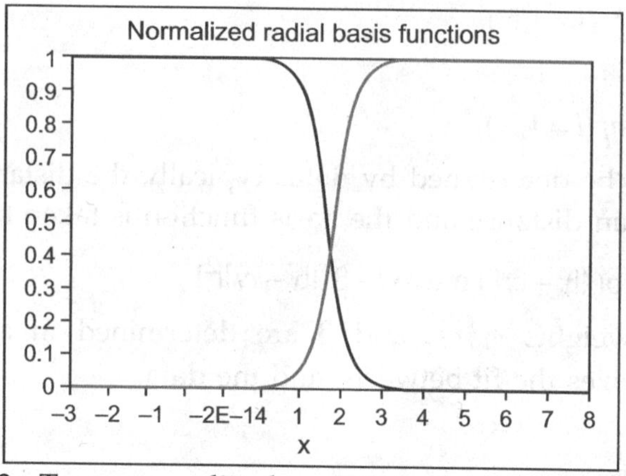

Figure 3: Two normalized radial basis functions in one input

dimension. The basis function centers are located at c1 = 0.75 and c2 = 3.25.

4.5.4 Theoretical motivation for normalization

There is theoretical justification for this architecture in the case of stochastic data flow. Assume a Stochastic kernel approximation for the joint probability density

$$P(x \wedge y) = \sum_{i=1}^{N} \rho(\|x - c_i\|)\, \sigma(|y - e_i|)$$

where the weights and ei are exemplars from the data and we require the kernels to be normalized

$$\int \rho(\|x - c_i\|)\, d^n x = 1$$

and

$$\int \sigma(|y - e_i|)\, dy = 1$$

The probability densities in the input and output spaces are

$$P(x) = \int P(x \wedge y)\, dy = \sum_{i=1}^{N} \rho(\|x - c_i\|)$$

and

$$P(y) = \int P(x \wedge y)\, d^n x = \sum_{i=1}^{N} \sigma(|y - e_i|)$$

The expectation of y given an input is

$$\varphi(x) \overset{\text{def}}{=} E(y \mid x) = \int y\, P'(y \mid x)\, dy$$

where

$$P(y \mid x)$$

is the conditional probability of y given . The conditional probability is related to the joint probability through Bayes theorem

$$P(y \mid x) = \frac{P(x \wedge y)}{P(x)}$$

which yields

$$\varphi(x) = \int y \frac{P(x \wedge y)}{P(x)} dy$$

This becomes

$$\varphi(x) = \frac{\sum_{i=1}^{N} a_i \rho(\|x - c_i\|)}{\sum_{i=1}^{N} \rho(\|x - c_i\|)} = \sum_{i=1}^{N} a_i u(\|x - c_i\|)$$

- when the integrations are performed.

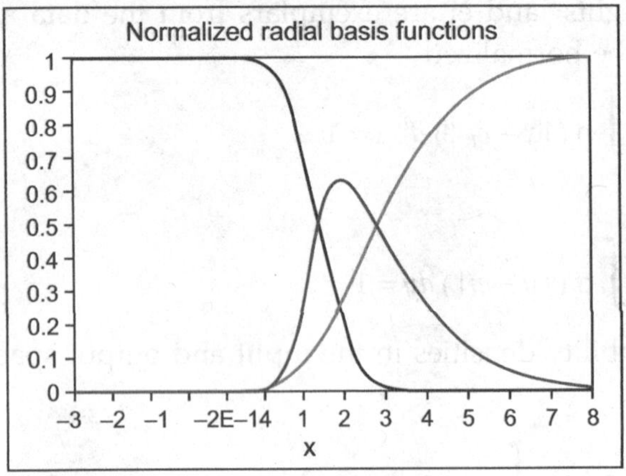

Figure 4: Three normalized radial basis functions in one input dimension. The additional basis function has center at c3 = 2.75

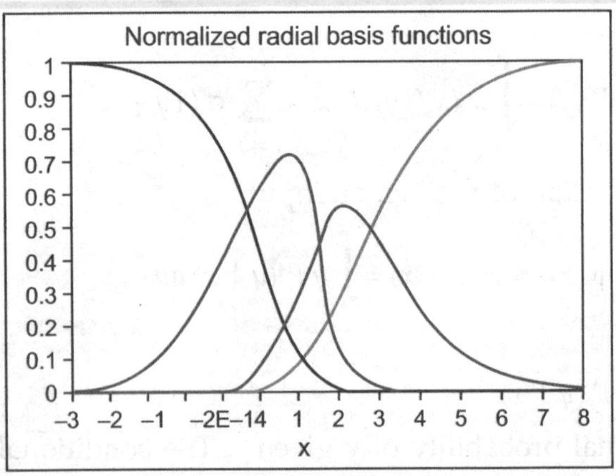

Figure 5: Four normalized radial basis functions in one input dimension. The fourth basis function has center at c4 = 0. Note that the first basis function (dark blue) has become localized.

4.5.5 Local linear models

It is sometimes convenient to expand the architecture to include local linear models. In that case the architectures become, to first order,

$$\varphi(x) = \sum_{i=1}^{N} (a_i + b_i \,.\, (x - c_i))\, \rho\, (\,\|x - c_i\,\|)$$

and

$$\varphi(x) = \sum_{i=1}^{N} (a_i + b_i \,.\, (x - c_i))\, \rho\, (\,\|x - c_i\,\|)$$

in the unnormalized and normalized cases, respectively. Here are weights to be determined. Higher order linear terms are also possible.

This result can be written

$$\varphi(x) = \sum_{i=1}^{2N} \sum_{j=1}^{n} e_{ij}\, v_{ij}\, (x - c_i)$$

where

$$e_{ij} = \begin{cases} a_i, & \text{if } i \in [1, N] \\ b_{ij}, & \text{if } i \in [N+1, 2N] \end{cases}$$

and

$$v_{ij}(x - c_i) \overset{\text{def}}{=} \begin{cases} \delta_{1j}\, \rho\, (\,\|x - c_i\,\|)\,, & \text{if } i \in [1, N] \\ (x_{ij} - c_{ij})\, \rho\, (\,\|x - c_i\,\|)\,, & \text{if } i \in [N+1, 2N] \end{cases}$$

in the unnormalized case and

$$v_{ij}(x - c_i) \overset{\text{def}}{=} \begin{cases} \delta_{1j}\, \rho\, (\,\|x - c_i\,\|)\,, & \text{if } i \in [1, N] \\ (x_{ij} - c_{ij})\, \rho\, (\,\|x - c_i\,\|)\,, & \text{if } i \in [N+1, 2N] \end{cases}$$

in the normalized case.

Here dij is a Kronecker delta function defined as

$$\delta_{ij} = \begin{cases} 1, & \text{if } i = j \\ 0, & \text{if } i \neq j \end{cases}$$

4.5.6 Objective functions

The weights, which we signify by , in the RBF architecture are found through optimization of an objective function. The most common objective function is the least squares function

$$K(w) \overset{\text{def}}{=} \sum_{i=1}^{\infty} K_t(w)$$

where

$$K_t(w) \overset{\text{def}}{=} [y(t) - \varphi(x(t), w)]^2.$$

We have explicitly included the dependence on the weights. Minimization of the least squares objective function by optimal choice of weights optimizes accuracy of fit.

There are occasions in which multiple objectives, such as smoothness as well as accuracy, must be optimized. In that case it is useful to optimize a regularized objective function such as

$$H(w) \overset{\text{def}}{=} K(w) + \lambda S(w) \overset{\text{def}}{=} \sum_{i=1}^{\infty} H_t(w)$$

where

$$S(w) \overset{\text{def}}{=} \sum_{i=1}^{\infty} S_t(w)$$

and

$$H_t(w) \overset{\text{def}}{=} K_t(w) + \lambda S_t(w)$$

where optimization of S maximizes smoothness and ? is known as a regularization parameter.

4.5.7 Training

Training the centers and weights to optimize the objective function is typically done in hybrid fashion by first fixing the basis funtion centers and then optimizing the weights. In the sequential training the weights are updated at each time step as data streams in.

Training the basis function centers

Basis function centers can be either randomly sampled among the input instances or found by clustering the samples and choosing the the cluster means as the centers.

Gradient descent training of the linear weights

The simplest training algorithm is Gradient descent. In gradient descent training the weights are adjusted at each time step by moving them in a direction opposite from the gradient of the objective function

$$w(t+1) = w(t) - v\frac{d}{dw}H_t(w)$$

where V is a "learning parameter."

For the case of training the linear weights, ai, the algorithm becomes

$$a_i(t+1) = a_i(t) + v\,[y(t) - \varphi(x(t), w]\,\rho\,(\|x(t) - c_i\|)$$

in the unnormalized case and

$$a_i(t+1) = a_i(t) + v\,[y(t) - \varphi(x(t), w]\,\rho\,(\|x(t) - c_i\|)$$

in the normalized case.

For local-linear-architectures gradient-descent training is

$$e_{ij}(t+1) = e_{ij}(t) + v\,[y(t) - \varphi(x(t), w)]\,v_{ij}(x(t) - c_i)$$

Projection operator training of the linear weights

For the case of training the linear weights, ai and eij, the algorithm becomes

$$a_i(t+1) = a_i(t) + v\,[y(t) - \varphi(x(t), w)]\frac{\rho\,(\|x(t) - c_i\|)}{\sum_{i=1}^{N} \rho^2(\|x(t) - c_i\|)}$$

in the unnormalized case and

$$a_i(t+1) = a_i(t) + v\,[y(t) - \varphi(x(t), w)]\frac{\rho\,(\|x(t) - c_i\|)}{\sum_{i=1}^{N} \rho^2(\|x(t) - c_i\|)}$$

in the normalized case and

$$a_i(t+1) = a_i(t) + v\,[y(t) - \varphi(x(t), w)]\frac{\rho\,(\|x(t) - c_i\|)}{\sum_{i=1}^{N} \rho^2(\|x(t) - c_i\|)}$$

in the local-linear case.

For one basis function, projection operator training reduces to Newton's method.

Examples

Logistic map

The basic properties of radial basis functions can be illustrated with a simple mathematical map, the logistic map, which maps the unit interval onto itself. It can be used to generate a convenient prototype data stream. The logistic map can be used to explore function approximation, time series prediction, and control theory. The map originated from the field of population dynamics and became the prototype chaotic time series. The map, in the fully chaotic regime, is given by

$$w(t+1) \overset{\text{def}}{=} f[x(t)] = rx(t)[1 - x(t)]$$

where t is a time index. The value of x at time t+1 is a parabolic function of x at time t. This equation represents the underlying geometry of the chaotic time series generated by the logistic map.

Generation of the time series from this equation is the forward problem. The examples here illustrate the inverse problem; identification of the the underlying dynamics, or fundamental equation, of the logistic map from exemplars of the time series. The goal is to find an estimate

$$x(t+1) = f[x(t)] \approx \varphi(t) = \varphi[x(t)]$$

- for f.

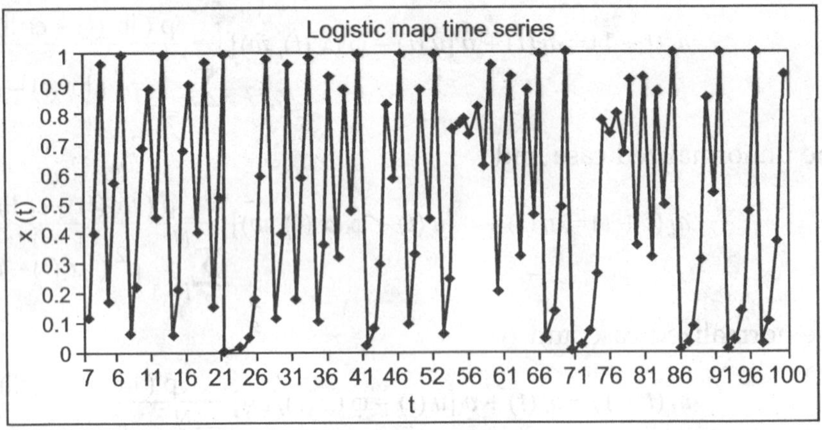

Figure 6: Logistic map time series. Repeated iteration of the logistic map generates a chaotic time series. The values lie between zero and one. Displayed here are the 100 training points used to train the examples in this section. The weights c are the first five points from this time series.

4.5.8 Time series prediction

Once the underlyting geometry of the time series is estimated as in the previous examples, a prediction for the time series can be made by iteration:

$$\varphi(0) = x(1)$$

$$x(t) \approx \varphi(t-1)$$

$$x(t+1) \approx \varphi(t) = \varphi[\varphi(t-1)].$$

A comparison of the actual and estimated time series is displayed in the figure. The estimated times series starts out at time zero with an exact knowledge of x(0). It then uses the estimate of the dynamics to update the the time series estimate for several time steps.

- Note that the estimate is accurate for only a few time steps. This is a general characteristic of chaotic time series. This is a property of the sensitive dependence on initial conditions common to chaotic time series. A small initial error is amplified with time. A measure of the divergence of time series with nearly identical initial conditions is known as the Lyapunov exponent.

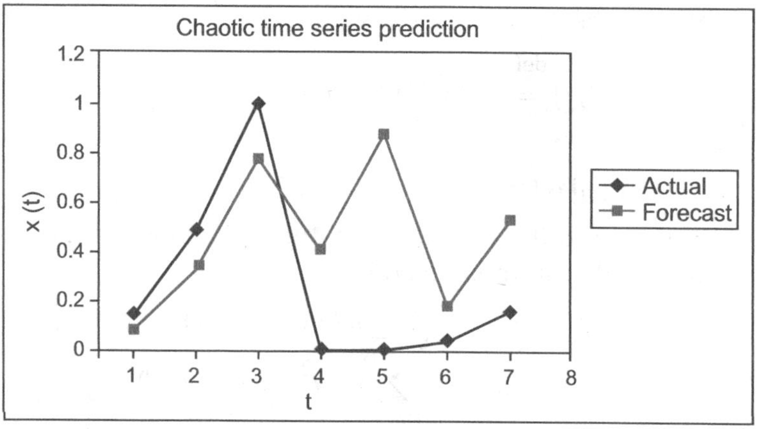

Figure 9 : Normalized basis functions. The Logistic map (blue) and the approximation to the logistic map (red) as a function of time. Note that the approximation is good for only a few time steps. This is a general characterisitc of chaotic time series.

Control of a chaotic time series

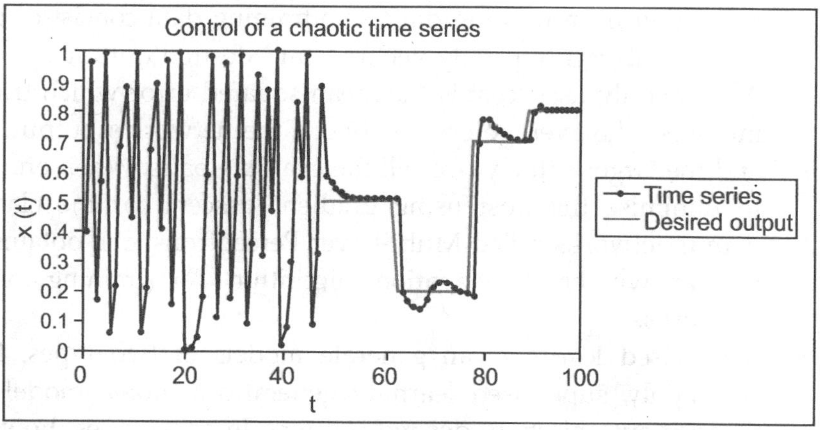

Figure 10: Control of the logistic map. The system is allowed to evolve naturally for 49 time steps. At time 50 control is turned on. The desired trajectory for the time series is red. The system under control learns the underlying dynamics and drives the time series to the desired output. The architecture is the same as for the time series prediction

example.

We assume the output of the logistic map can be manipulated through a control parameter c[x(t),t] such that

$$x(t+1) = 4x(t)\,[1 - x(t)] + c\,[x(t), t].$$

The goal is to choose the control parameter in such a way as to drive the time series to a desired output d(t). This can be done if we choose the control paramer to be

$$c\,[x(t), t] \overset{\text{def}}{=} -\,\varphi\,[x(t)] + d\,(t+1)$$

where

$$\varphi\,[x(t)] \approx f\,[x(t)] = x(t+1) - c\,[x(t), t]$$

is an approximation to the underlying natural dynamics of the system.

The learning algorithm is given by

$$a_i(t+1) = a_i(t) + v\,\varepsilon \frac{u\,(\|x(t) - c_i\|)}{\sum_{i=1}^{N} u^2\,(\|x(t) - c_i\|)}$$

where

$$\varepsilon \overset{\text{def}}{=} f\,[x(t)] - \varphi\,[x(t)] = x(t+1) - c\,[x(t), t] - \varphi\,[x(t)] = x(t+1) - d\,(t+1).$$

4.6 Summary

- Supervised learning is a machine learning technique for creating a function from training data. The training data consist of pairs of input objects (typically vectors), and desired outputs.
- A commonly used cost is the mean-squared error which tries to minimise the average error between the network's output, f(x), and the target value y over all the example pairs. When one tries to minimise this cost using gradient descent for the class of neural networks called Multi-Layer Perceptrons, one obtains the well-known backpropagation algorithm for training neural networks.
- Supervised learning can generate models of two types. Most commonly, supervised learning generates a global model that maps input objects to desired outputs. In some cases, however, the map is implemented as a set of local models (such as in case-based reasoning or the nearest neighbor algorithm).
- A perceptron can be created using any values for the activated and deactivated states as long as the threshold value lies between

the two. Most perceptrons have outputs of 1 or -1 with a threshold of 0 and there is some evidence that such networks can be trained more quickly than networks created from nodes with different activation and deactivation values.

- Multi-layer networks use a variety of learning techniques, the most popular being back-propagation. Here the output values are compared with the correct answer to compute the value of some predefined error-function. By various techniques the error is then fed back through the network.
- A radial basis function (RBF) is a real-valued function whose value depends only on the distance from the origin. They are used in function approximation, time series prediction, and control. In artificial neural networks radial basis functions are utilized as activation functions.
- RBF networks have the advantage of not suffering from local minima in the same way as multi-layer perceptrons. This is because the only parameters that are adjusted in the learning process are the linear mapping from hidden layer to output layer.
- RBF networks have the disadvantage of requiring good coverage of the input space by radial basis functions. RBF centres are determined with reference to the distribution of the input data, but without reference to the prediction task. As a result, representational resources may be wasted on areas of the input space that are irrelevant to the learning task.
- RBF networks typically have 3 layers, the input layer, the hidden layer with the RBF non-linearity and a linear output layer. The most popular choice for the non-linearity is the Gaussian. RBF networks have the advantage of not being locked into local minima as do the MLP networks.
- Basis function centers can be either randomly sampled among the input instances or found by clustering the samples and choosing the the cluster means as the centers.
- The simplest training algorithm is Gradient descent. In gradient descent training the weights are adjusted at each time step by moving them in a direction opposite from the gradient of the objective function.

Chapter No. 5

Unsupervised learning

In unsupervised learning we are given some data x, and the cost function to be minimised can be any function of the data x and the network's output, f. The cost function is determined by the task formulation. Most applications fall within the domain of estimation problems such as statistical modelling, compression, filtering, blind source separation and clustering.

As a trivial example, consider the model f(x) = a, where a is a constant and the cost C = (E[x] - f(x))2. Minimising this cost will give us a value of that is equal to the mean of the data. The cost function can be much more complicated. Its form depends on the application: For example in compression it could be related to the mutual information between x and y. In statistical modelling, it could be related to the posterior probability of the model given the data.

Tasks that fall within the paradigm of unsupervised learning are in general estimation problems; the applications include clustering, the estimation of statistical distributions, compression and filtering.

5.1 Winner-takes-all networks

A winner-takes-all Network tailored to the maximum clique problem, a well-known intractable combinatorial optimization problem that has practical applications in several real world domains. The analysis yields tight bounds for the parameter settings to ensure energy descent to feasible solutions. To verify the theoretical results we employ a fast annealing schedule to the WTA algorithm and show the effectiveness of the proposed approach for large scaled problems in extensive computer simulations.

A winner-takes-all (WTA) network is a simple type of an unsupervised competitive learning network. In WTA networks, the desired output vector has a single active unit because the output nodes are said to compete with each other to be the one to fire. A number of approaches for this feature have been proposed, and the simplest and probably most commonly used solution uses lateral inhibition. Such a network is depicted in Figure. There are other kinds of competitive learning networks, for instance, cluster input vector patterns.

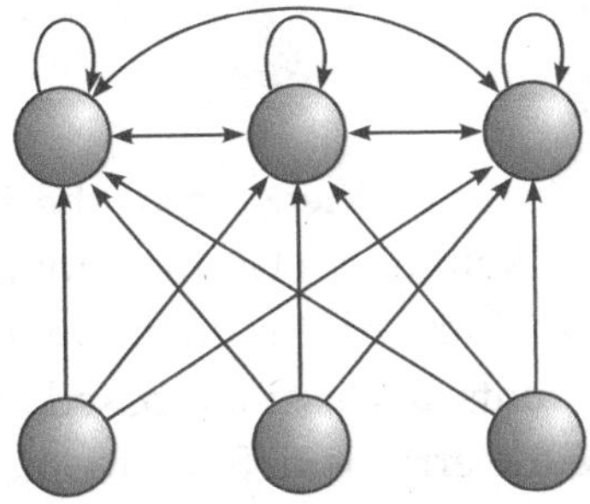

Fig 5.1 : winner take all implementation using lateral inhibition

In this network, each output unit corresponds to exactly one input unit. Every input unit excites its corresponding output unit while inhibiting all other output units. Therefore, the strongest input unit will cause its corresponding unit to have a comparatively high activation value, while it significantly reduces the activation values of all other output neurons. The extra excitatory self-loops as well as the inhibitory connections between the output units have been added in order to increase the stability of the network. In a truly parallel system, if two input neurons had the same activation value, the outcome of the network would be undefined and quite possibly oscillating between the two corresponding output units. However, given that artificial neural networks are mostly simulated on serial computers, this problem is eliminated with these connections.

The simplicity of this approach has its drawbacks. Unless the lateral weights and non-linear activation functions of the output units are chosen well, the output may not be as black-and-white as desired. It would be desirable for the winning output unit to be the only one with a positive activation. However, given analog input data, this is almost impossible to achieve without the loss of generality. With help of the self-loops and well-chosen connection strengths, the network can be configured such that it allows stabilization of the output vector, but due to the nature of neural networks, parallel computing, and analog data, the result may not always be as precise as the outcome of a computational algorithm.

In a controller of greater complexity than the one built here, a more robust solution to winner selection has to be used. Possibilities here include auto-associator networks, cascaded lateral inhibition, or minimum distance automata. For the purposes of the developed controller, however, the proposed approach conveniently combines functionality with simplicity.

5.2 Hamming Networks

The Hamming network is an extension of the Hopfield network in that it adds a maximum likelihood classifier to the frond end. This network was developed by Richard Lippman in the mid 1980's. The Hamming network implements a classifier based upon least error for binary input vectors, where the error is defined by the Hamming distance. The Hamming distance is defined as the number of bits, which differ between two corresponding, fixed-length input vectors. One input vector is the noiseless example pattern, the other is a pattern corrupted by real-world events. In this network architecture, the output categories are defined by a noiseless, pattern-filled training set. In the recall mode any incoming input vectors are then assigned to the category for which the distance between the examples input vectors and the current input vector is minimum.

The Hamming network has three layers. There is an example network shown in Figure 5.2. The network uses an input layer with as many nodes as there are separate binary features. It has a category layer, which is the Hopfield layer, with as many nodes as there are categories, or classes. This differs significantly from the formal Hopfield architecture, which has as many nodes in the middle layer as there are input nodes. And finally, there is an output layer, which matches the number of nodes in the category layer.

The network is simple feed forward architecture with the input layer fully connected to the category layer. Each processing element in the category layer is connected back to every other element in that same layer, as well as to a direct connection to the output processing element. The output from the category layer to the output layer is done through competition.

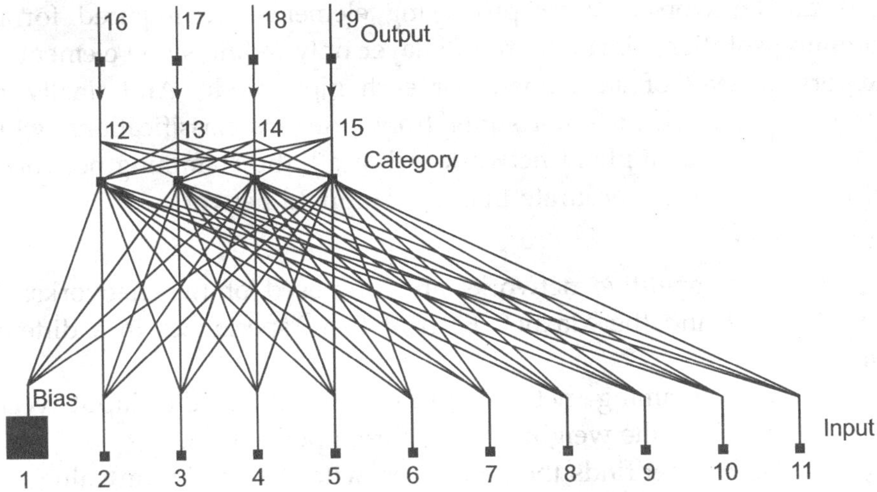

Figure 5.2. A Hamming Network Example.

The learning of a Hamming network is similar to the Hopfield methodology in that it requires a single-pass training set. However, in this supervised paradigm, the desired training pattern is impressed upon the input layer while the desired class to which the vector belongs is impressed upon the output layer. Here the output contains only the category output to which the input vector belongs. Again, the recursive nature of the Hopfield layer provides a means of adjusting all connection weights.

The connection weights are first set in the input to category layer such that the matching scores generated by the outputs of the category processing elements are equal to the number of input nodes minus the Hamming distances to the example input vectors. These matching scores range from zero to the total number of input elements and are highest for those input vectors which best match the learned patterns. The category layer's recursive connection weights are trained in the same manner as in the Hopfield network. In normal feed forward operation an input vector is applied to the input layer and must be presented long enough to allow the matching score outputs of the lower input to category subnet to settle. This will initialize the input to the Hopfield function in the category layer and allow that portion of the subnet to find the closest class to which the input vector belongs. This layer is competitive, so only one output is enabled at a time.

The Hamming network has a number of advantages over the Hopfield network. It implements the optimum minimum error classifier when input bit errors are random and independent. So, the Hopfield with its random set up nature can only be as good a solution as the Hamming, or it can be worse. Fewer processing elements are required for the Hamming solution, since the middle layer only requires one element per category, instead of an element for each input node. And finally, the Hamming network does not suffer from spurious classifications, which may occur in the Hopfield network. All in all, the Hamming network is both faster and more accurate than the Hopfield network.

5.2.1 Maxnet:

Simple competitive networks are composed of two networks: the Hemming net and the Maxnet. Each of them specializes in a different function:

- The Hemming net measures how much the input vector resembles the weight vector of each perceptron.
- The maxnet finds the perceptron with the maximum value.

In order to understand how these two seemingly unrelated networks function together, we need to examine more closely the details of each one.

5.2.2 The Hemming net:

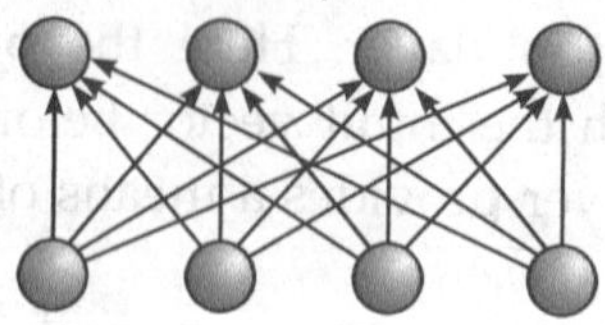

Fig 5.3 : Hamming net

Each perceptron at the top layer of the Hemming net calculates a weighted sum of the input values. This weighted sum can be interpreted as the dot product of the input vector and the weight vector.

$\Sigma wi = w \cdot i = \|w\| \, \|i\| \cos \theta$, where i and w are the input vector and the weight vector respectively.

If w and i are of unit length, then the dot product depends only on cos theta. Since the cosine function increases as the angle decreases, the dot product gets bigger when the two vectors are close to each other (the angle between them is small). Hence the weighted sum each perceptron calculates is a measure of how close its weight vector resembles the input vector.

5.2.3 The Maxnet :

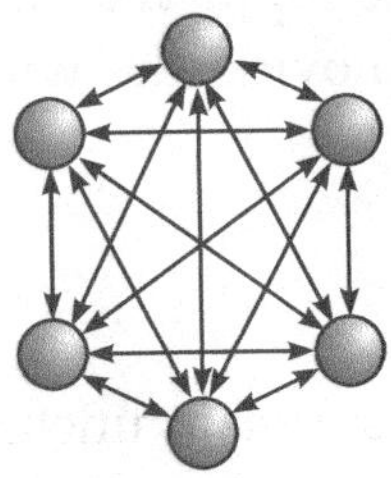

Fig 5.4 : Maxnet

The maxnet is a fully connected network with each node connecting to every other nodes, including itself. The basic idea is that the nodes compete against each other by sending out inhibiting signals to each other.

This is done by setting the weights of the connections between different nodes to be negative and applying the following algorithm:

Algorithm

```
left the value of node i be x
until (xi doesn't change){
        foreach i{
                xsubi = xi + Σ w xj   where w is negative
                            i≠j
        }
}
```

Using the above algorithm, all nodes converge to 0 except for the node with the maximum initial value. In this way the maxnet finds out the node with the maximum value.

Putting them together:

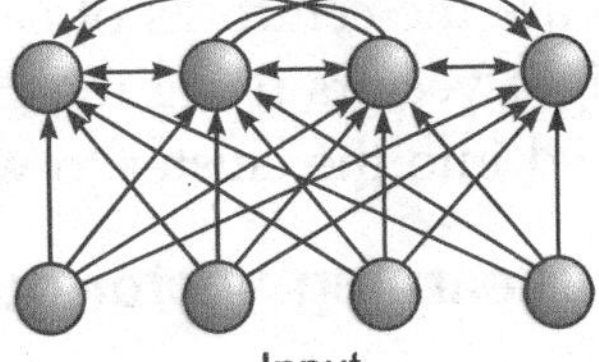

Fig. 5.4 : A Simple Competitive network.

In a simple competitive network, a Maxnet connects the top nodes of the Hemming net. Whenever an input is presented, the Hemming net finds out the cdistanced of the weight vector of each node from the input vector via the dot product, while the Maxnet selects the node with the greatest dot product. In this way, the whole network selects the node with its weight vector closest to the input vector, i.e. the winner.

The network learns by moving the winning weight vector towards the input vector:

$$w_{new} = w_{old} + n\,(i - w_{old})$$

while the other weight vectors remain unchanged.

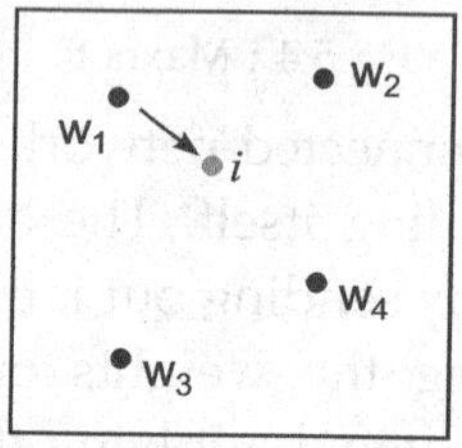

Fig. 5.6 : The winner learns by moving towards the input vector.

This process is repeated for all the samples for many times. If the samples are in clusters, then every time the winning weight vector moves towards a particular sample in one of the clusters. Eventually each of the weight vectors would converge to the centroid of one cluster. At this point, the training is complete.

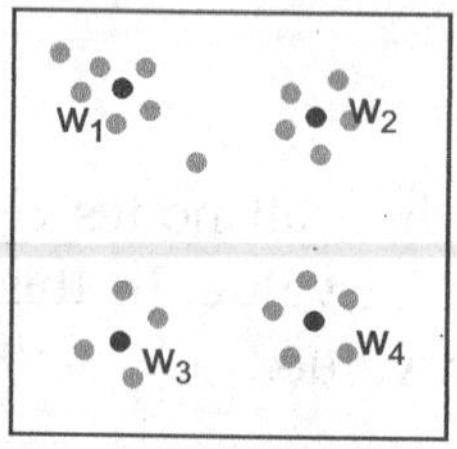

Fig. 5.7 : After training, the weight vectors become centroids of various clusters.

When new samples are presented to a trained net, it is compared to the weight vectors which are the centroids of each cluster. By measuring the distance from the weight vectors using the Hemming net, the sample would be correctly grouped into the cluster to which it is closest.

5.3 Simple competitive learning vector-quantization

In competitive networks, output units compete for the right to respond.

Goal: method of clustering - divide the data into a number of clusters such that the inputs in the same cluster are in some sense similar.

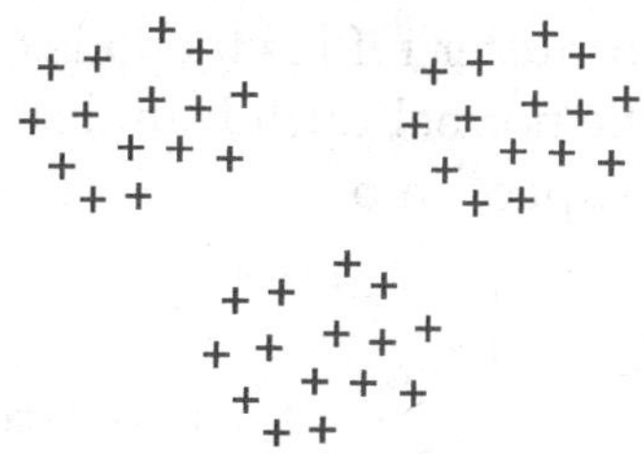

A basic competitive learning network has one layer of input nodes and one layer of output nodes. Binary valued outputs are often (but not always) used. There are as many output nodes as there are classes. Often (but not always) there are lateral inhibitory connections between the output nodes.(in simulations, the function of the lateral connections can be replaced with a different algorithm)

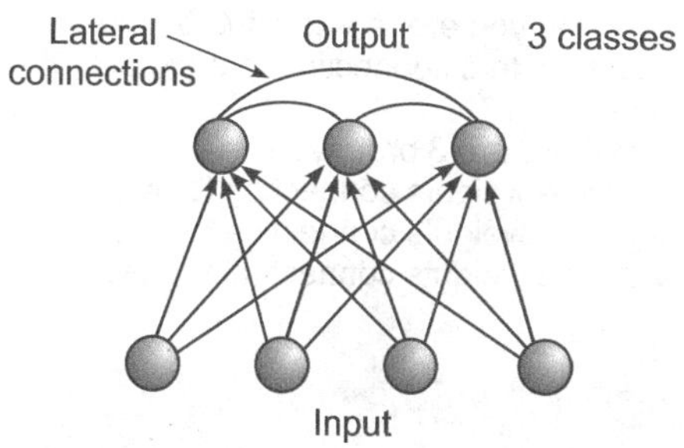

Since the output units complete with one another to turn on, they are often called *"winner-take-all"* units

The output units are also often called grandmother cells. The term grandmother cell comes from discussions as to whether your brain might contain cells that fire only when you encounter your maternal grandmother, or whether such higher level concepts are more distributed.

5.3.1 Vector Quantization (VQ)

Vector quantization is one example of competitive learning. The goal here is to have the network "discover" structure in the data by finding how the data is clustered. The results can be used for data encoding and compression. One such method for doing this is called vector quantization.

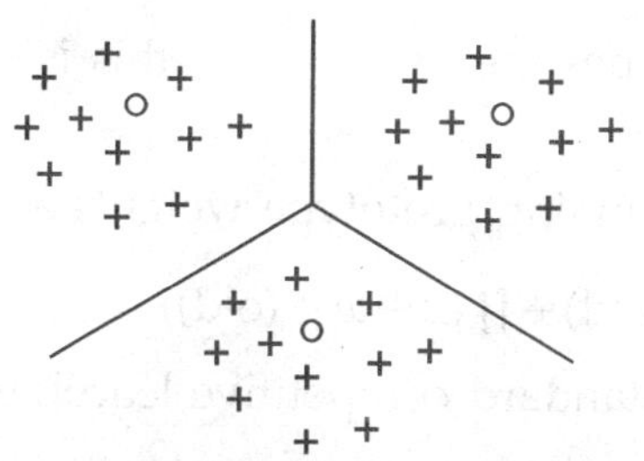

M = 3
o = prototype vector
+ = input data

In vector quantization, we assume there is a codebook which is defined by a set of M prototype vectors. (M is chosen by the user and the initial prototype vectors are chosen arbitrarily).

An input belongs to cluster i if i is the index of the closest prototype (closest in the sense of the normal Euclidean distance). This has the effect of dividing up the input space into a Voronoi tesselation.

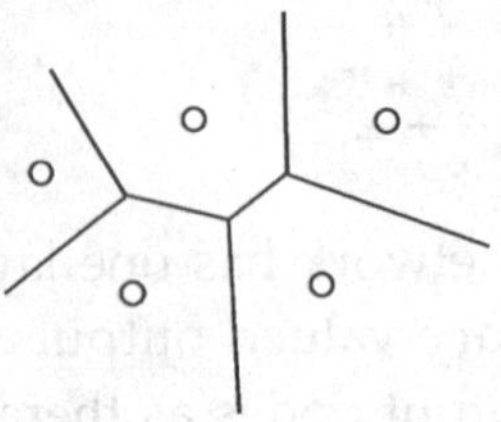

5.3.2 Implementing Vector Quantization with a Network

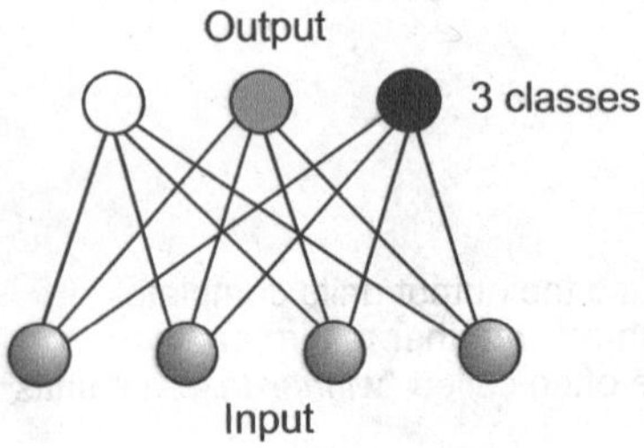

The prototype are represented by the weight vectors connecting to each output node.
Here there are 3 prototype:
w_1 = the weights connecting to output 1
w_2 = the weights connecting to output 2
w_3 = the weights connecting to output 3

Algorithm:

- Choose the number of clusters M
- Initialize the prototypes w*1,... w*m (one simple method for doing this is to randomly choose M vectors from the input data)
- Repeat until stopping criterion is satisfied:
  - o Randomly pick an input x
  - o Determine the "winning" node k by finding the prototype vector that satisfies

    $| w*_k - x | <= | w*_i - x |$ (for all i)

    note: if the prototypes are normalized, this is equivalent to maximizing w*i x
  - o Update only the winning prototype weights according to

    $w*_k \text{(new)} = w*_k \text{(old)} + [] (x - w*_k \text{(old)})$

    This is called the standard competitive learning rule.

5.3.3 Vector Quantization and Data Compression

Vector quantization can be used for (lossy) data compression. If we are sending information over a phone line, we

- Initially send the codebook vectors
- For each input, we send the index of the class that the input belongs

For a large amount of data, this can be a significant reduction. If M=64, then it takes only 6 bits to encode the index. If the data itself consists of floating point numbers (4 bytes) there is an 80% reduction (100*(1 - 6/32)).

5.3.4 Learning Vector Quantization (LVQ)

This is a supervised version of vector quantization. Classes are predefined and we have a set of labeled data. The goal is to determine a set of prototypes the best represent each class.

5.4 Counter-Propagation Network

The first counter-propagation network consisted of a bi-directional mapping between the input and output layers. In essence, while data is presented to the input layer to generate a classification pattern on the output layer, the output layer in turn would accept an additional input vector and generate an output classification on the network's input layer. The network got its name from this counter-posing flow of information through its structure. Most developers use a unit-flow variant of this formal representation of counter-propagation. In other words. There is only one feed forward path from input layer to output layer.

An example network is shown in Figure 5.8 the unit-directional counter-propagation network has three layers. If the inputs are not already normalized before they enter the network, a fourth layer is sometimes added. The main layers include an input buffer layer, a self-organizing Kohonen layer, and an output layer, which uses the Delta Rule to modify its incoming connection weights. Sometimes this layer is called a Grossberg Outstar layer.

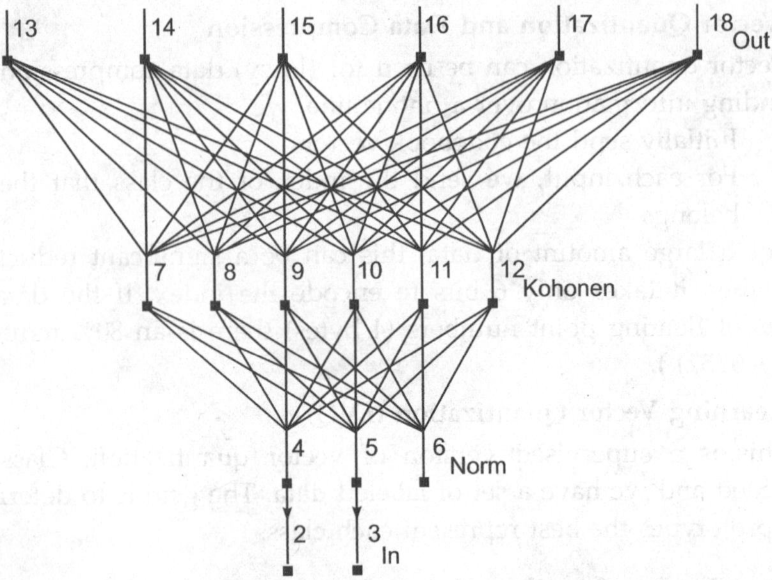

Figure 5.8 An Example Counter-propagation Network.

The size of the input layer depends upon how many separable parameters define the problem. With too few, the network may not generalize sufficiently. With too many, the processing time takes too long.

5.5 Adaptive resonance theory

The adaptive resonance theory network topology is protected by a patent held by the University of Boston. Developed by Stephen Grossberg in the mid 1970's, the network creates categories of input data based on adaptive resonance. The topology is biologically plausible and uses an unsupervised learning function. It analyses behaviorally significant input data and detects possible features or classifies patterns in the input vector.

This network was the basis for many other network paradigms, such as counter-propagation and bi-directional associative memory networks. The heart of the adaptive resonance network consists of two highly interconnected layers of processing elements located between an input and output layer. Each input pattern to the lower resonance layer will induce an expected pattern to be sent from the upper layer to the lower layer to influence the next input. This creates a "resonance" between the lower and upper layers to facilitate network adaption of patterns.

The network is normally used in biological modeling, however, some engineering applications do exist. The major limitation to the network architecture is its noise susceptibility. Even a small amount of noise on the input vector confuses the pattern matching capabilities of a trained network.

5.6 Kohonen's self-organizing maps

Kohonon's SOMs are a type of unsupervised learning. The goal is to discover some underlying structure of the data. However, the kind of structure we are looking for is very different than, say, PCA or vector quantization.

Kohonen's SOM is called a topology-preserving map because there is a topological structure imposed on the nodes in the network. A topological map is simply a mapping that preserves neighborhood relations. In the nets we have studied so far, we have ignored the geometrical arrangements of output nodes. Each node in a given layer has been identical in that each is connected with all of the nodes in the upper and/or lower layer. We are now going to take into consideration that physical arrangement of these nodes. Nodes that are "close" together are going to interact differently than nodes that are "far" apart.

What do we mean by "close" and "far"? We can think of organizing the output nodes in a line or in a planar configuration.

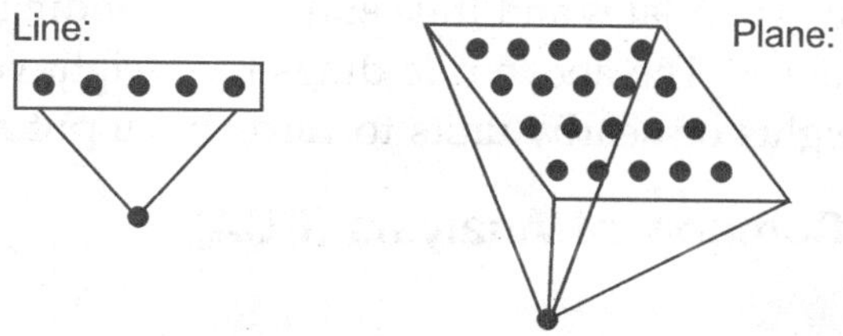

The goal is to train the net so that nearby outputs correspond to nearby inputs.

Example: if x1 and x2 are two input vectors and t1 and t2 are the locations of the corresponding winning output nodes, then t1 and t2 should be close if x1 and x2 are similar. A network that performs this kind of mapping is called a feature map. In the brain, neurons tend to cluster in groups. The connections within the group are much greater than the connections with the neurons outside of the group. Kohonen's network tries to mimics this in a simple way.

5.6.1 Algorithm for Kohonon's Self Organizing Map

- Assume output nodes are connected in an array (usually 1 or 2 dimensional)
- Assume that the network is fully connected - all nodes in input layer are connected to all nodes in output layer.

- Use the competitive learning algorithm as follows:
  - o Randomly choose an input vector x
  - o Determine the "winning" output node i, where wi is the weight vector connecting the inputs to output node i. Note: the above equation is equivalent to wi x = wk x only if the weights are normalized.

$$|w_i - x| \leq |w_k - x| \quad \forall k$$

  - o Given the winning node i, the weight update is

$$w_k\,(\text{new}) = w_k\,(\text{old}) + \mu\, N\,(i, k)\,(x - w_k)$$

Where is called the neighborhood function that has value 1 when i=k and falls off with the distance |rk - ri| between units i and k in the output array. Thus, units close to the winner as well as the winner itself, have their weights updated appreciably. Weights associated with far away output nodes do not change significantly. It is here that the topological information is supplied. Nearby units receive similar updates and thus end up responding to nearby input patterns. The above rule drags the weight vector wi and the weights of nearby units towards the input x.

5.7 Principal Component Analysis (PCA)

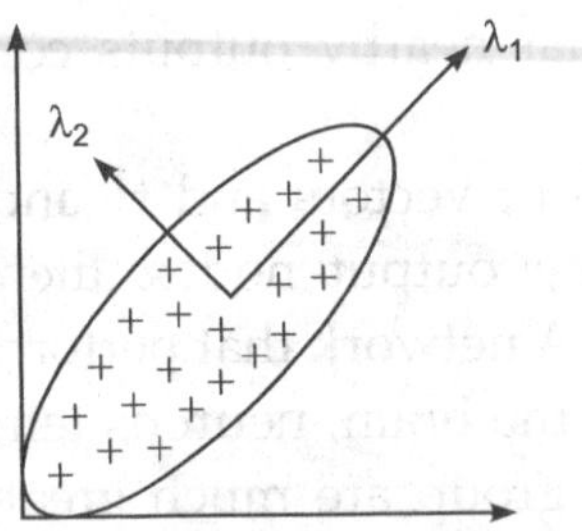

Projecting the data onto the direction λ_1 would cause the least amount of information loss.

How do we find the λ_1 direction?

The []1 direction corresponds to

- The direction of largest variance of the data.
- The eigenvector associated with the largest eigenvalue of the correlation matrix (<x x^T>).

If we have n dimensional data, we can compress it down to m dimensions by projecting it down to the space spanned by Eigen vectors of the m largest eigenvalues.The methods that can be used for finding these directions is called Principal Component Analysis (PCA).

5.7.1 Finding the Principal Components using an Auto associative Network

An auto associative network is a network whose inputs and targets are the same. That is, the net must find a mapping from an input to itself. When the number of hidden nodes is smaller than the number of input node, the network is forced to learn an efficient low dimensional representation of the data.

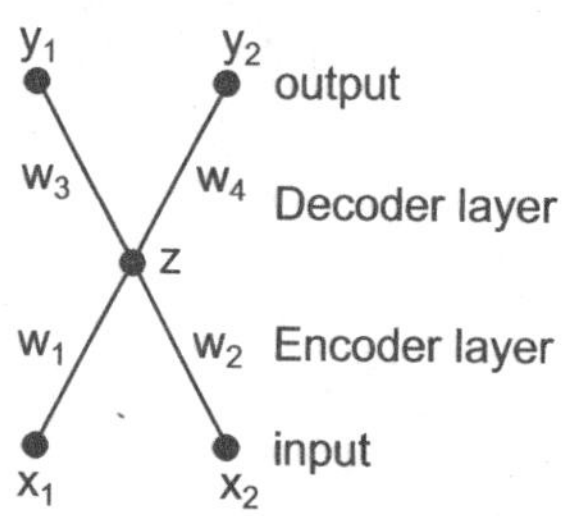

The encoded internal representation is z:
$z = w_1 \times 1 + w_2 \times 2$
which is line in (x_1, x_2) space.

Thus, a point (x_1, x_2) is mapped onto a 1-D space representation by z.

To decode the point we have
$y_1 = z\,w_3,\ y_2 = z\,w_4$

Example: Image Compression

- 64 inputs: 8x8 pixel regions of an image specified to 8 bit precision
- 16 hidden units
- 64 outputs: targets = inputs

Trained on randomly selected patches of an image (150,000 training steps). It was then tested on the entire image patch by patch using the entire set of non overlapping patches.

5.7.2 Nonlinear Compression Techniques

Two layer networks perform a projection of the data onto a linear subspace. In this case, the encoding and decoding portions of the network are really single layer linear networks.This works well in some cases. However, many datasets lie on lower dimensional subspaces that are not linear.

Example :

A helix is 1-D, however, it does not line on a 1-D linear subspace.

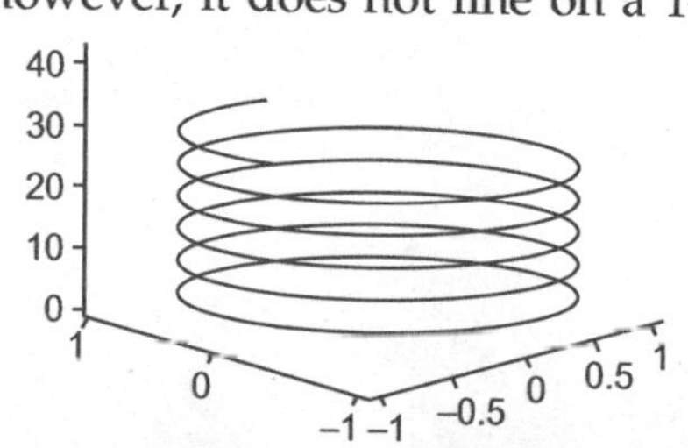

To solve this problem we can let the encoding and decoding portions each be multilayer networks. In this way we obtain nonlinear projections of the data.

Chapter No. 6

Models of Artificial Neural Network

6.1 Associated models

6.1.1 Hopfield Network:

A Hopfield net is a form of recurrent artificial neural network invented by John Hopfield. Hopfield nets serve as content-addressable memory systems with binary threshold units. They are guaranteed to converge to a stable state.

Structure

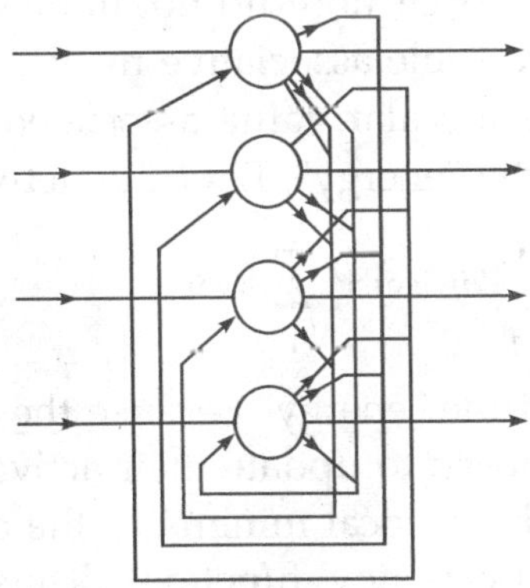

Fig. 6.1 : A Hopfield net with four nodes.

The units in Hopfield nets are binary threshold units, i.e. the units only take on two different values for their states and the value is determined by whether or not the units' input exceeds their threshold. Hopfield nets can either have units that take on values of 1 or -1, or units that take on values of 1 or 0. So, the two possible definitions for unit i's activation, ai, are :

$$(1)\ a_i \leftarrow \begin{cases} 1 & \text{if } \Sigma_j w_{ij} s_j > \theta_1, \\ -1 & \text{otherwise.} \end{cases}$$

$$(2)\ a_i \leftarrow \begin{cases} 1 & \text{if } \Sigma_j w_{ij} s_j > \theta_1, \\ 0 & \text{otherwise.} \end{cases}$$

Where :

- wij is the strength of the connection weight from unit j to unit i (the weight of the connection).
- sj is the state of unit j.
- i is the threshold of unit i.

The connections in a Hopfield net typically have the following restrictions:

- $w_{ij} = 0, \forall i$ (no unit has a connection with itself)
- $w_{ij} = w_{ji}\ \forall i, j$ (connections are symmetric)

The requirement that weights be symmetric is typically used, as it will guarantee that the energy function decreases monotonically while following the activation rules, and the network may exhibit some periodic or chaotic behaviour if non-symmetric weights are used. However, Hopfield found that this chaotic behaviour was confined to relatively small parts of the phase space, and did not impair the network's abilities to act as a content-addressable associative memory system.

Hopfield nets have a scalar value associated with each state of the network referred to as the "energy", E, of the network, where:

$$E = -\frac{1}{2}\sum_{i<j} w_{ij}\, s_i\, s_j + \sum_i \theta_i\, s_i$$

This value is called the "energy" because the definition ensures that if units are randomly chosen to update their activations the network will converge to states which are local minima in the energy function (which is considered to be a Lyapunov function). Thus, if a state is a local minimum in the energy function it is a stable state for the network. Note that this energy function belongs to a general class of models in physics, under the name of Ising models.

Running

At each step, pick a node at random. The node's behavior is then deterministic: it moves to a state to minimize the energy of itself and its neighbors. (In contrast, the Boltzmann machine has a stochastic update rule.)

Training

Training a Hopfield net involves lowering the energy of states that the net should "remember". This allows the net to serve as a content addressable memory system, that is to say, the network will converge to a "remembered" state if it is given only part of the state. For example, if we train a Hopfield net with five units so that the state (1, 0, 1, 0, 1) is an energy minimum, and we give the network the state (1, 0, 0, 0, 1) it will converge to (1, 0, 1, 0, 1). Thus, the network is properly trained when the energy of states which the network should remember are local minima.

6.1.2 brain-in-a-box network

Brain in a box is a small code size application offering to Cocoa developers the Capabilities to create artificial back propagation neural networks (BNN). Designed on client/server architecture, brain in a box runs in the background waiting for Client requests such as creation of a new BNN, learning it, running it and so on.

A Bundle release of Brain in a box can also be used for "private" applications. All communication between client applications and the server (client requests and Server feedbacks) is based on Apple's Distributed Object technology. Brain in a box is based on client/server architecture. It means you can create a Back propagation neural network on remote computer as well as on your own computer. Because of its multithreaded design, Brain in a box server is able to treat several

Requests (creation, learn, run...) at once. Brain in a box is specially written for MacOS X Cocoa environment; all APIs are accessible in Objective-C and bring elegant ways to Configure your neural networks. This document brings support for those who want use Brain in a box in their application. It shows how the server works, what messages can be sent or received and how the back propagation architecture is implemented in the server.

There are two Brains in a box objects:

- An executable object running in the background and able to treat different client Applications.
- A bundle object for those who want to create and distribute their own neural network Application.

Brain in a box capability

Brain in a box server Create new back propagation network Possibility to create multiple instances of a back propagation network.

Load patterns

Possibility to load several set of patterns in one network.

Run operation

As the learn operation, real time feedback comes when a network is running.

Learn operation

With real time feedback from each component of the network, weight of links, Nodes values and errors, global network performances, current pattern in learning. Several learn operations can be processed at once. It's possible to test the network While the learning. During the learning, some parameters can be modified Such as tolerance, momentum, learning rate.

Load a back propagation network from file

It provides reusability of all of your networks.

Real time feedback

Each client application receives appropriated information's depending On the process. The information can concern a particular link or node as Well as the entire network.

6.1.3 Boltzman machine

The Boltzmann machine is similar in function and operation to the Hopfield network with the addition of using a simulated annealing technique when determining the original pattern. The Boltzmann machine incorporates the concept of simulated annealing to search the pattern layer's state space for a global minimum. Because of this, the machine will gravitate to an improved set of values over time as data iterates through the system.

Ackley, Hinton, and Sejnowski developed the Boltzmann learning rule in 1985. Like the Hopfield network, the Boltzmann machine has an associated state space energy based upon the connection weights in the pattern layer. The processes of learning a training set full of patterns involves the minimization of this state space energy. Because of this, the machine will gravitate to an improved set of values for the connection weights while data iterates through the system.

The Boltzmann machine requires a simulated annealing schedule, which is added to the learning process of the network. Just as in physical annealing, temperatures start at higher values and decreases over time. The increased temperature adds an increased noise factor into each processing element in the pattern layer. Typically, the final temperature is zero. If the network fails to settle properly, adding more iteration at lower temperatures may help to get to an optimum solution.

Boltzmann machine learning at high temperature behaves much like a random model and at low temperatures it behaves like a deterministic model. Because of the random component in annealed learning, a processing element can sometimes assume a new state value that increases rather than decreases the overall energy of the system. This mimics physical annealing and is helpful in escaping local minima and moving toward a global minimum.

As with the Hopfield network, once a set of patterns are learned, a partial pattern can be presented to the network and it will complete the missing information. The limitation on the number of classes, being less than fifteen percent of the total processing elements in the pattern layer, still applies.

Structure

A Boltzmann machine, like a Hopfield Network, is a network of units with an "energy" defined for the network. Unlike Hopfield nets, Boltzmann machine units are binary and stochastic. The global energy, E, in a Boltzmann machine is identical in form to that of a Hopfield network:

$$E = -\sum_{i<j} w_{ij}\, s_i\, s_j + \sum_i \theta_i\, s_i$$

Where :

- wij is the connection strength between unit j and unit i.
- si is the state, , of unit i.
- ?i is the threshold of unit i.

The connections in a Boltzmann machine have two restrictions:

- $w_{ij} = 0, \forall i$. (No unit has a connection with itself.)
- $w_{ij} = w_{ji}\ \forall i, j$. (All connections are symmetric.)

Thus, the difference in the global energy that results from a single unit i being 0 versus 1, written ?Ei, is given by:

$$\Delta E_i = \sum_j w_{ij}\, s_j = \theta_i$$

A Boltzmann machine is made up of stochastic units. The probability, pi of the i-th unit being on is given by :

$$p_i = 1/(1 + \exp(-\Delta E_i/T))$$

where the scalar T is referred to as the temperature of the system.

The network is run by repeatedly choosing a unit and setting its state according to the above formula. After running for long enough at a certain temperature, the probability of a global state of the network will depend only upon that global state's energy, according to a Boltzmann Distribution. This means that log-probabilities of global states become linear in their energies. This relationship is true when the machine is "at thermal equilibrium", meaning that the probability distribution of global states has converged. If we start running the network from a high temperature, and gradually decrease it until we reach a thermal equilibrium at a low temperature, we are guaranteed to converge to a distribution where the energy level fluctuates around the global minimum. This process is called simulated annealing.

If we want to train the network so that the chance it will converge to a global state is according to an external distribution that we have over these states, we need to set the weights so that the global states with the highest probabilities will get the lowest energies. This is done by the following training procedure.

Training

The units in the Boltzmann Machine are divided into "visible" units, V, and "hidden" units, H. The visible units are those which receive information from the "environment", i.e. our training set is a bunch of binary vectors over the set V. The distribution over the training set is denoted P + (V).

On the Boltzmann Machine side, as recalled, the distribution over the global states is converging as we reach a thermal equilibrium. We denote the converged distribution, after we marginalize it over the visible units V, as P - (V).

Our goal is to approximate the "real" distribution P + (V) using the P - (V) which will be produced (eventually) by the machine. To measure how similar the two distributions are we use the Kullback-Leibler distance, G:

$$G = \sum_{v} P^{+}(i) \ln \frac{P^{+}(v)}{P^{-}(v)}$$

Where the sum is over all the possible states of V. G is a function of the weights, since they determine the energy of a state, and the energy determines P - (v), as promised by the Boltzmann distribution. Hence, we can use a gradient descent algorithm over G, so a given weight, wij is changed by subtracting the partial derivative of G with respect to the weight.

There are two phases to Boltzmann machine training, and we switch iteratively between them. One is the "positive" phase where the visible units' states are clamped to a particular binary state vector sampled from the training set (according to P +). The other is the "negative" phase where the network is allowed to run freely, i.e. no units have their state determined by external data. Surprisingly enough, the gradient with respect to a given weight, wij, is given by the very simple equation:

$$\frac{\partial G}{\partial w_{ij}} = -\frac{1}{T}\,[p_{ij}^{+} - p_{ij}^{-}]$$

Where :

- p_{ij}^{+} is the probability of units i and j both being on when the machine is at equilibrium on the positive phase.
- p_{ij}^{-} is the probability of units i and j both being on when the machine is at equilibrium on the negative phase.

This result follows from the fact that at the thermal equilibrium the probability P - (s) of any global state s when the network is free-running is given by the Boltzmann distribution (hence the name "Boltzmann machine").

Remarkably, this learning rule is fairly biologically plausible because the only information needed to change the weights is provided by "local" information. That is, the connection (or synapse biologically speaking) does not need information about anything other than the two neurons it connects. This is far more biologically realistic than the information needed by a connection in many other neural network training algorithms, such as backpropagation.

The training of a Boltzmann machines can also be viewed as an application of the EM algorithm, which is heavily used in machine learning. We are given an incomplete dataset (we only know the values of the visible units). At the positive phase, we estimate the completed data based on the current parameters of the system (the weights). Later, the weights are updated to maximize the probability of the network producing the completed data.

Problems

If it worked, the Boltzmann machine would be a sort of universal computational medium, able to solve nearly any learning problem. For instance, if trained on photographs, the machine would model the distribution of photographs, and could use that model to, for example, complete a partial photograph.

Unfortunately, there is a serious practical problem with the Boltzmann machine, namely that the learning seems to stop working correctly when the machine is scaled up to anything larger than a trivial machine. This is due to a number of effects, the most important of which are:

- the time the machine must be run for in order to collect equilibrium statistics grows exponentially with the machine's size, and with the magnitude of the connection strengths
- connection strengths are more plastic when the units being connected have activation probabilities intermediate between zero and one, leading to a so-called variance trap. The net effect is that noise causes the connection strengths to random walk until the activities saturate.

History

The Boltzmann machine is a Monte Carlo version of the Hopfield network. The idea of using annealed Ising models for inference is often thought to have originated from Geoff Hinton. However some claim that an earlier version of the same idea is present in Douglas Hofstadter's Copycat project, described in the following two papers:

- Hofstadter, Douglas R., The Copycat Project: An Experiment in Nondeterminism and Creative Analogies. MIT Artificial Intelligence Laboratory Memo No. 755, January 1984.
- Hofstadter, Douglas R., A Non-Deterministic Approach to Analogy, Involving the Ising Model of Ferromagnetism. In E. Caianiello, ed. The Physics of Cognitive Processes. Teaneck, NJ: World Scientific, 1987.

Others, without meaning to disparage Douglas Hofstadter's contributions to the field or any potential claims of independent discovery, contend that the following papers describe the idea and that 1983 is earlier than 1984:

- Geoffrey E. Hinton and Terrence J. Sejnowski, Analyzing Cooperative Computation. In Proceedings of the 5th Annual Congress of the Cognitive Science Society, Rochester, NY, May 1983.
- Geoffrey E. Hinton and Terrence J. Sejnowski, Optimal Perceptual Inference. In Proceedings of the IEEE conference on

Computer Vision and Pattern Recognition (CVPR), pages 448-453, IEEE Computer Society, Washington DC, June 1983.

Recent Progress

Although learning is impractical in general Boltzmann machines, it can be made quite efficient in an architecture called the "Restricted Boltzmann Machine" or "RBM" which does not allow connections between hidden units. After learning one RBM, the activities of its hidden units can be treated as data for training a higher-level RBM. This method of stacking RBM's makes it possible to learn many layers of hidden units efficiently and as each new layer is added the overall generative model gets better. Examples of multilayer RBM models of hand-written digits and faces.

Expectation-maximization algorithm

An expectation-maximization (EM) algorithm is used in statistics for finding maximum likelihood estimates of parameters in probabilistic models, where the model depends on unobserved latent variables. EM alternates between performing an expectation (E) step, which computes an expectation of the likelihood by including the latent variables as if they were observed, and a maximization (M) step, which computes the maximum likelihood estimates of the parameters by maximizing the expected likelihood found on the E step. The parameters found on the M step are then used to begin another E step, and the process is repeated.

Applications

EM is frequently used for data clustering in machine learning and computer vision. In psychometry, EM is almost indispensable for estimating item parameters and latent abilities of item response theory models.

Specification of the EM procedure

Let denote incomplete data consisting of values of observable variables and the missing data. Together, and form the complete data. can either be actual missing measurements or a hidden variable that would make the problem easier if its value were known. For instance, in mixture models, the likelihood formula would be much more convenient if mixture components that "generated" the samples were known.

Estimate unobservable data

Let be the joint probability distribution (continuous case) or probability mass function (discrete case) of the complete data with parameters given by the vector ?: . This function then also gives the complete data likelihood. Further, note that the conditional distribution of the missing data given the observed can be expressed as:

$$p(x \mid y, \theta) = \frac{p(y, x \mid \theta)}{p(y \mid \theta)} = \frac{p(y \mid x, \theta)\, p(x \mid \theta)}{\int p(y \mid x, \theta)\, p(x \mid \theta)\, dx}$$

when using the Bayes rule and law of total probability. This formulation only requires knowledge of the observation likelihood given the unobservable data $p(y \mid x, \theta)$, as well as the probability of the unobservable data $p(x \mid \theta)$.

Maximize expected log-likelihood for the complete dataset

An EM algorithm will then iteratively improve an initial estimate ?0 and construct new estimates $\theta_1, \ldots, \theta_n, \ldots$. An individual re-estimation step that derives θ_{n+1} from θ_n takes the following form :

$$\theta_{n+1} = arg \max_{\theta} E_x [\log p(y, x \mid \theta) \mid y],$$

where $E_x[\cdot]$ denotes the conditional expectation of $\log p(y, x \mid \theta)$ being taken with ? in the conditional distribution of x fixed at ?n. Log-likelihood $\log p(y, x \mid \theta)$ is often used instead of true likelihood $p(y, x \mid \theta)$ because it leads to easier formulas, but still attains its maximum at the same point as the likelihood.

In other words, θ_{n+1} is the value that maximizes (M) the conditional expectation (E) of the complete data log-likelihood given the observed variables under the previous parameter value. This expectation is usually denoted as Q(θ). In the continuous case, it would be given by

$$Q(\theta) = E_x [\log p(y, x \mid \theta) \mid y] = \int_{-\infty}^{\infty} p(x \mid y, \theta_n) \log p(y, x \mid \theta)\, dx$$

Speaking of an expectation (E) step is a bit of a misnomer. What is calculated in the first step are the fixed, data-dependent parameters of the function Q. Once the parameters of Q are known, it is fully determined and is maximized in the second (M) step of an EM algorithm.

Properties

It can be shown that an EM iteration does not decrease the observed data likelihood function. However, there is no guarantee that the sequence converges to a maximum likelihood estimator. For multimodal distributions, this means that an EM algorithm will converge to a local maximum (or saddle point) of the observed data likelihood function, depending on starting values. There are a variety of heuristic approaches for escaping a local maximum such as using several different random initial estimates, ?0, or applying simulated annealing.

EM is particularly useful when maximum likelihood estimation of a complete data model is easy. If closed-form estimators exist, the M step is often trivial. A classic example is maximum likelihood estimation of a finite mixture of Gaussians, where each component of the mixture can be estimated trivially if the mixing distribution is known.

"Expectation-maximization" is a description of a class of related algorithms, not a specific algorithm; EM is a recipe or meta-algorithm which is used to devise particular algorithms. The Baum-Welch algorithm is an example of an EM algorithm applied to hidden Markov models. Another example is the EM algorithm for fitting a mixture density model.

An EM algorithm can also find maximum a posteriori (MAP) estimates, by performing MAP estimation in the M step, rather than maximum likelihood. There are other methods for finding maximum likelihood estimates, such as gradient descent, conjugate gradient or variations of the Gauss-Newton method. Unlike EM, such methods typically require the evaluation of first and/or second derivatives of the likelihood function.

Incremental versions

The classic EM procedure is to replace both Q and ? with their optimal possible (argmax) values at each iteration. However it can be shown that simply finding Q and ? to give some improvement over their current value will also ensure successful convergence.

For example, to improve Q, we could restrict the space of possible functions to a computationally simple distribution such as a factorial distribution,

$$Q = \prod_i Q_i ,$$

Thus at each E step we compute the variational approximation of Q.

To improve ?, we could use any hill-climbing method, and not worry about finding the optimal ?, just some improvement. This method is also known as Generalized EM (GEM).

Relation to variational Bayes methods

EM is a partially non-Bayesian, maximum likelihood method. Its final result gives a probability distribution over the latent variables (in the Bayesian style) together with a point estimate for ? (either a maximum likelihood estimate or a posterior mode). We may want a fully Bayesian version of this, giving a probability distribution over ? as well as the latent variables. In fact the Bayesian approach to inference is simply to treat ? as another latent variable. In this paradigm, the distinction between the E and M steps disappears. If we use the factorized Q approximation,we may iterate over each latent variable (now including ?) and optimize them one at a time. There are now k steps per iteration, where k is the number of latent variables. For graphical models this is easy to do as each variable's new Q depends only on its Markov blanket, so local message passing can be used for efficient inference.

Example: Mixture Gaussian

Assume that the samples $y_1, \ldots, y_m$, where $y_j \in R^i$, are drawn from the gaussians , such that

$$P(y \mid x_i, \theta) = N(\mu_1, \sigma_i) = (2\pi)^{-i/2} \mid \sigma_i \mid^{-1/2} \exp\left(-\frac{1}{2}(y-\mu_i)^T \sigma_i^{-1} (y-\mu_i)\right)$$

The model you are trying to estimate is

$$\theta = \{\mu_1, \ldots, \mu_n, \sigma_1, \ldots, \sigma_n, P(x_i), \ldots, P(x_n)\}$$

E-step :

Estimation for unobserved event (which Gaussian is used), conditioned on the observation, using the values from the last maximisation step:

$$P(x_i \mid y_j, \theta_t) = \frac{p(x_i, y_j \mid \theta_t)}{p(y_j \mid \theta_t)} = \frac{p(y_j \mid x_i, \theta_t)' P(x_i \mid \theta_t)}{\sum_{k=1}^{n} p(y_j \mid x_k, \theta_t) P(x_k \mid \theta_t)}$$

M-step

You want to maximise the expected log-likelihood of the joint event:

$$Q(\theta) = E_x\left[\ln \prod_{j=1}^{m} p\,(y_j\,, x \mid \theta) \mid y_j\right]$$

$$= E_x\left[\sum_{j=1}^{m} \ln p\,(y_j\,, x \mid \theta) \mid y_j\right]$$

$$= \sum_{j=1}^{m} E_x\left[\ln p\,(y_j\,, x \mid \theta) \mid y_j\right]$$

$$= \sum_{j=1}^{m} \sum_{i=1}^{m} P\,(x_i \mid y_j\,, \theta_t) \ln p\,(x_i\,, y_j \mid \theta)$$

If we expand the probability of the joint event, we get

$$Q\,(\theta) = \sum_{j=1}^{m} \sum_{i=1}^{n} P\,(x_i \mid y_j\,, \theta_t) \ln\,(p\,(y_j \mid x_i\,, \theta)\,P\,(x_i \mid \theta))$$

You have a constraint

$$\sum_{i=1}^{n} P\,(x_i \mid \theta) = 1$$

If we add a Lagrange multiplier, and expand the pdf, we get

$$L\,(\theta) = \left(\sum_{j=1}^{m} \sum_{i=1}^{n} P\,(x_i \mid y_j\,, \theta_t)\right.$$
$$\left.\left(-\frac{l}{2}\ln\,(2\pi) - \frac{1}{2}\ln\,|\sigma_i| - \frac{1}{2}(y_j - \mu_i)^T \sigma_i^{-1}\,(y_j - 1)\right)\right.$$

To find the new estimate ?t + 1, you find a maxima where $\frac{\partial L\,(\theta)}{\partial\theta} = 0.$

New estimate for mean (using some differentiation rules from matrix calculus) :

$$\frac{\partial L(\theta)}{\partial \mu_i} = \sum_{j=1}^{m} P\,(x_i \mid y_j\,, \theta_t)\left(-\frac{\partial}{\partial\,\mu_i}\frac{1}{2}(y_j - \mu_i)^T \sigma_i^{-1}\,(y_j - \mu_i)\right)$$

$$= \sum_{j=1}^{m} P(x_i \mid y_j, \theta_t)\left(-\frac{1}{2}(\sigma_i^{-1} + \sigma_i^{-T})(y_j - \mu_i)(-1)\right)$$

$$= \sum_{j=1}^{m} P(x_i \mid y_j, \theta_t)(\sigma_i^{-1}(y_j - \mu_i))$$

$$= 0$$

$$\Downarrow$$

$$\sum_{j=1}^{m} P(x_i \mid y_j, \theta_t)\,\sigma_i^{-1}\,\mu_i = \sum_{j=1}^{m} P(x_i \mid y_j, \theta_t)\,\sigma_i^{-1}\,y_j$$

$$\Downarrow$$

$$\mu_i \sum_{j=1}^{m} P(x_i \mid y_j, \theta_t) = \sum_{j=1}^{m} P(x_i \mid y_j, \theta_t)\,y_j$$

$$\Downarrow$$

$$\mu_i = \frac{\sum_{j=1}^{m} P(x_i \mid y_j, \theta_t)\,y_j}{\sum_{j=1}^{m} P(x_i \mid y_j, \theta_t)}$$

New estimate for covariance:

$$\frac{\partial L(\theta)}{\partial \sigma_i} = \sum_{j=1}^{m} P(x_i \mid y_j, \theta_t)\left(-\frac{\partial}{\partial \sigma_i}\frac{1}{2}\ln|\sigma_i| - \frac{\partial}{\partial \sigma_i}\frac{1}{2}(y_j - \mu_i)^T \sigma_i^{-1}(y_j - \mu_i)\right)$$

$$= \sum_{j=1}^{m} P(x_i \mid y_j, \theta_t)\left(-\frac{1}{2}(\sigma_i^{-1} + \sigma_i^{-T})(y_j - \mu_i)(-1)\right)$$

$$= 0$$

$$\Downarrow$$

$$\sum_{j=1}^{m} P(x_i \mid y_j, \theta_t)\,\sigma_i^{-1}\,\mu_i = \sum_{j=1}^{m} P(x_i \mid y_j, \theta_t)\,\sigma_i^{-1}(y_j - \mu_i)(y_i - \mu_i)^T \sigma_i^{-1}$$

$$\Downarrow$$

$$\sum_{j=1}^{m} P(x_i \mid y_j, \theta_t) = \sum_{j=1}^{m} P(x_i \mid y_j, \theta_t)\,\sigma_i^{-1}(y_j - \mu_i)(y_j - \mu_i)^T$$

$$\Downarrow$$

$$\sigma_i = \frac{\sum_{j=1}^{m} P(x_i \mid y_j, \theta_t)(y_j - \mu_i)(y_j - \mu_i)^T}{\sum_{j=1}^{m} P(x_i \mid y_j, \theta_t)}$$

New estimate for class probability:

$$\frac{\partial L(\theta)}{\partial P(x_i \mid \theta)} = \left(\sum_{j=1}^{m} P(x_i \mid y_j, \theta_t) \frac{\partial \ln P(x_i \mid \theta)}{\partial P(x_i \mid \theta)} \right)$$

$$= \left(\sum_{j=1}^{m} P(x_i \mid y_j, \theta_t) \frac{2}{P(x_i \mid \theta)} \right) - \lambda$$

$$= 0$$

$$\Downarrow$$

$$\sum_{j=1}^{m} P(x_i \mid y_j, \theta_t) \frac{1}{P(x_i \mid \theta)} = \lambda$$

$$\Downarrow$$

$$P(x_i \mid \theta) = \frac{1}{\lambda} \sum_{j=1}^{m} P(x_i \mid y_j, \theta_t)$$

Inserting into the constraint :

$$\sum_{j=1}^{n} P(x_i \mid \theta) = \sum_{j=1}^{n} \frac{1}{\lambda} \sum_{j=1}^{m} P(x_i \mid y_j, \theta_t)$$

$$= 1$$

$$\Downarrow$$

$$\lambda = \sum_{i=1}^{n} \sum_{j=1}^{m} P(x_i \mid y_j, \theta_t)$$

Inserting ^ into the our estimate :

$$P(x_i \mid \theta) = \frac{1}{\lambda} \sum_{j=1}^{m} P(x_i \mid y_j, \theta_t)$$

$$= \frac{\sum_{j=1}^{m} P(x_i \mid y_j, \theta_t)}{\sum_{j=1}^{n} \sum_{j=1}^{m} P(x_i \mid y_j, \theta_t)}$$

These estimates now become our ?t + 1, to be used in the next estimation step.

6.2 Optimization methods

6.2.1 Hopfield networks for-TSP

This describes a simple version of the Hopfield network for optimizing the traveling salesman problem.

Hopfield Network Basics

1. The Hopfield network was originally designed for pattern storage and recognition (stores patterns, then recognizes noisy or incomplete versions of the pattern). This is called an auto-associative network.
2. It was originally a binary network (binary inputs and outputs).
3. The Hopfield network is fully interconnected, that is, all neurons are connected to all other neurons (there are no "layers).
4. The weights are symmetric, so that the weight from neuron 1 to neuron 2 is identical to the weight from neuron 2 to neuron 1.
5. The Hopfield networks works on an energy idea, where the network changes its outputs to find the low energy state. The energy equation is of the form of a
   Lyapunov equation, which only accepts "moves" which lower the energy and
   theoretically converges to a low energy state.
6. The network calculates the energy through the product of the outputs (0 or 1) and the interconnecting weights.
7. Hopfield networks for pattern storage find their weights through calculation using the patterns to be stored. There is no iterative training.
8. The Hopfield's capacity for accurate pattern storage is poor and is usually about 0.15 * number of neurons.

Hopfield Version for TSP

This version is based on using a consensus function, which is to be maximized. This is the same as minimizing the energy function. Each neuron, x, is either on (output = 1) or off (output = 0). The consensus, C, is calculated by:

C= E(WijXiXj)

1. The number of neurons in the network is N2, where N is the number of cities. For a TSP with N cities, there are N! tours where N!/2 are unique.
2. These are arranged in an N x N matrix where the row is the city and the column is the position in the tour.
3. A valid tour will have one and exactly one neuron "on" in each row and each column.
4. Connecting the "on" cities in order constructs the tour.
5. Weights are set according to the problem. There are three main types of weights:
   a. Each neuron has its own positive bias weight.
   b. Each neuron has a negative (inhibitatory) weight to each of the other neurons in its row and its column.
   c. Each neuron has a negative weight to other possible cities just before it and just after it on the tour. This weight is equal to (or correlated with) Euclidean distance. Since the tour makes a loop, the final column is connected to the first column by distance weights.
6. Outputs of nodes change one by one and only changes that increase consensus are accepted. (A probabilistic version, the "Boltzmann Machine", accepts changes that lower consensus probabilistically using a simulated annealing function).

6.2.2 solution of simultaneous linear equations

Any linear equation can be put in the form

$$c_1x_1 + c_2x_2 + \ldots + c_nx_n = c_0.$$

Where n is the number of variables, the variables are x1, x2, ... , xn, and c0, c1, ... , cn are constants.

A system is just a collection of such linear equations, and to solve a system look for the values of the variables, which make all the equations true simultaneously. For instance, if x and y are the variables, then an example system of linear equations is

$$5x - 2y = 4$$

$$x + 2y = 8$$

There are various ways of solving this system, and they lead to the unique solution where x = 2 and y = 3. We'll look next at a common algorithm for solving systems of simultaneous equations called elimination.

Elimination: the first example

The algorithm of elimination for solving a system of simultaneous linear equations is not difficult and has been discovered more than once.

There are three classes of corn, of which three bundles of the first class, two of the second and one of the third make 39 measures. Two of the first, three of the second and one of the third make 34 measures. And one of the first, two of the second and three of the third make 26 measures. How many measures of grain are contained in one bundle of each class?

It is quite clear that this artificial problem was constructed just to illustrate the method. Each class of corn, or grain, is bundled in different sizes and the problem is to decide what sizes the different classes are bundled in. In modern algebraic notation, we can let x denote the number of measures of grain in the first class, y the number in the second class, and z the number in the third. Then we would have three equations in three unknowns that we would write as

$$3x + 2y + z = 39$$

$$2x + 3y + z = 34$$

$$x + 2y + 3z = 26$$

This is very similar to the ancient Chinese method except they wrote in columns and did not use variables. In fact, the ancient Chinese method uses what we would call matrices.

Rule. Arrange the 3, 2, and 1 bundles of the three classes and the 39 measures of the grains at the right. Arrange other conditions in the middle and at the left.

This arrangement took place on a counting board using rods to indicate the numbers. It would look something like this.

1	2	3
2	3	2
3	1	1
26	34	39

Putting the numbers in rows rather than columns, and starting at the top instead of the right, we get the matrix of coefficients of the system of simultaneous linear equations that appears above.

3	2	1	39
2	3	1	34
1	2	3	26

This matrix contains all the information of the system of equations so long as we remember what the rows and columns mean. But we don't have to write down all the variables, so it's more concise.

For the rest of the translation of the solution in the Jiuzhang suanshu, I'll use rows instead of columns to be consistent with the modern practice. The solution proceeds:

With the first class in the first row multiply currently the middle row, and directly leave out.

This may be a little obscure, but the ancient Chinese method is a way of avoiding fractions. It means that you multiply the middle row by 3 (the first class in the first row) and subtract the first row from the second until a 0 is reached in the first entry of the second row. (Yes, the ancient Chinese had a 0 for this purpose; zero was just an empty space in that particular place on the counting board.) So we triple each entry of the second row to get 6 9 3 102, then subtract the first row from it twice, and the second row becomes 0 5 1 24. We now have this matrix.

3	2	1	39
0	5	1	24
1	2	3	26

The whole purpose of that operation is to get a 0 just where we got it.

Again multiply the next, and directly leave out.

In other words do the same thing with the first and third row in order to get a 0 at the beginning of the third row. So we multiply the third row by 3 to get 3 6 9 78, then subtract the first from it to get 0 4 8 39. We now have this matrix.

3	2	1	39
0	5	1	24
0	4	8	39

Then with what remains of the second class in the second row, directly leave out.

So we do the same thing with the second and third rows to get a 0 in the second entry of the third row. That is, multiply the third row by 5 to get 0 20 40 195, then subtract 4 times the second row from it to get 0 0 36 99.

3	2	1	39
0	5	1	34
0	0	36	26

This is what we call echelon form, a steplike form where the leading nonzero entries are further to the right in each row. We've finished the first stage of the algorithm of elimination. The next stage finds the answers starting with the third unknown and working backwards with back substitutions.

Of the quantities that do not vanish, make the first the divisor and the next the dividend, that is, of the third class.

So 99 divided by 36 will give z, the number of measures of grain in the third class. This quotient can be simplified to 11/4. We have

3	2	1	39
0	5	1	24
0	0	4	11

To find the second class, with the divisor multiply the measure in the middle row and leave out from it the dividends for the third and second classes. The remainder being divided by the number of bundles of the first class gives the dividend for the first class.

Multiply the second row 0 5 1 24 by 4 to get 0 20 4 96, then subtract the third row from it to get 0 20 0 85. Then y is 85 divided by 20, and that can be simplified to 17/4. The matrix is now

3	2	1	39
0	4	0	34
0	0	4	26

To find the first class, also with the divisor multiply the measures in the first row and leave out from it the dividends for the third and second classes. The remainder being divided by the number of bundles of the first class gives the dividend for the first class.

Multiply the first row 3 2 1 39 by 4 to get 12 8 4 156 and subtract the third row to get 12 8 0 145. Then subtract twice the second row from that to get 12 0 0 111. We have

12	0	0	111
0	4	0	17
0	0	4	11

Divide the dividends of the three classes by the divisor and we get their respective measures.

We get the answers 9 1/4, 4 1/4, and 2 3/4, for the measures of grain in the three classes.

A second example

The first example was probably chosen because it doesn't involve negative numbers. But sometimes the method involves negative numbers even when the final answer doesn't.

There are three kinds of corn. The grains contained in two, three and four bundles, respectively, of these classes of corn, are not sufficient to make a whole measure. If however we add to them one bundle of the second, third, and first classes, respectively, then the grains would become full one measure in each case. How many measures of grain does then each one bundle of the different classes contain?

This problem takes a little interpretation. If you take two bundles of the first class, it doesn't make a measure of grain, but two bundles of the first plus one of the second does. Similarly, three of the second plus one of the third makes one whole measure, and four of the third plus one of the first makes a whole measure. That gives us three equations in three unknowns.

$$2x + y = 1$$

$$3y + z = 1$$

$$x + 4z = 1$$

As a matrix this looks like

2	1	0	1
0	3	1	1
1	0	4	1

First, we'll put it in echelon form. There already is a 0 at the beginning of the second row. We need to get a 0 at the beginning of the third row. For this example, let's follow the ancient Chinese method that avoids fractions as long as possible. Double the third row to get 2 0 8 2, and subtract the first row from it.

2	1	0	1
0	3	1	1
0	-1	8	1

You might wonder how the ancient Chinese dealt with negative numbers like the -1 that appears in the third row. They had no problem with them. According to Lui Hui (c. 263 C.E.) who wrote about the Jiuzhang suanshu, red rods were used for positive numbers and black rods for negative numbers. He also explained how to add and subtract positive and negative numbers.

For this problem, we can continue by tripling the third row to get 0 -3 24 3, and then adding the second row to it.

2	1	0	1
0	3	1	1
0	0	25	4

The matrix is now in echelon form. We know z = 4/25. We can continue to avoid fractions if we multiply the second row by 25 to get 0 75 25 25 and subtracting the third from it.

2	1	0	1
0	75	0	7
0	0	25	4

We now have y = 21/75 = 7/25. Multiply the first row by 25 to get 50 25 0 25, and subtract the second row 0 25 0 7 from it.

50	0	0	18
0	25	0	7
0	0	25	4

Therefore, x = 18/50 = 9/25. We've solved the problem. The solution is: one bundle of the first class contains x = 9/25 measures of grain, one bundle of the second class contains y = 7/25 measures of grain, and one bundle of the third class contains z = 4/25 measures of grain.

Fractions earlier in the method

Modern computers have no difficulty with fractions (except roundoff error), so it's not necessary to postpone using them until the end of the algorithm. They can be introduced in the first stage of finding the echelon form of the matrix. Just make sure the leading nonzero entry of a row is made to be 1. For example, begin with this system of linear equations (also from the Jiuzhang suanshu).

$$2x + 5y - 13z = 1000$$

$$3x - 9y + 3z = 0$$

$$-5x + 6y + 8z = -600$$

As a matrix this looks like

2	5	-13	1000
3	9	3	0
-5	6	8	-600

We can begin by putting a 1 at the beginning of the first row by dividing that row by 2.

1	2.5	-6.5	500
3	-9	3	0
-5	6	8	-600

Now subtract 3 times the first row from the second, and add 5 times the first row to the third. That will make the first entries in the second and third rows both 0.

1	2.5	-6.5	500
0	-16.5	22.5	-1500
0	16.5	-24.5	1900

Next, divide the second row by -16.5 to put a 1 in its first nonzero entry. We can wait on the third row until later.

1	2.5	-6.5	500
0	1	-1.3636	90.909
0	18.5	-24.5	1900

(Note that we've only kept five significant figures. You would think that would be enough, but we'll see how that small roundoff error makes a larger error in the final answer.)

Now subtract 18.5 times the second row from the third.

1	2.5	-6.5	500
0	1	-1.3636	90.909
0	0	7766	1900

(The error is building up. The .7266 should be .727272...)

Divide the third row by .7266 so its leading nonzero entry becomes 1.

1	2.5	-6.5	500
0	1	-1.3636	90.909
0	18.5	-24.5	1900

(The correct entry in the last row is 300, not 300.275.)

The matrix is now in echelon form where the first nonzero entry in each row is a 1. We know what z is, 300.275. We can back substitute. Add 1.3636 times the third row to the second row, and add 6.5 times the third row to the first row.

1	2.5	0	2451.79
0	1	0	500.364
0	0	1	300.275

Subtract 2.5 times the second row from the first row.

1	2.5	0	2451.79
0	1	0	500.364
0	0	1	300.275

Thus, the solution is that x = 1200.88, y = 500.364, and z = 300.275.

The fractions are due to roundoff error. The actual solution is x = 1200, y = 500, and z = 300. Even though our computations were done with five significant figures, our final answer is only correct to three significant figures. Typical modern calculators keep a couple extra digits of accuracy to hide the roundoff error. Usually that's enough, but not always. Perhaps the original method which delays division to the end of the algorithm is a better method.

Summary of the method, and wrinkles

There are two stages to the elimination algorithm. The first is to put the matrix into echelon form, a steplike form where the leading nonzero entries are further to the right in each row. If you want, you can make each of those nonzero entries equal to 1. The second stage is sometimes called "back substitution" and it makes sure there are only zeros above the leading nonzero entries. Both stages only use one operation, and that is to add or subtract a multiple of one row from another row. (It's really only one operation since subtracting a multiple is the same as adding the negative multiple.) The final stage is a division (if it wasn't done before) to make the leading nonzero entries all equal to 1. The answer is then evident.

Of course, there are shortcuts and exceptions. The order of the rows in the matrix is irrelevant, so you can decide which one goes first. If there's a 1 as the first entry of some row other than the first, you might just as well make that row the first and save yourself some division. For example, in the matrix

4	2	-3	12
-3	0	5	-4
1	5	-8	0

start off by making the third row the first. You don't actually have to exchange the rows; it's enough to treat the third row as the first. You can do something similar with the columns, but you can get pretty confused if you do that. (You must remember which column refers to which variable.)

One time when you have to treat some other row as the first is when the first leads off with a 0. For instance, in the matrix

0	2	24	200
3	-5	-6	350
-4	4	7	-600

you have to make either the second or the third row into the first row.

Now a wrinkle. In many applications, there is a unique solution, that is, there is only one way to assign values to the variables so that the equations are simultaneously true. But not in all applications. Sometimes, there are no solutions at all, and sometimes there are infinitely many solutions. Here's a coefficient matrix for a system of linear equations that has no solution.

2	-3	4	8
3	2	6	5
5	-1	10	4

Note that if you sum the first two rows, then you get 5 -1 10 13. That says 5x - y + 10z = 13. But the third row says 5x - y + 10z = 4. Since 13 does not equal 4, there is no solution. If you were to go through the algorithm of elimination, you end up with the matrix

1	0	2	31/13
0	1	0	-14/13
0	0	0	1

The important thing to notice is that the last row is a contradiction. It says 0 = 1. There are no values of x, y, and z to make that true. So, there are no solutions to the system. When one of the rows has all zeros in it except the final number, that means the system has no solutions.

Next, let's look at a system where there are infinitely many solutions. Take the last example, but change the last entry in the last row to 13.

2	-3	4	8
3	2	6	5
5	-1	10	13

Note now how the third row is the sum of the previous two. If you follow through the method of elimination, you end up with the matrix

1	0	2	31/13
0	1	0	-14/13
0	0	0	0

The last row says 0 = 0, and that is no condition whatsoever on the values of x, y, and z. The question is: what do you do at this point? The second row says y = -14/13, and the first row says x -2z = 31/13, that is to say, x = 2z + 31/13. Those are the conditions on x and y, but there are no conditions on z. That means you can take any value of z you want, set y to -14/13, and set x to 2z + 31/13, and you get a solution to the system of equations. There are infinitely many solutions. When the solutions are described that way, we say that they are parameterized by z.

6.2.3 Iterated Gradient descent

The Gradient Descent Rule is similar to the Delta Rule in that the derivative of the transfer function is still used to modify the delta error before it is applied to the connection weights. Here, however, an additional proportional constant tied to the learning rate is appended to the final modifying factor acting upon the weight. This rule is commonly used, even though it converges to a point of stability very slowly.

It has been shown that different learning rates for different layers of network help the learning process converge faster. In these tests, the learning rates for those layers close to the output were set lower than those layers near the input. This is especially important for applications where the input data is not derived from a strong underlying model.

Gradient descent is an optimization algorithm. To find a local minimum of a function using gradient descent, one takes steps proportional to the negative of the gradient (or the approximate gradient) of the function at the current point. If instead one takes steps proportional to the gradient, one approaches a local maximum of that function; the procedure is then known as gradient ascent.

Gradient descent is also known as steepest descent, or the method of steepest descent. When known as the latter, gradient descent should not be confused with the method of steepest descent for approximating integrals.

6.2.4 simulated annealing

Simulated annealing (SA) is a generic probabilistic meta-algorithm for the global optimization problem, namely locating a good approximation to the global optimum of a given function in a large search space. It was independently invented by S. Kirkpatrick, C. D. Gelatt and M. P. Vecchi in 1983, and by V. Cern} in 1985.

The name and inspiration come from annealing in metallurgy, a technique involving heating and controlled cooling of a material to increase the size of its crystals and reduce their defects. The heat causes the atoms to become unstuck from their initial positions (a local minimum of the internal energy) and wander randomly through states of higher energy; the slow cooling gives them more chances of finding configurations with lower internal energy than the initial one.

By analogy with this physical process, each step of the SA algorithm replaces the current solution by a random "nearby" solution, chosen with a probability that depends on the difference between the corresponding function values and on a global parameter T (called the temperature), that is gradually decreased during the process. The dependency is such that the current solution changes almost randomly when T is large, but increasingly "downhill" as T goes to zero. The allowance for "uphill" moves saves the method from becoming stuck at local minima-which are the bane of greedier methods.

In the simulated annealing (SA) method, each point s of the search space is compared to a state of some physical system, and the function E(s) to be minimized is interpreted as the internal energy of the system in that state. Therefore the goal is to bring the system, from an arbitrary initial state, to a state with the minimum possible energy.

Simulated quenching and tuning

A reference to the use of SA does not always mean that SA is the algorithm being used. Any true SA algorithm has an associated proof of (weak) ergodicity, which means that theoretically one can actually find a global optimum. Many SA algorithms are quite slow, so in practice many users simply speed up the algorithm, but in the process they also void their SA proof. If the modified Simulated Quenching (SQ) works, fine, but it should not be called SA. SA is often used for hard problems where the chances are reduced for being trapped in local minima. SA also is used in problems with complex constraints since the method of rejection is simply applied to keep the sampling within the constrained region(s). In practice, when the need is clear to use a sampling technique, it is best to do at least a few long runs with SA, and then use SQ modifications to speed up calculations as long as the same results are achieved. To apply any generic sampling technique like SA over many classes of nonlinear problems, it should be expected that tuning of some basic search parameters will be required.

The basic iteration

At each step, the SA heuristic considers some neighbour s′ of the current state s, and probabilistically decides between moving the system to state s′ or staying put in state s. The probabilities are chosen so that the system ultimately tends to move to states of lower energy. Typically this step is repeated until the system reaches a state which is good enough for the application, or until a given computation budget has been exhausted.

The neighbours of a state

The neighbours of each state are specified by the user, usually in an application-specific way. For example, in the traveling salesman problem, each state is typically defined as a particular tour (a permutation of the cities to be visited); then one could define two tours to be neighbours if and only if one can be converted to the other by interchanging a pair of adjacent cities.

Transition probabilities

The probability of making the transition from the current state: s to a candidate new state: s′ is a function P(e,e′,T) of the energies e = E(s) and e′ = E(s′) of the two states, and of a global time-varying parameter T called the temperature.

One essential requirement for the transition probability P is that it must be nonzero when e′ e, meaning that the system may move to the new state even when it is worse (has a higher energy) than the current one. It is this feature that prevents the method from becoming stuck in a local minimum - a state whose energy is far from being minimum, but is still less than that of any neighbour.

On the other hand, when T goes to zero, the probability P(e,e′,T) must tend to zero if e′ e, and to a positive value if e′ e. That way, for sufficiently small values of T, the system will increasingly favor moves that go "downhill" (to lower energy values), and avoid those that go "uphill". In particular, when T becomes 0, the procedure will reduce to the greedy algorithm - which makes the move if and only if it goes downhill.

The P function is usually chosen so that the probability of accepting a move decreases when the difference e′ - e increases - that is, small uphill moves are more likely than large ones. However, this requirement is not strictly necessary, provided that the above requirements are met.

Given these properties, the evolution of the state s depends crucially on the temperature T. Roughly speaking, the evolution of s is sensitive only to coarser energy variations when T is large, and to finer variations when T is small.

The annealing schedule

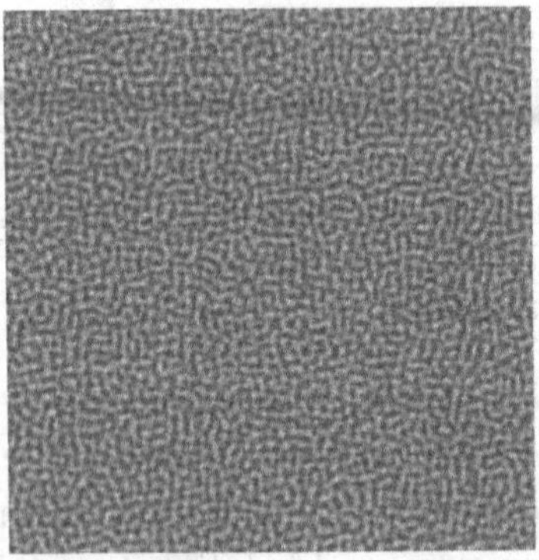

An image with random pixels, using simulated annealing to swap pairs of pixels. Similar colours attract at short range and repel at slightly less short range. Fast cooling schedule.

Possibly resembles an amorphous solid.

An image with random pixels, using simulated annealing to swap pairs of pixels. Similar colours attract at short range and repel at slightly less short range. Slow cooling schedule. Possibly resembles a crystalline solid.

Another essential feature of the SA method is that the temperature is gradually reduced as the simulation proceeds. Initially, T is set to a high value (or infinity), and it is decreased at each step according to some annealing schedule - which may be specified by the user, but must end with T = 0 towards the end of the allotted time budget. In this way, the system is expected to wander initially towards a broad region of the search space containing good solutions, ignoring small features of the energy function; then drift towards low-energy regions that become narrower and narrower; and finally move downhill according to the steepest descent heuristic.

In plain English

Given an incredibly hard problem, such as finding a set of 100 numbers that fit some characteristic, for which attempting to brute-force the problem would result in several million years worth of computation, this technique attempts to quickly find a "pretty good" answer by adjusting the current set (in this case some random sequence of 100 numbers) until a better answer is found (the way the adjustment is done depends on the problem). The new set of numbers, or "neighbour", if more optimal, is then used as the current set and the process is repeated.

Sometimes a problem may arise when one approaches what is known as a local minimum, in this case, a set of numbers that is the "most optimized" for its current region. In an attempt to find a better optimization, this technique may use various methods to jump out of the current pit, such as searching for better optimizations randomly by a factor of the inverse amount of the previous adjustment.

Keep in mind that implementations of this method are strictly problem specific, and so the way in which one finds an optimization will vary from problem to problem.

Convergence to optimum

It can be shown that, for any given finite problem, the probability that the simulated annealing algorithm terminates with the global optimal solution approaches 1 as the annealing schedule is extended. This theoretical result is, however, not particularly helpful, since the annealing time required to ensure a significant probability of success will usually exceed the time required for a complete search of the solution space.

Pseudo-code

The following pseudo-code implements the simulated annealing heuristic, as described above, starting from state s0 and continuing to a maximum of kmax steps or until a state with energy emax or less is found. The call neighbour(s) should generate a randomly chosen neighbour of a given state s; the call random() should return a random value in the range [0,1). The annealing schedule is defined by the call temp(r), which should yield the temperature to use, given the fraction r of the time budget that has been expended so far.

```
s := s0; e := E(s)                    // Initial state, energy.
k := 0                                // Energy evaluation count.
while k  kmax and e  emax             // While time remains & not good
                                         enough :
  sn := neighbour(s)                  // Pick some neighbour.
  en := E(sn)                         // Compute its energy.
  if random()  P(e, en,               //  Should we move to it?
  temp(k/kmax)) then
    s := sn; e := en                  //   Yes, change state.
  k := k + 1                          //  One more evaluation done
return s                              // Return current solution
```

Saving the best solution seen

As in any metaheuristic, one should keep track of the best solution seen so far, in a separate state variable. Namely:

```
s := s0; e := E(s)                    // Initial state, energy.
sb := s; eb := e                      // Initial "best" solution
k := 0                                // Energy evaluation count.
while k  kmax and e  emax             // While time remains & not good
                                         enough:
 sn := neighbour(s)                   //  Pick some neighbour.
 en := E(sn)                          //  Compute its energy.
 if en  eb then                       //  Is this a new best?
   sb := sn; eb := en                 //    Yes, save it.
 if random()  P(e, en,                //  Should we move to it?
 temp(k/kmax)) then
   s := sn; e := en                   //    Yes, change state.
 k := k + 1                           //  One more evaluation done
return sb                             // Return the best solution found.
```

While copying the state may be an expensive operation, this step happens only on a small fraction of the moves, so the change is usually worth the cost.

Restarts

Sometimes it is better to move back to a solution that was significantly better rather than always moving from the current state. This is called restarting. To do this we set s and e to sb and eb and perhaps restart the annealing schedule. The decision to restart could be based on a fixed number of steps, or based on the current energy being too high from the best energy so far.

Selecting the parameters

In order to apply the SA method to a specific problem, one must specify the state space, the neighbour selection method (which enumerates the candidates for the next state s'), the probability transition function, and the annealing schedule. These choices can have a significant impact on the method's effectiveness. Unfortunately, there are no choices that will be good for all problems, and there is no general way to find the best choices for a given problem. About the only guidance available is that choices that maximize the correlation between the energies of neighbouring states can lead to better solutions. It has therefore been observed that applying the SA method is more an art than a science.

State neighbours

The neighbour selection method is particularly critical. The method may be modeled as a search graph - where the states are vertices, and there is an edge from each state to each of its neighbours. Roughly speaking, it must be possible to go from the initial state to a "good enough" state by a relatively short path on this graph, and such a path must be as likely as possible to be followed by the SA iteration.

In practice, one tries to achieve this criterion by using a search graph where the neighbours of s are expected to have about the same energy as s. Thus, in the traveling salesman problem above, generating the neighbour by swapping two adjacent cities is expected to be more effective than swapping two arbitrary cities. It is true that reaching the goal can always be done with only n - 1 general swaps, while it may take as many as n(n - 1) / 2 adjacent swaps. However, if one were to apply a random general swap to a fairly good solution, one would almost certainly get a large energy increase, and thus an extremely low probability of a swap. The probability of swapping two adjacent cities is more likely to have a smaller energy increase, and thus a much greater probability of a swap. In fact, the swap probability is so much greater in the latter case that the choice of adjacent cities leads to a more efficient algorithm. This is a special case of the general heuristic that "more correlated landscapes are better", as noted above.

Transition probabilities

The transition probability function P is not as critical as the neighbourhood graph, provided that it follows the general requirements of the SA method stated before. Since the probabilities depend on the temperature T, in practice the same probability function is used for all problems, and the annealing schedule is adjusted accordingly.

In the original formulation of the method by Kirkpatrick et. al, the transition probability P(e,e′,T) was defined as 1 if e′ e (i.e., downhill moves were always performed); otherwise, the probability would be: exp((e - e′) / T).

This formula was said to come from the Metropolis-Hastings algorithm, used here to generate samples from the Maxwell-Boltzmann distribution governing the distribution of energies of molecules in a gas. However, there is no mathematical justification for using this particular formula in SA. Even the physical analogy is misleading: since the neighbours are tested sequentially in the SA algorithm, the actual probability of the SA algorithm moving from a state s to a state s' definitely is not given by that formula.

Annealing schedule

The annealing schedule is less critical than the neighbourhood function, but still must be chosen with care. The initial temperature must be large enough to make the uphill and downhill transition probabilities about the same. To do that, one must have some estimate of the difference e' - e for a random state and its neighbours.

The temperature must then decrease so that it is zero, or nearly zero, at the end of the allotted time. A popular choice is the exponential schedule, where the temperature decreases by a fixed factor a 1 at each step.

Related methods

Tabu search (TS) is similar to simulated annealing, in that both traverse the solution space by testing neighbours of the current solution. In order to prevent cycling, the TS algorithm maintains a "tabu list" of solutions already seen, and moves to those solutions are suppressed.

Stochastic hill climbing (SH) runs many hill-climbing searches from random initial locations. Genetic algorithms (GA) maintain a pool of solutions rather than just one. New candidate solutions are generated not only by "mutation" (as in SA), but also by "combination" of two solutions from the pool. Probabilistic criteria, similar to those used in SA, are used to select the candidates for mutation or combination, and for discarding excess solutions from the pool. Ant colony optimization (ACO) uses many ants (or agents) to traverse the solution space and find locally productive areas.

The cross-entropy method (CE) generates candidates solutions via a parameterized probability distribution. The parameters are updated via cross-entropy minimization, so as to generate better samples in the next iteration. Stochastic optimization is an umbrella set of methods that includes simulated annealing and numerous other approaches.

Quantum annealing

In performing annealing, one may use quantum fluctuations instead of thermal fluctuations. The resulting method is known as quantum annealing. It has been demonstrated experimentally as well as theoretically, that quantum annealing can indeed outperform thermal annealing in certain cases, specifically, where the potential energy (cost) landscape consists of very high but thin barriers surrounding shallow local minima. Since thermal transition probabilities (~exp(- ? / kBT) , where T is temperature, kB is Boltzmann constant) depend only on the height ? of the barriers, it is very difficult for thermal fluctuations to get the system out from such local minima. But quantum tunneling probabilities through a barrier depend not only the height ? of the barrier, but also on its width w; if the barriers are thin enough, quantum fluctuations may bring the system out of the shallow local minima surrounded by them.

Stochastic tunneling

As mentioned above, getting out of local minima becomes increasingly difficult for a simulated annealing run. Stochastic tunneling is a particular successful attempt to overcome this problem, by pushing the optimization run out of local minima, 'tunneling' through barriers.

Thermodynamic Simulated Annealing

One of the theoretical bases on SA (Simulated Annealing) consists of reaching equilibrium at each temperature. In order to achieve this goal, the annealing schedule of SA goes along a sequence of temperatures for cooling the system, while a number of rearrangements are attempted to recover equilibrium at each one. Commonly, both the cooling rule and the number of movements per temperature are experimentally adjusted to provide high performance in a specific problem. Thermodynamic Simulated Annealing (TSA) provides an alternative method to perform the cooling close to equilibrium. The temperature in TSA is free to evolve (i.e. not controlled), but continuously updated from the variation of state functions as the internal energy and entropy according to the thermodynamic laws. Thereby, TSA achieves straightforward the high quality results of fine-tuned SA tools.

6.2.5 Genetic algorithm

A genetic algorithm is a search technique used in computing to find true or approximate solutions to optimization and search problems, and is often abbreviated as GA. Genetic algorithms are categorized as global search heuristics. Genetic algorithms are a particular class of evolutionary algorithms that use techniques inspired by evolutionary biology such as inheritance, mutation, selection, and crossover (also called recombination).

Genetic algorithms are implemented as a computer simulation in which a population of abstract representations (called chromosomes or the genotype or the genome) of candidate solutions (called individuals, creatures, or phenotypes) to an optimization problem evolves toward better solutions. Traditionally, solutions are represented in binary as strings of 0s and 1s, but other encodings are also possible. The evolution usually starts from a population of randomly generated individuals and happens in generations. In each generation, the fitness of every individual in the population is evaluated, multiple individuals are stochastically selected from the current population (based on their fitness), and modified (recombined and possibly mutated) to form a new population. The new population is then used in the next iteration of the algorithm.

Genetic algorithms find application in computer science, engineering, economics,chemistry, physics, mathematics and other fields.

GA procedure

A typical genetic algorithm requires two things to be defined:

1. A genetic representation of the solution domain,
2. A fitness function to evaluate the solution domain.

A standard representation of the solution is as an array of bits. Arrays of other types and structures can be used in essentially the same way. The main property that makes these genetic representations convenient is that their parts are easily aligned due to their fixed size, that facilitates simple crossover operation. Variable length representations were also used, but crossover implementation is more complex in this case. Tree-like representations are explored in Genetic programming and free-form representations are explored in HBGA.

The fitness function is defined over the genetic representation and measures the quality of the represented solution. The fitness function is always problem dependent. For instance, in the knapsack problem we want to maximize the total value of objects that we can put in a knapsack of some fixed capacity. A representation of a solution might be an array of bits, where each bit represents a different object, and the value of the bit (0 or 1) represents whether or not the object is in the knapsack. Not every such representation is valid, as the size of objects may exceed the capacity of the knapsack. The fitness of the solution is the sum of values of all objects in the knapsack if the representation is valid, or 0 otherwise. In some problems, it is hard or even impossible to define the fitness expression; in these cases, interactive genetic algorithms are used.

Once we have the genetic representation and the fitness function defined, GA proceeds to initialize a population of solutions randomly, then improve it through repetitive application of mutation, crossover, and selection operators.

Initialization

Initially many individual solutions are randomly generated to form an initial population. The population size depends on the nature of the problem, but typically contains several hundreds or thousands of possible solutions. Traditionally, the population is generated randomly, covering the entire range of possible solutions.Occasionally, the solutions may be "seeded" in areas where optimal solutions are likely to be found.

Selection

During each successive epoch, a proportion of the existing population is selected to breed a new generation. Individual solutions are selected through a fitness-based process, where fitter solutions (as measured by a fitness function) are typically more likely to be selected. Certain selection methods rate the fitness of each solution and preferentially select the best solutions. Other methods rate only a random sample of the population, as this process may be very time-consuming.

Most functions are stochastic and designed so that a small proportion of less fit solutions are selected. This helps keep the diversity of the population large, preventing premature convergence on poor solutions. Popular and well-studied selection methods include roulette wheel selection and tournament selection.

Reproduction

The next step is to generate a second generation population of solutions from those selected through genetic operators: crossover (also called recombination), and/or mutation.

For each new solution to be produced, a pair of "parent" solutions is selected for breeding from the pool selected previously. By producing a "child" solution using the above methods of crossover and mutation, a new solution is created which typically shares many of the characteristics of its "parents". New parents are selected for each child, and the process continues until a new population of solutions of appropriate size is generated.

These processes ultimately result in the next generation population of chromosomes that is different from the initial generation. Generally the average fitness will have increased by this procedure for the population, since only the best organisms from the first generation are selected for breeding, along with a small proportion of less fit solutions, for reasons already mentioned above.

Termination

This generational process is repeated until a termination condition has been reached. Common terminating conditions are

- A solution is found that satisfies minimum criteria
- Fixed number of generations reached
- Allocated budget (computation time/money) reached
- The highest ranking solution's fitness is reaching or has reached a plateau such that successive iterations no longer produce better results
- Manual inspection
- Combinations of the above

Pseudo-code algorithm

- Choose initial population
- Evaluate the fitnesses of individuals in the population
- Repeat
- Select best-ranking individuals to reproduce
- Breed new generation through crossover and mutation (genetic operations) and give birth to offspring
- Evaluate the individual fitnesses of the offspring
- Replace worst ranked part of population with offspring
- Until terminating condition

Observations

There are several general observations about the generation of solutions via a genetic algorithm:

- In many problems with sufficient complexity, GAs may have a tendency to converge towards local optima rather than the global optimum of the problem. The likelihood of this occurring depends on the shape of the fitness landscape: certain problems may provide an easy ascent towards a global optimum, others may make it easier for the function to find the local optima. This problem may be alleviated by using a different fitness function, increasing the rate of mutation, or by using selection techniques that maintain a diverse population of solutions.

- Operating on dynamic data sets is difficult, as genomes begin to converge early on towards solutions which may no longer be valid for later data. Several methods have been proposed to remedy this by increasing genetic diversity somehow and preventing early convergence, either by increasing the probability of mutation when the solution quality drops (called triggered hypermutation), or by occasionally introducing entirely new, randomly generated elements into the gene pool (called random immigrants). Recent research has also shown the benefits of using biological exaptation (or preadaptation) in solving this problem.
- GAs cannot effectively solve problems in which the only fitness measure is right/wrong, as there is no way to converge on the solution. (No hill to climb). In these cases, a random search may find a solution as quickly as a GA.
- Selection is clearly an important genetic operator, but opinion is divided over the importance of crossover versus mutation. Some argue that crossover is the most important, while mutation is only necessary to ensure that potential solutions are not lost. Others argue that crossover in a largely uniform population only serves to propagate innovations originally found by mutation, and in a non-uniform population crossover is nearly always equivalent to a very large mutation (which is likely to be catastrophic).
- Often, GAs can rapidly locate good solutions, even for difficult search spaces.
- For specific optimization problems and problem instantiations, simpler optimization algorithms may find better solutions than genetic algorithms (given the same amount of computation time). Alternative and complementary algorithms include simulated annealing, hill climbing, and swarm intelligence (e.g.: ant colony optimization, particle swarm optimization).
- As with all current machine learning problems it is worth tuning the parameters such as mutation probability, recombination probability and population size to find reasonable settings for the problem class being worked on. A very small mutation rate may lead to genetic drift (which is non-ergodic in nature) or premature convergence of the genetic algorithm in a local optimum. A mutation rate that is too high may lead to loss of good solutions. There are theoretical but not yet practical upper

and lower bounds for these parameters that can help guide selection.

- The implementation and evaluation of the fitness function is an important factor in the speed and efficiency of the algorithm.

Variants

The simplest algorithm represents each chromosome as a bit string. Typically, numeric parameters can be represented by integers, though it is possible to use floating point representations. The basic algorithm performs crossover and mutation at the bit level. Other variants treat the chromosome as a list of numbers which are indexes into an instruction table, nodes in a linked list, hashes, objects, or any other imaginable data structure. Crossover and mutation are performed so as to respect data element boundaries. For most data types, specific variation operators can be designed. Different chromosomal data types seem to work better or worse for different specific problem domains.

When bit strings representations of integers are used, Gray coding is often employed. In this way, small changes in the integer can be readily effected through mutations or crossovers. This has been found to help prevent premature convergence at so called Hamming walls, in which too many simultaneous mutations (or crossover events) must occur in order to change the chromosome to a better solution.

Other approaches involve using arrays of real-valued numbers instead of bit strings to represent chromosomes. Theoretically, the smaller the alphabet, the better the performance, but paradoxically, good results have been obtained from using real-valued chromosomes.

A slight, but very successful variant of the general process of constructing a new population is to allow some of the better organisms from the current generation to carry over to the next, unaltered. This strategy is known as elitist selection.

Parallel implementations of genetic algorithms come in two flavours. Coarse grained parallel genetic algorithms assume a population on each of the computer nodes and migration of individuals among the nodes. Fine grained parallel genetic algorithms assume an individual on each processor node which acts with neighboring individuals for selection and reproduction. Other variants, like genetic algorithms for online optimization problems, introduce time-dependence or noise in the fitness function.

Problem domains

Problems which appear to be particularly appropriate for solution by genetic algorithms include timetabling and scheduling problems, and many scheduling software packages are based on GAs. GAs have also been applied to engineering. Genetic algorithms are often applied as an approach to solve global optimization problems.

As a general rule of thumb genetic algorithms might be useful in problem domains that have a complex fitness landscape as recombination is designed to move the population away from local optima that a traditional hill climbing algorithm might get stuck in.

History

Computer simulations of evolution started with Nils Aall Barricelli in 1954. Barricelli was simulating the evolution of automata that played a simple card game. Starting in 1957, the Australian quantitative geneticist Alex Fraser published a series of papers on simulation of artificial selection of organisms with multiple loci controlling a measurable trait. From these beginnings, computer simulation of evolution by biologists became more common in the early 1960s, and the methods were described in books by Fraser and Burnell (1970) and Crosby (1973). Many early papers are reprinted by Fogel (1998).

Although Barricelli had also used evolutionary simulation as a general optimization method, genetic algorithms became a widely recognized optimization method as a result of the work of John Holland in the early 1970s, and particularly his 1975 book. His work originated with studies of cellular automata, conducted by Holland and his colleagues at the University of Michigan. Research in GAs remained largely theoretical until the mid-1980s, when The First International Conference on Genetic Algorithms was held at The University of Illinois. As academic interest grew, the dramatic increase in desktop computational power allowed for practical application of the new technique. In 1989, The New York Times writer John Markoff wrote about Evolver, the first commercially available desktop genetic algorithm. Custom computer applications began to emerge in a wide variety of fields, and these algorithms are now used by a majority of Fortune 500 companies to solve difficult scheduling, data fitting, trend spotting and budgeting problems, and virtually any other type of combinatorial optimization problem.

Related techniques

- Ant colony optimization (ACO) uses many ants (or agents) to traverse the solution space and find locally productive areas. While usually inferior to genetic algorithms and other forms of local search, it is able to produce results in problems where no global or up-to-date perspective can be obtained, and thus the other methods cannot be applied.
- Bacteriologic Algorithms (BA) inspired by evolutionary ecology and, more particularly, bacteriologic adaptation. Evolutionary ecology is the study of living organisms in the context of their environment, with the aim of discovering how they adapt. Its basic concept is that in a heterogeneous environment, you can't find one individual that fits the whole environment. So, you need to reason at the population level. BAs have shown better results than GAs on problems such as complex positioning problems (antennas for cell phones, urban planning, and so on) or data mining (see http://www.irisa.fr/triskell/publis/2005/Baudry05d.pdf).
- Cross-entropy method The Cross-entropy (CE) method generates candidates solutions via a parameterized probability distribution. The parameters are updated via cross-entropy minimization, so as to generate better samples in the next iteration.
- Evolution strategies (ES) evolve linear individuals by means of mutation. ES algorithms are designed particulary to solve problems in the real-value domain.
- Extremal optimization (EO) Unlike GAs, which work with a population of candidate solutions, EO evolves a single solution and makes local modifications to the worst components. This requires that a suitable representation be selected which permits individual solution components to be assigned a quality measure ("fitness"). The governing principle behind this algorithm is that of emergent improvement through selectively removing low-quality components and replacing them with a randomly selected component. This is decidedly at odds with a GA that selects good solutions in an attempt to make better solutions.
- Genetic programming (GP) is a related technique popularized by John Koza in which computer programs, rather than function parameters, are optimized. Genetic programming often uses tree-based internal data structures to represent the computer

programs for adaptation instead of the list structures typical of genetic algorithms.

- Interactive genetic algorithms (IGA) are genetic algorithms that use human evaluation. They are usually applied to domains where it is hard to design a computational fitness function, for example, evolving images, music, artistic designs and forms to fit users' aesthetic preference.
- Memetic algorithm (MA), also called hybrid genetic algorithm among others, is a relatively new evolutionary method where local search is applied during the evolutionary cycle. The idea of memetic algorithms comes from memes, which-unlike genes-can adapt themselves. In some problem areas they are shown to be more efficient than traditional evolutionary algorithms.
- Simulated annealing (SA) is a related global optimization technique that traverses the search space by testing random mutations on an individual solution. A mutation that increases fitness is always accepted. A mutation that lowers fitness is accepted probabilistically based on the difference in fitness and a decreasing temperature parameter.
- In Simulated Annealing parlance, one speaks of seeking the lowest energy instead of the maximum fitness. SA can also be used within a standard GA algorithm by starting with a relatively high rate of mutation and decreasing it over time along a given schedule.
- Stochastic optimization is an umbrella set of methods that includes GAs and numerous other approaches.
- Tabu search (TS) is similar to Simulated Annealing in that both traverse the solution space by testing mutations of an individual solution. While simulated annealing generates only one mutated solution, tabu search generates many mutated solutions and moves to the solution with the lowest energy of those generated.
- In order to prevent cycling and encourage greater movement through the solution space, a tabu list is maintained of partial or complete solutions. It is forbidden to move to a solution that contains elements of the tabu list, which is updated as the solution traverses the solution space.

Applications

- Artificial Creativity

- Automated design, including research on composite material design and multi-objective design of automotive components for crashworthiness, weight savings, and other characteristics.
- Automated design of mechatronic systems using bond graphs and genetic programming (NSF).
- Automated design of industrial equipment using catalogs of exemplar lever patterns.
- Calculation of Bound states and Local-density approximations.
- Chemical kinetics (gas and solid phases)
- Configuration applications, particularly physics applications of optimal molecule configurations for particular systems like C60 (buckyballs).
- Container loading optimization.
- Code-breaking, using the GA to search large solution spaces of ciphers for the one correct decryption.
- Design of water distribution systems.
- Distributed computer network topologies.
- Electronic circuit design, known as Evolvable hardware.
- File allocation for a distributed system.
- JGAP: Java Genetic Algorithms Package, also includes support for Genetic Programming
- Parallelization of GAs/GPs including use of hierarchical decomposition of problem domains and design spaces nesting of irregular shapes using feature matching and GAs.
- Game Theory Equilibrium Resolution.
- Learning Robot behavior using Genetic Algorithms.
- Learning fuzzy rule base using genetic algorithms.
- Linguistic analysis, including Grammar Induction and other aspects of Natural Language Processing (NLP) such as word sense disambiguation.
- Mobile communications infrastructure optimization.
- Molecular Structure Optimization (Chemistry).
- Multiple population topologies and interchange methodologies.
- Optimisation of data compression systems, for example using wavelets.
- Protein folding and protein/ligand docking.
- Plant floor layout.
- Representing rational agents in economic models such as the cobweb model.
- Scheduling applications, including job-shop scheduling. The objective being to schedule jobs in a sequence dependent or

non-sequence dependent setup environment in order to maximize the volume of production while minimizing penalties such as tardiness.

- Software engineering
- Solving the machine-component grouping problem required for cellular manufacturing systems.
- Tactical asset allocation and international equity strategies.
- Timetabling problems, such as designing a non-conflicting class timetable for a large university.
- Training artificial neural networks when pre-classified training examples are not readily obtainable (neuroevolution).
- Traveling Salesman Problem.
- Robot learning, obstacle avoidance.

6.3 Summary

- A Hopfield net is a form of recurrent artificial neural network invented by John Hopfield. Hopfield nets serve as content-addressable memory systems with binary threshold units. They are guaranteed to convarge to a stable state.
- The requirement that weights be symmetric is typically used, as it will guarantee that the energy function decreases monotonically while following the activation rules, and the network may exhibit some periodic or chaotic behaviour if non-symmetric weights are used.
- Training a Hopfield net involves lowering the energy of states that the net should "remember". This allows the net to serve as a content addressable memory system, that is to say, the network will converge to a "remembered" state if it is given only part of the state.
- The Boltzmann machine is similar in function and operation to the Hopfield network with the addition of using a simulated annealing technique when determining the original pattern. The Boltzmann machine incorporates the concept of simulated annealing to search the pattern layer's state space for a global minimum. Because of this, the machine will gravitate to an improved set of values over time as data iterates through the system.
- Simulated annealing (SA) is a generic probabilistic meta-algorithm for the global optimization problem, namely locating a good approximation to the global optimum of a given function in a large search space.

- The name and inspiration come from annealing in metallurgy, a technique involving heating and controlled cooling of a material to increase the size of its crystals and reduce their defects.
- A genetic algorithm is a search technique used in computing to find true or approximate solutions to optimization and search problems, and is often abbreviated as GA. Genetic algorithms are categorized as global search heuristics. Genetic algorithms are a particular class of evolutionary algorithms that use techniques inspired by evolutionary biology such as inheritance, mutation, selection, and crossover (also called recombination).

6.4 Review Questions

1. Discuss Models of Artificial Neural Network and How They Work.
2. Discuss the associated models and its types.
3. Discuss the Major Components of an optimization models.
4. Discuss the Iterated radiant descent.
5. Discuss the simulated annealing.
6. Discuss the genetic algorithms.
7. Discuss the solution of simultaneous linear equations.

—•—•—•—•—•—

Chapter No.7

Network Selection

Because all artificial neural networks are based on the concept of neurons, connections and transfer functions, there is a similarity between the different structures or architectures of neural networks. The majority of the variations stem from the various learning rules and how those rules modify a network's typical topology. The following sections outline some of the most common artificial neural networks. They are organized in very rough categories of application. These categories are not meant to be exclusive, they are merely meant to separate out some of the confusion over networks architectures and their best matches to specific applications.

Basically, most applications of neural networks fall into the following five categories:

1. Prediction
2. Classification
3. Data association
4. Data conceptualization
5. Data filtering

Network Type	Networks	Use for Network
Prediction	• Back-propagation • Delta Bar Delta • Extended Delta Bar Delta • Directed Random Search • Higher Order Neural Networks • Self-organizing map into Back-propagation	Use input values to predict some output (e.g. pick the best stocks in the market, predict weather, identify people with cancer risks etc.)
Classification	• Learning Vector Quantization • Counter-propagation • Probabilistic Neural Networks	Use input values to determine the classification (e.g. is the input the letter A, is the blob of video data a plane and what kind of plane is it)
Data Association	• Hopfield • Boltzmann Machine • Hamming Network • Bi-directional associative Memory • Spation-temporal Pattern Recognition	Like Classification but it also recognizes data that contains errors (e.g. not only identify the characters that were scanned but identify when the scanner isn't working properly)
Data Conceptualization	• Adaptive Resonance Network • Self Organizing Map	Analyze the inputs so that grouping relationships can be inferred (e.g. extract from a database the names of those most likely to buy a particular product)
Data Filtering	• Recirculation	Smooth an input signal (e.g. take the noise out of a telephone signal)

Table 7.1 Network Selector Table

Table 7.1 shows the differences between these network categories and shows which of the more common network topologies belong to which primary category. This chart is intended as a guide and is not meant to be all-inclusive. While there are many other network derivations, this chart only includes the architectures explained within this section of this report. Some of these networks, which have been grouped by application, have been used to solve more than one type of problem.

Feed forward back-propagation in particular has been used to solve almost all types of problems and indeed is the most popular for the first four categories. The next five subsections describe these five network types.

7.1 Networks for Prediction

The most common use for neural networks is to project what will most likely happen. There are many applications where prediction can help in setting priorities. For example, the emergency room at a hospital can be a hectic place. To know whom needs the most time critical help can enable a more successful operation. Basically, all organizations must establish priorities, which govern the allocation of their resources. This projection of the future is what drove the creation of networks of prediction.

7.1.1. Feed forward, Back-Propagation.

The feed forward, back-propagation architecture was developed in the early 19709s by several independent sources. This independent co-development was the result of a proliferation of articles and talks at various conferences, which stimulated the entire industry. Currently, this synergistically developed back-propagation architecture is the most popular, effective, and easy to earn model for complex, multi-layered networks. This network is used more than all other combined. It is used in many different types of applications. This architecture has spawned a large class of network types with many different topologies and training methods. Its greatest strength is in non-linear solutions to ill-defined problems.

The typical back-propagation network has an input layer, an output layer, and at least one hidden layer. There is no theoretical limit on the number of hidden layers but typically there is just one or two. Some work has been done which indicates that a minimum of four layers (three hidden layers plus an output layer) are required to solve problems of any complexity. Each layer is fully connected to the succeeding layer, as shown in Figure 7.1. (Note: all of the drawings of networks in section 5 are from NeuralWare9s Neural Works Professional II/Plus artificial neural network development tool.)

The in and out layers indicate the flow of information during recall. Recall is the process of putting input data into a trained network and receiving the answer. Back-propagation is not used during recall, but only when the network is learning a training set.

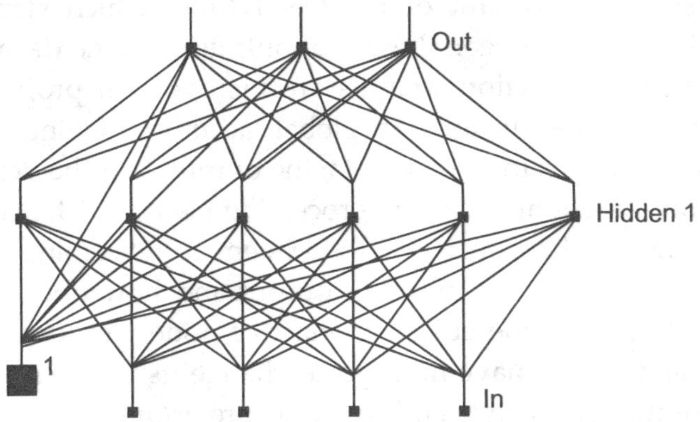

Figure 7.1 An Example Feed forward Back-propagation Network

The number of layers and the number of processing element per layer are important decisions. These parameters to a feed forward, back-propagation topology are also the most ethereal. They are the 3art2 of the network designer. There is no quantifiable, best answer to the layout of the network for any particular application. There are only general rules picked up over time and followed by most researchers and engineers applying this architecture of their problems.

Rule One: As the complexity in the relationship between the input data and the desired output increases, then the number of the processing elements in the hidden layer should also increase.

Rule Two: If the process being modeled is separable into multiple stages, then additional hidden layer(s) may be required. If the process is not separable into stages, then additional layers may simply enable memorization and not a true general solution.

Rule Three: The amount of training data available sets an upper bound for the number of processing elements in the hidden layers. To calculate this upper bound, use the number of input output pair examples in the training set and divide that number by the total number of input and output processing elements in the network. Then divide that result again by a scaling factor between five and ten. Larger scaling factors are used for relatively noisy data. Extremely noisy data may require a factor of twenty or even fifty, while very clean input data with an exact relationship to the output might drop the factor to around two. It is important that the hidden layers have few processing elements. Too many artificial neurons and the training set will be memorized. If that happens then no generalization of the data trends will occur, making the network useless on new data sets.

Once the above rules have been used to create a network, the process of teaching begins. This teaching process for a feed forward network normally uses some variant of the Delta Rule, which starts with the calculated difference between the actual outputs and the desired outputs. Using this error, connection weights are increased in proportion to the error times a scaling factor for global accuracy. Doing this for an individual node means that the inputs, the output, and the desired output all have to be present at the same processing element. The complex part of this learning mechanism is for the system to determine which input contributed the most to an incorrect output and how does that element get changed to correct the error. An inactive node would not contribute to the error and would have no need to change its weights.

To solve this problem, training inputs are applied to the input layer of the network, and desired outputs are compared at the output layer. During the learning process, a forward sweep is made through the network, and the output of each element is computed layer by layer. The difference between the output of the final layer and the desired output is back-propagated to the previous layer(s), usually modified by the derivative of the transfer function, and the connection weights are normally adjusted using the Delta Rule. This process proceeds for the previous layer(s) until the input layer is reached.

There are many variations to the learning rules for back-propagation network. Different error functions, transfer functions, and even the modifying method of the derivative of the transfer function can be used. The concept of momentum error was introduced to allow for more prompt learning while minimizing unstable behavior. Here, the error function, or delta weight equation, is modified so that a portion of the previous delta weight is fed through to the current delta weight. This acts, in engineering terms, as a low-pass filter on the delta weight terms since general trends are reinforced whereas oscillatory behavior is canceled out. This allows a low, normally slower, learning coefficient to be used, but creates faster learning.

Another technique that has an effect on convergence speed is to only update the weights after many pairs of inputs and their desired outputs are presented to the network, rather than after every presentation. This is referred to as cumulative back-propagation because the delta weights are not accumulated until the complete set of pairs is presented. The number of input-output pairs that are presented during the accumulation is referred to as a 3epoch2. This epoch may correspond either to the complete set of training pairs or to a subset.

There are limitations to the feed forward, back-propagation architecture. Back-propagation requires lots of supervised training, with lots of input-output examples. Additionally, the internal mapping procedures are not well understood, and there is no guarantee that the system will converge to an acceptable solution. At times, the learning gets stuck in a local minimum, limiting the best solution. This occurs when the network systems finds an error that is lower than the surrounding possibilities but does not finally get to the smallest possible error. Many learning applications add a term to the computations to bump or jog the weights past shallow barriers and find the actual minimum rather than a temporary error pocket.

Typical feed forward, back-propagation applications include speech synthesis from text, robot arms, evaluation of bank loans, image processing, knowledge representation, forecasting and prediction, and multi-target tracking. Each month more back-propagation solutions are announced in the trade journals.

7.1.2 Delta Bar Delta

The delta bar delta network utilizes the same architecture as a back-propagation network. The difference of delta bar delta lies in its unique algorithmic method of learning. Delta bar delta was developed by Robert Jacobs to improve the learning rate of standard feed forward, back-propagation networks.

As outlined above, the back-propagation procedure is based on a steepest descent approach, which minimizes the network9s prediction error during the process where the connection weights to each artificial neuron are changed. The standard learning rates are applied on a layer-by-layer basis and the momentum term is usually assigned globally. Some back-propagation approaches allow the learning rates to gradually decrease as large quantities of training sets pass through the network. Although this method is successful in solving many applications, the convergence rate of the procedure is still too slow to be used on some practical problems.

The delta bar delta paradigm uses a learning method where each weight has its own self-adapting coefficient. It also does not use the momentum factor of the back-propagation architecture. The remaining operations of the network, such as feed forward recall, are identical to the normal back-propagation architecture. Delta bar delta is a heuristic approach to training artificial networks. What that means is that past error values can be used to infer future calculated error values. Knowing the probable errors enables the system to take intelligence steps in adjusting the weights.

However, this process is complicated in that empirical evidence suggests that each weight may have quite different effects on the overall error. Jacobs then suggested the common sense notion that the back-propagation learning rules should account for these variations in the effect on the overall error. In other words, every connection weight of a network should have its own learning rate. The claim is that the step size appropriate for one connection weight may not be appropriate for all weights in that layer.

Further, these learning rates should be allowed to vary over time. By assigning a learning rate to each connection and permitting this learning rate to change continuously over time, more degrees of freedom are introduced to reduce the time to convergence. Rules, which directly apply to this algorithm, are straightforward and easy to implement. Each connection weight has its own learning rate. These learning rates are varied based on the current error information found with standard back-propagation. When the connection weight changes, if the local error has the same sign for several consecutive time steps, the learning rate for that connection is linearly increased. Incrementing linearly prevents the learning rates from becoming too large too fast. When the local error changes signs frequently, the learning rate is decreased geometrically. Decrementing geometrically ensures that the connection learning rates are always positive. Further, they can be decreased more rapidly in regions where the change in error is large.

By permitting different learning rates for each connection weight in a network, a steepest descent search (in the direction of the negative gradient) is no longer being performed. Instead, the connection weights are updated on the basis of the partial derivatives of the error with respect to the weight itself. It is also based on an estimate of the curvature of the error surface2 in the vicinity of the current point weight value. Additionally, the weight changes satisfy the locality constraint, that is, they require information only from the processing elements to which they are connected.

7.1.3 Extended Delta Bar Delta:

Ali Minai and Ron Williams developed the extended delta bar delta algorithm as a natural outgrowth from Jacob's work. Here, they enhance the delta bar delta by applying an exponential decay to the learning rate increase, add the momentum component back in, and put a cap on the learning rate and momentum coefficient. As discussed in the section on back-propagation, momentum is a factor used to smooth the learning rate.

It is a term added to the standard weight change, which is proportional to the previous weight change. In this way, good general trends are reinforced, and oscillations are dampened.

The learning rate and the momentum rate for each weight have separate constants controlling their increase and decrease. Once again, the sign of the current error is used to indicate whether an increase or decrease is appropriate. The adjustment for decrease is identical in form to that of Delta Bar Delta. However, the learning rate and momentum rate increases are modified to be exponentially decreasing functions of the magnitude of the weighted gradient components. Thus, greater increases will be applied in areas of small slope or curvature than in areas of high curvature. This is a partial solution to the jump problem of delta bar delta.

To take a step further to prevent wild jumps and oscillations in the weights, ceilings are placed on the individual connection learning rates and momentum rates. And finally, a memory with a recovery feature is built into the algorithm. When in use, after each epoch presentation of the training data, the accumulated error is evaluated. If the error is less than the previous minimum error, the weights are saved in memory as the current best. A tolerance parameter controls the recovery phase. Specifically, if the current error exceeds the minimum previous error, modified by the tolerance parameter, than all connection weight values revert stochastically to the stored best set of weights in memory. Furthermore, the learning and momentum rates are decreased to begin the recovery process.

7.1.4 Directed Random Search.

The previous architectures were all based on learning rules, or paradigms, which are based on calculus. Those paradigms use a gradient descent technique to adjust each of the weights. The architecture of the directed random search, however, uses a standard feed forward recall structure, which is not based on back-propagation. Instead, the directed random search adjusts the weights randomly. To provide some order to this process a direction component is added to the random step, which insures that the weights tend toward a previously successful search direction. All processing elements are influenced individually.

This random search paradigm has several important features. Basically, it is fast and easy to use if the problem is well understood and relatively small. The reason that the problem has to be well understood is that the best results occur when the initial weights, the first guesses, are within close proximity to the best weights. It is fast because the algorithm cycles through its training much more quickly than calculus-bases techniques (i.e., the delta rule and its variations), since no error terms are computed for the intermediate processing elements. Only the output error is calculated. This learning rule is easy to use because there are only two key parameters associated with it. But the problem needs to result in a small network because if the number of connections becomes high, then the training process becomes long and cumbersome.

To facilitate keeping the weights within the compact region where the algorithm works best, an upper bound is required on the weight's magnitude. Yet, by setting the weight's bounds reasonably high, the network is still allowed to seek what is not exactly known - the true global optimum. The second key parameter to this learning rule involves the initial variance of the random distribution of the weights. In most of the commercial packages there is a vendor recommended number for this initial variance parameter. Yet, the setting of this number is not all that important as the self-adjusting feature of the directed random search has proven to be robust over a wide range of initial variances.

There are four key components to a random search network. They are the random step, the reversal step, a directed component, and a self-adjusting variance.

Random Step: A random value is added to each weight. Then, the entire training set is run through the network, producing a "prediction error." If this new total training set error is less than the previous best prediction error, the current weight values (which include the random step) becomes the new set of "best" weights. The current prediction error is then saved as the new, best prediction error.

Reversal Step: If the random step's results are worse than the previous best, then the same random value is subtracted from the original weight value. This produces a set of weights that is in the opposite direction to the previous random step. If the total "prediction error" is less than the previous best error, the current weight values of the reversal step are stored as the best weights. The current prediction error is also saved as the new, best prediction error. If both the forward and reverse steps fail, a completely new set of random values are added to the best weights and the process is then begun again.

Directed Component: To add in convergence a set of directed components is created, based on the outcomes of the forward and reversal steps. These directed components reflect the history of success or failure for the previous random steps. The directed components, which are initialized to zero, are added to the random components at each step in the procedure. Directed components provide a "common sense, let's go this way" element to the search. It has been found that the addition of these directed components provide a dramatic performance improvement to convergence.

Self-adjusting Variance: An initial variance parameter is specified to control the initial size (or length) of the random steps, which are added to the weights. An adaptive mechanism changes the variance parameter based on the current relative success rate or failure rate. The learning rule assumes that the current size of the steps for the weights is in the right direction if it records several consecutive successes, and it then expands to try even larger steps. Conversely, if it detects several consecutive failures it contracts the variance to reduce the step size.

For small to moderately sized networks, a directed random search produces good solutions in a reasonable amount of time. The training is automatic, requiring little, if any, user interaction. The number of connection weights imposes a practical limit on the size of a problem that this learning algorithm can effectively solve. If a network has more than 200 connection weights, a directed random search can require a relatively long training time and still end up yielding an acceptable solution.

7.1.5 Higher-order Neural Network or Functional-link Network.

Either name is given to neural networks, which expand the standard feed forward, back-propagation architecture to include nodes at the input layer, which provide the network with a more complete understanding of the input. Basically, the inputs are transformed in a well-understood mathematical way so that the network does not have to learn some basic math functions. These functions do enhance the network's understanding of a given problem. These mathematical functions transform the inputs via higher-order functions such as squares, cubes, or sines. It is from the very name of these functions, higher-order or functionally linked mappings, that the two names for this same concept were derived.

This technique has been shown to dramatically improve the learning rates of some applications. An additional advantage to this extension of back-propagation is that these higher order functions can be applied to other derivations - delta bar delta, extended delta bar delta, or any other enhanced feed forward, back-propagation networks.

There are two basic ways of adding additional input nodes. First, the cross products of the input terms can be added into the model. This is also called the output product or tensor model, where each component of the input pattern multiplies the entire input pattern vector. A reasonable way to do this is to add all interaction terms between input values. For example, for a back-propagation network with three inputs (A, B and C), the cross products would include: AA, BB, CC, AB, AC, and BC. This example adds second-order terms to the input structure of the network. Third-order terms, such as ABC, could also be added.

The second method for adding additional input nodes is the functional expansion of the base inputs. Thus, a back-propagation model with A, B and C might be transformed into a higher-order neural network model with inputs: A, B, C, SIN (A), COS (B), LOG(C), MAX (A, B, C), etc. In this model, input variables are individually acted upon by appropriate functions. Many different functions can be used. The overall effect is to provide the network with an enhanced representation of the input. It is even possible to combine the tensor and functional expansion models together.

No new information is added, but the representation of the inputs is enhanced. Higher-order representation of the input data can make the network easier to train. The joint or functional activations become directly available to the model. In some cases, a hidden layer is no longer needed. However, there are limitations to the network model. Many more input nodes must be processed to use the transformations of the original inputs. With higher-order systems, the problem is exacerbated. Yet, because of the finite processing time of computers, it is important that the inputs are not expanded more than is needed to get an accurate solution.

Functional-link networks were developed by Yoh-Han Pao and are documented in his book, Adaptive Pattern Recognition and Neural Networks. Pao draws a distinction between truly adding higher order terms in the sense that some of these terms represent joint activations versus functional expansion, which increases the dimension of the representation space without adding joint activations. While most developers recognize the difference, researchers typically treat these two aspects in the same way. Pao has been awarded a patent for the functional-link network, so its commercial use may require royalty licensing.

7.2 Self-Organizing Map into Back-Propagation.

A hybrid network uses a self-organizing map to conceptually separate the data before that data is used in the normal back-propagation manner. This map helps to visualize topologies and hierarchical structures of higher-order input spaces before they are entered into the feed forward, back-propagation network. The change to the input is similar to having an automatic functional-link input structure. This self-organizing map trains in an unsupervised manner. The rest of the network goes through its normal supervised training.

7.3 Networks for Classification

The previous section describes networks that attempt to make projections of the future. But understanding trends and what impacts those trends might have is only one of several types of applications. The second class of applications is classification. A network that can classify could be used in the medical industry to process both lab results and doctor-recorded patience symptoms to determine the most likely disease. Other applications can separate the "tire kicker" inquiries from the requests for information from real buyers.

7.3.1 Learning Vector Quantization.

This network topology was originally suggested by Tuevo Kohonen in the mid 80's, well after his original work in self-organizing maps. Both this network and self-organizing maps are based on the Kohonen layer, which is capable of sorting items into appropriate categories of similar objects. Specifically, Learning Vector Quantization is a artificial neural network model used both for classification and image segmentation problems.

Topologically, the network contains an input layer, a single Kohonen layer and an output layer. An example network is shown in Figure 7.2. The output layer has as many processing elements as there are distinct categories, or classes. The Kohonen layer has a number of processing elements grouped for each of these classes. The number of processing elements per class depends upon the complexity of the input-output relationship. Usually, each class will have the same number of elements throughout the layer. It is the Kohonen layer that learns and performs relational classifications with the aid of a training set.

This network uses supervised learning rules. However, these rules vary significantly from the back-propagation rules. To optimize the learning and recall functions, the input layer should contain only one processing element for each separable input parameter. Higher-order input structures could also be used.

Learning Vector Quantization classifies its input data into groupings that it determines. Essentially, it maps an n-dimensional space into an m-dimensional space. That is it takes n inputs and produces m outputs. The networks can be trained to classify inputs while preserving the inherent topology of the training set. Topology preserving maps preserve nearest neighbor relationships in the training set such that input patterns which have not been previously learned will be categorized by their nearest neighbors in the training data.

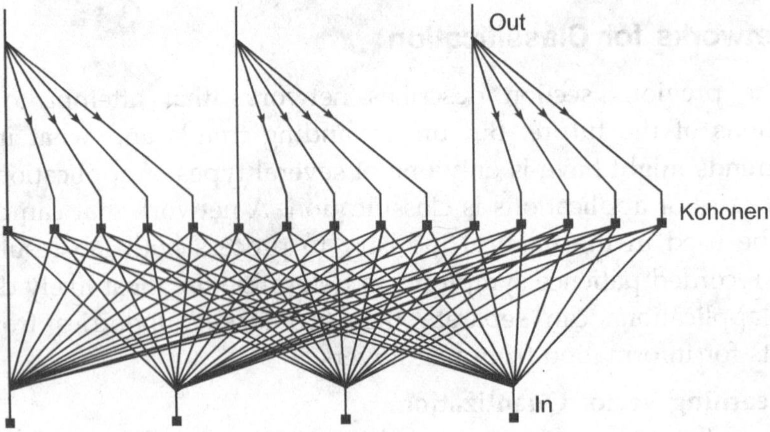

Figure 7.2. An Example Learning Vector Quantization Network.

In the training mode, this supervised network uses the Kohonen layer such that the distance of a training vector to each processing element is computed and the nearest processing element is declared the winner. There is only one winner for the whole layer. The winner will enable only one output-processing element to fire, announcing the class or category the input vector belonged to. If the winning element is in the expected class of the training vector, it is reinforced toward the training vector. If the winning element is not in the class of the training vector, the connection weights entering the processing element are moved away from the training vector. This later operation is referred to as repulsion. During this training process, individual processing elements assigned to a particular class migrate to the region associated with their specific class.

During the recall mode, the distance of an input vector to each processing element is computed and again the nearest element is declared the winner. That in turn generates one output, signifying a particular class found by the network.

There are some shortcomings with the Learning Vector Quantization architecture. Obviously, for complex classification problems with similar objects or input vectors, the network requires a large Kohonen layer with many processing elements per class. This can be overcome with selectively better choices for, or higher-order representation of, the input parameters.

The learning mechanisms have some weaknesses, which have been addressed by variants to the paradigm. Normally these variants are applied at different phases of the learning process. They imbue a conscience mechanism, a boundary adjustment algorithm, and an attraction function at different points while training the network.

The simple form of the Learning Vector Quantization network suffers from the defect that some processing elements tend to win too often while others, in effect, do nothing. This particularly happens when the processing elements begin far from the training vectors. Here, some elements are drawn in close very quickly and the others remain permanently far away. To alleviate this problem, a conscience mechanism is added so that a processing element, which wins too often, develops a "guilty conscience" and is penalized. The actual conscience mechanism is a distance bias, which is added to each processing element. This distance bias is proportional to the difference between the win frequency of an element and the average processing element win frequency. As the network progresses along its learning curve, this bias proportionality factors needs to be decreased.

The boundary adjustment algorithm is used to refine a solution once a relatively good solution has been found. This algorithm affects the cases when the winning processing element is in the wrong class and the second best processing element is in the right class. A further limitation is that the training vector must be near the midpoint of space joining these two processing elements. The winning wrong processing element is moved away from the training vector and the second place element is moved toward the training vector. This procedure refines the boundary between regions where poor classifications commonly occur.

In the early training of the Learning Vector Quantization network, it is some times desirable to turn off the repulsion. The winning processing element is only moved toward the training vector if the training vector and the winning processing element are in the same class. This option is particularly helpful when a processing element must move across a region having a different class in order to reach the region where it is needed.

7.3.2 Counter-propagation Network.

Robert Hecht-Nielsen developed the counter-propagation network as a means to combine an unsupervised Kohonen layer with a teachable output layer. This is yet another topology to synthesize complex classification problems, while trying to minimize the number of processing elements and training time. The operation for the counter-propagation network is similar to that of the Learning Vector Quantization network in that the middle Kohonen layer acts as an adaptive look-up table, finding the closest fit to an input stimulus and outputting its equivalent mapping.

The first counter-propagation network consisted of a bi-directional mapping between the input and output layers. In essence, while data is presented to the input layer to generate a classification pattern on the output layer, the output layer in turn would accept an additional input vector and generate an output classification on the network's input layer. The network got its name from this counter-posing flow of information through its structure. Most developers use a unit-flow variant of this formal representation of counter-propagation. In other words. There is only one feed forward path from input layer to output layer.

An example network is shown in Figure 7.3. The unit-directional counter-propagation network has three layers. If the inputs are not already normalized before they enter the network, a fourth layer is sometimes added. The main layers include an input buffer layer, a self-organizing Kohonen layer, and an output layer, which uses the Delta Rule to modify its incoming connection weights. Sometimes this layer is called a Grossberg Outstar layer.

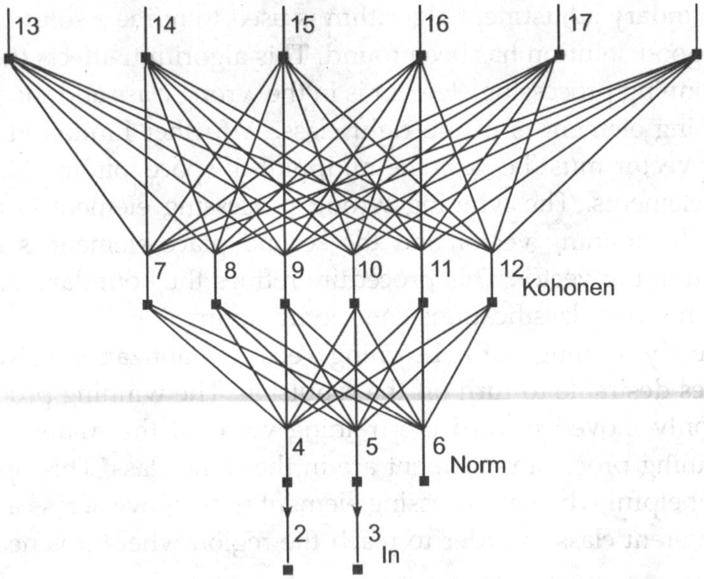

Figure 7.3. An Example Counter-propagation Network.

The size of the input layer depends upon how many separable parameters define the problem. With too few, the network may not generalize sufficiently. With too many, the processing time takes too long.

For the network to operate properly, the input vector must be normalized. This means that for every combination of input values, the total "length" of the input vector must add up to one. This can be done with a preprocessor, before the data is entered into the counter-propagation network. Or, a normalization layer can be added between the input and Kohonen layers. The normalization layer requires one processing element for each input, plus one more for a balancing element. This layer modifies the input set before going to the Kohonen layer to guarantee that all input sets combine to the same total.

Normalization of the inputs is necessary to insure that the Kohonen layer finds the correct class for the problem. Without normalization, larger input vectors bias many of the Kohonen processing elements such that weaker value input sets cannot be properly classified. Because of the competitive nature of the Kohonen layer, the larger value input vectors overpower the smaller vectors. Counter-propagation uses a standard Kohonen paradigm, which self-organizes the input sets into classification zones. It follows the classical Kohonen learning law described in section 4.2 of this report. This layer acts as a nearest neighbor classifier in that the processing elements in the competitive layer autonomously adjust their connection weights to divide up the input vector space in approximate correspondence to the frequency with which the inputs occur. There needs to be at least as many processing elements in the Kohonen layer as output classes. The Kohonen layer usually has many more elements than classes simply because additional processing elements provide a finer resolution between similar objects.

The output layer for counter-propagation is basically made up of processing elements, which learn to produce an output when a particular input is applied. Since the Kohonen layer includes competition, only a single output is produced for a given input vector. This layer provides a way of decoding that input to a meaningful output class. It uses the Delta Rule to back-propagate the error between the desired output class and the actual output generated with the training set. The errors only adjust the connection weights coming into the output layer. The Kohonen layer is not affected.

Since only one output from the competitive Kohonen layer is active at a time and all other elements are zero, the only weight adjusted for the output processing elements are the ones connected to the winning element in the competitive layer. In this way the output layer learns to reproduce a certain pattern for each active processing element in the competitive layer. If several competitive elements belong to the same class, that output processing element will evolve weights in response to those competitive processing elements and zero for all others.

There is a problem, which could arise with this architecture. The competitive Kohonen layer learns without any supervision. It does not know what class it is responding to. This means that it is possible for a processing element in the Kohonen layer to learn to take responsibility for two or more training inputs, which belong to different classes. When this happens, the output of the network will be ambiguous for any inputs, which activate this processing element. To alleviate this problem, the processing elements in the Kohonen layer could be pre-conditioned to learn only about a particular class.

7.3.3 Probabilistic Neural Network.

The probabilistic neural network was developed by Donald Specht. His network architecture was first presented in two papers, Probabilistic Neural Networks for Classification, Mapping or Associative Memory and Probabilistic Neural Networks, released in 1988 and 1990, respectively. This network provides a general solution to pattern classification problems by following an approach developed in statistics, called Bayesian classifiers. Bayes theory, developed in the 1950's, takes into account the relative likelihood of events and uses a priori information to improve prediction. The network paradigm also uses Parzen Estimators, which were developed to construct the probability density functions required by Bayes theory.

The probabilistic neural network uses a supervised training set to develop distribution functions within a pattern layer. These functions, in the recall mode, are used to estimate the likelihood of an input feature vector being part of a learned category, or class. The learned patterns can also be combined, or weighted, with the a priori probability, also called the relative frequency, of each category to determine the most likely class for a given input vector. If the relative frequency of the categories is unknown, then all categories can be assumed to be equally likely and the determination of category is solely based on the closeness of the input feature vector to the distribution function of a class.

An example of a probabilistic neural network is shown in Figure 7.4. This network has three layers. The network contains an input layer, which has as many elements as there are separable parameters needed to describe the objects to be classified. It has a pattern layer, which organizes the training set such that each input vector is represented by an individual processing element. And finally, the network contains an output layer, called the summation layer, which has as many processing elements as there are classes to be recognized. Each element in this layer combines via processing elements within the pattern layer, which relate to the same class and prepares that category for output. Sometimes a fourth layer is added to normalize the input vector, if the inputs are not already normalized before they enter the network. As with the counter-propagation network, the input vector must be normalized to provide proper object separation in the pattern layer.

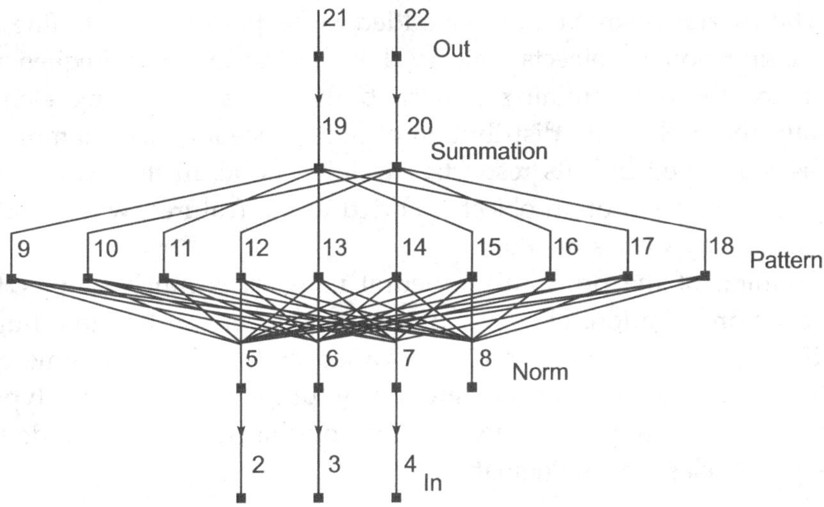

Figure 7.4. A Probabilistic Neural Network Example.

As mentioned earlier, the pattern layer represents a neural implementation of a version of a Bayes classifier, where the class dependent probability density functions are approximated using a Parzen estimator. This approach provides an optimum pattern classifier in terms of minimizing the expected risk of wrongly classifying an object. With the estimator, the approach gets closer to the true underlying class density functions as the number of training samples increases, so long as the training set is an adequate representation of the class distinctions.

In the pattern layer, there is a processing element for each input vector in the training set. Normally, there are equal amounts of processing elements for each output class. Otherwise, one or more classes may be skewed incorrectly and the network will generate poor results. Each processing element in the pattern layer is trained once. An element is trained to generate a high output value when an input vector matches the training vector. The training function may include a global smoothing factor to better generalize classification results. In any case, the training vectors do not have to be in any special order in the training set, since the category of a particular vector is specified by the desired output of the input. The learning function simply selects the first untrained processing element in the correct output class and modifies its weights to match the training vector.

The pattern layer operates competitively, where only the highest match to an input vector wins and generates an output. In this way, only one classification category is generated for any given input vector. If the input does not relate well to any patterns programmed into the pattern layer, no output is generated.

The Parzen estimation can be added to the pattern layer to fine tune the classification of objects, this is done by adding the frequency of occurrence for each training pattern built into a processing element. Basically, the probability distribution of occurrence for each example in a class is multiplied into its respective training node. In this way, a more accurate expectation of an object is added to the features, which make it recognizable as a class member.

Training of the probabilistic neural network is much simpler than with back-propagation. However, the pattern layer can be quite huge if the distinction between categories is varied and at the same time quite similar is special areas. There are many proponents for this type of network, since the groundwork for optimization is founded in well-known, classical mathematics.

7.4 Networks for Data Association

The previous class of networks, classification, is related to networks for data association. In data association, classification is still done. For example, a character reader will classify each of its scanned inputs. However, an additional element exists for most applications. That element is the fact that some data is simply erroneous. Credit card applications might have been rendered unreadable by water stains. The scanner might have lost its light source. The card itself might have been filled out by a five year old. Networks for data association recognize these occurrences as simply bad data and they recognize that this bad data can span all classifications.

7.4.1 Hopfield Network.

John Hopfield first presented his crossbar associative network in 1982 at the National Academy of Sciences. In honor of Hopfield's success and his championing of neural networks in general, this network paradigm is usually referred to as a Hopfield Network. The network can be conceptualized in terms of its energy and the physics of dynamic systems. A processing element in the Hopfield layer will change state only if the overall "energy" of the state space is reduced. In other words, the state of a processing element will vary depending whether the change will reduce the overall "frustration level" of the network. Primary applications for this sort of network have included associative, or content-addressable, memories and a whole set of optimization problems, such as the combinatory best route for a traveling salesman.

The Figure 7.5 outlines a basic Hopfield network. The original network had each processing element operate in a binary format. This is where the elements compute the weighted sum of the inputs and quantize the output to a zero or one. These restrictions were later relaxed, in that the paradigm can use a sigmoid-based transfer function for finer class distinction. Hopfield himself showed that the resulting network is equivalent to the original network designed in 1982.

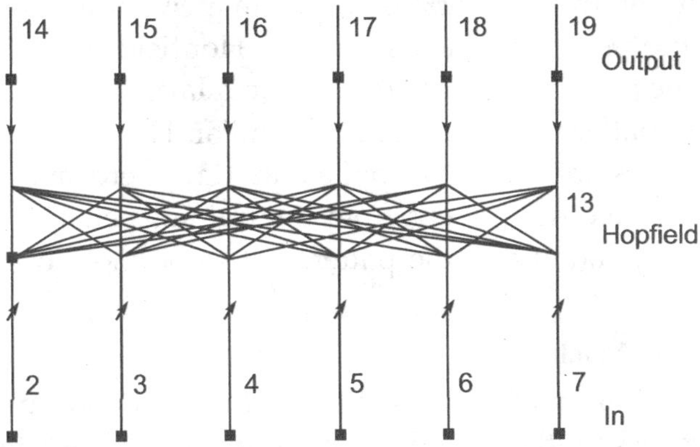

Figure 7.5. A Hopfield Network Example.

The Hopfield network uses three layers; an input buffer, a Hopfield layer, and an output layer. Each layer has the same number of processing elements. The inputs of the Hopfield layer are connected to the outputs of the corresponding processing elements in the input buffer layer through variable connection weights. The outputs of the Hopfield layer are connected back to the inputs of every other processing element except itself. They are also connected to the corresponding elements in the output layer. In normal recall operation, the network applies the data from the input layer through the learned connection weights to the Hopfield layer. The Hopfield layer oscillates until some fixed number of cycles has been completed, and the current state of that layer is passed on to the output layer. This state matches a pattern already programmed into the network.

The learning of a Hopfield network requires that a training pattern be impressed on both the input and output layers simultaneously. The recursive nature of the Hopfield layer provides a means of adjusting all of the connection weights. The learning rule is the Hopfield Law, where connections are increased when both the input and output of an Hopfield element are the same and the connection weights are decreased if the output does not match the input. Obviously, any non-binary implementation of the network must have a threshold mechanism in the transfer function, or matching input-output pairs could be too rare to train the network properly.

The Hopfield network has two major limitations when used as a content addressable memory. First, the number of patterns that can be stored and accurately recalled is severely limited. If too many patterns are stored, the network may converge to a novel spurious pattern different from all programmed patterns. Or, it may not converge at all. The storage capacity limit for the network is approximately fifteen percent of the number of processing elements in the Hopfield layer. The second limitation of the paradigm is that the Hopfield layer may become unstable if the common patterns it shares are too similar. Here an example pattern is considered unstable if it is applied at time zero and the network converges to some other pattern from the training set. This problem can be minimized by modifying the pattern set to be more orthogonal with each other.

7.4.2 Boltzmann Machine.

The Boltzmann machine is similar in function and operation to the Hopfield network with the addition of using a simulated annealing technique when determining the original pattern. The Boltzmann machine incorporates the concept of simulated annealing to search the pattern layer's state space for a global minimum. Because of this, the machine will gravitate to an improved set of values over time as data iterates through the system.

Ackley, Hinton, and Sejnowski developed the Boltzmann learning rule in 1985. Like the Hopfield network, the Boltzmann machine has an associated state space energy based upon the connection weights in the pattern layer. The processes of learning a training set full of patterns involves the minimization of this state space energy. Because of this, the machine will gravitate to an improved set of values for the connection weights while data iterates through the system.

The Boltzmann machine requires a simulated annealing schedule, which is added to the learning process of the network. Just as in physical annealing, temperatures start at higher values and decreases over time. The increased temperature adds an increased noise factor into each processing element in the pattern layer. Typically, the final temperature is zero. If the network fails to settle properly, adding more iteration at lower temperatures may help to get to a optimum solution.

Boltzmann machine learning at high temperature behaves much like a random model and at low temperatures it behaves like a deterministic model. Because of the random component in annealed learning, a processing element can sometimes assume a new state value that increases rather than decreases the overall energy of the system. This mimics physical annealing and is helpful in escaping local minima and moving toward a global minimum.

As with the Hopfield network, once a set of patterns are learned, a partial pattern can be presented to the network and it will complete the missing information. The limitation on the number of classes, being less than fifteen percent of the total processing elements in the pattern layer, still applies.

7.4.3 Hamming Network.

The Hamming network is an extension of the Hopfield network in that it adds a maximum likelihood classifier to the frond end. This network was developed by Richard Lippman in the mid 1980's. The Hamming network implements a classifier based upon least error for binary input vectors, where the Hamming distance defines the error. The Hamming distance is defined as the number of bits, which differ between two corresponding, fixed-length input vectors. One input vector is the noiseless example pattern, the other is a pattern corrupted by real-world events.

In this network architecture, the output categories are defined by a noiseless, pattern-filled training set. In the recall mode any incoming input vectors are then assigned to the category for which the distance between the examples input vectors and the current input vector is minimum.

The Hamming network has three layers. There is an example network shown in Figure 7.6. The network uses an input layer with as many nodes as there are separate binary features. It has a category layer, which is the Hopfield layer, with as many nodes as there are categories, or classes. This differs significantly from the formal Hopfield architecture, which has as many nodes in the middle layer as there are input nodes. And finally, there is an output layer, which matches the number of nodes in the category layer.

The network is simple feed forward architecture with the input layer fully connected to the category layer. Each processing element in the category layer is connected back to every other element in that same layer, as well as to a direct connection to the output processing element. The output from the category layer to the output layer is done through competition.

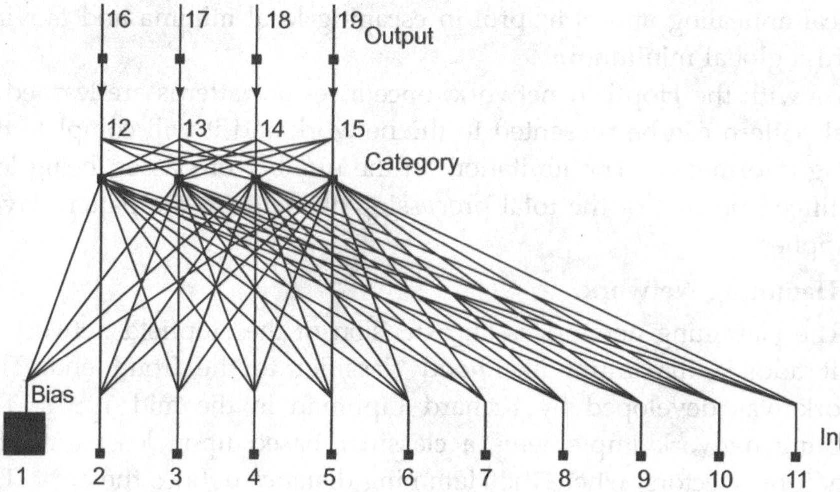

Figure 7.6. A Hamming Network Example.

The learning of a Hamming network is similar to the Hopfield methodology in that it requires a single-pass training set. However, in this supervised paradigm, the desired training pattern is impressed upon the input layer while the desired class to which the vector belongs is impressed upon the output layer. Here the output contains only the category output to which the input vector belongs. Again, the recursive nature of the Hopfield layer provides a means of adjusting all connection weights.

The connection weights are first set in the input to category layer such that the matching scores generated by the outputs of the category processing elements are equal to the number of input nodes minus the Hamming distances to the example input vectors. These matching scores range from zero to the total number of input elements and are highest for those input vectors which best match the learned patterns. The category layer's recursive connection weights are trained in the same manner as in the Hopfield network. In normal feed forward operation an input vector is applied to the input layer and must be presented long enough to allow the matching score outputs of the lower input to category subnet to settle. This will initialize the input to the Hopfield function in the category layer and allow that portion of the subnet to find the closest class to which the input vector belongs. This layer is competitive, so only one output is enabled at a time.

The Hamming network has a number of advantages over the Hopfield network. It implements the optimum minimum error classifier when input bit errors are random and independent. So, the Hopfield with its random set up nature can only be as good a solution as the Hamming, or it can be worse. Fewer processing elements are required for the Hamming solution, since the middle layer only requires one element per category, instead of an element for each input node. And finally, the Hamming network does not suffer from spurious classifications, which may occur in the Hopfield network. All in all, the Hamming network is both faster and more accurate than the Hopfield network.

7.4.4 Bi-directional Associative Memory.

This network model was developed by Bart Kosko and again generalizes the Hopfield model. A set of paired patterns is learned with the patterns represented as bipolar vectors. Like the Hopfield, when a noisy version of one pattern is presented, the closest pattern associated with it is determined.

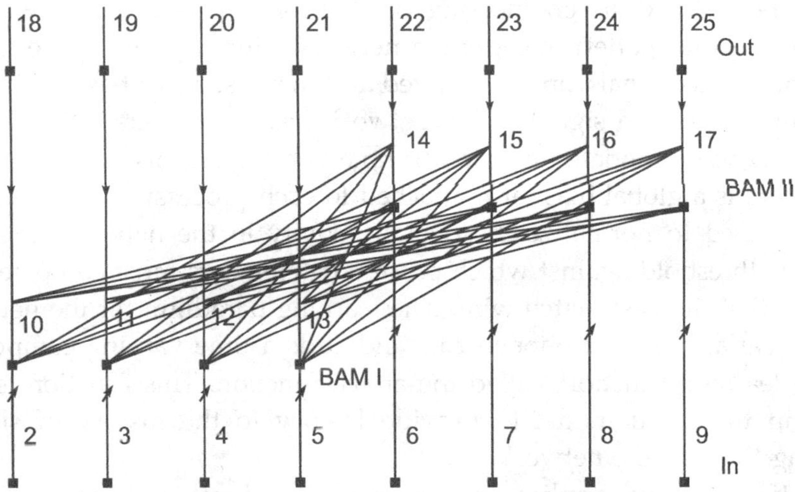

Figure 7.7. Bi-directional Associative Memory Example.

A diagram of an example bi-directional associative memory is shown in Figure 7.7. It has as many inputs as output processing nodes. The two hidden layers are made up of two separate associated memories and represent the size of two input vectors. The two lengths need not be the same, although this example shows identical input vector lengths of four each. The middle layers are fully connected to each other. The input and output layers are for implementation purposes the means to enter and retrieve information from the network. Kosko original work targeted the bi-directional associative memory layers for optical processing, which would not need formal input and output structures.

The middle layers are designed to store associated pairs of vectors. When a noisy pattern vector is impressed upon the input, the middle layers oscillate back and forth until a stable equilibrium state is reached.

This state, providing the network is not over trained, corresponds to the closest learned association and will generate the original training pattern on the output. Like the Hopfield network, the bi-directional associative memory network is susceptible to incorrectly finding a trained pattern when complements of the training set are used as the unknown input vector.

7.4.5 Spatio-Temporal Pattern Recognition (Avalanche).

This network as shown in Figure 7.8 came out of Stephen Grossberg's work in the early 1970's. It basically was developed to explain certain cognitive processes for recognizing time varying sequences of events. In his work at the time he called this network paradigm an "Avalanche" network. Robert Hecht-Nielsen became interested in how this network could be applied to engineering applications. The outcome was the spatio-temporal pattern recognition network. Here, specific patterns, for example audio signals, are memorized and then used as a basis to classify incoming repetitive signals. This network has parameters, which allow tuning to accommodate detection of time varying signals.

Here is a global bias term attached to each processing element. This term is used to normalize the overall activity in the network. It sets a variable threshold against which processing elements must compete, and insures that the best match wins. The learning paradigm for the network uses a variant of the Kohonen rule and adds a time varying component to the learning function, called the attack function. This function is also used in the recall mode, to provide latency to the history of signals passing through the network.

The primary application of spatio-temporal pattern networks appears to be in the area of recognizing repetitive audio signals. One group in General Dynamics has applied this network to classify types of ships based on the sounds their propellers make. Another characteristic of the network is that because of the slow decay of the attack function, even though the periodicity of the input signal varied by as much as a factor of two, the network was still able to correctly classify the propeller signals.

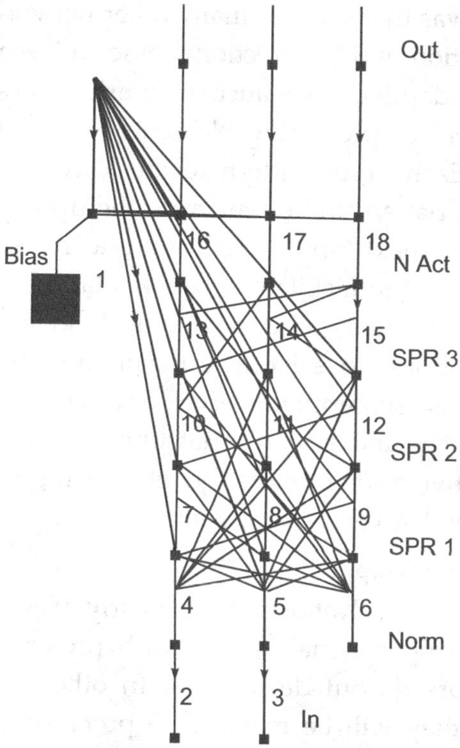

Figure 7.8. A Spatio-temporal Pattern Network Example

7.5 Networks for Data Conceptualization

Another network type is data conceptualization. In many applications data is not just classified, for not all applications involve data that can fit within a class, not all applications read characters or identify diseases. Some applications need to group data that may, or may not be, clearly definable. An example of this is in the processing of a database for a mailing list of potential customers. Customers might exist within all classifications, yet they might be concentrated within a certain age group and certain income levels. Also, in real life, other information might stretch and twist the region, which contains the vast majority of potential buyers. This process is data conceptualization. It simply tries to identify a group as best as it can.

7.5.1 Adaptive Resonance Network.

Developed by Stephen Grossberg in the mid 1970's, the network creates categories of input data based on adaptive resonance. The topology is biologically plausible and uses an unsupervised learning function. It analyses behaviorally significant input data and detects possible features or classifies patterns in the input vector.

This network was the basis for many other network paradigms, such as counter-propagation and bi-directional associative memory networks. The heart of the adaptive resonance network consists of two highly interconnected layers of processing elements located between an input and output layer. Each input pattern to the lower resonance layer will induce an expected pattern to be sent from the upper layer to the lower layer to influence the next input. This creates a "resonance" between the lower and upper layers to facilitate network adaption of patterns.

The network is normally used in biological modeling, however, some engineering applications do exist. The major limitation to the network architecture is its noise susceptibility. Even a small amount of noise on the input vector confuses the pattern matching capabilities of a trained network. The adaptive resonance theory network topology is protected by a patent held by the University of Boston.

7.5.2 Self-Organizing Map.

Developed by Teuvo Kohonen in the early 1980's, the input data is projected to a two-dimensional layer, which preserves order, compacts spare data, and spreads out dense data. In other words, if two input vectors are close, they will be mapped to processing elements that are close together in the two-dimensional Kohonen layer that represents the features or clusters of the input data. Here, the processing elements represent a two-dimensional map of the input data.

The primary use of the self-organizing map is to visualize topologies and hierarchical structures of higher-order dimensional input spaces. The self-organizing network has been used to create area-filled curves in two-dimensional space created by the Kohonen layer. The Kohonen layer can also be used for optimization problems by allowing the connection weights to settle out into a minimum energy pattern.

A key difference between this network and many other networks is that the self-organizing map learns without supervision. However, when the topology is combined with other neural layers for prediction or categorization, the network first learns in an unsupervised manner and then switches to a supervised mode for the trained network to which it is attached.

An example self-organizing map network is shown in Figure 7.9. The self-organizing map has typically two layers. The input layer is fully connected to a two-dimensional Kohonen layer. The output layer shown here is used in a categorization problem and represents three classes to which the input vector can belong. This output layer typically learns using the delta rule and is similar in operation to the counter-propagation paradigm.

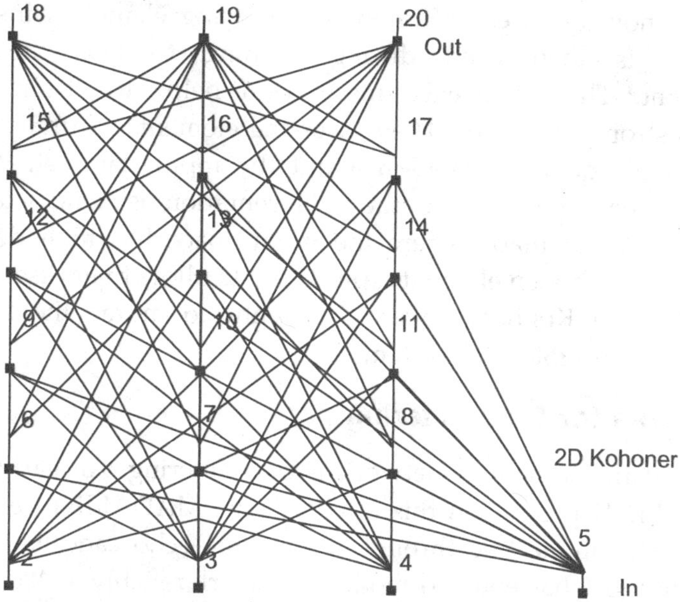

Figure 7.9. An Example Self-organizing Map Network.

The Kohonen layer processing elements each measure the Euclidean distance of its weights from the incoming input values. During recall, the Kohonen element with the minimum distance is the winner and outputs a one to the output layer, if any. This is a competitive win, so all other processing elements are forced to zero for that input vector. Thus the winning processing element is, in a measurable way, the closest to the input value and thus represents the input value in the Kohonen two-dimensional map. So the input data, which may have many dimensions, comes to be represented by a two-dimensional vector, which preserves the order of the higher dimensional input data. This can be thought of as an order-preserving projection of the input space onto the two-dimensional Kohonen layer.

During training, the Kohonen processing element with the smallest distance adjusts its weight to be closer to the values of the input data. The neighbors of the winning element also adjust their weights to be closer to the same input data vector. The adjustment of neighboring processing elements is instrumental in preserving the order of the input space. Training is done with the competitive Kohonen learning law described in counter-propagation.

The problem of having one processing element take over for a region and representing too much input data exists in this paradigm. As with counter-propagation, this problem is solved by a conscience mechanism built into the learning function. The conscience rule depends on keeping a record of how often each Kohonen processing element wins and this information is then used during training to bias the distance measurement. This conscience mechanism helps the Kohonen layer achieve its strongest benefit. The processing elements naturally represent approximately equal information about the input data set. Where the input space has sparse data, the representation is compacted in the Kohonen space, or map. Where the input space has high density, the representative Kohonen elements spread out to allow finer discrimination. In this way the Kohonen layer is thought to mimic the knowledge representation of biological systems.

7.6 Networks for Data Filtering

The last major type of network is data filtering. An early network, the MADALINE, belongs in this category. The MADALINE removed the echoes from a phone line through a dynamic echo cancellation circuit. More recent work has enabled modems to work reliably at 4800 and 9600 baud through dynamic equalization techniques. Both of these applications utilize neural networks, which were incorporated into special purpose chips.

7.6.1 Recirculation.

Recirculation networks were introduced by Geoffrey Hinton and James McClelland as a biologically plausible alternative to back-propagation networks. In a back-propagation network, errors are passed backwards through the same connections that are used in the feed forward mechanism with an additional scaling by the derivative of the feed forward transfer function. This makes the back-propagation algorithm difficult to implement in electronic hardware.

In a recirculation network, data is processed in one direction only and learning is done using only local knowledge. In particular, the knowledge comes from the state of the processing element and the input value on the particular connection to be adapted. Recirculation networks use unsupervised learning so no desired output vector is required to be presented at the output layer. The network is auto-associative, where there are the same number of outputs as inputs.

This network has two layers between the input and output layers, called the visible and hidden layers. The purpose of the learning rule is to construct in the hidden layer an internal representation of the data presented at the visible layer. An important case of this is to compress the input data by using fewer processing elements in the hidden layer. In this case, the hidden representation can be considered a compressed version of the visible representation. The visible and hidden layers are fully connected to each other in both directions. Also, each element in both the hidden and visible layers are connected to a bias element. These connections have variable weights, which learn in the same manner as the other variable weights in the network.

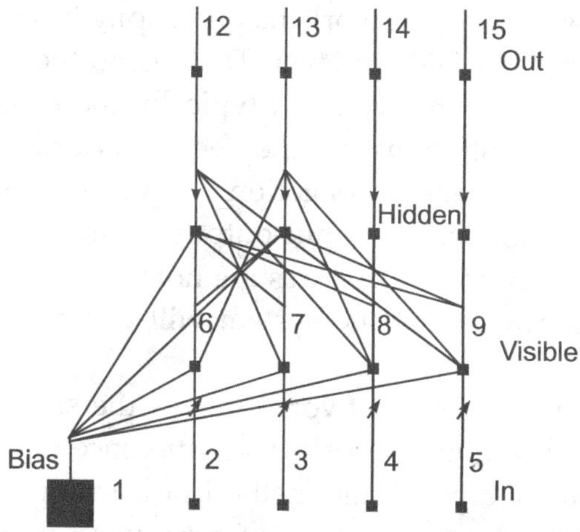

Figure 7.10. An Example Recirculation Network.

The learning process for this network is similar to the bi-directional associative memory technique. Here, the input data is presented to the visible layer and passed on to the hidden layer. The hidden layer passes the incoming data back to the visible, which in turn passes the results back to the hidden layer and beyond to the output layer. It is the second pass through the hidden layer where learning occurs. In this manner the input data is recalculated through the network architecture.

During training, the output of the hidden layer at the first pass is the encoded version of the input vector. The output of the visible layer on the next pass is the reconstruction of the original input vector from the encoded vector on the hidden layer. The aim of the learning is to reduce the error between the reconstructed vector and the input vector. This error is also reflected in the difference between the outputs of the hidden layer at the first and final passes since a good reconstruction will mean that the same values are passed to the hidden layer both times around. Learning seeks to reduce the reconstruction error at the hidden layer also.

In most applications of the network, an input data signal is smoothed by compressing then reconstructing the input vector on the output layer. The network acts as a low band pass filter whose transition point is controlled by the number of hidden nodes.

7.7 Summary

a. Feed forward network is used more than all other combined. It is used in many different types of applications. This architecture has spawned a large class of network types with many different topologies and training methods. Its greatest strength is in non-linear solutions to ill-defined problems.

b. Back-propagation network has an input layer, an output layer, and at least one hidden layer. There is no theoretical limit on the number of hidden layers but typically there is just one or two.

c. There are limitations to the feed forward, back-propagation architecture. Back-propagation requires lots of supervised training, with lots of input-output examples. Additionally, the internal mapping procedures are not well understood, and there is no guarantee that the system will converge to an acceptable solution.

d. The delta bar delta network utilizes the same architecture as a back-propagation network. The difference of delta bar delta lies in its unique algorithmic method of learning.

e. A hybrid network uses a self-organizing map to conceptually separate the data before that data is used in the normal back-propagation manner. This map helps to visualize topologies and hierarchical structures of higher-order input spaces before they are entered into the feed forward, back-propagation network.

f. Learning Vector Quantization classifies its input data into groupings that it determines. Essentially, it maps an n-dimensional space into an m-dimensional space. That is it takes n inputs and produces m outputs.

g. The probabilistic neural network uses a supervised training set to develop distribution functions within a pattern layer. These functions, in the recall mode, are used to estimate the likelihood of an input feature vector being part of a learned category, or class.

h. The Boltzmann machine is similar in function and operation to the Hopfield network with the addition of using a simulated annealing technique when determining the original pattern. The Boltzmann machine incorporates the concept of simulated annealing to search the pattern layer's state space for a global minimum. Because of this, the machine will gravitate to an improved set of values over time as data iterates through the system.

7.8 Review Questions

1. Discuss Feed forward, Back-Propagation and How They Work .
2. Discuss the Delta Bar Delta and Extended Delta Bar Delta.
3. Discuss the Higher-order Neural Network or Functional-link Network.
4. Discuss the Self-Organizing Map into Back-Propagation.
5. Discuss the Learning Vector Quantization
6. Discuss the Counter-propagation Network.
7. Discuss the Networks for Data Association.
8. Discuss the Networks for Data Filtering & Recirculation.

Chapter No. 8

How Artificial Neural Networks Are Being Used

Artificial neural networks are undergoing the change that occurs when a concept leaves the academic environment and is thrown into the harsher world of users who simply want to get a job done. Many of the networks now being designed are statistically quite accurate but they still leave a bad taste with users who expect computers to solve their problems absolutely. These networks might be 85% to 90% accurate. Unfortunately, few applications tolerate that level of error. While researchers continue to work on improving the accuracy of their "creations," some explorers are finding uses for the current technology.

In reviewing this state of the art, it is hard not to be overcome by the bright promises or tainted by the unachieved realities. Currently, neural networks are not the user interface, which translates spoken works into instructions for a machine, but some day they will. Someday, VCRs, home security systems, CD players, and word processors will simply be activated by voice. Touch screen and voice editing will replace the word processors of today while bringing spreadsheets and data bases to a level of usability pleasing to most everyone. But for now, neural networks are simply entering the marketplace in niches where their statistical accuracy is valuable as they await what will surely come.

Many of these niches indeed involve applications where answers are nebulous. Loan approval is one. Financial institutions make more money by having the lowest bad loan rate they can achieve. Systems that are "90% accurate" might be an improvement over the current selection process. Indeed, some banks have proven that the failure rate on loans approved by neural networks is lower than those approved by some of there best traditional methods. Also, some credit card companies are using neural networks in their application screening process.

This newest method of seeking the future by analyzing past experiences has generated its own unique problems. One of those problems is to provide a reason behind the computer-generated answer, say as to why a particular loan application was denied. As mentioned throughout this report, the inner workings of neural networks are "black boxes." Some people have even called the use of neural networks "voodoo engineering." To explain how a network learned and why it recommends a particular decision has been difficult. To facilitate this process of justification, several neural network tool makers have provided programs which explain which input through which node dominates the decision making process. From that information, experts in the application should be able to infer the reason that a particular piece of data is important.

Besides this filling of niches, neural network work is progressing in other more promising application areas. The next section of this report goes through some of these areas and briefly details the current work. This is done to help stimulate within the reader the various possibilities where neural networks might offer solutions, possibilities such as language processing, character recognition, image compression, pattern recognition among others.

8.1 Language Processing

Language processing encompasses a wide variety of applications. These applications include text-to-speech conversion, auditory input for machines, automatic language translation, secure voice keyed locks, automatic transcription, aids for the deaf, aids for the physically disabled, which respond to voice commands, and natural language processing.

Many companies and universities are researching how a computer, via ANNs, could be programmed to respond to spoken commands. The potential economic rewards are a proverbial gold mine. If this capability could be shrunk to a chip, that chip could become part of almost any electronic device sold today. Literally hundreds of millions of these chips could be sold.

This magic-like capability needs to be able to understand the 50,000 most commonly spoken words. Currently, according to the academic journals, most of the hearing-capable neural networks are trained to only one talker. These one-talker, isolated-word recognizers can recognize a few hundred words. Within the context of speech, with pauses between each word, they can recognize up to 20,000 words.

Some researchers are touting even greater capabilities, but due to the potential reward the true progress, and methods involved, are being closely held. The most highly touted, and demonstrated, speech-parsing system comes from the Apple Corporation. This network, according to an April 1992 Wall Street Journal article, can recognize most any person's speech through a limited vocabulary. This works continues in Corporate America (particularly venture capital land), in the universities, and in Japan.

8.2 Character Recognition

Character recognition is another area in which neural networks are providing solutions. Some of these solutions are beyond simply academic curiosities. HNC Inc., according to a HNC spokesman, markets a neural network based product that can recognize hand printed characters through a scanner. This product can take cards, like a credit card application form, and put those recognized characters into a database. This product has been out for two and a half years. It is 98% to 99% accurate for numbers, a little less for alphabetical characters. Currently, the system is built to highlight characters below a certain percent probability of being right so that a user can manually fill in what the computer could not. This product is in use by banks, financial institutions, and credit card companies.

Odin Corp., according to a press release in the November 4, 1991 Electronic Engineering Times, has also proved capable of recognizing characters, including cursive. This capability utilizes Odin's propriatory Quantum Neural Network software package called, QNspec. It has proven uncannily successful in analyzing reasonably good handwriting. It actually benefits from the cursive stroking.

The largest amount of research in the field of character recognition is aimed at scanning oriental characters into a computer. Currently, these characters require four or five keystrokes each. This complicated process elongates the task of keying a page of text into hours of drudgery. Several vendors are saying they are close to commercial products that can scan pages.

8.3 Image (data) Compression

A number of studies have been done proving that neural networks can do real-time compression and decompression of data. These networks are auto associative in that they can reduce eight bits of data to three and then reverse that process upon restructuring to eight bits again. However, they are not loss less. Because of this losing of bits they do not favorably compete with more traditional methods.

8.4 Pattern Recognition

Recently, a number of pattern recognition applications have been written about in the general press. The Wall Street Journal has featured a system that can detect bombs in luggage at airports by identifying, from small variances, patterns from within specialized sensor's outputs. Another article reported on how a physician had trained a back-propagation neural network on data collected in emergency rooms from people who felt that they were experiencing a heart attack to provide a probability of a real heart attack versus a false alarm. His system is touted as being a very good discriminator in an arena where priority decisions have to be made all the time.

Another application involves the grading of rare coins. Digitized images from an electronic camera are fed into a neural network. These images include several angles of the front and back. These images are then compared against known patterns, which represent the various grades for a coin. This system has enabled a quick evaluation for about $15 as opposed to the standard three-person evaluation, which costs $200. The results have shown that the neural network recommendations are as accurate as the people-intensive grading method.

Yet, by far the biggest use of neural networks as a recognizer of patterns is within the field known as quality control. A number of automated quality applications are now in use. These applications are designed to find that one in a hundred or one in a thousand part that is defective. Human inspectors become fatigued or distracted. Systems now evaluate solder joints, welds, cuttings, and glue applications. One car manufacturer is now even prototyping a system that evaluates the color of paints. This system digitizes pictures of new batches of paint to determine if they are the right shades.

Another major area where neural networks are being built into pattern recognition systems is as processors for sensors. Sensors can provide so much data that the few meaningful pieces of information can become lost. People can lose interest as they stare at screens looking for "the needle in the haystack." Many of these sensor-processing applications exist within the defense industry. These neural network systems have been shown successful at recognizing targets. These sensor processors take data from cameras, sonar systems, seismic recorders, and infrared sensors. That data is then used to identify probable phenomenon.

Another field related to defense sensor processing is the recognition of patterns within the sensor data of the medical industry. A neural network is now being used in the scanning of PAP smears. This network is trying to do a better job at reading the smears than can the average lab technician. Missed diagnoses are a too common problem throughout this industry. In many cases, a professional must perceive patterns from noise, such as identifying a fracture from an X-ray or cancer from a X-ray "shadow." Neural networks promise, particularly when faster hardware becomes available, help in many areas of the medical profession where data is hard to read.

8.5 Signal Processing

Neural networks' promise for signal processing has resulted in a number of experiments in various university labs. Neural networks have proven capable of filtering out noise. Widrow's MADALINE was the first network applied to a real-world problem. It eliminates noise from phone lines.

Another application is a system that can detect engine misfire simply from the noise. This system, developed by Odin Corp, works on engines up to 10,000 RPMS. The Odin system satisfies the California Air Resources Board's mandate that by 1994 new automobiles will have to detect misfire in real time. Misfires are suspected of being a leading cause of pollution. The Odin solution requires 3 kbytes of software running on a Motorola 68030 microprocessor.

8.6 Financial

Neural networks are making big inroads into the financial worlds. Banking, credit card companies, and lending institutions deal with decisions that are not clear-cut. They involve learning and statistical trends.

The loan approval process involves filling out forms, which hopefully can enable a loan officer to make a decision. The data from these forms is now being used by neural networks, which have been trained on the data from past decisions. Indeed, to meet government requirements as to why applications are being denied, these packages are providing information on what input, or combination of inputs, weighed heaviest on the decision.

Credit card companies are also using similar back-propagation networks to aid in establishing credit risks and credit limits. In the world of direct marketing, neural networks are being applied to databases so that these phone peddlers can achieve higher ordering rates from those annoying calls that most of us receive at dinner time. (A probably more lucrative business opportunity awaits the person who can devise a system, which will tailor all of the databases in the world so that certain phone numbers are never selected.)

Neural networks are being used in all of the financial markets - stock, bonds, international currency, and commodities. Some users are cackling that these systems just make them "see green," money that is. Indeed, neural networks are reported to be highly successful in the Japanese financial markets. Daiichi Kangyo Bank has reported that for government bond transactions, neural networks have boosted their hit rate from 60% to 75%. Daiwa research Institute has reported a neural net system, which has scored 20% better than the Nikkei average. Daiwa Securities' stock prediction system has boosted the companies hit rate from 70% to 80%.

8.7 Servo Control

Controlling complicated systems is one of the more promising areas of neural networks. Most conventional control systems model the operation of all the system's processes with one set of formulas. To customize a system for a specific process, those formulas must be manually tuned. It is an intensive process, which involves the tweaking of parameters until a combination is found that produces the desired results. Neural networks offer two advantages. First, the statistical model of neural networks is more complex that a simple set of formulas, enabling it to handle a wider variety of operating conditions without having to be retuned. Second, because neural networks learn on their own, they don't require control system's experts, just simply enough historical data so that they can adequately train themselves.

Within the oil industry a neural network has been applied to the refinery process. The network controls the flow of materials and is touted to do that in a more vigilant fashion than distractible humans.

NASA is working on a system to control the shuttle during in-flight maneuvers. This system is known as Martingale's Parametric Avalanche (a spatio-temporal pattern recognition network as explained in section 5.3.5). Another prototype application is known as ALVINN, for Autonomous Land Vehicle in a Neural Network. This project has mounted a camera and a laser range finder on the roof of a vehicle, which is being taught to stay in the middle of a winding road.

British Columbia Hydroelectric funded a prototype network to control operations of a power-distribution substation that was so successful at optimizing four large synchronous condensers that it refused to let its supplier, Neural Systems, take it out.

8.8 How to Determine if an Application is a Neural Network Candidate

As seen by the sections above, neural networks are being successfully applied in a number of areas. Each of these applications can be grouped into two broad categories. These categories offer a test for anyone who is considering using neural networks. Basically, a potential application should be examined for the following two criteria:

1. Can a neural network replace existing technologies in an area where small improvements in performance can result in a major economic impact? Examples of applications which meet this criteria are:
   - o Loan approvals
   - o Credit card approvals
   - o Financial market predictions
   - o Potential customer analysis for the creation of mailing lists
2. Can a neural network be used in an area where current technologies have proven inadequate to making a system viable? Examples of applications which meet this criteria are:
   - o Speech recognition
   - o Text recognition
   - o Target analysis

The most successful applications have been focused on a single problem in a high value, high volume, or a strategically important application.

The easiest implementation of neural networks occur in solutions where they can be made to be "plug compatible" with existing systems. To simply replace an existing element of a system with a neural network eases an installation. It also increases the likelihood of success. These "plug compatible" solutions might be at the front end of many systems where neural networks can recognize patterns and classify data.

8.9 Summary

- Character recognition is another area in which neural networks are providing solutions. Some of these solutions are beyond simply academic curiosities. HNC Inc., according to a HNC spokesman, markets a neural network based product that can recognize hand printed characters through a scanner.

- Language processing encompasses a wide variety of applications. These applications include text-to-speech conversion, auditory input for machines, automatic language translation, secure voice keyed locks, automatic transcription, aids for the deaf, aids for the physically disabled, which respond to voice commands, and natural language processing.
- Character recognition is another area in which neural networks are providing solutions. Some of these solutions are beyond simply academic curiosities. HNC Inc., according to a HNC spokesman, markets a neural network based product that can recognize hand printed characters through a scanner.
- The largest amount of research in the field of character recognition is aimed at scanning oriental characters into a computer. Currently, these characters require four or five keystrokes each. This complicated process elongates the task of keying a page of text into hours of drudgery. Several vendors are saying they are close to commercial products that can scan pages.
- Another major area where neural networks are being built into pattern recognition systems is as processors for sensors. Sensors can provide so much data that the few meaningful pieces of information can become lost. People can lose interest as they stare at screens looking for "the needle in the haystack." Many of these sensor-processing applications exist within the defense industry.
- Another field related to defense sensor processing is the recognition of patterns within the sensor data of the medical industry. A neural network is now being used in the scanning of PAP smears. This network is trying to do a better job at reading the smears than can the average lab technician.

8.10 Review Questions

1. Discuss the Hardware Accelerators.
2. Discuss the Language Processing.
3. Discuss the Character Recognition.
4. Explain the Image (data) Compression.
5. Explain the Pattern Recognition.
6. Discuss the Signal Processing.
7. Discuss the Financial & Servo Control.
8. How to Determine if an Application is a Neural Network Candidate.

Chapter No. 9
Emerging Technologies

If the 21st Century is to be the age of intelligent machines, then artificial neural networks will become an integral part of life. In order that software engineers can lead us to this "promised life" they must begin by utilizing the emerging technology of Neural Networks. To do that they must optimize their time by using already implemented hardware and commercial software packages while anticipating what is still to come. To accomplish this understanding, this section is broken into two pieces - what currently exists and what implementers think the next developments will be.

9.1 What Currently Exists

Currently, a number of vendors exist within the marketplace. These vendors are each seeking a share of the neural network business. Some of them do that by hitching their wagon to other packages within the industry. Neural network products exist which are simply add-ons to the popular databases and spreadsheets. Other products are geared for particular operating systems on particular machines. There are vendors of neural network development tools for most machines. The most popular tools work on either Apple's Macintosh or the IBM PC standard.

Some of these packages are geared toward particular applications such as image processing. Others are general but lack good data routing capabilities. Each of these companies are identifying their weaknesses and are working on them. It is an exciting time for them, with both the rewards and risks high.

In choosing a development tool software engineer needs to beware of this emerging field. Most products are not evolved into the user-friendly routines that draw raves. This is a young field. Its very volatility has created a confusing set of offerings, and features within offerings, which will ultimately be relegated to the trash.

9.1.1 Development Systems.

Good development systems allow a user to prototype a network, train it, tweak it, and use it. These systems run on the standard range of computers. These packages usually don't run on specialized hardware, although some vendors have packaged fast RISC processors into special neural processing boards. Usually, these packages are simply tools, which create networks that prove concepts but may be way too slow to run.

9.1.2 Hardware Accelerators.

The key to the continued evolution of neural networking lies in the hardware. Traditional hardware does not enable the massive parallelism that is required by neural networks. There are several approaches that are being worked on. One is to develop a processor which is specifically tailored to performing the tasks of individual artificial neurons. Another approach is to package fast processors, primarily Risks, onto a hardware accelerator. These processors can be packed many to a board to facilitate the parallel nature of neural networks. Other accelerator boards simply provide more horsepower for sequential processing.

Accelerator board products are being developed both independently and by the makers of neural network development systems. Each has specific characteristics that lend themselves to particular resolutions.

9.1.3 Dedicated Neural Processors.

Dedicated neural processors are processors with specific capabilities that enable their use in neural networks. Several of the large chip manufacturers have developed neural processors. Some of these processors were created specifically for the development system vendors. Some of these chips package a number of simplistic neurons onto one chip. Others incorporate proprietary concepts, such as creating a specific type of fuzzy neuron. These chips come in many broad technologies - analog, digital, hybrid, and optical. There is no clear winner to date.

9.2 What the Next Developments Will Be?

The vendors within the industry predict that migration from tools to applications will continue. In particular, the trend is to move toward hybrid systems. These systems will encompass other types of processes, such as fuzzy logic, expert systems, and kinetic algorithms. Indeed, several manufactures are working on "fuzzy neurons."

The greatest interest is on merging fuzzy logic with neural networks. Fuzzy logic incorporates the inexactness of life into mathematics. In life most pieces of data do not exactly fit into certain categories. For instance, a person is not just short or tall. He can be kind of short, pretty tall, a little above average, or very tall. Fuzzy logic takes these real-world variations into account. In potential application of neural networks, in systems, which solve real problems, this fuzziness is a large part of the problem. In automating a car, to stop is not to slam on the brakes; to speed up is not to "burn rubber." To help neural networks accommodate this fuzziness of life, some researchers are developing fuzzy neurons. These neurons do not simply give yes/no answers. They provide a more fuzzy answer.

Systems built with fuzzy neurons may be initialized to what an expert thinks are the rules and the weights for a given application. This merging of expert systems and fuzzy logic with neural networks utilizes the strength of all three disciplines to provide a better system than either can provide themselves. Expert systems have the problem that most experts don't exactly understand all of the nuances of an application and, therefore, are unable to clearly state rules, which define the entire problem to someone else. But the neural network doesn't care that the rules are not exact, for neural networks can then learn, and then correct, the expert's rules. It can add nodes for concepts that the expert might not understand. It can tailor the fuzzy logic, which defines states like tall, short, fast, or slow. It can tweak itself until it can meet the user-identified state of being a workable tool. In short, hybrid systems are the future.

9.3 Summary

In summary, artificial neural networks are one of the promises for the future in computing. They offer an ability to perform tasks outside the scope of traditional processors. They can recognize patterns within vast data sets and then generalize those patterns into recommended courses of action. Neural networks learn, they are not programmed.

Yet, even though they are not traditionally programmed, the designing of neural networks does require a skill. It requires an "art." This art involves the understanding of the various network topologies, current hardware, current software tools, the application to be solved, and a strategy to acquire the necessary data to train the network. This art further involves the selection of learning rules, transfer functions, summation functions, and how to connect the neurons within the network.

Then, the art of neural networking requires a lot of hard work as data is fed into the system, performances are monitored, processes tweaked, connections added, rules modified, and on and on until the network achieves the desired results.

These desired results are statistical in nature. The network is not always right. It is for that reason that neural networks are finding themselves in applications where humans are also unable to always be right. Neural networks can now pick stocks, cull marketing prospects, approve loans, deny credit cards, tweak control systems, grade coins, and inspect work.

Yet, the future holds even more promises. Neural networks need faster hardware. They need to become part of hybrid systems, which also utilize fuzzy logic and expert systems. It is then that these systems will be able to hear speech, read handwriting, and formulate actions. They will be able to become the intelligence behind robots that never tire nor become distracted. It is then that they will become the leading edge in an age of "intelligent" machines.

9.4 Review Questions

1. Discuss the Emerging Technologies
   - o What Currently Exists
     * Development Systems.
     * Hardware Accelerators.
     * Dedicated Neural Processors.
2. What the Next Developments Will Be.
3. Discuss the Networks for Data Filtering & Recirculation.

Chapter No. 10

Software Architecture

In spite of the interest in software architecture as a field of research, there is little agreement among researchers as to what exactly should be included in the definition of architecture. In many cases, this has led to important aspects of architectural design being overlooked by past research. This chapter defines a self-consistent terminology for software architecture based on an examination of existing definitions within the literature and my own insight with respect to network-based application architectures. Each definition, highlighted within a box for ease of reference, is followed by a discussion of how it is derived from, or compares to, related research.

10.1 Run-time Abstraction

Software architecture is an abstraction of the run-time elements of a software system during some phase of its operation. A system may be composed of many levels of abstraction and many phases of operation, each with its own software architecture.

At the heart of software architecture is the principle of abstraction: hiding some of the details of a system through encapsulation in order to better identify and sustain its properties. A complex system will contain many levels of abstraction, each with its own architecture. Architecture represents an abstraction of system behavior at that level, such that architectural elements are delineated by the abstract interfaces they provide to other elements at that level. Within each element may be found another architecture, defining the system of sub-elements that implement the behavior represented by the parent element's abstract interface. This recursion of architectures continues down to the most basic system elements: those that cannot be decomposed into less abstract elements.

In addition to levels of architecture, a software system will often have multiple operational phases, such as start-up, initialization, normal processing, re-initialization, and shutdown. Each operational phase has its own architecture. For example, a configuration file will be treated as a data element during the start-up phase, but won't be considered an architectural element during normal processing, since at that point the information it contained will have already been distributed throughout the system. It may, in fact, have defined the normal processing architecture. An overall description of system architecture must be capable of describing not only the operational behavior of the system's architecture during each phase, but also the architecture of transitions between phases.

Perry and Wolf define processing elements as "transformers of data," while Shaw et al. describe components as "the locus of computation and state." This is further clarified in Shaw and Clements "A component is a unit of software that performs some function at run-time. Examples include programs, objects, processes, and filters." This raises an important distinction between software architecture and what is typically referred to as software structure: the former is an abstraction of the run-time behavior of a software system, whereas the latter is a property of the static software source code. Although there are advantages to having the modular structure of the source code match the decomposition of behavior within a running system, there are also advantages to having independent software components be implemented using parts of the same code (e.g., shared libraries). We separate the view of software architecture from that of the source code in order to focus on the software's run-time characteristics independent of a given component's implementation. Therefore, architectural design and source code structural design, though closely related, are separate design activities. Unfortunately, some descriptions of software architecture fail to make this distinction.

10.2 Elements

Software architecture is defined by a configuration of architectural elements--components, connectors, and data--constrained in their relationships in order to achieve a desired set of architectural properties.

A comprehensive examination of the scope and intellectual basis for software architecture can be found in Perry and Wolf. They present a model that defines software architecture as a set of architectural elements that have a particular form, explicated by a set of rationale. Architectural elements include processing, data, and connecting elements. Form is defined by the properties of the elements and the relationships among the elements -- that is, the constraints on the elements. The rationale provides the underlying basis for the architecture by capturing the motivation for the choice of architectural style, the choice of elements, and the form.

My definitions for software architecture are an elaborated version of those within the Perry and Wolf model, except that I exclude rationale. Although rationale is an important aspect of software architecture research and of architectural description in particular, including it within the definition of software architecture would imply that design documentation is part of the run-time system. The presence or absence of rationale can influence the evolution of architecture, but, once constituted, the architecture is independent of its reasons for being. Reflective systems can use the characteristics of past performance to change future behavior, but in doing so they are replacing one lower-level architecture with another lower-level architecture, rather than encompassing rationale within those architectures.

As an illustration, consider what happens to a building if its blueprints and design plans are burned. Does the building immediately collapse? No, since the properties by which the walls sustain the weight of the roof remain intact. Architecture has, by design, a set of properties that allow it to meet or exceed the system requirements. Ignorance of those properties may lead to later changes, which violate the architecture, just as the replacement of a load-bearing wall with a large window frame may violate the structural stability of a building. Thus, instead of rationale, our definition of software architecture includes architectural properties. Rationale explicates those properties, and lack of rationale may result in gradual decay or degradation of the architecture over time, but the rationale itself is not part of the architecture.

A key feature of the model in Perry and Wolf is the distinction of the various element types. Processing elements are those that perform transformations on data, data elements are those that contain the information that is used and transformed, and connecting elements are the glue that holds the different pieces of the architecture together. I use the more prevalent terms of components and connectors to refer to processing and connecting elements, respectively.

Garlan and Shaw describe architecture of a system as a collection of computational components together with a description of the interactions between these components--the connectors. This model is expanded upon in Shaw et al. The architecture of a software system defines that system in terms of components and of interactions among those components. In addition to specifying the structure and topology of the system, the architecture shows the intended correspondence between the system requirements and elements of the constructed system. Further elaboration of this definition can be found in Shaw and Garlan.

What is surprising about the Shaw et al. model is that, rather than defining the software's architecture as existing within the software, it is defining a description of the software's architecture as if that were the architecture. In the process, software architecture as a whole is reduced to what is commonly found in most informal architecture diagrams: boxes (components) and lines (connectors). Data elements, along with many of the dynamic aspects of real software architectures, are ignored. Such a model is incapable of adequately describing network-based software architectures, since the nature, location, and movement of data elements within the system is often the single most significant determinant of system behavior.

10.2.1 Components

A component is an abstract unit of software instructions and internal state that provides a transformation of data via its interface. Components are the most easily recognized aspect of software architecture. Perry and Wolf's processing elements are defined as those components that supply the transformation on the data elements. Garlan and Shaw describe components simply as the elements that perform computation. Our definition attempts to be more precise in making the distinction between components and the software within connectors.

A component is an abstract unit of software instructions and internal state that provides a transformation of data via its interface. Example transformations include loading into memory from secondary storage, performing some calculation, translating to a different format, encapsulation with other data, etc. The behavior of each component is part of the architecture insofar as that behavior can be observed or discerned from the point of view of another component In other words, a component is defined by its interface and the services it provides to other components, rather than by its implementation behind the interface. Parnas would define this as the set of assumptions that other architectural elements can make about the component.

10.2.2 Connectors

A connector is an abstract mechanism that mediates communication, coordination, or cooperation among components. Perry and Wolf describe connecting elements vaguely as the glue that holds the various pieces of the architecture together. A more precise definition is provided by Shaw and Clements, A connector is an abstract mechanism that mediates communication, coordination, or cooperation among components.

Examples include shared representations, remote procedure calls, message-passing protocols, and data streams.

Perhaps the best way to think about connectors is to contrast them with components. Connectors enable communication between components by transferring data elements from one interface to another without changing the data. Internally, a connector may consist of a subsystem of components that transform the data for transfer, perform the transfer, and then reverse the transformation for delivery. However, the external behavioral abstraction captured by the architecture ignores those details. In contrast, a component may, but not always will, transform data from the external perspective.

10.2.3 Data

A data is an element of information that is transferred from a component, or received by a component, via a connector. As noted above, the presence of data elements is the most significant distinction between the model of software architecture defined by Perry and Wolf and the model used by much of the research labeled software architecture Boasson criticizes current software architecture research for its emphasis on component structures and architecture development tools, suggesting that more focus should be placed on data-centric architectural modeling.

A datum is an element of information that is transferred from a component, or received by a component, via a connector. Examples include byte-sequences, messages, marshaled parameters, and serialized objects, but do not include information that is permanently resident or hidden within a component. From the architectural perspective, a "file" is a transformation that a file system component might make from a "file name" datum received on its interface to a sequence of bytes recorded within an internally hidden storage system. Components can also generate data, as in the case of a software encapsulation of a clock or sensor.

The nature of the data elements within network-based application architecture will often determine whether or not a given architectural style is appropriate. This is particularly evident in the comparison of mobile code design paradigms, where the choice must be made between interacting with a component directly or transforming the component into a data element, transferring it across a network, and then transforming it back to a component that can be interacted with locally. It is impossible to evaluate such architecture without considering data elements at the architectural level.

10.3 Configurations

A configuration is the structure of architectural relationships among components, connectors, and data during a period of system run-time. Abowd et al. define architectural description as supporting the description of systems in terms of three basic syntactic classes: components, which are the locus of computation; connectors, which define the interactions between components; and configurations, which are collections of interacting components and connectors. Various style-specific concrete notations may be used to represent these visually, facilitate the description of legal computations and interactions, and constrain the set of desirable systems.

Strictly speaking, one might think of a configuration as being equivalent to a set of specific constraints on component interaction. For example, Perry and Wolf include topology in their definition of architectural form relationships. However, separating the active topology from more general constraints allows an architect to more easily distinguish the active configuration from the potential domain of all legitimate configurations.

10.4 Properties

The set of architectural properties of software architecture includes all properties that derive from the selection and arrangement of components, connectors, and data within the system. Examples include both the functional properties achieved by the system and non-functional properties, such as relative ease of evolution, reusability of components, efficiency, and dynamic extensibility, often referred to as quality attributes.

Properties are induced by the set of constraints within architecture. Constraints are often motivated by the application of a software engineering principle to an aspect of the architectural elements. For example, the uniform pipe-and-filter style obtains the qualities of reusability of components and configurability of the application by applying generality to its component interfaces -- constraining the components to a single interface type. Hence, the architectural constraint is "uniform component interface," motivated by the generality principle, in order to obtain two desirable qualities that will become the architectural properties of reusable and configurable components when that style is instantiated within architecture.

The goal of architectural design is to create architecture with a set of architectural properties that form a superset of the system requirements. The relative importance of the various architectural properties depends on the nature of the intended system..

10.5 Styles

An architectural style is a coordinated set of architectural constraints that restricts the roles/features of architectural elements and the allowed relationships among those elements within any architecture that conforms to that style.

Since architecture embodies both functional and non-functional properties, it can be difficult to directly compare architectures for different types of systems, or for even the same type of system set in different environments. Styles are a mechanism for categorizing architectures and for defining their common characteristics each style provides an abstraction for the interactions of components, capturing the essence of a pattern of interaction by ignoring the incidental details of the rest of the architecture. Perry and Wolf define architectural style as an abstraction of element types and formal aspects from various specific architectures, perhaps concentrating on only certain aspects of architecture. An architectural style encapsulates important decisions about the architectural elements and emphasizes important constraints on the elements and their relationships. This definition allows for styles that focus only on the connectors of an architecture, or on specific aspects of the component interfaces.

In contrast, Garlan and Shaw, Garlan et al., and Shaw and Clements all define style in terms of a pattern of interactions among typed components. Specifically, an architectural style determines the vocabulary of components and connectors that can be used in instances of that style, together with a set of constraints on how they can be combined This restricted view of architectural styles is a direct result of their definition of software architecture -- thinking of architecture as a formal description, rather than as a running system, leads to abstractions based only in the shared patterns of box and line diagrams. Abowd et al. go further and define this explicitly as viewing the collection of conventions that are used to interpret a class of architectural descriptions as defining an architectural style.

New architectures can be defined as instances of specific styles. Since architectural styles may address different aspects of software architecture, a given architecture may be composed of multiple styles. Likewise, combining multiple basic styles into a single coordinated style can form a hybrid style.

Some architectural styles are often portrayed as "silver bullet" solutions for all forms of software. However, a good designer should select a style that matches the needs of the particular problem being solved. Choosing the right architectural style for a network-based application requires an understanding of the problem domain and thereby the communication needs of the application, an awareness of the variety of architectural styles and the particular concerns they address, and the ability to anticipate the sensitivity of each interaction style to the characteristics of network-based communication.

Unfortunately, using the term style to refer to a coordinated set of constraints often leads to confusion. This usage differs substantially from the etymology of style, which would emphasize personalization of the design process. Loerke devotes a chapter to denigrating the notion that personal stylistic concerns have any place in the work of a professional architect. Instead, he describes styles as the critics' view of past architecture, where the available choice of materials, the community culture, or the ego of the local ruler was responsible for the architectural style, not the designer. In other words, Loerke views the real source of style in traditional building architecture to be the set of constraints applied to the design, and attaining or copying a specific style should be the least of the designer's goals. Since referring to a named set of constraints as a style makes it easier to communicate the characteristics of common constraints, we use architectural styles as a method of abstraction, rather than as an indicator of personalized design.

10.6 Patterns and Pattern Languages

In parallel with the software engineering research in architectural styles, the object-oriented programming community has been exploring the use of design patterns and pattern languages to describe recurring abstractions in object-based software development. A design pattern is defined as an important and recurring system construct. A pattern language is a system of patterns organized in a structure that guides the patterns' application. Both concepts are based on the writings of Alexander et al. with regard to building architecture.

The design space of patterns includes implementation concerns specific to the techniques of object-oriented programming, such as class inheritance and interface composition, as well as the higher-level design issues addressed by architectural styles. In some cases, architectural style descriptions have been recast as architectural patterns. However, a primary benefit of patterns is that they can describe relatively complex protocols of interactions between objects as a single abstraction thus including both constraints on behavior and specifics of the implementation. In general, a pattern, or pattern language in the case of multiple integrated patterns, can be thought of as a recipe for implementing a desired set of interactions among objects. In other words, a pattern defines a process for solving a problem by following a path of design and implementation choices.

Like software architectural styles, the software patterns research has deviated somewhat from its origin in building architecture. Indeed, Alexander's notion of patterns centers not on recurring arrangements of architectural elements, but rather on the recurring pattern of events--human activity and emotion--that take place within a space, with the understanding that a pattern of events cannot be separated from the space where it occurs Alexander's design philosophy is to identify patterns of life that are common to the target culture and determine what architectural constraints are needed to differentiate a given space such that it enables the desired patterns to occur naturally. Such patterns exist at multiple levels of abstraction and at all scales.

As an element in the world, each pattern is a relationship between a certain contexts, a certain system of forces, which occurs repeatedly in that context, and a certain spatial configuration, which allows these forces to resolve themselves. As an element of language, a pattern is an instruction, which shows how this spatial configuration can be used, over and over again, to resolve the given system of forces, wherever the context makes it relevant.

The pattern is, in short, at the same time a thing, which happens in the world, and the rule which tells us how to create that thing, and when we must create it. It is both a process and a thing; both a description of a thing which is alive, and a description of the process which will generate that thing.

In many ways, Alexander's patterns have more in common with software architectural styles than the design patterns of OOPL research. An architectural style, as a coordinated set of constraints, is applied to a design space in order to induce the architectural properties that are desired of the system. By applying a style, an architect is differentiating the software design space in the hope that the result will better match the forces inherent in the application, thus leading to system behavior that enhances the natural pattern rather than conflicting with it.

10.7 Views

In addition to the much architecture within a system, and the many architectural styles from which the architectures are composed, it is also possible to view architecture from many different perspectives. Perry and Wolf describe three important views in software architecture: processing, data, and connection views. A process view emphasizes the data flow through the components and some aspects of the connections among the components with respect to the data. A data view emphasizes the processing flow, with less emphasis on the connectors. A connection view emphasizes the relationship between components and the state of communication.

Multiple architectural views are common within case studies of specific architectures. One architectural design methodology, the 4+1 View Model, organizes the description of a software architecture using five concurrent views, each of which addresses a specific set of concerns.

10.8 Related Work

I include here only those areas of research that define software architecture or describe software architectural styles. Other areas for software architecture research include architectural analysis techniques, architecture recovery and re-engineering, tools and environments for architectural design, architecture refinement from specification to implementation, and case studies of deployed software architectures.

10.8.1 Design Methodologies

Most early research on software architecture was concentrated on design methodologies. For example, object-oriented design advocates a way to structure problems that leads naturally to an object-based architecture (or, more accurately, does not lead naturally to any other form of architecture). One of the first design methodologies to emphasize design at the architectural level is Jackson System Development, JSD intentionally structures the analysis of a problem so that it leads to a style of architecture that combines pipe-and-filter (data flow) and process control constraints. These design methodologies tend to produce only one style of architecture.

There has been some initial work investigating methodologies for the analysis and development of architectures. Kazman et al. have described design methods for eliciting the architectural aspects of a design through scenario-based analysis with SAAM and architectural trade-off analysis via ATAM. Shaw compares a variety of box-and-arrow designs for an automobile cruise control system, each done using a different design methodology and encompassing several architectural styles.

10.8.2 Handbooks for Design, Design Patterns, and Pattern Languages

Shaw advocates the development of architectural handbooks along the same lines as traditional engineering disciplines. The object-oriented programming community has taken the lead in producing catalogs of design patterns, as exemplified by the "Gang of Four" book and the essays edited by Coplien and Schmidt.

Software design patterns tend to be more problem-oriented than architectural styles. Shaw presents eight example architectural patterns based on the architectural styles described in including information on the kinds of problems best suited to each architecture. Buschmann et al. provide a comprehensive examination of the architectural patterns common to object-based development. Both references are purely descriptive and make no attempt to compare or illustrate the differences among architectural patterns.

Tepfenhart and Cusick use a two dimensional map to differentiate among domain taxonomies, domain models, architectural styles, frameworks, kits, design patterns, and applications. In the topology, design patterns are predefined design structures used as building blocks for software architecture, whereas architectural styles are sets of operational characteristics that identify an architectural family independent of application domain. However, they fail to define architecture itself.

10.8.3 Reference Models and Domain-specific Software Architectures (DSSA)

Reference models are developed to provide conceptual frameworks for describing architectures and showing how components are related to each other. The Object Management Architecture (OMA), developed by the OMG as a reference model for brokered distributed object architectures, specifies how objects are defined and created, how client applications invoke objects, and how objects can be shared and reused. The emphasis is on management of distributed objects, rather than efficient application interaction.

Hayes-Roth et al. define domain-specific software architecture (DSSA) as comprising: (a) a reference architecture, which describes a general computational framework for a significant domain of applications, (b) a component library, which contains reusable chunks of domain expertise, and (c) an application configuration method for selecting and configuring components within the architecture to meet particular application requirements. Tracz provides a general overview of DSSA.

DSSA projects have been successful at transferring architectural decisions to running systems by restricting the software development space to a specific architectural style that matches the domain requirements. Examples include ADAGE for avionics, AIS for adaptive intelligent systems, and MetaH for missile guidance, navigation, and control systems. DSSA emphasize reuse of components within a common architectural domain, rather than selecting an architectural style that is specific to each system.

10.8.4 Architecture Description Languages (ADL)

Most of the recent published work regarding software architectures is in the area of architecture description languages (ADL). An ADL is, according to Medvidovic and Taylor a language that provides features for the explicit specification and modeling of a software system's conceptual architecture, including at a minimum: components, component interfaces, connectors, and architectural configurations.

Darwin is a declarative language, which is intended to be a general-purpose notation for specifying the structure of systems composed of diverse components using diverse interaction mechanisms. Darwin's interesting qualities are that it allows the specification of distributed architectures and dynamically composed architectures.

UniCon is a language and associated toolset for composing architecture from a restricted set of component and connector examples. Wright provides a formal basis for specifying the interactions between architectural components by specifying connector types by their interaction protocols.

Like design methodologies, ADLs often introduce specific architectural assumptions that may impact their ability to describe some architectural styles, and may conflict with the assumptions in existing middleware. In some cases, an ADL is designed specifically for a single architectural style, thus improving its capacity for specialized description and analysis at the cost of generality. For example, C2SADEL is an ADL designed specifically to describe architectures developed in the C2 style. In contrast, ACME is an ADL that attempts to be as generic as possible, but with the trade-off being that it doesn't support style-specific analysis and the building of actual applications; rather, its focus is on the interchange among analysis tools.

10.8.5 Formal Architectural Models

Abowd et al. claim that architectural styles can be described formally in terms of a small set of mappings from the syntactic domain of architectural descriptions (box-and-line diagrams) to the semantic domain of architectural meaning. However, this assumes that the architecture is the description, rather than an abstraction of a running system.

Inverardi and Wolf use the Chemical Abstract Machine (CHAM) formalism to model software architecture elements as chemicals whose reactions are controlled by explicitly stated rules. It specifies the behavior of components according to how they transform available data elements and uses composition rules to propagate the individual transformations into an overall system result. While this is an interesting model, it is unclear as to how CHAM could be used to describe any form of architecture whose purpose goes beyond transforming a data stream.

Rapid is a concurrent, event-based simulation language specifically designed for defining and simulating system architectures. The simulator produces a partially ordered set of events that can be analyzed for conformance to the architectural constraints on interconnection. Le Mitayerpresents formalism for the definition of architectures in terms of graphs and graph grammars.

10.9 Summary

This chapter examined the background for software architecture. Introducing and formalizing a consistent set of terminology for software architecture concepts is necessary to avoid the confusion between architecture and architecture description that is common in the literature, particularly since much of the prior research on architecture excludes data as an important architectural element. We concluded with a survey of other research related to software architecture and architectural styles.

The next two chapters continue our discussion of background material by focusing on network-based application architectures and describing how styles can be used to guide their architectural design, followed by a survey of common architectural styles using a classification methodology that highlights the architectural properties induced when the styles are applied to an architecture for network-based hypermedia.

10.10 Review Question

1. Discuss the Software Architecture & Run-time Abstraction.
2. Discuss the Design Methodologies.
3. Discuss the Patterns and Pattern Languages.
4. Explain the Architecture Description Languages (ADL).
5. Explain the Formal Architectural Models.

Chapter No. 11

Network-based Application Architectures

This chapter continues our discussion of background material by focusing on network-based application architectures and describing how styles can be used to guide their architectural design.

11.1 Scope

Architecture is found at multiple levels within software systems. This dissertation examines the highest level of abstraction in software architecture, where the interactions among components are capable of being realized in network communication. We limit our discussion to styles for network-based application architectures in order to reduce the dimensions of variance among the styles studied.

11.1.1 Network-based vs. Distributed

The primary distinction between network-based architectures and software architectures in general is that communication between components is restricted to message passing, or the equivalent of message passing if a more efficient mechanism can be selected at run-time based on the location of components.

Tanenbaum and van Renesse make a distinction between distributed systems and network-based systems: a distributed system is one that looks to its users like an ordinary centralized system, but runs on multiple, independent CPUs. In contrast, network-based systems are those capable of operation across a network, but not necessarily in a fashion that is transparent to the user. In some cases it is desirable for the user to be aware of the difference between an action that requires a network request and one that is satisfiable on their local system, particularly when network usage implies an extra transaction cost. This dissertation covers network-based systems by not limiting the candidate styles to those that preserve transparency for the user.

11.1.2 Application Software vs. Networking Software

Another restriction on the scope of this dissertation is that we limit our discussion to application architectures, excluding the operating system, networking software, and some architectural styles that would only use a network for system support (e.g., process control styles. Applications represent the "business-aware" functionality of a system.

Application software architecture is an abstraction level of an overall system, in which the goals of a user action are representable as functional architectural properties. For example, a hypermedia application must be concerned with the location of information pages, performing requests, and rendering data streams. This is in contrast to a networking abstraction, where the goal is to move bits from one location to another without regard to why those bits are being moved. It is only at the application level that we can evaluate design trade-offs based on the number of interactions per user action, the location of application state, the effective throughput of all data streams (as opposed to the potential throughput of a single data stream), the extent of communication being performed per user action, etc.

11.2 Evaluating the Design of Application Architectures

One of the goals of this dissertation is to provide design guidance for the task of selecting or creating the most appropriate architecture for a given application domain, keeping in mind that an architecture is the realization of an architectural design and not the design itself. Architecture can be evaluated by its run-time characteristics, but we would obviously prefer an evaluation mechanism that could be applied to the candidate architectural designs before having to implement all of them. Unfortunately, architectural designs are notoriously hard to evaluate and compare in an objective manner. Like most artifacts of creative design, architectures are normally presented as a completed work, as if the design simply sprung fully formed from the architect's mind. In order to evaluate an architectural design, we need to examine the design rationale behind the constraints it places on a system, and compare the properties derived from those constraints to the target application's objectives.

The first level of evaluation is set by the application's functional requirements. For example, it makes no sense to evaluate the design of process control architecture against the requirements of a distributed hypermedia system, since the comparison is moot if the architecture would not function. Although this will eliminate some candidates, in most cases there will remain many other architectural designs that are capable of meeting the application's functional needs. The remainder differs by their relative emphasis on the non-functional requirements--the degree to which each architecture would support the various non-functional architectural properties that have been identified as necessary for the system. Since properties are created by the application of architectural constraints, it is possible to evaluate and compare different architectural designs by identifying the constraints within each architecture, evaluating the set of properties induced by each constraint, and comparing the cumulative properties of the design to those properties required of the application.

As described in the previous chapter, an architectural style is a coordinated set of architectural constraints that has been given a name for ease of reference. Each architectural design decision can be seen as an application of a style. Since the addition of a constraint may derive a new style, we can think of the space of all possible architectural styles as a derivation tree, with its root being the null style (empty set of constraints). When their constraints do not conflict, styles can be combined to form hybrid styles, eventually culminating in a hybrid style that represents a complete abstraction of the architectural design. An architectural design can therefore be analyzed by breaking-down its set of constraints into a derivation tree and evaluating the cumulative effect of the constraints represented by that tree. If we understand the properties induced by each basic style, then traversing the derivation tree gives us an understanding of the overall design's architectural properties. The specific needs of an application can then be matched against the properties of the design. Comparison becomes a relatively simple matter of identifying which architectural design satisfies the most desired properties for that application.

Care must be taken to recognize when the effects of one constraint may counteract the benefits of some other constraint. Nevertheless, it is possible for an experienced software architect to build such a derivation tree of architectural constraints for a given application domain, and then use the tree to evaluate many different architectural designs for applications within that domain. Thus, building a derivation tree provides a mechanism for architectural design guidance.

The evaluation of architectural properties within a tree of styles is specific to the needs of a particular application domain because the impact of a given constraint is often dependent on the application characteristics.

For example, the pipe-and-filter style enables several positive architectural properties when used within a system that requires data transformations between components, whereas it would add nothing but overhead to a system that consists only of control messages. Since it is rarely useful to compare architectural designs across different application domains, the simplest means of ensuring consistency is to make the tree domain-specific.

Design evaluation is frequently a question of choosing between trade-offs. Perry and Wolf describe a method of recognizing trade-offs explicitly by placing a numeric weight against each property to indicate its relative importance to the architecture, thus providing a normalized metric for comparing candidate designs. However, in order to be a meaningful metric, each weight would have to be carefully chosen using an objective scale that is consistent across all properties. In practice, no such scale exists. Rather than having the architect fiddle with weight values until the result matches their intuition, I prefer to present all of the information to the architect in a readily viewable form, and let the architect's intuition be guided by the visual pattern.

11.3 Architectural Properties of Key Interest

This section describes the architectural properties used to differentiate and classify architectural styles in this dissertation. It is not intended to be a comprehensive list. I have included only those properties that are clearly influenced by the restricted set of styles surveyed. Additional properties, sometimes referred to as software qualities, are covered by most textbooks on software engineering; Bass et al. examine qualities in regards to software architecture.

11.3.1 Performance

One of the main reasons to focus on styles for network-based applications is because component interactions can be the dominant factor in determining user-perceived performance and network efficiency. Since the architectural style influences the nature of those interactions, selection of an appropriate architectural style can make the difference between success and failure in the deployment of a network-based application.

The performance of a network-based application is bound first by the application requirements, then by the chosen interaction style, followed by the realized architecture, and finally by the implementation of each component. In other words, software cannot avoid the basic cost of achieving the application needs; e.g., if the application requires that data be located on system A and processed on system B, then the software cannot avoid moving that data from A to B. Likewise, an architecture cannot be any more efficient than its interaction style allows; e.g., the cost of multiple interactions to move the data from A to B cannot be any less than that of a single interaction from A to B. Finally, regardless of the quality of an architecture, no interaction can take place faster than a component implementation can produce data and its recipient can consume data.

11.3.1.1 Network Performance

Network performance measures are used to describe some attributes of communication. Throughput is the rate at which information, including both application data and communication overhead, is transferred between components. Overhead can be separated into initial setup overhead and per-interaction overhead, a distinction that is useful for identifying connectors that can share setup overhead across multiple interactions (amortization). Bandwidth is a measure of the maximum available throughput over a given network link. Usable bandwidth refers to that portion of bandwidth, which is actually available to the application.

Styles impact network performance by their influence on the number of interactions per user action and the granularity of data elements. A style that encourages small, strongly typed interactions will be efficient in an application involving small data transfers among known components, but will cause excessive overhead within applications that involve large data transfers or negotiated interfaces. Likewise, a style that involves the coordination of multiple components arranged to filter a large data stream will be out of place in an application that primarily requires small control messages.

11.3.1.2 User-perceived Performance

User-perceived performance differs from network performance in that the performance of an action is measured in terms of its impact on the user in front of an application rather than the rate at which the network moves information. The primary measures for user-perceived performance are latency and completion time.

Latency is the time period between initial stimulus and the first indication of a response. Latency occurs at several points in the processing of a network-based application action: 1) the time needed for the application to recognize the event that initiated the action; 2) the time required to setup the interactions between components; 3) the time required to transmit each interaction to the components; 4) the time required to process each interaction on those components; and, 5) the time required to complete sufficient transfer and processing of the result of the interactions before the application is able to begin rendering a usable result. It is important to note that, although only (3) and (5) represent actual network communication; all five points can be impacted by the architectural style. Furthermore, multiple component interactions per user action are additive to latency unless they take place in parallel.

Completion is the amount of time taken to complete an application action. Completion time is dependent upon all of the aforementioned measures. The difference between an action's completion time and its latency represents the degree to which the application is incrementally processing the data being received. For example, a Web browser that can render a large image while it is being received provides significantly better user-perceived performance than one that waits until the entire image is completely received prior to rendering, even though both experience the same network performance.

It is important to note that design considerations for optimizing latency will often have the side-effect of degrading completion time, and vice versa. For example, compression of a data stream can produce a more efficient encoding if the algorithm samples a significant portion of the data before producing the encoded transformation, resulting in a shorter completion time to transfer the encoded data across the network. However, if this compression is being performed on-the-fly in response to a user action, then buffering a large sample before transfer may produce an unacceptable latency. Balancing these trade-offs can be difficult, particularly when it is unknown whether the recipient cares more about latency (e.g., Web browsers) or completion (e.g., Web spiders).

11.3.1.3 Network Efficiency

An interesting observation about network-based applications is that the best application performance is obtained by not using the network. This essentially means that the most efficient architectural styles for a network-based application are those that can effectively minimize use of the network when it is possible to do so, through reuse of prior interactions (caching), reduction of the frequency of network interactions in relation to user actions (replicated data and disconnected operation), or by removing the need for some interactions by moving the processing of data closer to the source of the data (mobile code).

The impact of the various performance issues is often related to the scope of distribution for the application. The benefits of a style under local conditions may become drawbacks when faced with global conditions.

Thus, the properties of a style must be framed in relation to the interaction distance: within a single process, across processes on a single host, inside a local-area network (LAN), or spread across a wide-area network (WAN). Additional concerns become evident when interactions across a WAN, where a single organization is involved, are compared to interactions across the Internet, involving multiple trust boundaries.

11.3.2 Scalability

Scalability refers to the ability of the architecture to support large numbers of components, or interactions among components, within an active configuration. Scalability can be improved by simplifying components, by distributing services across many components (decentralizing the interactions), and by controlling interactions and configurations as a result of monitoring. Styles influence these factors by determining the location of application state, the extent of distribution, and the coupling between components.

Scalability is also impacted by the frequency of interactions, whether the load on a component is distributed evenly over time or occurs in peaks, whether an interaction requires guaranteed delivery or a best-effort, whether a request involves synchronous or asynchronous handling, and whether the environment is controlled or anarchic (i.e., can you trust the other components?).

11.3.3 Simplicity

The primary means by which architectural styles induce simplicity is by applying the principle of separation of concerns to the allocation of functionality within components. If functionality can be allocated such that the individual components are substantially less complex, then they will be easier to understand and implement. Likewise, such separation eases the task of reasoning about the overall architecture. I have chosen to lump the qualities of complexity, understandability, and verifiability under the general property of simplicity, since they go hand-in-hand for a network-based system.

Applying the principle of generality to architectural elements also improves simplicity, since it decreases variation within architecture. Generality of connectors leads to middleware.

11.3.4 Modifiability

Modifiability is about the ease with which a change can be made to application architecture. Modifiability can be further broken down into evolvability, extensibility, customizability, configurability, and reusability, as described below. A particular concern of network-based systems is dynamic modifiability, where the modification is made to a deployed application without stopping and restarting the entire system.

Even if it were possible to build a software system that perfectly matches the requirements of its users, those requirements will change over time just as society changes over time. Because the components participating in a network-based application may be distributed across multiple organizational boundaries, the system must be prepared for gradual and fragmented change, where old and new implementations coexist, without preventing the new implementations from making use of their extended capabilities.

11.3.4.1 Evolvability

Evolvability represents the degree to which a component implementation can be changed without negatively impacting other components. Static evolution of components generally depends on how well the architectural abstraction is enforced by the implementation, and thus is not something unique to any particular architectural style. Dynamic evolution, however, can be influenced by the style if it includes constraints on the maintenance and location of application state. The same techniques used to recover from partial failure conditions in a distributed system can be used to support dynamic evolution.

11.3.4.2 Extensibility

Extensibility is defined as the ability to add functionality to a system. Dynamic extensibility implies that functionality can be added to a deployed system without impacting the rest of the system. Extensibility is induced within an architectural style by reducing the coupling between components, as exemplified by event-based integration.

11.3.4.3 Customizability

Customizability refers to the ability to temporarily specialize the behavior of an architectural element, such that it can then perform an unusual service. A component is customizable if one client of that component's services can extend it without adversely impacting other clients of that component. Styles that support customization may also improve simplicity and scalability, since service components can be reduced in size and complexity by directly implementing only the most frequent services and allowing infrequent services to be defined by the client. Customizability is a property induced by the remote evaluation and code-on-demand styles.

11.3.4.4 Configurability

Configurability is related to both extensibility and reusability in that it refers to post-deployment modification of components, or configurations of components, such that they are capable of using a new service or data element type. The pipe-and-filter and code-on-demand styles are two examples that induce configurability of configurations and components, respectively.

11.3.4.5 Reusability

Reusability is a property of application architecture if its components, connectors, or data elements can be reused, without modification, in other applications. The primary mechanisms for inducing reusability within architectural styles is reduction of coupling (knowledge of identity) between components and constraining the generality of component interfaces. The uniform pipe-and-filter style exemplifies these types of constraints.

11.3.5 Visibility

Styles can also influence the visibility of interactions within a network-based application by restricting interfaces via generality or providing access to monitoring. Visibility in this case refers to the ability of a component to monitor or mediate the interaction between two other components. Visibility can enable improved performance via shared caching of interactions, scalability through layered services, reliability through reflective monitoring, and security by allowing the interactions to be inspected by mediators (e.g., network firewalls). The mobile agent style is an example where the lack of visibility may lead to security concerns.

This usage of the term visibility differs from that in Ghezzi et al., where they are referring to visibility into the development process rather than the product.

11.3.6 Portability

Software is portable if it can run in different environments. Styles that induce portability include those that move code along with the data to be processed, such as the virtual machine and mobile agent styles, and those that constrain the data elements to a set of standardized formats.

11.3.7 Reliability

Reliability, within the perspective of application architectures, can be viewed as the degree to which architecture is susceptible to failure at the system level in the presence of partial failures within components, connectors, or data. Styles can improve reliability by avoiding single points of failure, enabling redundancy, allowing monitoring, or reducing the scope of failure to a recoverable action.

11.4 Summary

This chapter examined the scope of the dissertation by focusing on network-based application architectures and describing how styles can be used to guide their architectural design. It also defined the set of architectural properties that will be used throughout the rest of the dissertation for the comparison and evaluation of architectural styles.

The next chapter presents a survey of common architectural styles for network-based application software within a classification framework that evaluates each style according to the architectural properties it would induce if applied to an architecture for a prototypical network-based hypermedia system.

11.5 Review Questions

1. Explain the Network-based Application Architectures.
2. Explain the Scope.
3. Discuss the Network-based vs. Distributed.
4. Discuss Application Software vs. Networking Software
5. Discuss the Evaluating the Design of Application Architectures
6. Explain the Architectural Properties of Key Interest
7. Write short notes on
   (i) Performance (ii) Scalability
   (iii) Simplicity (iv) Modifiability.

Chapter No. 12

Network-based Architectural Styles

This chapter presents a survey of common architectural styles for network-based application software within a classification framework that evaluates each style according to the architectural properties it would induce if applied to architecture for a prototypical network-based hypermedia system.

12.1Classification Methodology

The purpose of building software is not to create a specific topology of interactions or use a particular component type -- it is to create a system that meets or exceeds the application needs. The architectural styles chosen for a system's design must conform to those needs, not the other way around. Therefore, in order to provide useful design guidance, a classification of architectural styles should be based on the architectural properties induced by those styles.

12.1.1 Selection of Architectural Styles for Classification

The set of architectural styles included in the classification is by no means comprehensive of all possible network-based application styles. Indeed, merely adding an architectural constraint to any one of the styles surveyed can form a new style. My goal is to describe a representative sample of styles, particularly those already identified within the software architecture literature, and provide a framework by which other styles can be added to the classification as they are developed.

I have intentionally excluded styles that do not enhance the communication or interaction properties when combined with one of the surveyed styles to form a network-based application. For example, the blackboard architectural style consists of a central repository and a set of components (knowledge sources) that operate opportunistically upon the repository. Blackboard architecture can be extended to a network-based system by distributing the components, but the properties of such an extension are entirely based on the interaction style chosen to support the distribution -- notifications via event-based integration, polling a la client-server, or replication of the repository. Thus, there would be no added value from including it in the classification, even though the hybrid style is network-capable.

12.1.2 Style-induced Architectural Properties

My classification uses relative changes in the architectural properties induced by each style as a means of illustrating the effect of each architectural style when applied to a system for distributed hypermedia. Note that the evaluation of a style for a given property depends on the type of system interaction being studied, as described in Section 8.2 The architectural properties are relative in the sense that adding an architectural constraint may improve or reduce a given property, or simultaneously improve one aspect of the property and reduce some other aspect of the property. Likewise, improving one property may lead to the reduction of another.

Although our discussion of architectural styles will include those applicable to a wide range of network-based systems, our evaluation of each style will be based on its impact upon an architecture for a single type of software: network-based hypermedia systems. Focusing on a particular type of software allows us to identify the advantages of one style over another in the same way that a designer of a system would evaluate those advantages. Since we do not intend to declare any single style as being universally desirable for all types of software, restricting the focus of our evaluation simply reduces the dimensions over which we need to evaluate. Evaluating the same styles for other types of application software is an open area for future research.

12.1.3 Visualization

I use a table of style versus architectural properties as the primary visualization for this classification. The table values indicate the relative influence that the style for a given row has on a column's property. Minus (-) symbols accumulate for negative influences and plus (+) symbols for positive, with plus-minus (1) indicating that it depends on some aspect of the problem domain. Although this is a gross simplification of the details presented in each section, it does indicate the degree to which a style has addressed (or ignored) an architectural property.

An alternative visualization would be a property-based derivation graph for classifying architectural styles. The styles would be classified according to how they are derived from other styles, with the arcs between styles illustrated by architectural properties gained or lost. The starting point of the graph would be the null style (no constraints). It is possible to derive such a graph directly from the descriptions.

12.2 Data-flow Styles

Table 12-2: Evaluation of Data-flow Styles for Network-based Hypermedia

Style	Derivation													
PF			±			+	+	+		+	+			
UPF	PF	-	±			+	+	+		+	+	+		

12.2.1 Pipe and Filter (PF)

In a pipe and filter style, each component (filter) reads streams of data on its inputs and produces streams of data on its outputs, usually while applying a transformation to the input streams and processing them incrementally so that output begins before the input is completely consumed This style is also referred to as a one-way data flow network. The constraint is that a filter must be completely independent of other filters (zero coupling): it must not share state, control thread, or identity with the other filters on its upstream and downstream interfaces.

Abowd et al. provide an extensive formal description of the pipe and filter style using the Z language. The Khoros software development environment for image processing provides a good example of using the pipe and filter style to build a range of applications.

Garlan and Shaw describe the advantageous properties of the pipe and filter style as follows. First, PF allows the designer to understand the overall input/output of the system as a simple composition of the behaviors of the individual filters (simplicity). Second, PF supports reuse: any two filters can be hooked together, provided they agree on the data that is being transmitted between them (reusability). Third, PF systems can be easily maintained and enhanced: new filters can be added to existing systems (extensibility) and old filters can be replaced by improved ones (evolvability). Fourth, they permit certain kinds of specialized analysis (verifiability), such as throughput and deadlock analysis. Finally, they naturally support concurrent execution (user-perceived performance).

Disadvantages of the PF style include:

- Propagation delay is added through long pipelines.
- Batch sequential processing occurs if a filter cannot incrementally process its inputs.
- No interactivity is allowed.
- A filter cannot interact with its environment because it cannot know that any particular output stream shares a controller with any particular input stream. These properties decrease user-perceived performance if the problem being addressed does not fit the pattern of a data flow stream.

One aspect of PF styles that is rarely mentioned is that there is an implied "invisible hand" that arranges the configuration of filters in order to establish the overall application. A network of filters is typically arranged just prior to each activation, allowing the application to specify the configuration of filter components based on the task at hand and the nature of the data streams (configurability). This controller function is considered a separate operational phase of the system, and hence a separate architecture, even though one cannot exist without the other.

12.2.2 Uniform Pipe and Filter (UPF)

The uniform pipe and filter style adds the constraint that all filters must have the same interface. The primary example of this style is found in the Unix operating system, where filter processes have an interface consisting of one input data stream of characters (stdin) and two output data streams of characters (stdout and stderr). Restricting the interface allows independently developed filters to be arranged at will to form new applications. It also simplifies the task of understanding how a given filter works.

A disadvantage of the uniform interface is that it may reduce network performance if the data needs to be converted to or from its natural format.

12.3 Replication Styles

Table 12-3: Evaluation of Replication Styles for Network-based Hypermedia

Style	Derivation													
RR			+		+									
$	RR		+	+	+	+								

12.3.1 Replicated Repository (RR)

Systems based on the replicated repository style improve the accessibility of data and scalability of services by having more than one process provide the same service. These decentralized servers interact to provide clients the illusion that there is just one, centralized service. Distributed file systems, such as XMS, and remote versioning systems, like CVS [www.cyclic.com], are the primary examples.

Improved user-perceived performance is the primary advantage, both by reducing the latency of normal requests and enabling disconnected operation in the face of primary server failure or intentional roaming off the network. Simplicity remains neutral; since the complexity of replication is offset by the savings of allowing network-unaware components to operate transparently on locally replicated data. Maintaining consistency is the primary concern.

12.3.2 Cache ($)

A variant of replicated repository is found in the cache style: replication of the result of an individual requests such that it may be reused by later requests. This form of replication is most often found in cases where the potential data set far exceeds the capacity of any one client, as in the WWW, or where complete access to the repository is unnecessary. Lazy replication occurs when data is replicated upon a not-yet-cached response for a request, relying on locality of reference and commonality of interest to propagate useful items into the cache for later reuse. Active replication can be performed by pre-fetching cacheable entries based on anticipated requests.

Caching provides slightly less improvement than the replicated repository style in terms of user-perceived performance, since more requests will miss the cache and only recently accessed data will be available for disconnected operation. On the other hand, caching is much easier to implement, doesn't require as much processing and storage, and is more efficient because data is transmitted only when it is requested. The cache style becomes network-based when it is combined with a client-stateless-server style.

12.4 Hierarchical Styles

Table 12-4: Evaluation of Hierarchical Styles for Network-based Hypermedia

Style	Derivation													
CS					+	+	+							
LS			-		+		+				+		+	
LCS	CS+LS		-		+	+	+				+		+	
CSS	CS	-			+	+	+					+		+
C$SS	CSS+$	-	±	+	+	+	+					+		+
LC$SS	LCS+C$SS	-	±	+	+++	+	+				+	+	+	+
=RS	CS			+	-	+	+					-		
RDA	CS			+	-	-						+		-

12.4.1 Client-Server (CS)

The client-server style is the most frequently encountered of the architectural styles for network-based applications. A server component, offering a set of services, listens for requests upon those services. A client component, desiring that a service be performed, sends a request to the server via a connector. The server either rejects or performs the request and sends a response back to the client. A variety of client-server systems are surveyed by Sinha and Umar.

Andrews describes client-server components as follows: A client is a triggering process; a server is a reactive process. Clients make requests that trigger reactions from servers. Thus, a client initiates activity at times of its choosing; it often then delays until its request has been serviced. On the other hand, a server waits for requests to be made and then reacts to them. A server is usually a non-terminating process and often provides service to more than one client.

Separation of concerns is the principle behind the client-server constraints. A proper separation of functionality should simplify the server component in order to improve scalability. This simplification usually takes the form of moving all of the user interface functionality into the client component. The separation also allows the two types of components to evolve independently, provided that the interface doesn't change.

The basic form of client-server does not constrain how application state is partitioned between client and server components. It is often referred to by the mechanisms used for the connector implementation, such as remote procedure call or message-oriented middleware.

12.4.2 Layered System (LS) and Layered-Client-Server (LCS)

A layered system is organized hierarchically, each layer providing services to the layer above it and using services of the layer below it. Although layered system is considered a "pure" style, its use within network-based systems is limited to its combination with the client-server style to provide layered-client-server.

Layered systems reduce coupling across multiple layers by hiding the inner layers from all except the adjacent outer layer, thus improving evolvability and reusability. Examples include the processing of layered communication protocols, such as the TCP/IP and OSI protocol stacks, and hardware interface libraries. The primary disadvantage of layered systems is that they add overhead and latency to the processing of data, reducing user-perceived performance.

Layered-client-server adds proxy and gateway components to the client-server style. A proxy acts as a shared server for one or more client components, taking requests and forwarding them, with possible translation, to server components. A gateway component appears to be a normal server to clients or proxies that request its services, but is in fact forwarding those requests, with possible translation, to its "inner-layer" servers. These additional mediator components can be added in multiple layers to add features like load balancing and security checking to the system.

Architectures based on layered-client-server are referred to as two-tiered, three-tiered, or multi-tiered architectures in the information systems literature.

LCS is also a solution to managing identity in a large-scale distributed system, where complete knowledge of all servers would be prohibitively expensive. Instead, servers are organized in layers such that each client handles rarely used services by intermediaries rather than directly.

12.4.3 Client-Stateless-Server (CSS)

The client-stateless-server style derives from client-server with the additional constraint that no session state is allowed on the server component. Each request from client to server must contain all of the information necessary to understand the request, and cannot take advantage of any stored context on the server. Session state is kept entirely on the client.

These constraints improve the properties of visibility, reliability, and scalability. Visibility is improved because a monitoring system does not have to look beyond a single request datum in order to determine the full nature of the request. Reliability is improved because it eases the task of recovering from partial failures Scalability is improved because not having to store state between requests allows the server component to quickly free resources and further simplifies implementation.

The disadvantage of client-stateless-server is that it may decrease network performance by increasing the repetitive data (per-interaction overhead) sent in a series of requests, since that data cannot be left on the server in a shared context.

12.4.4 Client-Cache-Stateless-Server (CCSS)

The client-cache-stateless-server style derives from the client-stateless-server and cache styles via the addition of cache components. A cache acts as a mediator between client and server in which the responses to prior requests can, if they are considered cacheable, be reused in response to later requests that are equivalent and likely to result in a response identical to that in the cache if the request were to be forwarded to the server. An example system that makes effective use of this style is Sun Microsystems' NFS.

The advantage of adding cache components is that they have the potential to partially or completely eliminate some interactions, improving efficiency and user-perceived performance.

12.4.5 Layered-Client-Cache-Stateless-Server (LCCSS)

The layered-client-cache-stateless-server style derives from both layered-client-server and client-cache-stateless-server through the addition of proxy and/or gateway components. An example system that uses an LCCSS style is the Internet domain name system (DNS).

The advantages and disadvantages of LCCSS are simply a combination of those for LCS and CCSS. However, note that we don't count the contributions of the CS style twice, since the benefits are not additive if they come from the same ancestral derivation.

12.4.6 Remote Session (RS)

The remote session style is a variant of client-server that attempts to minimize the complexity, or maximize the reuse, of the client components rather than the server component. Each client initiates a session on the server and then invokes a series of services on the server, finally exiting the session. Application state is kept entirely on the server. This style is typically used when it is desired to access a remote service using a generic client (e.g., TELNET) or via an interface that mimics a generic client (e.g., FTP).

The advantages of the remote session style are that it is easier to centrally maintain the interface at the server, reducing concerns about inconsistencies in deployed clients when functionality is extended, and improves efficiency if the interactions make use of extended session context on the server. The disadvantages are that it reduces scalability of the server, due to the stored application state, and reduces visibility of interactions, since a monitor would have to know the complete state of the server.

12.4.7 Remote Data Access (RDA)

The remote data access style is a variant of client-server that spreads the application state across both client and server. A client sends a database query in a standard format, such as SQL, to a remote server. The server allocates a workspace and performs the query, which may result in a very large data set. The client can then make further operations upon the result set (such as table joins) or retrieve the result one piece at a time. The client must know about the data structure of the service to build structure-dependent queries.

The advantages of remote data access are that a large data set can be iteratively reduced on the server side without transmitting it across the network, improving efficiency, and visibility is improved by using a standard query language. The disadvantages are that the client needs to understand the same database manipulation concepts as the server implementation (lacking simplicity) and storing application context on the server decreases scalability. Reliability also suffers, since partial failure can leave the workspace in an unknown state. Transaction mechanisms (e.g., two-phase commit) can be used to fix the reliability problem, though at a cost of added complexity and interaction overhead.

12.5 Mobile Code Styles

Mobile code styles use mobility in order to dynamically change the distance between the processing and source of data or destination of results. These styles are comprehensively examined in Fuggetta et al. A site abstraction is introduced at the architectural level, as part of the active configuration, in order to take into account the location of the different components. Introducing the concept of location makes it possible to model the cost of an interaction between components at the design level. In particular, an interaction between components that share the same location is considered to have negligible cost when compared to an interaction involving communication through the network. By changing its location, a component may improve the proximity and quality of its interaction, reducing interaction costs and thereby improving efficiency and user-perceived performance.

In all of the mobile code styles, a data element is dynamically transformed into a component. Fuggetta et al.use an analysis that compares the code's size as a data element to the savings in normal data transfer in order to determine whether mobility is desirable for a given action. This would be impossible to model from an architectural standpoint if the definition of software architecture excludes data elements.

Table 12-5: Evaluation of Mobile Code Styles for Network-based Hypermedia

Style	Derivation													
VM						±		+				-	+	
REV	CS+VM			+	-	±		+	+			-	+	-
COD	CS+VM		+	+	+	±		+		+		-		
LCODC$SS	LC$SS+COD	-	+	+	+4+	+±+	+	+		+	+	±	+	+
MA	REV+COS		+	+		±		+	+	+		-	+	

12.5.1 Virtual Machine (VM)

Underlying all of the mobile code styles is the notion of a virtual machine, or interpreter, style. The code must be executed in some fashion, preferably within a controlled environment to satisfy security and reliability concerns, which is exactly what the virtual machine style provides. It is not, in itself, a network-based style, but it is commonly used as such when combined with a component in the client-server style (REV and COD styles).

Virtual machines are commonly used as the engine for scripting languages, including general-purpose languages like Perl and task-specific languages like PostScript. The primary benefits are the separation between instruction and implementation on a particular platform (portability) and ease of extensibility. Visibility is reduced because it is hard to know what an executable will do simply by looking at the code. Simplicity is reduced due to the need to manage the evaluation environment, but that may be compensated in some cases as a result of simplifying the static functionality.

12.5.2 Remote Evaluation (REV)

In the remote evaluation style, derived from the client-server and virtual machine styles, a client component has the know-how necessary to perform a service, but lacks the resources (CPU cycles, data source, etc.) required, which happen to be located at a remote site. Consequently, the client sends the know-how to a server component at the remote site, which in turn executes the code using the resources available there. The results of that execution are then sent back to the client. The remote evaluation style assumes that the provided code will be executed in a sheltered environment, such that it won't impact other clients of the same server aside from the resources being used.

The advantages of remote evaluation include the ability to customize the server component's services, which provides for improved extensibility and customizability, and better efficiency when the code can adapt its actions to the environment inside the server (as opposed to the client making a series of interactions to do the same). Simplicity is reduced due to the need to manage the evaluation environment, but that may be compensated in some cases as a result of simplifying the static server functionality. Scalability is reduced; this can be improved with the server's management of the execution environment (killing long-running or resource-intensive code when resources are tight), but the management function itself leads to difficulties regarding partial failure and reliability. The most significant limitation, however, is the lack of visibility due to the client sending code instead of standardized queries. Lack of visibility leads to obvious deployment problems if the server cannot trust the clients.

12.5.3 Code on Demand (COD)

In the code-on-demand style, a client component has access to a set of resources, but not the know-how on how to process them. It sends a request to a remote server for the code representing that know-how, receives that code, and executes it locally.

The advantages of code-on-demand include the ability to add features to a deployed client, which provides for improved extensibility and configurability, and better user-perceived performance and efficiency when the code can adapt its actions to the client's environment and interact with the user locally rather than through remote interactions. Simplicity is reduced due to the need to manage the evaluation environment, but that may be compensated in some cases as a result of simplifying the client's static functionality. Scalability of the server is improved, since it can off-load work to the client that would otherwise have consumed its resources. Like remote evaluation, the most significant limitation is the lack of visibility due to the server sending code instead of simple data. Lack of visibility leads to obvious deployment problems if the client cannot trust the servers.

12.5.4 Layered-Code-on-Demand-Client-Cache-Stateless-Server (LCODC$SS)

As an example of how some architecture are complementary, consider the addition of code-on-demand to the layered-client-cache-stateless-server style discussed above. Since the code can be treated as just another data element, this does not interfere with the advantages of the LC$SS style. An example is the Hot Java Web browser [java.sun.com], which allows applets and protocol extensions to be downloaded as typed media.

The advantages and disadvantages of LCODC$SS are just a combination of those for COD and LC$SS. We could go further and discuss the combination of COD with other CS styles, but this survey is not intended to be exhaustive (nor exhausting).

12.5.5 Mobile Agent (MA)

In the mobile agent style, an entire computational component is moved to a remote site, along with its state, the code it needs, and possibly some data required to perform the task. This can be considered a derivation of the remote evaluation and code-on-demand styles, since the mobility works both ways.

The primary advantage of the mobile agent style, beyond those already described for REV and COD is that there is greater dynamism in the selection of when to move the code. An application can be in the midst of processing information at one location when it decides to move to another location; presumably in order to reduce the distance between it and the next set of data it wishes to process. In addition, the reliability problem of partial failure is reduced because the application state is in one location at a time .

12.6 Peer-to-Peer Styles

Table 12-6: Evaluation of Peer-to-Peer Styles for Network-based Hypermedia

Style	Derivation													
EBI				+	- -	±	+	+		+	+	-		-
C2	EBI+LCS		-	+		+	+	+		+	+	±	+	±
DO	CS+CS	-		+			+	+		+	+	-		-
BDO	DO+LCS	-	-				+	+		+	+	-	+	

12.6.1 Event-based Integration (EBI)

The event-based integration style, also known as the implicit invocation or event system style, reduces coupling between components by removing the need for identity on the connector interface. Instead of invoking another component directly, a component can announce (or broadcast) one or more events. Other components in a system can register interest in that type of event and, when the event is announced, the system itself invokes all of the registered components. Examples include the Model-View-Controller paradigm in Smalltalk-80and the integration mechanisms of many software engineering environments, including Field, Soft Bench, and Polylith.

The event-based integration style provides strong support for extensibility through the ease of adding new components that listen for events, for reuse by encouraging a general event interface and integration mechanism, and for evolution by allowing components to be replaced without affecting the interfaces of other components. Like pipe-and-filter systems, a higher-level configuring architecture is needed for the "invisible hand" that places components on the event interface. Most EBI systems also include explicit invocation as a complementary form of interaction. For applications that are dominated by data monitoring, rather than data retrieval, EBI can improve efficiency by removing the need for polling interactions.

The basic form of EBI system consists of one event bus to which all components listen for events of interest to them. Of course, this immediately leads to scalability issues with regard to the number of notifications, event storms as other components broadcast as a result of events caused by that notification, and a single point of failure in the notification delivery system. This can be ameliorated though the use of layered systems and filtering of events, at the cost of simplicity.

Other disadvantages of EBI systems are that it can be hard to anticipate what will happen in response to an action (poor understandability) and event notifications are not suitable for exchanging large-grain data,Also, there is no support for recovery from partial failure.

12.6.2 C2 architectural style

The C2 architectural style is directed at supporting large-grain reuse and flexible composition of system components by enforcing substrate independence. It does so by combining event-based integration with layered-client-server. Asynchronous notification messages going down, and asynchronous request messages going up, are the sole means of intercommoning communication. This enforces loose coupling of dependency on higher layers (service requests may be ignored) and zero coupling with lower levels (no knowledge of notification usage), improving control over the system without losing most of the advantages of EBI.

Notifications are announcements of a state change within a component. C2 does not constrain what should be included with a notification: a flag, a delta of state change, or a complete state representation is all possibilities. A connector's primary responsibility is the routing and broadcasting of messages; its secondary responsibility is message filtering. The introduction of layered filtering of messages solves the EBI problems with scalability, while improving evolvability and reusability as well. Heavyweight connectors that include monitoring capabilities can be used to improve visibility and reduce the reliability problems of partial failure.

12.6.3 Distributed Objects

The distributed objects style organizes a system as a set of components interacting as peers. An object is an entity that encapsulates some private state information or data, a set of associated operations or procedures that manipulate the data, and possibly a thread of control, so that collectively they can be considered a single unit. In general, an object's state is completely hidden and protected from all other objects. The only way it can be examined or modified is by making a request or invocation on one of the object's publicly accessible operations. This creates a well-defined interface for each object, enabling the specification of an object's operations to be made public while at the same time keeping the implementation of its operations and the representation of its state information private, thus improving evolvability.

An operation may invoke other operations, possibly on other objects. These operations may in turn make invocations on others, and so on. A chain of related invocations is referred to as an action. State is distributed among the objects. This can be advantageous in terms of keeping the state where it is most likely to be up-to-date, but has the disadvantage in that it is difficult to obtain an overall view of system activity (poor visibility).

In order for one object to interact with another, it must know the identity of that other object. When the identity of an object changes, it is necessary to modify all other objects that explicitly invoke it. There must be some controller object that is responsible for maintaining the system state in order to complete the application requirements. Central issues for distributed object systems include: object management, object interaction management, and resource management.

Object systems are designed to isolate the data being processed. As a consequence, data streaming is not supported in general. However, this does provide better support for object mobility when combined with the mobile agent style.

12.6.4 Brokered Distributed Objects

In order to reduce the impact of identity, modern distributed object systems typically use one or more intermediary styles to facilitate communication. This includes event-based integration and brokered client/server. The brokered distributed object style introduces name resolver components whose purpose is to answer client object requests for general service names with the specific name of an object that will satisfy the request. Although improving reusability and evolvability, the extra level of indirection requires additional network interactions, reducing efficiency and user-perceived performance.

Brokered distributed object systems are currently dominated by the industrial standards development of CORBA within the OMG and the international standards development of Open Distributed Processing (ODP) within ISO/IEC.

In spite of all the interest associated with distributed objects, they fare poorly when compared to most other network-based architectural styles. They are best used for applications that involve the remote invocation of encapsulated services, such as hardware devices, where the efficiency and frequency of network interactions is less a concern.

12.7 Limitations

Each architectural style promotes a certain type of interaction among components. When components are distributed across a wide-area network, use or misuse of the network drives application usability. By characterizing styles by their influence on architectural properties, and particularly on the network-based application performance of a distributed hypermedia system, we gain the ability to better choose a software design that is appropriate for the application. There are, however, a couple limitations with the chosen classification.

The first limitation is that the evaluation is specific to the needs of distributed hypermedia. For example, many of the good qualities of the pipe-and-filter style disappear if the communication is fine-grained control messages, and are not applicable at all if the communication requires user interactivity. Likewise, layered caching only adds to latency, without any benefit, if none of the responses to client requests are cacheable. This type of distinction does not appear in the classification, and is only addressed informally in the discussion of each style. I believe this limitation can be overcome by creating separate classification tables for each type of communication problem. Example problem areas would include, among others, large grain data retrieval, remote information monitoring, search, remote control systems, and distributed processing.

A second limitation is with the grouping of architectural properties. In some cases, it is better to identify the specific aspects of, for example, understandability and verifiability induced by an architectural style, rather than lumping them together under the rubric of simplicity. This is particularly the case for styles, which might improve verifiability at the expense of understandability. However, the more abstract notion of a property also has value as a single metric, since we do not want to make the classification so specific that no two styles impact the same category. One solution would be a classification that presented both the specific properties and a summary property.

Regardless, this initial survey and classification is a necessary prerequisite to any further classifications that might address its limitations.

12.8 Related Work

12.8.1 Classification of Architectural Styles and Patterns

The area of research most directly related to this chapter is the identification and classification of architectural styles and architecture-level patterns.

Shaw describes a few architectural styles, later expanded in Garlan and Shaw. A preliminary classification of these styles is presented in Shaw and Clements and repeated in Bass et al., in which a two-dimensional, tabular classification strategy is used with control and data issues as the primary axes, organized by the following categories of features: which kinds of components and connectors are used in the style; how control is shared, allocated, and transferred among the components; how data is communicated through the system; how data and control interact; and, what type of reasoning is compatible with the style. The primary purpose of the taxonomy is to identify style characteristics, rather than to assist in their comparison. It concludes with a small set of "rules of thumb" as a form of design guidance.

the Shaw and Clements classification does not assist in evaluating designs in a way that is useful to an application designer. The problem is that the purpose of building software is not to build a specific shape, topology or component type, so organizing the classification in that fashion does not help a designer find a style that corresponds to their needs. It also mixes the essential differences among styles with other issues, which have only incidental significance, and obscures the derivation relationships among styles. Furthermore, it does not focus on any particular type of architecture, such as network-based applications. Finally, it does not describe how styles can be combined, or the effect of their combination.

Buschmann and Meunier describe a classification scheme that organizes patterns according to granularity of abstraction, functionality, and structural principles. The granularity of abstraction separates patterns into three categories: architectural frameworks (templates for architectures), design patterns, and idioms. Their classification addresses some of the same issues as this dissertation, such as separation of concerns and structural principles that lead to architectural properties, but only covers two of the architectural styles described here. Their classification is considerably expanded in Buschmann et al.with more extensive discussion of architectural patterns and their relation to software architecture.

Zimmer organizes design patterns using a graph based on their relationships, making it easier to understand the overall structure of the patterns in the Gamma et al. catalog. However, the patterns classified are not architectural patterns, and the classification is based exclusively on derivation or uses relationships rather than on architectural properties.

12.8.2 Distributed Systems and Programming Paradigms

Andrews surveys how processes in a distributed program interact via message passing. He defines concurrent programs, distributed programs, kinds of processes in a distributed program (filters, clients, servers, peers), interaction paradigms, and communication channels. Interaction paradigms represent the communication aspects of software architectural styles. He describes paradigms for one-way data flow through networks of filters (pipe-and-filter), client-server, heartbeat, probe/echo, broadcast, token passing, replicated servers, and replicated workers with bag of tasks. However, the presentation is from the perspective of multiple processes cooperating on a single task, rather than general network-based architectural styles.

Sullivan and Notkin provide a survey of implicit invocation research and describe its application to improving the evolution quality of software tool suites. Barrett et al. present a survey of event-based integration mechanisms by building a framework for comparison and then seeing how some systems fit within that framework. Rosenblum and Wolf investigate a design framework for Internet-scale event notification. All are concerned with the scope and requirements of an EBI style, rather than providing solutions for network-based systems.

Fuggetta et al. provide a thorough examination and classification of mobile code paradigms. This chapter builds upon their work to the extent that I compare the mobile code styles with other network-capable styles, and place them within a single framework and set of architectural definitions.

12.8.3 Middleware

Bernstein defines middleware as a distributed system service that includes standard programming interfaces and protocols. These services are called middleware because they act as a layer above the OS and networking software and below industry-specific applications. Umar presents an extensive treatment of the subject.

Architecture research regarding middleware focuses on the problems and effects of integrating components with off-the-shelf middleware. Di Nitto and Rosenblum describe how the usage of middleware and predefined components can influence the architecture of a system being developed and, conversely, how specific architectural choices can constrain the selection of middleware. Dashofy et al. discuss the use of middleware with the C2 style.

Garlan et al. point out some of the architectural assumptions within off-the-shelf components, examining the authors' problems with reusing subsystems in creating the Aesop tool for architectural design. They classify the problems into four main categories of assumptions that can contribute to architectural mismatch: nature of components, nature of connectors, global architectural structure, and construction process.

12.9 Summary

This chapter has presented a survey of common architectural styles for network-based application software within a classification framework that evaluates each style according to the architectural properties it would induce if applied to architecture for a prototypical network-based hypermedia system. The next chapter uses the insight garnered from this survey and classification to hypothesize methods for developing and evaluating an architectural style to guide the design of improvements for the modern World Wide Web architecture.

Table 12-9: Evaluation Summary

Style	Derivation													
PF			±			+	+	+		+	+			
UPF	PF	-	±			+	+	+		+	+	+		
RR														
$	RR													
CS														
LS														
LCS														
CSS														
C$SS														
LC$SS														
RS														
RDA														
VM														
REV														
COD														
LCODC$SS														
MA														

12.10 Review Questions

1. Explain the Network-based Architectural Styles.
2. Discuss the Classification Methodology &Selection of Architectural Styles for Classification
3. Explain the Style-induced Architectural Properties & Visualization.
4. Explain Data-flow Styles & Pipe and Filter (PF).
5. Write short notes on-
   (i) Uniform Pipe and Filter (UPF)
   (ii) Replication Styles
   (iii) Replicated Repository (RR)
   (iv) Cache ($)
   (v) Hierarchical Styles
   (vi) Client-Server (CS)
6. Explain the Layered System (LS) and Layered-Client-Server (LCS) & Client-Stateless-Server (CSS)
7. Explain the Client-Cache-Stateless-Server (C$SS)& Layered-Client-Cache-Stateless-Server (LC$SS).
8. Explain the following-
   (i) Remote Session (RS) (ii) Remote Data Access (RDA)
   (iii) Mobile Code Styles (iv) Virtual Machine (VM)
   (v) Remote Evaluation (REV).

—•—•—•—•—•—

Chapter No. 13

Designing the Web Architecture: Problems and Insights

This chapter presents the requirements of the World Wide Web architecture and the problems faced in designing and evaluating proposed improvements to its key communication protocols. We use the insights garnered from the survey and classification of architectural styles for network-based hypermedia systems to hypothesize methods for developing an architectural style that would be used to guide the design of improvements for the modern Web architecture.

13.1 WWW Application Domain Requirements

Berners-Lee writes that the "Web's major goal was to be a shared information space through which people and machines could communicate." What was needed was a way for people to store and structure their own information, whether permanent or ephemeral in nature, such that it could be usable by themselves and others, and to be able to reference and structure the information stored by others so that it would not be necessary for everyone to keep and maintain local copies.

The intended end-users of this system were located around the world, at various university and government high-energy physics research labs connected via the Internet. Their machines were a heterogeneous collection of terminals, workstations, servers and supercomputers, requiring a Hodge podge of operating system software and file formats. The information ranged from personal research notes to organizational phone listings. The challenge was to build a system that would provide a universally consistent interface to this structured information, available on as many platforms as possible, and incrementally deployable as new people and organizations joined the project.

13.1.1 Low Entry-barrier

Since participation in the creation and structuring of information was voluntary, a low entry-barrier was necessary to enable sufficient adoption. This applied to all users of the Web architecture: readers, authors, and application developers.

Hypermedia was chosen as the user interface because of its simplicity and generality: the same interface can be used regardless of the information source, the flexibility of hypermedia relationships (links) allows for unlimited structuring, and the direct manipulation of links allows the complex relationships within the information to guide the reader through an application. Since information within large databases is often much easier to access via a search interface rather than browsing, the Web also incorporated the ability to perform simple queries by providing user-entered data to a service and rendering the result as hypermedia.

For authors, the primary requirement was that partial availability of the overall system must not prevent the authoring of content. The hypertext authoring language needed to be simple and capable of being created using existing editing tools. Authors were expected to keep such things as personal research notes in this format, whether directly connected to the Internet or not, so the fact that some referenced information was unavailable, either temporarily or permanently, could not be allowed to prevent the reading and authoring of information that was available. For similar reasons, it was necessary to be able to create references to information before the target of that reference was available. Since authors were encouraged to collaborate in the development of information sources, references needed to be easy to communicate, whether in the form of e-mail directions or written on the back of a napkin at a conference.

Simplicity was also a goal for the sake of application developers. Since all of the protocols were defined as text, communication could be viewed and interactively tested using existing network tools. This enabled early adoption of the protocols to take place in spite of the lack of standards.

13.1.2 Extensibility

While simplicity makes it possible to deploy an initial implementation of a distributed system, extensibility allows us to avoid getting stuck forever with the limitations of what was deployed. Even if it were possible to build a software system that perfectly matches the requirements of its users, those requirements will change over time just as society changes over time. A system intending to be as long-lived as the Web must be prepared for change.

13.1.3 Distributed Hypermedia

Hypermedia is defined by the presence of application control information embedded within, or as a layer above, the presentation of information. Distributed hypermedia allows the presentation and control information to be stored at remote locations. By its nature, user actions within a distributed hypermedia system require the transfer of large amounts of data from where the data is stored to where it is used. Thus, the Web architecture must be designed for large-grain data transfer.

The usability of hypermedia interaction is highly sensitive to user-perceived latency: the time between selecting a link and the rendering of a usable result. Since the Web's information sources are distributed across the global Internet, the architecture needs to minimize network interactions (round-trips within the data transfer protocols).

13.1.4 Internet-scale

The Web is intended to be an Internet-scale distributed hypermedia system, which means considerably more than just geographical dispersion. The Internet is about interconnecting information networks across multiple organizational boundaries. Suppliers of information services must be able to cope with the demands of anarchic scalability and the independent deployment of software components.

13.1.4.1 Anarchic Scalability

Most software systems are created with the implicit assumption that the entire system is under the control of one entity, or at least that all entities participating within a system are acting towards a common goal and not at cross-purposes. Such an assumption cannot be safely made when the system runs openly on the Internet. Anarchic scalability refers to the need for architectural elements to continue operating when they are subjected to an unanticipated load, or when given malformed or maliciously constructed data, since they may be communicating with elements outside their organizational control. The architecture must be amenable to mechanisms that enhance visibility and scalability.

The anarchic scalability requirement applies to all architectural elements. Clients cannot be expected to maintain knowledge of all servers. Servers cannot be expected to retain knowledge of state across requests. Hypermedia data elements cannot retain "back-pointers," an identifier for each data element that references them, since the number of references to a resource is proportional to the number of people interested in that information. Particularly newsworthy information can also lead to "flash crowds": sudden spikes in access attempts as news of its availability spreads across the world.

Security of the architectural elements, and the platforms on which they operate, also becomes a significant concern. Multiple organizational boundaries implies that multiple trust boundaries could be present in any communication. Intermediary applications, such as firewalls, should be able to inspect the application interactions and prevent those outside the security policy of the organization from being acted upon. The participants in an application interaction should either assume that any information received is untrusted, or require some additional authentication before trust can be given. This requires that the architecture be capable of communicating authentication data and authorization controls. However, since authentication degrades scalability, the architecture's default operation should be limited to actions that do not need trusted data: a safe set of operations with well-defined semantics.

13.1.4.2 Independent Deployment

Multiple organizational boundaries also means that the system must be prepared for gradual and fragmented change, where old and new implementations co-exist without preventing the new implementations from making use of their extended capabilities. Existing architectural elements need to be designed with the expectation that later architectural features will be added. Likewise, older implementations need to be easily identified so that legacy behavior can be encapsulated without adversely impacting newer architectural elements. The architecture as a whole must be designed to ease the deployment of architectural elements in a partial, iterative fashion, since it is not possible to force deployment in an orderly manner.

13.2 Problem

In late 1993, it became clear that more than just researchers would be interested in the Web. Adoption had occurred first in small research groups, spread to on-campus dorms, clubs, and personal home pages, and later to the institutional departments for campus information. When individuals began publishing their personal collections of information, on whatever topics they might feel fanatic about, the social network-effect launched an exponential growth of websites that continues today. Commercial interest in the Web was just beginning, but it was clear by then that the ability to publish on an international scale would be irresistible to businesses.

Although elated by its success, the Internet developer community became concerned that the rapid growth in the Web's usage, along with some poor network characteristics of early HTTP, would quickly outpace the capacity of the Internet infrastructure and lead to a general collapse. This was worsened by the changing nature of application interactions on the Web. Whereas the initial protocols were designed for single request-response pairs, new sites used an increasing number of in-line images as part of the content of Web pages, resulting in a different interaction profile for browsing. The deployed architecture had significant limitations in its support for extensibility, shared caching, and intermediaries, which made it difficult to develop ad-hoc solutions to the growing problems. At the same time, commercial competition within the software market led to an influx of new and occasionally contradictory feature proposals for the Web's protocols.

Working groups within the Internet Engineering Taskforce were formed to work on the Web's three primary standards: URI, HTTP, and HTML. The charter of these groups was to define the subset of existing architectural communication that was commonly and consistently implemented in the early Web architecture, identify problems within that architecture, and then specify a set of standards to solve those problems. This presented us with a challenge: how do we introduce a new set of functionality to an architecture that is already widely deployed, and how do we ensure that its introduction does not adversely impact, or even destroy, the architectural properties that have enabled the Web to succeed?

13.3 Approach

The early Web architecture was based on solid principles--separation of concerns, simplicity, and generality--but lacked an architectural description and rationale. The design was based on a set of informal hypertext notes two early papers oriented towards the user community, and archived discussions on the Web developer community mailing list (www-talk@info.cern.ch). In reality, however, the only true description of the early Web architecture was found within the implementations of libwww (the CERN protocol library for clients and servers), Mosaic (the NCSA browser client), and an assortment of other implementations that interoperated with them.

An architectural style can be used to define the principles behind the Web architecture such that they are visible to future architects. As discussed in Chapter 1, a style is a named set of constraints on architectural elements that induces the set of properties desired of the architecture. The first step in my approach, therefore, is to identify the constraints placed within the early Web architecture that are responsible for its desirable properties.

> Hypothesis I: The design rationale behind the WWW architecture can be described by an architectural style consisting of the set of constraints applied to the elements within the Web architecture.

Additional constraints can be applied to an architectural style in order to extend the set of properties induced on instantiated architectures. The next step in my approach is to identify the properties desirable in an Internet-scale distributed hypermedia system, select additional architectural styles that induce those properties, and combine them with the early Web constraints to form a new, hybrid architectural style for the modern Web architecture.

> Hypothesis II: Constraints can be added to the WWW architectural style to derive a new hybrid style that better reflects the desired properties of a modern Web architecture.

Using the new architectural style as a guide, we can compare proposed extensions and modifications to the Web architecture against the constraints within the style. Conflicts indicate that the proposal would violate one or more of the design principles behind the Web. In some cases, the conflict could be removed by requiring the use of a specific indicator whenever the new feature is used, as is often done for HTTP extensions that impact the default cache ability of a response. For severe conflicts, such as a change in the interaction style, the same functionality would either be replaced with a design more conducive to the Web's style, or the proposer would be told to implement the functionality as a separate architecture running in parallel to the Web.

> Hypothesis III: Proposals to modify the Web architecture can be compared to the updated WWW architectural style and analyzed for conflicts prior to deployment.

Finally, the updated Web architecture, as defined by the revised protocol standards that have been written according to the guidelines of the new architectural style, is deployed through participation in the development of the infrastructure and middleware software that make up the majority of Web applications. This included my direct participation in software development for the Apache HTTP server project and the libwww-perl client library, as well as indirect participation in other projects by advising the developers of the W3C libwww and jigsaw projects, the Netscape Navigator, Lynx, and MSIE browsers, and dozens of other implementations, as part of the IETF discourse.

Although I have described this approach as a single sequence, it is actually applied in a non-sequential, iterative fashion. That is, over the past six years I have been constructing models, adding constraints to the architectural style, and testing their affect on the Web's protocol standards via experimental extensions to client and server software. Likewise, others have suggested the addition of features to the architecture that were outside the scope of my then-current model style, but not in conflict with it, which resulted in going back and revising the architectural constraints to better reflect the improved architecture. The goal has always been to maintain a consistent and correct model of how I intend the Web architecture to behave, so that it could be used to guide the protocol standards that define appropriate behavior, rather than to create an artificial model that would be limited to the constraints originally imagined when the work began.

13.4 Summary

This chapter presented the requirements of the World Wide Web architecture and the problems faced in designing and evaluating proposed improvements to its key communication protocols. The challenge is to develop a method for designing improvements to architecture such that the improvements can be evaluated prior to their deployment. My approach is to use an architectural style to define and improve the design rationale behind the Web's architecture, to use that style as the acid test for proving proposed extensions prior to their deployment, and to deploy the revised architecture via direct involvement in the software development projects that have created the Web's infrastructure.

The next chapter introduces and elaborates the Representational State Transfer (REST) architectural style for distributed hypermedia systems, as it has been developed to represent the model for how the modern Web should work. REST provides a set of architectural constraints that, when applied as a whole, emphasizes scalability of component interactions, generality of interfaces, independent deployment of components, and intermediary components to reduce interaction latency, enforce security, and encapsulate legacy systems.

13.5 Review Questions

1. Explain the Designing of Web Architecture & also Problems and Insights.
2. Explain the WWW Application Domain Requirements
3. Discuss the following-
   (i) Low Entry-barrier
   (ii) Extensibility
   (iii) Distributed Hypermedia
   (iv) Internet-scale & Problem Approach.

—•—•—•—•—•—

Chapter No. 14

Representational State Transfer (REST)

This chapter introduces and elaborates the Representational State Transfer (REST) architectural style for distributed hypermedia systems, describing the software engineering principles guiding REST and the interaction constraints chosen to retain those principles, while contrasting them to the constraints of other architectural styles. REST is a hybrid style derived from several of the network-based architectural styles and combined with additional constraints that define a uniform connector interface. The software architecture framework is used to define the architectural elements of REST and examine sample process, connector, and data views of prototypical architectures.

14.1 Deriving REST

The design rationale behind the Web architecture can be described by an architectural style consisting of the set of constraints applied to elements within the architecture. By examining the impact of each constraint as it is added to the evolving style, we can identify the properties induced by the Web's constraints. Additional constraints can then be applied to form a new architectural style that better reflects the desired properties of a modern Web architecture. This section provides a general overview of REST by walking through the process of deriving it as an architectural style. Later sections will describe in more detail the specific constraints that compose the REST style.

14.1.1 Starting with the Null Style

There are two common perspectives on the process of architectural design, whether it be for buildings or for software. The first is that a designer starts with nothing--a blank slate, whiteboard, or drawing board--and builds-up architecture from familiar components until it satisfies the needs of the intended system. The second is that a designer starts with the system needs as a whole, without constraints, and then incrementally identifies and applies constraints to elements of the system in order to differentiate the design space and allow the forces that influence system behavior to flow naturally, in harmony with the system. Where the first emphasizes creativity and unbounded vision, the second emphasizes restraint and understanding of the system context. REST has been developed using the latter process. Figures 14.1 through 14.8 depict this graphically in terms of how the applied constraints would differentiate the process view of architecture as the incremental set of constraints is applied.

The Null style is simply an empty set of constraints. From an architectural perspective, the null style describes a system in which there are no distinguished boundaries between components. It is the starting point for our description of REST.

Figure 14.1. Null style

14.1.2 Client-Server

The first constraints added to our hybrid style are those of the client-server architectural style. Separation of concerns is the principle behind the client-server constraints. By separating the user interface concerns from the data storage concerns, we improve the portability of the user interface across multiple platforms and improve scalability by simplifying the server components. Perhaps most significant to the Web, however, is that the separation allows the components to evolve independently, thus supporting the Internet-scale requirement of multiple organizational domains.

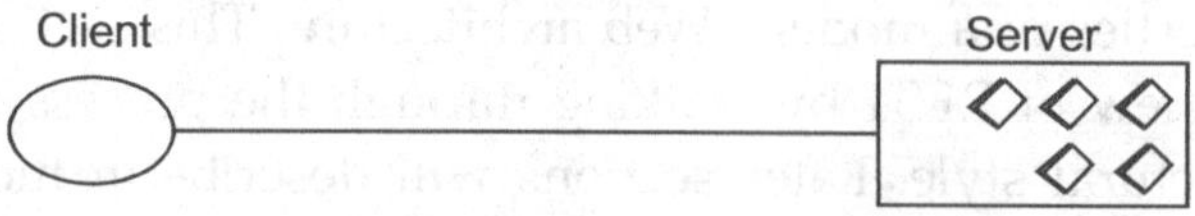

Figure 14.2. Client-Server

14.1.3 Stateless

We next add a constraint to the client-server interaction: communication must be stateless in nature, as in the client-stateless-server (CSS) style of, such that each request from client to server must contain all of the information necessary to understand the request, and cannot take advantage of any stored context on the server. Session state is therefore kept entirely on the client.

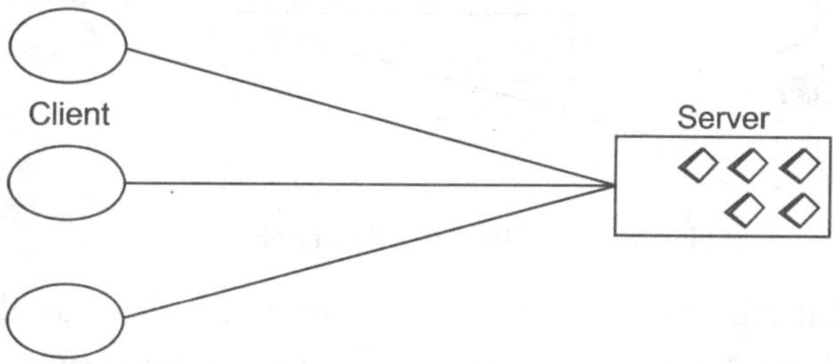

Figure 14.3. Client-Stateless-Server

This constraint induces the properties of visibility, reliability, and scalability. Visibility is improved because a monitoring system does not have to look beyond a single request datum in order to determine the full nature of the request. Reliability is improved because it eases the task of recovering from partial failures, capability is improved because not having to store state between requests allows the server component to quickly free resources, and further simplifies implementation because the server doesn't have to manage resource usage across requests.

Like most architectural choices, the stateless constraint reflects a design trade-off. The disadvantage is that it may decrease network performance by increasing the repetitive data (per-interaction overhead) sent in a series of requests, since that data cannot be left on the server in a shared context. In addition, placing the application state on the client-side reduces the server's control over consistent application behavior, since the application becomes dependent on the correct implementation of semantics across multiple client versions.

14.1.4 Cache

In order to improve network efficiency, we add cache constraints to form the client-cache-stateless-server style of. Cache constraints require that the data within a response to a request be implicitly or explicitly labeled as cacheable or non-cacheable. If a response is cacheable, then a client cache is given the right to reuse that response data for later, equivalent requests.

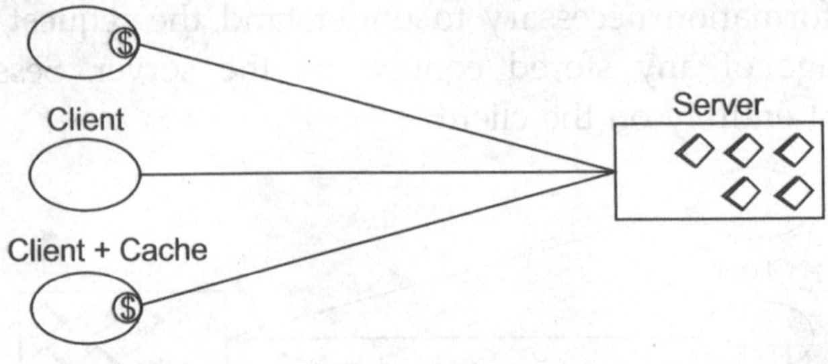

Figure 14.4. Client-Cache-Stateless-Server

The advantage of adding cache constraints is that they have the potential to partially or completely eliminate some interactions, improving efficiency, scalability, and user-perceived performance by reducing the average latency of a series of interactions. The trade-off, however, is that a cache can decrease reliability if stale data within the cache differs significantly from the data that would have been obtained had the request been sent directly to the server.

The early Web architecture, as portrayed by the diagram in, was defined by the client-cache-stateless-server set of constraints. That is, the design rationale presented for the Web architecture prior to 1994 focused on stateless client-server interaction for the exchange of static documents over the Internet. The protocols for communicating interactions had rudimentary support for non-shared caches, but did not constrain the interface to a consistent set of semantics for all resources. Instead, the Web relied on the use of a common client-server implementation library (CERN libwww) to maintain consistency across Web applications.

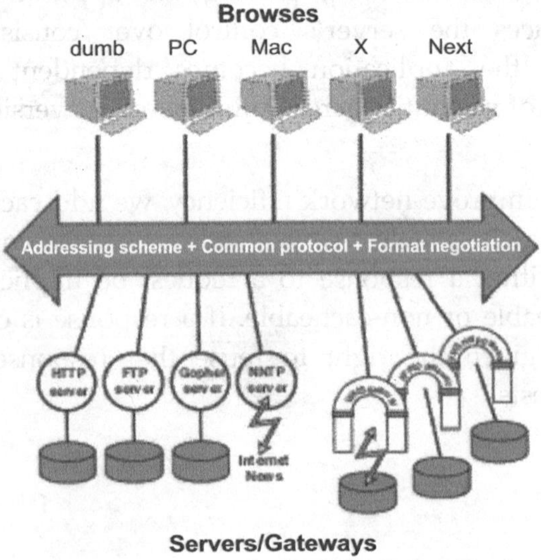

Figure 14.5. Early WWW Architecture Diagram

Developers of Web implementations had already exceeded the early design. In addition to static documents, requests could identify services that dynamically generated responses, such as image-maps [Kevin Hughes] and server-side scripts. Work had also begun on intermediary components, in the form of proxies and shared caches, but extensions to the protocols were needed in order for them to communicate reliably. The following sections describe the constraints added to the Web's architectural style in order to guide the extensions that form the modern Web architecture.

14.1.5 Uniform Interface

The central feature that distinguishes the REST architectural style from other network-based styles is its emphasis on a uniform interface between components. By applying the software engineering principle of generality to the component interface, the overall system architecture is simplified and the visibility of interactions is improved. Implementations are decoupled from the services they provide, which encourages independent evolvability. The trade-off, though, is that a uniform interface degrades efficiency, since information is transferred in a standardized form rather than one, which is specific to an application's needs. The REST interface is designed to be efficient for large-grain hypermedia data transfer, optimizing for the common case of the Web, but resulting in an interface that is not optimal for other forms of architectural interaction.

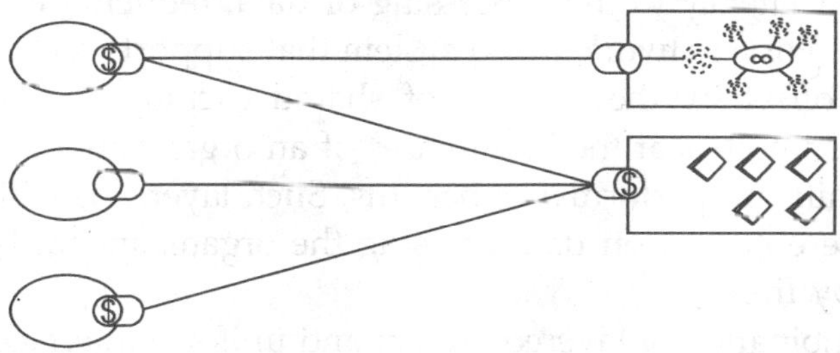

Client connector: Client + Cache: Server connector: Server + Cache:

Figure 14.6. Uniform-Client-Cache-Stateless-Server

In order to obtain a uniform interface, multiple architectural constraints are needed to guide the behavior of components. REST is defined by four interface constraints: identification of resources; manipulation of resources through representations; self-descriptive messages; and, hypermedia as the engine of application state.

14.1.6 Layered System

In order to further improve behavior for Internet-scale requirements, we add layered system constraints, the layered system style allows an architecture to be composed of hierarchical layers by constraining component behavior such that each component cannot "see" beyond the immediate layer with which they are interacting. By restricting knowledge of the system to a single layer, we place a bound on the overall system complexity and promote substrate independence. Layers can be used to encapsulate legacy services and to protect new services from legacy clients, simplifying components by moving infrequently used functionality to a shared intermediary. Intermediaries can also be used to improve system scalability by enabling load balancing of services across multiple networks and processors.

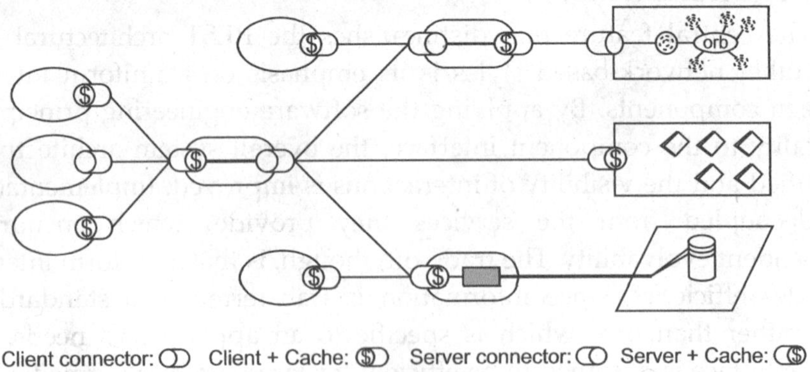

Figure 14.7

The primary disadvantage of layered systems is that they add overhead and latency to the processing of data, reducing user-perceived performance. For a network-based system that supports cache constraints, this can be offset by the benefits of shared caching at intermediaries. Placing shared caches at the boundaries of an organizational domain can result in significant performance benefits. Such layers also allow security policies to be enforced on data crossing the organizational boundary, as is required by firewalls.

The combination of layered system and uniform interface constraints induces architectural properties similar to those of the uniform pipe-and-filter style Although REST interaction is two-way, the large-grain data flows of hypermedia interaction can each be processed like a data-flow network, with filter components selectively applied to the data stream in order to transform the content as it passes. Within REST, intermediary components can actively transform the content of messages because the messages are self-descriptive and their semantics are visible to intermediaries.

14.1.7 Code-On-Demand

The final addition to our constraint set for REST comes from the code-on-demand style of. REST allows client functionality to be extended by downloading and executing code in the form of applets or scripts. This simplifies clients by reducing the number of features required to be pre-implemented. Allowing features to be downloaded after deployment improves system extensibility. However, it also reduces visibility, and thus is only an optional constraint within REST.

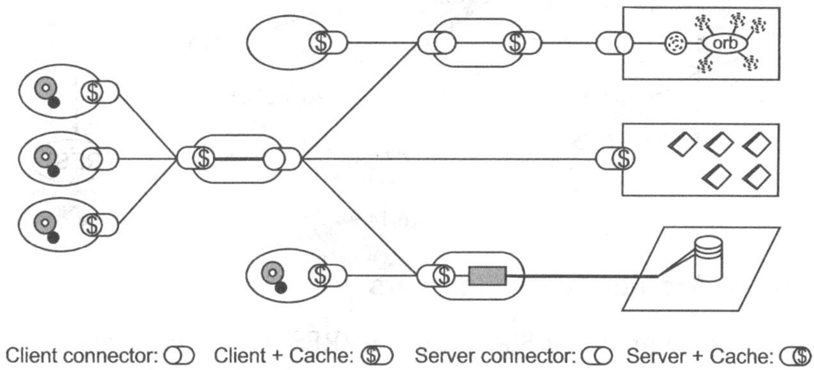

Figure 14.8. REST

The notion of an optional constraint may seem like an oxymoron. However, it does have a purpose in the architectural design of a system that encompasses multiple organizational boundaries. It means that the architecture only gains the benefit (and suffers the disadvantages) of the optional constraints when they are known to be in effect for some realm of the overall system. For example, if all of the client software within an organization is known to support Java applets , then services within that organization can be constructed such that they gain the benefit of enhanced functionality via downloadable Java classes. At the same time, however, the organization's firewall may prevent the transfer of Java applets from external sources, and thus to the rest of the Web it will appear as if those clients do not support code-on-demand. An optional constraint allows us to design an architecture that supports the desired behavior in the general case, but with the understanding that it may be disabled within some contexts.

14.1.8 Style Derivation Summary

REST consists of a set of architectural constraints chosen for the properties they induce on candidate architectures. Although each of these constraints can be considered in isolation, describing them in terms of their derivation from common architectural styles makes it easier to understand the rationale behind their selection. depicts the derivation of REST's constraints graphically in terms of the network-based architectural styles.

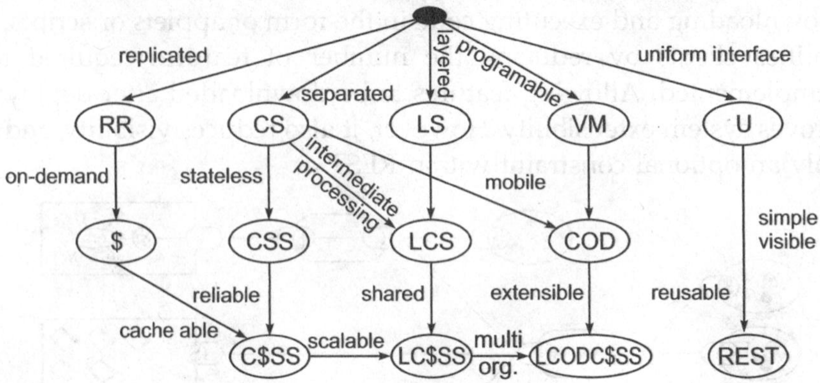

Figure 14.9

14.2 REST Architectural Elements

The Representational State Transfer (REST) style is an abstraction of the architectural elements within a distributed hypermedia system. REST ignores the details of component implementation and protocol syntax in order to focus on the roles of components, the constraints upon their interaction with other components, and their interpretation of significant data elements. It encompasses the fundamental constraints upon components, connectors, and data that define the basis of the Web architecture, and thus the essence of its behavior as a network-based application.

14.2.1 Data Elements

Unlike the distributed object style, where all data is encapsulated within and hidden by the processing components, the nature and state of an architecture's data elements is a key aspect of REST. The rationale for this design can be seen in the nature of distributed hypermedia. When a link is selected, information needs to be moved from the location where it is stored to the location where it will be used by, in most cases, a human reader. This is unlike many other distributed processing paradigms, where it is possible, and usually more efficient, to move the "processing agent" (e.g., mobile code, stored procedure, search expression, etc.) to the data rather than move the data to the processor.

A distributed hypermedia architect has only three fundamental options: (1) render the data where it is located and send a fixed-format image to the recipient; (2) encapsulate the data with a rendering engine and send both to the recipient; (3) send the raw data to the recipient along with metadata that describes the data type, so that the recipient can choose their own rendering engine.

Each option has its advantages and disadvantages. Option 1, the traditional client-server style , allows all information about the true nature of the data to remain hidden within the sender, preventing assumptions from being made about the data structure and making client implementation easier. However, it also severely restricts the functionality of the recipient and places most of the processing load on the sender, leading to scalability problems. Option 2, the mobile object style, provides information hiding while enabling specialized processing of the data via its unique rendering engine, but limits the functionality of the recipient to what is anticipated within that engine and may vastly increase the amount of data transferred. Option 3 allows the sender to remain simple and scalable while minimizing the bytes transferred, but loses the advantages of information hiding and requires that both sender and recipient understand the same data types.

REST provides a hybrid of all three options by focusing on a shared understanding of data types with metadata, but limiting the scope of what is revealed to a standardized interface. REST components communicate by transferring a representation of a resource in a format matching one of an evolving set of standard data types, selected dynamically based on the capabilities or desires of the recipient and the nature of the resource. Whether the representation is in the same format as the raw source, or is derived from the source, remains hidden behind the interface. The benefits of the mobile object style are approximated by sending a representation that consists of instructions in the standard data format of an encapsulated rendering engine (e.g., Java). REST therefore gains the separation of concerns of the client-server style without the server scalability problem, allows information hiding through a generic interface to enable encapsulation and evolution of services, and provides for a diverse set of functionality through downloadable feature-engines.

REST's data elements are summarized in Table 14-1.

Table 14-1: REST Data Elements

Data Element	Modern Web Examples
Resource	The intended conceptual target of a hypertext reference
Resource identifier	URL, URN
Representation	HTML document, JPEG image
Representation metadata	Media type, last-modified time
Resource metadata	Source link, alternates, vary
Control data	If-modified-since, cache-control

14.2.1.1 Resources and Resource Identifiers

The key abstraction of information in REST is a resource. Any information that can be named can be a resource: a document or image, a temporal service (e.g. "today's weather in Los Angeles"), a collection of other resources, a non-virtual object (e.g. a person), and so on. In other words, any concept that might be the target of an author's hypertext reference must fit within the definition of a resource. A resource is a conceptual mapping to a set of entities, not the entity that corresponds to the mapping at any particular point in time.

More precisely, a resource R is a temporally varying membership function MR(t), which for time t maps to a set of entities, or values, which are equivalent. The values in the set may be resource representations and/or resource identifiers. A resource can map to the empty set, which allows references to be made to a concept before any realization of that concept exists -- a notion that was foreign to most hypertext systems prior to the Web. Some resources are static in the sense that, when examined at any time after their creation, they always correspond to the same value set. Others have a high degree of variance in their value over time. The only thing that is required to be static for a resource is the semantics of the mapping, since the semantics is what distinguishes one resource from another.

For example, the "authors' preferred version" of an academic paper is a mapping whose value changes over time, whereas a mapping to "the paper published in the proceedings of conference X" is static. These are two distinct resources, even if they both map to the same value at some point in time. The distinction is necessary so that both resources can be identified and referenced independently. A similar example from software engineering is the separate identification of a version-controlled source code file when referring to the "latest revision", "revision number 1.2.7", or "revision included with the Orange release."

This abstract definition of a resource enables key features of the Web architecture. First, it provides generality by encompassing many sources of information without artificially distinguishing them by type or implementation. Second, it allows late binding of the reference to a representation, enabling content negotiation to take place based on characteristics of the request. Finally, it allows an author to reference the concept rather than some singular representation of that concept, thus removing the need to change all existing links whenever the representation changes (assuming the author used the right identifier).

REST uses a resource identifier to identify the particular resource involved in an interaction between components. REST connectors provide a generic interface for accessing and manipulating the value set of a resource, regardless of how the membership function is defined or the type of software that is handling the request. The naming authority that assigned the resource identifier, making it possible to reference the resource, is responsible for maintaining the semantic validity of the mapping over time (i.e., ensuring that the membership function does not change).

Traditional hypertext systems, which typically operate in a closed or local environment, use unique node or document identifiers that change every time the information changes, relying on link servers to maintain references separately from the content. Since centralized link servers are an anathema to the immense scale and multi-organizational domain requirements of the Web, REST relies instead on the author choosing a resource identifier that best fits the nature of the concept being identified. Naturally, the quality of an identifier is often proportional to the amount of money spent to retain its validity, which leads to broken links as ephemeral (or poorly supported) information moves or disappears over time.

14.2.1.2 Representations

REST components perform actions on a resource by using a representation to capture the current or intended state of that resource and transferring that representation between components. A representation is a sequence of bytes, plus representation metadata to describe those bytes. Other commonly used but less precise names for a representation include: document, file, and HTTP message entity, instance, or variant.

A representation consists of data, metadata describing the data, and, on occasion, metadata to describe the metadata (usually for the purpose of verifying message integrity). Metadata is in the form of name-value pairs, where the name corresponds to a standard that defines the value's structure and semantics. Response messages may include both representation metadata and resource metadata: information about the resource that is not specific to the supplied representation.

Control data defines the purpose of a message between components, such as the action being requested or the meaning of a response. It is also used to parameterize requests and override the default behavior of some connecting elements. For example, cache behavior can be modified by control data included in the request or response message.

Depending on the message control data, a given representation may indicate the current state of the requested resource, the desired state for the requested resource, or the value of some other resource, such as a representation of the input data within a client's query form, or a representation of some error condition for a response. For example, remote authoring of a resource requires that the author send a representation to the server, thus establishing a value for that resource that can be retrieved by later requests. If the value set of a resource at a given time consists of multiple representations, content negotiation may be used to select the best representation for inclusion in a given message.

The data format of a representation is known as a media type. A representation can be included in a message and processed by the recipient according to the control data of the message and the nature of the media type. Some media types are intended for automated processing, some are intended to be rendered for viewing by a user, and a few are capable of both. Composite media types can be used to enclose multiple representations in a single message.

The design of a media type can directly impact the user-perceived performance of a distributed hypermedia system. Any data that must be received before the recipient can begin rendering the representation adds to the latency of an interaction. A data format that places the most important rendering information up front, such that the initial information can be incrementally rendered while the rest of the information is being received, results in much better user-perceived performance than a data format that must be entirely received before rendering can begin.

For example, a Web browser that can incrementally render a large HTML document while it is being received provides significantly better user-perceived performance than one that waits until the entire document is completely received prior to rendering, even though the network performance is the same. Note that the rendering ability of a representation can also be impacted by the choice of content. If the dimensions of dynamically sized tables and embedded objects must be determined before they can be rendered, their occurrence within the viewing area of a hypermedia page will increase its latency.

14.2.2 Connectors

REST uses various connector types, summarized in Table 14-2, to encapsulate the activities of accessing resources and transferring resource representations. The connectors present an abstract interface for component communication, enhancing simplicity by providing a clean separation of concerns and hiding the underlying implementation of resources and communication mechanisms. The generality of the interface also enables substitutability: if the users' only access to the system is via an abstract interface, the implementation can be replaced without impacting the users. Since a connector manages network communication for a component, information can be shared across multiple interactions in order to improve efficiency and responsiveness.

Table 14-2: REST Connectors

Connector	Modern Web Examples
Client	Libwww, libwww-perl
Server	Libwww, Apache API, NSAPI
Cache	Browser cache, Akamai cache network
Resolver	Bind (DNS lookup library)
Tunnel	SOCKS, SSL after HTTP CONNECT

All REST interactions are stateless. That is, each request contains all of the information necessary for a connector to understand the request, independent of any requests that may have preceded it. This restriction accomplishes four functions: (1) it removes any need for the connectors to retain application state between requests, thus reducing consumption of physical resources and improving scalability; (2) it allows interactions to be processed in parallel without requiring that the processing mechanism understand the interaction semantics; (3) it allows an intermediary to view and understand a request in isolation, which may be necessary when services are dynamically rearranged; and, (4) it forces all of the information that might factor into the reusability of a cached response to be present in each request.

The connector interface is similar to procedural invocation, but with important differences in the passing of parameters and results. The in-parameters consist of request control data, a resource identifier indicating the target of the request, and an optional representation. The out-parameters consist of response control data, optional resource metadata, and an optional representation. From an abstract viewpoint the invocation is synchronous, but both in and out-parameters can be passed as data streams. In other words, processing can be invoked before the value of the parameters is completely known, thus avoiding the latency of batch processing large data transfers.

The primary connector types are client and server. The essential difference between the two is that a client initiates communication by making a request, whereas a server listens for connections and responds to requests in order to supply access to its services. A component may include both client and server connectors.

A third connector type, the cache connector, can be located on the interface to a client or server connector in order to save cacheable responses to current interactions so that they can be reused for later requested interactions. A cache may be used by a client to avoid repetition of network communication, or by a server to avoid repeating the process of generating a response, with both cases serving to reduce interaction latency. A cache is typically implemented within the address space of the connector that uses it.

Some cache connectors are shared, meaning that its cached responses may be used in answer to a client other than the one for which the response was originally obtained. Shared caching can be effective at reducing the impact of "flash crowds" on the load of a popular server, particularly when the caching is arranged hierarchically to cover large groups of users, such as those within a company's intranet, the customers of an Internet service provider, or Universities sharing a national network backbone. However, shared caching can also lead to errors if the cached response does not match what would have been obtained by a new request. REST attempts to balance the desire for transparency in cache behavior with the desire for efficient use of the network, rather than assuming that absolute transparency is always required.

A cache is able to determine the cacheability of a response because the interface is generic rather than specific to each resource. By default, the response to a retrieval request is cacheable and the responses to other requests are non-cacheable. If some form of user authentication is part of the request, or if the response indicates that it should not be shared, then the response is only cacheable by a non-shared cache. A component can override these defaults by including control data that marks the interaction as cacheable, non-cacheable or cacheable for only a limited time.

A resolver translates partial or complete resource identifiers into the network address information needed to establish an inter-component connection. For example, most URI include a DNS hostname as the mechanism for identifying the naming authority for the resource. In order to initiate a request, a Web browser will extract the hostname from the URI and make use of a DNS resolver to obtain the Internet Protocol address for that authority. Another example is that some identification schemes (e.g., URN) require an intermediary to translate a permanent identifier to a more transient address in order to access the identified resource. Use of one or more intermediate resolvers can improve the longevity of resource references through indirection, though doing so adds to the request latency.

The final form of connector type is a tunnel, which simply relays communication across a connection boundary, such as a firewall or lower-level network gateway. The only reason it is modeled as part of REST and not abstracted away as part of the network infrastructure is that some REST components may dynamically switch from active component behavior to that of a tunnel. The primary example is an HTTP proxy that switches to a tunnel in response to a CONNECT method request , thus allowing its client to directly communicate with a remote server using a different protocol, such as TLS, that doesn't allow proxies. The tunnel disappears when both ends terminate their communication.

14.2.3 Components

REST components, summarized in Table 14-3, are typed by their roles in an overall application action.

Table 14-3: REST Components

Component	Modern Web Examples
Origin server	Apache httpd, Microsoft IIS
Gateway	Squid, CGI, Reverse Proxy
Proxy	CERN Proxy, Netscape Proxy, Gauntlet
User agent	Netscape Navigator, Lynx, MOM spider

A user agent uses a client connector to initiate a request and becomes the ultimate recipient of the response. The most common example is a Web browser, which provides access to information services and renders service responses according to the application needs.

An origin server uses a server connector to govern the namespace for a requested resource. It is the definitive source for representations of its resources and must be the ultimate recipient of any request that intends to modify the value of its resources. Each origin server provides a generic interface to its services as a resource hierarchy. The resource implementation details are hidden behind the interface.

Intermediary components act as both a client and a server in order to forward, with possible translation, requests and responses. A proxy component is an intermediary selected by a client to provide interface encapsulation of other services, data translation, performance enhancement, or security protection. A gateway (a.k.a., reverse proxy) component is an intermediary imposed by the network or origin server to provide an interface encapsulation of other services, for data translation, performance enhancement, or security enforcement. Note that the difference between a proxy and a gateway is that a client determines when it will use a proxy.

14.3 REST Architectural Views

Now that we have an understanding of the REST architectural elements in isolation, we can use architectural views to describe how the elements work together to form architecture. Three types of view--process, connector, and data--are useful for illuminating the design principles of REST.

14.3.1 Process View

A process view of architecture is primarily effective at eliciting the interaction relationships among components by revealing the path of data as it flows through the system. Unfortunately, the interaction of a real system usually involves an extensive number of components, resulting in an overall view that is obscured by the details. Provides a sample of the process view from a REST-based architecture at a particular instance during the processing of three parallel requests.

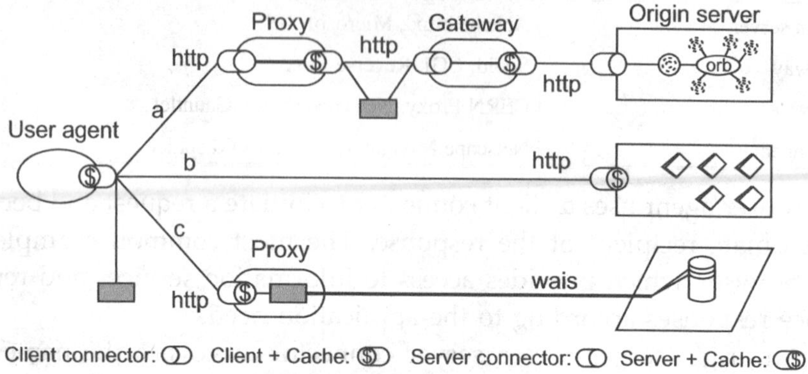

Figure 14.10. REST architectural views.

REST's client-server separation of concerns simplifies component implementation, reduces the complexity of connector semantics, improves the effectiveness of performance tuning, and increases the scalability of pure server components. Layered system constraints allow intermediaries--proxies, gateways, and firewalls--to be introduced at various points in the communication without changing the interfaces between components, thus allowing them to assist in communication translation or improve performance via large-scale, shared caching. REST enables intermediate processing by constraining messages to be self-descriptive: interaction is stateless between requests, standard methods and media types are used to indicate semantics and exchange information, and responses explicitly indicate cache ability.

Since the components are connected dynamically, their arrangement and function for a particular application action has characteristics similar to a pipe-and-filter style. Although REST components communicate via bi-directional streams, the processing of each direction is independent and therefore susceptible to stream transducers (filters). The generic connector interface allows components to be placed on the stream based on the properties of each request or response.

Services may be implemented using a complex hierarchy of intermediaries and multiple distributed origin servers. The stateless nature of REST allows each interaction to be independent of the others, removing the need for an awareness of the overall component topology, an impossible task for Internet-scale architecture, and allowing components to act as either destinations or intermediaries, determined dynamically by the target of each request. Connectors need only be aware of each other's existence during the scope of their communication, though they may cache the existence and capabilities of other components for performance reasons.

14.3.2 Connector View

A connector view of an architecture concentrates on the mechanics of the communication between components. For a REST-based architecture, we are particularly interested in the constraints that define the generic resource interface.

Client connectors examine the resource identifier in order to select an appropriate communication mechanism for each request. For example, a client may be configured to connect to a specific proxy component, perhaps one acting as an annotation filter, when the identifier indicates that it is a local resource. Likewise, a client can be configured to reject requests for some subset of identifiers.

REST does not restrict communication to a particular protocol, but it does constrain the interface between components, and hence the scope of interaction and implementation assumptions that might otherwise be made between components. For example, the Web's primary transfer protocol is HTTP, but the architecture also includes seamless access to resources that originate on pre-existing network servers, including FTP, Gopher and WAIS. Interaction with those services is restricted to the semantics of a REST connector. This constraint sacrifices some of the advantages of other architectures, such as the stateful interaction of a relevance feedback protocol like WAIS, in order to retain the advantages of a single, generic interface for connector semantics. In return, the generic interface makes it possible to access a multitude of services through a single proxy. If an application needs the additional capabilities of another architecture, it can implement and invoke those capabilities as a separate system running in parallel, similar to how the Web architecture interfaces with "telnet" and "mailto" resources.

14.3.3 Data View

A data view of architecture reveals the application state as information flows through the components. Since REST is specifically targeted at distributed information systems, it views an application as a cohesive structure of information and control alternatives through which a user can perform a desired task. For example, looking-up a word in an on-line dictionary is one application, as is touring through a virtual museum, or reviewing a set of class notes to study for an exam. Each application defines goals for the underlying system, against which the system's performance can be measured.

Component interactions occur in the form of dynamically sized messages. Small or medium-grain messages are used for control semantics, but the bulk of application work is accomplished via large-grain messages containing a complete resource representation. The most frequent form of request semantics is that of retrieving a representation of a resource, which can often be cached for later reuse.

REST concentrates all of the control state into the representations received in response to interactions. The goal is to improve server scalability by eliminating any need for the server to maintain an awareness of the client state beyond the current request. An application's state is therefore defined by its pending requests, the topology of connected components (some of which may be filtering buffered data), the active requests on those connectors, the data flow of representations in response to those requests, and the processing of those representations as they are received by the user agent.

An application reaches a steady-state whenever it has no outstanding requests; i.e., it has no pending requests and all of the responses to its current set of requests have been completely received or received to the point where they can be treated as a representation data stream. For a browser application, this state corresponds to a "web page," including the primary representation and ancillary representations, such as in-line images, embedded applets, and style sheets. The significance of application steady states is seen in their impact on both user-perceived performance and the burstiness of network request traffic.

The user-perceived performance of a browser application is determined by the latency between steady-states: the period of time between the selection of a hypermedia link on one web page and the point when usable information has been rendered for the next web page. The optimization of browser performance is therefore centered around reducing this communication latency.

Since REST-based architectures communicate primarily through the transfer of representations of resources, latency can be impacted by both the design of the communication protocols and the design of the representation data formats. The ability to incrementally render the response data as it is received is determined by the design of the media type and the availability of layout information (visual dimensions of in-line objects) within each representation.

An interesting observation is that the most efficient network request is one that doesn't use the network. In other words, the ability to reuse a cached response results in a considerable improvement in application performance. Although use of a cache adds some latency to each individual request due to lookup overhead, the average request latency is significantly reduced when even a small percentage of requests result in usable cache hits.

The next control state of an application resides in the representation of the first requested resource, so obtaining that first representation is a priority. REST interaction is therefore improved by protocols that "respond first and think later." In other words, a protocol that requires multiple interactions per user action, in order to do things like negotiate feature capabilities prior to sending a content response, will be perceptively slower than a protocol that sends whatever is most likely to be optimal first and then provides a list of alternatives for the client to retrieve if the first response is unsatisfactory.

The application state is controlled and stored by the user agent and can be composed of representations from multiple servers. In addition to freeing the server from the scalability problems of storing state, this allows the user to directly manipulate the state (e.g., a Web browser's history), anticipate changes to that state (e.g., link maps and perfecting of representations), and jump from one application to another (e.g., bookmarks and URI-entry dialogs).

The model application is therefore an engine that moves from one state to the next by examining and choosing from among the alternative state transitions in the current set of representations. Not surprisingly, this exactly matches the user interface of a hypermedia browser. However, the style does not assume that all applications are browsers. In fact, the application details are hidden from the server by the generic connector interface, and thus a user agent could equally be an automated robot performing information retrieval for an indexing service, a personal agent looking for data that matches certain criteria, or a maintenance spider busy patrolling the information for broken references or modified content.

14.4 Related Work

Bass, et al. devote a chapter on architecture for the World Wide Web, but their description only encompasses the implementation architecture within the CERN/W3C developed libwww (client and server libraries) and Jigsaw software. Although those implementations reflect many of the design constraints of REST, having been developed by people familiar with the Web's architectural design and rationale, the real WWW architecture is independent of any single implementation. The modern Web is defined by its standard interfaces and protocols, not how those interfaces and protocols are implemented in a given piece of software.

The REST style draws from many preexisting distributed process paradigms communication protocols, and software fields. REST component interactions are structured in a layered client-server style, but the added constraints of the generic resource interface create the opportunity for substitutability and inspection by intermediaries. Requests and responses have the appearance of a remote invocation style, but REST messages are targeted at a conceptual resource rather than an implementation identifier.

Several attempts have been made to model the Web architecture as a form of distributed file system (e.g., WebNFS) or as a distributed object system. However, they exclude various Web resource types or implementation strategies as being "not interesting," when in fact their presence invalidates the assumptions that underlie such models. REST works well because it does not limit the implementation of resources to certain predefined models, allowing each application to choose an implementation that best matches its own needs and enabling the replacement of implementations without impacting the user.

The interaction method of sending representations of resources to consuming components has some parallels with event-based integration

(EBI) styles. The key difference is that EBI styles are push-based. The component containing the state (equivalent to an origin server in REST) issues an event whenever the state changes, whether or not any component is actually interested in or listening for such an event. In the REST style, consuming components usually pull representations. Although this is less efficient when viewed as a single client wishing to monitor a single resource, the scale of the Web makes an unregulated push model infeasible.

The principled use of the REST style in the Web, with its clear notion of components, connectors, and representations, relates closely to the C2 architectural style. The C2 style supports the development of distributed, dynamic applications by focusing on structured use of connectors to obtain substrate independence. C2 applications rely on asynchronous notification of state changes and request messages. As with other event-based schemes, C2 is nominally push-based, though C2 architecture could operate in REST's pull style by only emitting a notification upon receipt of a request. However, the C2 style lacks the intermediary-friendly constraints of REST, such as the generic resource interface, guaranteed stateless interactions, and intrinsic support for caching.

14.5 Summary

This chapter introduced the Representational State Transfer (REST) architectural style for distributed hypermedia systems. REST provides a set of architectural constraints that, when applied as a whole, emphasizes scalability of component interactions, generality of interfaces, independent deployment of components, and intermediary components to reduce interaction latency, enforce security, and encapsulate legacy systems. I described the software engineering principles guiding REST and the interaction constraints chosen to retain those principles, while contrasting them to the constraints of other architectural styles.

The next chapter presents an evaluation of the REST architecture through the experience and lessons learned from applying REST to the design, specification, and deployment of the modern Web architecture. This work included authoring the current Internet standards-track specifications of the Hypertext Transfer Protocol (HTTP/1.1) and Uniform Resource Identifiers (URI), and implementing the architecture through the libwww-perl client protocol library and Apache HTTP server.

14.6 Review Questions

1. Explain the Representational State Transfer (REST).
2. Write short notes
   - REST Architectural Elements
   - Data Elements
   - Connectors
   - Components
   - REST Architectural Views
   - Process View
   - Connector View.

—•—•—•—•—

Chapter No. 15

Experience and Evaluation

Since 1994, the REST architectural style has been used to guide the design and development of the architecture for the modern Web. This chapter describes the experience and lessons learned from applying REST while authoring the Internet standards for the Hypertext Transfer Protocol (HTTP) and Uniform Resource Identifiers (URI), the two specifications that define the generic interface used by all component interactions on the Web, as well as from the deployment of these technologies in the form of the libwww-perl client library, the Apache HTTP Server Project, and other implementations of the protocol standards.

15.1 Standardizing the Web

The motivation for developing REST was to create an architectural model for how the Web should work, such that it could serve as the guiding framework for the Web protocol standards. REST has been applied to describe the desired Web architecture, help identify existing problems, compare alternative solutions, and ensure that protocol extensions would not violate the core constraints that make the Web successful. This work was done as part of the Internet Engineering Taskforce (IETF) and World Wide Web Consortium (W3C) efforts to define the architectural standards for the Web: HTTP, URI, and HTML.

My involvement in the Web standards process began in late 1993, while developing the libwww-perl protocol library that served as the client connector interface for MOM spider. At the time, the Web's architecture was described by a set of informal hypertext notes, two early introductory papers, draft hypertext specifications representing proposed features for the Web (some of which had already been implemented), and the archive of the public www-talk mailing list that was used for informal discussion among the participants in the WWW project worldwide. Each of the specifications were significantly out of date when compared with

Web implementations, mostly due to the rapid evolution of the Web after the introduction of the Mosaic graphical browser [NCSA]. Several experimental extensions had been added to HTTP to allow for proxies, but for the most part the protocol assumed a direct connection between the user agent and either an HTTP origin server or a gateway to legacy systems. There was no awareness within the architecture of caching, proxies, or spiders, even though implementations were readily available and running amok. Many other extensions were being proposed for inclusion in the next versions of the protocols.

At the same time, there was growing pressure within the industry to standardize on some version, or versions, of the Web interface protocols. The W3C was formed by Berners-Lee to act as a think-tank for Web architecture and to supply the authoring resources needed to write the Web standards and reference implementations, but the standardization itself was governed by the Internet Engineering Taskforce [www.ietf.org] and its working groups on URI, HTTP, and HTML. Due to my experience developing Web software, I was first chosen to author the specification for Relative URL, later teamed with Henrik Frystyk Nielsen to author the HTTP/1.0 specification, became the primary architect of HTTP/1.1, and finally authored the revision of the URL specifications to form the standard on URI generic syntax.

The first edition of REST was developed between October 1994 and August 1995, primarily as a means for communicating Web concepts as we wrote the HTTP/1.0 specification and the initial HTTP/1.1 proposal. It was iteratively improved over the next five years and applied to various revisions and extensions of the Web protocol standards. REST was originally referred to as the "HTTP object model," but that name would often lead to misinterpretation of it as the implementation model of an HTTP server. The name "Representational State Transfer" is intended to evoke an image of how a well-designed Web application behaves: a network of web pages (a virtual state-machine), where the user progresses through the application by selecting links (state transitions), resulting in the next page (representing the next state of the application) being transferred to the user and rendered for their use.

REST is not intended to capture all possible uses of the Web protocol standards. There are applications of HTTP and URI that do not match the application model of a distributed hypermedia system. The important point, however, is that REST does capture all of those aspects of a distributed hypermedia system that are considered central to the behavioral and performance requirements of the Web, such that optimizing behavior within the model will result in optimum behavior within the deployed Web architecture. In other words, REST is optimized for the common case so that the constraints it applies to the Web architecture will also be optimized for the common case.

15.2 REST Applied to URI

Uniform Resource Identifiers (URI) are both the simplest element of the Web architecture and the most important. URI have been known by many names: WWW addresses, Universal Document Identifiers, Universal Resource Identifiers, and finally the combination of Uniform Resource Locators (URL) and Names (URN) . Aside from its name, the URI syntax has remained relatively unchanged since 1992. However, the specification of Web addresses also defines the scope and semantics of what we mean by resource, which has changed since the early Web architecture. REST was used to define the term resource for the URI standard, as well as the overall semantics of the generic interface for manipulating resources via their representations.

15.2.1 Redefinition of Resource

The early Web architecture defined URI as document identifiers. Authors were instructed to define identifiers in terms of a document's location on the network. Web protocols could then be used to retrieve that document. However, this definition proved to be unsatisfactory for a number of reasons. First, it suggests that the author is identifying the content transferred, which would imply that the identifier should change whenever the content changes. Second, there exist many addresses that corresponded to a service rather than a document -- authors may be intending to direct readers to that service, rather than to any specific result from a prior access of that service. Finally, there exist addresses that do not correspond to a document at some periods of time, such as when the document does not yet exist or when the address is being used solely for naming, rather than locating, information.

The definition of resource in REST is based on a simple premise: identifiers should change as infrequently as possible. Because the Web uses embedded identifiers rather than link servers, authors need an identifier that closely matches the semantics they intend by a hypermedia reference, allowing the reference to remain static even though the result of accessing that reference may change over time. REST accomplishes this by defining a resource to be the semantics of what the author intends to identify, rather than the value corresponding to those semantics at the time the reference is created. It is then left to the author to ensure that the identifier chosen for a reference does indeed identify the intended semantics.

15.2.2 Manipulating Shadows

Defining resource such that a URI identifies a concept rather than a document leaves us with another question: how does a user access, manipulate, or transfer a concept such that they can get something useful when a hypertext link is selected? REST answers that question by defining the things that are manipulated to be representations of the identified resource, rather than the resource itself. An origin server maintains a mapping from resource identifiers to the set of representations corresponding to each resource. A resource is therefore manipulated by transferring representations through the generic interface defined by the resource identifier.

REST's definition of resource derives from the central requirement of the Web: independent authoring of interconnected hypertext across multiple trust domains. Forcing the interface definitions to match the interface requirements causes the protocols to seem vague, but that is only because the interface being manipulated is only an interface and not an implementation. The protocols are specific about the intent of an application action, but the mechanism behind the interface must decide how that intention affects the underlying implementation of the resource mapping to representations.

Information hiding is one of the key software engineering principles that motivate the uniform interface of REST. Because a client is restricted to the manipulation of representations rather than directly accessing the implementation of a resource, the implementation can be constructed in whatever form is desired by the naming authority without impacting the clients that may use its representations. In addition, if multiple representations of the resource exist at the time it is accessed, a content selection algorithm can be used to dynamically select a representation that best fits the capabilities of that client. The disadvantage, of course, is that remote authoring of a resource is not as straightforward as remote authoring of a file.

15.2.3 Remote Authoring

The challenge of remote authoring via the Web's uniform interface is due to the separation between the representation that can be retrieved by a client and the mechanism that might be used on the server to store, generate, or retrieve the content of that representation. An individual server may map some part of its namespace to a file system, which in turn maps to the equivalent of an inode that can be mapped into a disk location, but those underlying mechanisms provide a means of associating a resource to a set of representations rather than identifying the resource itself. Many different resources could map to the same representation, while other resources may have no representation mapped at all.

In order to author an existing resource, the author must first obtain the specific source resource URI: the set of URI that bind to the handler's underlying representation for the target resource. A resource does not always map to a singular file, but all resources that are not static are derived from some other resources, and by following the derivation tree an author can eventually find all of the source resources that must be edited in order to modify the representation of a resource. These same principles apply to any form of derived representation, whether it be from content negotiation, scripts, servlets, managed configurations, versioning, etc.

The resource is not the storage object. The resource is not a mechanism that the server uses to handle the storage object. The resource is a conceptual mapping -- the server receives the identifier (which identifies the mapping) and applies it to its current mapping implementation (usually a combination of collection-specific deep tree traversal and/or hash tables) to find the currently responsible handler implementation and the handler implementation then selects the appropriate action response based on the request content. All of these implementation-specific issues are hidden behind the Web interface; their nature cannot be assumed by a client that only has access through the Web interface.

For example, consider what happens when a Web site grows in user base and decides to replace its old Brand X server, based on an XOS platform, with a new Apache server running on Free BSD. The disk storage hardware is replaced. The operating system is replaced. The HTTP server is replaced. Perhaps even the method of generating responses for all of the content is replaced. However, what doesn't need to change is the Web interface: if designed correctly, the namespace on the new server can mirror that of the old, meaning that from the client's perspective, which only knows about resources and not about how they are implemented, nothing has changed aside from the improved robustness of the site.

15.2.4 Binding Semantics to URI

As mentioned above, a resource can have many identifiers. In other words, there may exist two or more different URI that have equivalent semantics when used to access a server. It is also possible to have two URI that result in the same mechanism being used upon access to the server, and yet those URI identify two different resources because they don't mean the same thing.

Semantics are a by-product of the act of assigning resource identifiers and populating those resources with representations. At no time whatsoever do the server or client software need to know or understand the meaning of a URI -- they merely act as a conduit through which the creator of a resource (a human naming authority) can associate representations with the semantics identified by the URI. In other words, there are no resources on the server; just mechanisms that supply answers across an abstract interface defined by resources. It may seem odd, but this is the essence of what makes the Web work across so many different implementations.

It is the nature of every engineer to define things in terms of the characteristics of the components that will be used to compose the finished product. The Web doesn't work that way. The Web architecture consists of constraints on the communication model between components, based on the role of each component during an application action. This prevents the components from assuming anything beyond the resource abstraction, thus hiding the actual mechanisms on either side of the abstract interface.

15.2.5 REST Mismatches in URI

Like most real-world systems, not all components of the deployed Web architecture obey every constraint present in its architectural design. REST has been used both as a means to define architectural improvements and to identify architectural mismatches. Mismatches occur when, due to ignorance or oversight, a software implementation is deployed that violates the architectural constraints. While mismatches cannot be avoided in general, it is possible to identify them before they become standardized.

Although the URI design matches REST's architectural notion of identifiers, syntax alone is insufficient to force naming authorities to define their own URI according to the resource model. One form of abuse is to include information that identifies the current user within all of the URI referenced by a hypermedia response representation. Such embedded user-ids can be used to maintain session state on the server, track user behavior by logging their actions, or carry user preferences across multiple actions (e.g., Hyper-G's gateways. However, by violating REST's constraints, these systems also cause shared caching to become ineffective, reduce server scalability, and result in undesirable effects when a user shares those references with others.

Another conflict with the resource interface of REST occurs when software attempts to treat the Web as a distributed file system. Since file systems expose the implementation of their information, tools exist to "mirror" that information across to multiple sites as a means of load balancing and redistributing the content closer to users. However, they can do so only because files have a fixed set of semantics (a named sequence of bytes) that can be duplicated easily. In contrast, attempts to mirror the content of a Web server as files will fail because the resource interface does not always match the semantics of a file system, and because both data and metadata are included within, and significant to, the semantics of a representation. Web server content can be replicated at remote sites, but only by replicating the entire server mechanism and configuration, or by selectively replicating only those resources with representations known to be static (e.g., cache networks contract with Web sites to replicate specific resource representations to the "edges" of the overall Internet in order to reduce latency and distribute load away from the origin server).

15.3 REST Applied to HTTP

The Hypertext Transfer Protocol (HTTP) has a special role in the Web architecture as both the primary application-level protocol for communication between Web components and the only protocol designed specifically for the transfer of resource representations. Unlike URI, there were a large number of changes needed in order for HTTP to support the modern Web architecture. The developers of HTTP implementations have been conservative in their adoption of proposed enhancements, and thus extensions needed to be proven and subjected to standards review before they could be deployed. REST was used to identify problems with the existing HTTP implementations, specify an interoperable subset of that protocol as HTTP/1.0, analyze proposed extensions for HTTP/1.1 , and provide motivating rationale for deploying HTTP/1.1.

The key problem areas in HTTP that were identified by REST included planning for the deployment of new protocol versions, separating message parsing from HTTP semantics and the underlying transport layer (TCP), distinguishing between authoritative and non-authoritative responses, fine-grained control of caching, and various aspects of the protocol that failed to be self-descriptive. REST has also been used to model the performance of Web applications based on HTTP and anticipate the impact of such extensions as persistent connections and content negotiation. Finally, REST has been used to limit the scope of standardized HTTP extensions to those that fit within the architectural model, rather than allowing the applications that misuse HTTP to equally influence the standard.

15.3.1 Extensibility

One of the major goals of REST is to support the gradual and fragmented deployment of changes within an already deployed architecture. HTTP was modified to support that goal through the introduction of versioning requirements and rules for extending each of the protocol's syntax elements.

15.3.1.1 Protocol Versioning

HTTP is a family of protocols, distinguished by major and minor version numbers, that share the name primarily because they correspond to the protocol expected when communicating directly with a service based on the "http" URL namespace. A connector must obey the constraints placed on the HTTP-version protocol element included in each message.

The HTTP-version of a message represents the protocol capabilities of the sender and the gross-compatibility (major version number) of the message being sent. This allows a client to use a reduced (HTTP/1.0) subset of features in making a normal HTTP/1.1 request, while at the same time indicating to the recipient that it is capable of supporting full HTTP/1.1 communication. In other words, it provides a tentative form of protocol negotiation on the HTTP scale. Each connection on a request/response chain can operate at its best protocol level in spite of the limitations of some clients or servers that are parts of the chain.

The intention of the protocol is that the server should always respond with the highest minor version of the protocol it understands within the same major version of the client's request message. The restriction is that the server cannot use those optional features of the higher-level protocol, which are forbidden to be sent to such an older-version client. There are no required features of a protocol that cannot be used with all other minor versions within that major version, since that would be an incompatible change and thus require a change in the major version. The only features of HTTP that can depend on a minor version number change are those that are interpreted by immediate neighbors in the communication, because HTTP does not require that the entire request/response chain of intermediary components speak the same version.

These rules exist to assist in the deployment of multiple protocol revisions and to prevent the HTTP architects from forgetting that deployment of the protocol is an important aspect of its design. They do so by making it easy to differentiate between compatible changes to the protocol and incompatible changes. Compatible changes are easy to deploy and communication of the differences can be achieved within the protocol stream. Incompatible changes are difficult to deploy because they require some determination of acceptance of the protocol before the protocol stream can commence.

15.3.1.2 Extensible Protocol Elements

HTTP includes a number of separate namespaces, each of which has differing constraints, but all of which share the requirement of being extensible without bound. Some of the namespaces are governed by separate Internet standards and shared by multiple protocols (e.g., URI schemes, media types, MIME header field names, charset values, language tags), while others are governed by HTTP, including the namespaces for method names, response status codes, non-MIME header field names, and values within standard HTTP header fields. Since early HTTP did not define a consistent set of rules for how changes within these namespaces could be deployed, this was one of the first problems tackled by the specification effort.

HTTP request semantics are signified by the request method name. Method extension is allowed whenever a standardizable set of semantics can be shared between client, server, and any intermediaries that may be between them. Unfortunately, early HTTP extensions, specifically the HEAD method, made the parsing of an HTTP response message dependent on knowing the semantics of the request method. This led to a deployment contradiction: if a recipient needs to know the semantics of a method before it can be safely forwarded by an intermediary, then all intermediaries must be updated before a new method can be deployed.

This deployment problem was fixed by separating the rules for parsing and forwarding HTTP messages from the semantics associated with new HTTP protocol elements. For example, HEAD is the only method for which the Content-Length header field has a meaning other than signifying the message body length, and no new method can change the message length calculation. GET and HEAD are also the only methods for which conditional request header fields have the semantics of a cache refresh, whereas for all other methods they have the meaning of a precondition.

Likewise, HTTP needed a general rule for interpreting new response status codes, such that new responses could be deployed without significantly harming older clients. We therefore expanded upon the rule that each status code belonged to a class signified by the first digit of its three-digit decimal number: 100-199 indicating that the message contains a provisional information response, 200-299 indicating that the request succeeded, 300-399 indicating that the request needs to be redirected to another resource, 400-499 indicating that the client made an error that should not be repeated, and 500-599 indicating that the server encountered an error, but that the client may get a better response later (or via some other server). If a recipient does not understand the specific semantics of the status code in a given message, then they must treat it in the same way as the x00 code within its class. Like the rule for method names, this extensibility rule places a requirement on the current architecture such that it anticipates future change. Changes can therefore be deployed onto an existing architecture with less fear of adverse component reactions.

15.3.1.3 Upgrade

The addition of the Upgrade header field in HTTP/1.1 reduces the difficulty of deploying incompatible changes by allowing the client to advertise its willingness for a better protocol while communicating in an older protocol stream. Upgrade was specifically added to support the selective replacement of HTTP/1.x with other, future protocols that might be more efficient for some tasks. Thus, HTTP not only supports internal extensibility, but also completes replacement of itself during an active connection. If the server supports the improved protocol and desires to switch, it simply responds with a 101 status and continues on as if the request were received in that upgraded protocol.

15.3.2 Self-descriptive Messages

REST constrains messages between components to be self-descriptive in order to support intermediate processing of interactions. However, there were aspects of early HTTP that failed to be self-descriptive, including the lack of host identification within requests, failure to syntactically distinguish between message control data and representation metadata, failure to differentiate between control data intended only for the immediate connection peer versus metadata intended for all recipients, lack of support for mandatory extensions, and the need for metadata to describe representations with layered encoding.

15.3.2.1 Host

One of the worst mistakes in the early HTTP design was the decision not to send the complete URI that is the target of a request message, but rather send only those portions that were not used in setting up the connection. The assumption was that a server would know its own naming authority based on the IP address and TCP port of the connection.

However, this failed to anticipate that multiple naming authorities might exist on a single server, which became a critical problem as the Web grew at an exponential rate and new domain names (the basis for naming authority within the http URL namespace) far exceeded the availability of new IP addresses.

The solution defined and deployed for both HTTP/1.0 and HTTP/1.1 was to include the target URL's host information within a Host header field of the request message. Deployment of this feature was considered so important that the HTTP/1.1 specification requires servers to reject any HTTP/1.1 request that doesn't include a Host field. As a result, there now exist many large ISP servers that run tens of thousands of name-based virtual host websites on a single IP address.

15.3.2.2 Layered Encoding

HTTP inherited its syntax for describing representation metadata from the Multipurpose Internet Mail Extensions (MIME). MIME does not define layered media types, preferring instead to only include the label of the outermost media type within the Content-Type field value. However, this prevents a recipient from determining the nature of an encoded message without decoding the layers. An early HTTP extension worked around this failing by listing the outer encoding separately within the Content-Encoding field and placing the label for the innermost media type in the Content-Type. That was a poor design decision, since it changed the semantics of Content-Type without changing its field name, resulting in confusion whenever older user agents encountered the extension.

A better solution would have been to continue treating Content-Type as the outermost media type, and use a new field to describe the nested types within that type. Unfortunately, the first extension was deployed before its faults were identified.

REST did identify the need for another layer of encoding: those placed on a message by a connector in order to improve its transferability over the network. This new layer, called a transfer encoding in reference to a similar concept in MIME, allows messages to be encoded for transfer without implying that the representation is encoded by nature. Transfer encoding can be added or removed by transfer agents, for whatever reason, without changing the semantics of the representation.

15.3.2.3 Semantic Independence

As described above, HTTP message parsing has been separated from its semantics. Message parsing, including finding and globing together the header fields, occurs entirely separate from the process of parsing the header field contents. In this way, intermediaries can quickly process and forward HTTP messages, and extensions can be deployed without breaking existing parsers.

15.3.2.4 Transport Independence

Early HTTP, including most implementations of HTTP/1.0, used the underlying transport protocol as the means for signaling the end of a response message. A server would indicate the end of a response message body by closing the TCP connection. Unfortunately, this created a significant failure condition in the protocol: a client had no means for distinguishing between a completed response and one that was truncated by some erroneous network failure. To solve this, the Content-Length header fields was redefined within HTTP/1.0 to indicate the message body length in bytes, whenever the length is known in advance, and the "chunked" transfer encoding was introduced to HTTP/1.1.

The chunked encoding allows a representation whose size is unknown at the beginning of its generation (when the header fields are sent) to have its boundaries delineated by a series of chunks that can be individually sized before being sent. It also allows metadata to be sent at the end of the message as trailers, enabling the creation of optional metadata at the origin while the message is being generated, without adding to response latency.

15.3.2.5 Size Limits

A frequent barrier to the flexibility of application-layer protocols is the tendency to over-specify size limits on protocol parameters. Although there always exist some practical limits within implementations of the protocol (e.g., available memory), specifying those limits within the protocol restricts all applications to the same limits, regardless of their implementation. The result is often a lowest-common-denominator protocol that cannot be extended much beyond the envisioning of its original creator.

There is no limit in the HTTP protocol on the length of URI, the length of header fields, the length of an representation, or the length of any field value that consists of a list of items. Although older Web clients have a well-known problem with URI that consist of more than 255 characters, it is sufficient to note that problem in the HTTP specification rather than require that all servers be so limited. The reason that this does not make for a protocol maximum is that applications within a controlled context (such as an intranet) can avoid those limits by replacing the older components.

Although we did not need to invent artificial limitations, HTTP/1.1 did need to define an appropriate set of response status codes for indicating when a given protocol element is too long for a server to process. Such response codes were added for the conditions of Request-URI too long, header field too long, and body too long. Unfortunately, there is no way for a client to indicate to a server that it may have resource limits, which leads to problems when resource-constrained devices, such as PDAs, attempt to use HTTP without a device-specific intermediary adjusting the communication.

15.3.2.6 Cache Control

Because REST tries to balance the need for efficient, low-latency behavior with the desire for semantically transparent cache behavior, it is critical that HTTP allow the application to determine the caching requirements rather than hard-code it into the protocol itself. The most important thing for the protocol to do is to fully and accurately describe the data being transferred, so that no application is fooled into thinking it has one thing when it actually has something else. HTTP/1.1 does this through the addition of the Cache-Control, Age, Etag, and Vary header fields.

15.3.2.7 Content Negotiation

All resources map a request (consisting of method, identifier, request-header fields, and sometimes a representation) to a response (consisting of a status code, response-header fields, and sometimes a representation). When an HTTP request maps to multiple representations on the server, the server may engage in content negotiation with the client in order to determine which one best meets the client's needs. This is really more of a "content selection" process than negotiation.

Although there were several deployed implementations of content negotiation, it was not included in the specification of HTTP/1.0 because there was no interoperable subset of implementations at the time it was published. This was partly due to a poor implementation within NCSA Mosaic, which would send 1KB of preference information in the header fields on every request, regardless of the negotiability of the resource. Since far less than 0.01% of all URI are negotiable in content, the result was substantially increased request latency for very little gain, which led to later browsers disregarding the negotiation features of HTTP/1.0.

Preemptive (server-driven) negotiation occurs when the server varies the response representation for a particular request method*identifier*status-code combination according to the value of the request header fields, or something external to the normal request parameters above. The client needs to be notified when this occurs, so that a cache can know when it is semantically transparent to use a particular cached response for a future request, and also so that a user agent can supply more detailed preferences than it might normally send once it knows they are having an effect on the response received. HTTP/1.1 introduced the Vary header field for this purpose. Vary simply lists the request header field dimensions under which the response may vary.

In preemptive negotiation, the user agent tells the server what it is capable of accepting. The server is then supposed to select the representation that best matches what the user agent claims to be its capabilities. However, this is a non-tractable problem because it requires not only information on what the UA will accept, but also how well it accepts each feature and to what purpose the user intends to put the representation. For example, a user that wants to view an image on screen might prefer a simple bitmap representation, but the same user with the same browser may prefer a PostScript representation if they intend to send it to a printer instead. It also depends on the user correctly configuring their browser according to their own personal content preferences. In short, a server is rarely able to make effective use of preemptive negotiation, but it was the only form of automated content selection defined by early HTTP.

HTTP/1.1 added the notion of reactive (agent-driven) negotiation. In this case, when a user agent requests a negotiated resource, the server responds with a list of the available representations. The user agent can then choose which one is best according to its own capabilities and purpose. The information about the available representations may be supplied via a separate representation (e.g., a 300 response), inside the response data (e.g., conditional HTML), or as a supplement to the "most likely" response. The latter works best for the Web because an additional interaction only becomes necessary if the user agent decides one of the other variants would be better. Reactive negotiation is simply an automated reflection of the normal browser model, which means it can take full advantage of all the performance benefits of REST.

Both preemptive and reactive negotiation suffers from the difficulty of communicating the actual characteristics of the representation dimensions (e.g., how to say that a browser supports HTML tables but not the INSERT element). However, reactive negotiation has the distinct advantages of not having to send preferences on every request, having more context information with which to make a decision when faced with alternatives, and not interfering with caches.

A third form of negotiation, transparent negotiation, is a license for an intermediary cache to act as an agent, on behalf of other agents, for selecting a better representation and initiating requests to retrieve that representation. The request may be resolved internally by another cache hit, and thus it is possible that no additional network request will be made. In so doing, however, they are performing server-driven negotiation, and must therefore add the appropriate Vary information so that other outbound caches won't be confused.

15.3.3 Performance

HTTP/1.1 focused on improving the semantics of communication between components, but there were also some improvements to user-perceived performance, albeit limited by the requirement of syntax compatibility with HTTP/1.0.

15.3.3.1 Persistent Connections

Although early HTTPS's single request/response per connection behavior made for simple implementations, it resulted in inefficient use of the underlying TCP transport due to the overhead of per-interaction set-up costs and the nature of TCP's slow-start congestion control algorithm. As a result, several extensions were proposed to combine multiple requests and responses within a single connection.

The first proposal was to define a new set of methods for encapsulating multiple requests within a single message (MGET, MHEAD, etc.) and returning the response as a MIME multipart. This was rejected because it violated several of the REST constraints. First, the client would need to know all of the requests it wanted to package before the first request could be written to the network, since a request body must be length-delimited by a content-length field set in the initial request header fields. Second, intermediaries would have to extract each of the messages to determine which ones it could satisfy locally. Finally, it effectively doubles the number of request methods and complicates mechanisms for selectively denying access to certain methods.

Instead, we adopted a form of persistent connections, which uses length-delimited messages in order to send multiple HTTP messages on a single connection. For HTTP/1.0, this was done using the "keep-alive" directive within the Connection header field. Unfortunately, that did not work in general because the header field could be forwarded by intermediaries to other intermediaries that do not understand keep-alive, resulting in a deadlock condition. HTTP/1.1 eventually settled on making persistent connections the default, thus signaling their presence via the HTTP-version value, and only using the connection-directive "close" to reverse the default.

It is important to note that persistent connections only became possible after HTTP messages were redefined to be self-descriptive and independent of the underlying transport protocol.

15.3.3.2 Write-through Caching

HTTP does not support write-back caching. An HTTP cache cannot assume that what gets written through it is the same as what would be retrievable from a subsequent request for that resource, and thus it cannot cache a PUT request body and reuse it for a later GET response. There are two reasons for this rule: 1) metadata might be generated behind-the-scenes, and 2) access control on later GET requests cannot be determined from the PUT request. However, since write actions using the Web are extremely rare, the lack of write-back caching does not have a significant impact on performance.

15.3.4 REST Mismatches in HTTP

There are several architectural mismatches present within HTTP, some due to 3rd-party extensions that were deployed external to the standards process and others due to the necessity of remaining compatible with deployed HTTP/1.0 components.

15.3.4.1 Differentiating Non-authoritative Responses

One weakness that still exists in HTTP is that there is no consistent mechanism for differentiating between authoritative responses, which are generated by the origin server in response to the current request, and non-authoritative responses that are obtained from an intermediary or cache without accessing the origin server. The distinction can be important for applications that require authoritative responses, such as the safety-critical information appliances used within the health industry, and for those times when an error response is returned and the client is left wondering whether the error was due to the origin or to some intermediary. Attempts to solve this using additional status codes did not succeed, since the authoritative nature is usually orthogonal to the response status.

HTTP/1.1 did add a mechanism to control cache behavior such that the desire for an authoritative response can be indicated. The 'no-cache' directive on a request message requires any cache to forward the request toward the origin server even if it has a cached copy of what is being requested. This allows a client to refresh a cached copy, which is known to be corrupted or stale. However, using this field on a regular basis interferes with the performance benefits of caching. A more general solution would be to require that responses be marked as non-authoritative whenever an action does not result in contacting the origin server. A Warning response header field was defined in HTTP/1.1 for this purpose (and others), but it has not been widely implemented in practice.

15.3.4.2 Cookies

An example of where an inappropriate extension has been made to the protocol to support features that contradict the desired properties of the generic interface is the introduction of site-wide state information in the form of HTTP cookies. Cookie interaction fails to match REST's model of application state, often resulting in confusion for the typical browser application.

An HTTP cookie is opaque data that can be assigned by the origin server to a user agent by including it within a Set-Cookie response header field, with the intention being that the user agent should include the same cookie on all future requests to that server until it is replaced or expires. Such cookies typically contain an array of user-specific configuration choices, or a token to be matched against the server's database on future requests. The problem is that a cookie is defined as being attached to any future requests for a given set of resource identifiers, usually encompassing an entire site, rather than being associated with the particular application state (the set of currently rendered representations) on the browser. When the browser's history functionality (the "Back" button) is subsequently used to back-up to a view prior to that reflected by the cookie, the browser's application state no longer matches the stored state represented within the cookie. Therefore, the next request sent to the same server will contain a cookie that misrepresents the current application context, leading to confusion on both sides.

Cookies also violate REST because they allow data to be passed without sufficiently identifying its semantics, thus becoming a concern for both security and privacy. The combination of cookies with the Referrer [sic] header field makes it possible to track a user as they browse between sites.

As a result, cookie-based applications on the Web will never be reliable. The same functionality should have been accomplished via anonymous authentication and true client-side state. A state mechanism that involves preferences can be more efficiently implemented using judicious use of context-setting URI rather than cookies, where judicious means one URI per state rather than an unbounded number of URI due to the embedding of a user-id. Likewise, the use of cookies to identify a user-specific "shopping basket" within a server-side database could be more efficiently implemented by defining the semantics of shopping items within the hypermedia data formats, allowing the user agent to select and store those items within their own client-side shopping basket, complete with a URI to be used for check-out when the client is ready to purchase.

15.3.4.3 Mandatory Extensions

HTTP header field names can be extended at will, but only when the information they contain is not required for proper understanding of the message. Mandatory header field extensions require a major protocol revision or a substantial change to method semantics, such as that proposed in. This is an aspect of the modern Web architecture, which does not yet match the self-descriptive messaging constraints of the REST architectural style, primarily because the cost of implementing a mandatory extension framework within the existing HTTP syntax exceeds any clear benefits that we might gain from mandatory extensions. However, it is reasonable to expect that mandatory field name extensions will be supported in the next major revision of HTTP, when the existing constraints on backwards-compatibility of syntax no longer apply.

15.3.4.4 Mixing Metadata

HTTP is designed to extend the generic connector interface across a network connection. As such, it is intended to match the characteristics of that interface, including the delineation of parameters as control data, metadata, and representation. However, two of the most significant limitations of the HTTP/1.x protocol family are that it fails to syntactically distinguish between representation metadata and message control information (both transmitted as header fields) and does not allow metadata to be effectively layered for message integrity checks.

REST identified these as limitations in the protocol early in the standardization process, anticipating that they would lead to problems in the deployment of other features, such as persistent connections and digest authentication. Workarounds were developed, including adding the Connection header field to identify per-connection control data that is unsafe to be forwarded by intermediaries, as well as an algorithm for the canonical treatment of header field digests.

15.3.4.5 MIME Syntax

HTTP inherited its message syntax from MIME in order to retain commonality with other Internet protocols and reuse many of the standardized fields for describing media types in messages. Unfortunately, MIME and HTTP have very different goals, and the syntax is only designed for MIME's goals.

In MIME, a user agent is sending a bunch of information, which is intended to be treated as a coherent whole, to an unknown recipient with which they never directly interact. MIME assumes that the agent would want to send all that information in one message, since sending multiple messages across Internet mail is less efficient. Thus, MIME syntax is constructed to package messages within a part or multipart in much the way postal carriers wraps packages in extra paper.

In HTTP, packaging different objects within a single message doesn't make any sense other than for secure encapsulation or packaged archives, since it is more efficient to make separate requests for those documents not already cached. Thus, HTTP applications use media types like HTML as containers for references to the "package" -- a user agent can then choose what parts of the package to retrieve as separate requests. Although it is possible that HTTP could use a multipart package in which only the non-URI resources were included after the first part, there hasn't been much demand for it.

The problem with MIME syntax is that it assumes the transport is lossy, deliberately corrupting things like line breaks and content lengths. The syntax is therefore verbose and inefficient for any system not based on a lossy transport, which makes it inappropriate for HTTP. Since HTTP/1.1 has the capability to support deployment of incompatible protocols, retaining the MIME syntax won't be necessary for the next major version of HTTP, even though it will likely continue to use the many standardized protocol elements for representation metadata.

15.3.5 Matching Responses to Requests

HTTP messages fail to be self-descriptive when it comes to describing which response belongs with which request. Early HTTP was based on a single request and response per connection, so there was no perceived need for message control data that would tie the response back to the request that invoked it. Therefore, the ordering of requests determines the ordering of responses, which means that HTTP relies on the transport connection to determine the match.

HTTP/1.1, though defined to be independent of the transport protocol, still assumes that communication takes place on a synchronous transport. It could easily be extended to work on an asynchronous transport, such as e-mail, through the addition of a request identifier. Such an extension would be useful for agents in a broadcast or multicast situation, where responses might be received on a channel different from that of the request. Also, in a situation where many requests are pending, it would allow the server to choose the order in which responses are transferred, such that smaller or more significant responses are sent first.

15.4 Technology Transfer

Although REST had its most direct influence over the authoring of Web standards, validation of its use as an architectural design model came through the deployment of the standards in the form of commercial-grade implementations.

15.4.1 Deployment experience with libwww-perl

My involvement in the definition of Web standards began with development of the maintenance robot MOM spider and its associated protocol library, libwww-perl. Modeled after the original libwww developed by Tim Berners-Lee and the WWW project at CERN, libwww-perl provided a uniform interface for making Web requests and interpreting Web responses for client applications written in the Perl language. It was the first Web protocol library to be developed independent of the original CERN project, reflecting a more modern interpretation of the Web interface than was present in older code bases. This interface became the basis for designing REST.

Libwww-perl consisted of a single request interface that used Perl's self-evaluating code features to dynamically load the appropriate transport protocol package based on the scheme of the requested URI. For example, when asked to make a "GET" request on the URL http://www.ebuilt.com/, libwww-perl would extract the scheme from the URL ("http") and use it to construct a call to wwwhttp'request (), using an interface that was common to all types of resources (HTTP, FTP, WAIS, local files, etc.). In order to achieve this generic interface, the library treated all calls in much the same way as an HTTP proxy. It provided an interface using Perl data structures that had the same semantics as an HTTP request, regardless of the type of resource.

Libwww-perl demonstrated the benefits of a generic interface. Within a year of its initial release, over 600 independent software developers were using the library for their own client tools, ranging from command-line download scripts to full-blown browsers. It is currently the basis for most Web system administration tools.

15.4.2 Deployment experience with Apache

As the specification effort for HTTP began to take the form of complete specifications, we needed server software that could both effectively demonstrate the proposed standard protocol and serve as a test-bed for worthwhile extensions. At the time, the most popular HTTP server (httpd) was the public domain software developed by Rob McCool at the National Center for Supercomputing Applications, University of

Illinois, and Urbana-Champaign (NCSA). However, development had stalled after Rob left NCSA in mid-1994, and many webmasters had developed their own extensions and bug fixes that were in need of a common distribution. A group of us created a mailing list for the purpose of coordinating our changes as "patches" to the original source. In the process, we created the Apache HTTP Server Project.

The Apache project is a collaborative software development effort aimed at creating a robust, commercial-grade, full-featured, open-source software implementation of an HTTP server. The project is jointly managed by a group of volunteers located around the world, using the Internet and the Web to communicate, plan, and develop the server and its related documentation. These volunteers are known as the Apache Group. More recently, the group formed the nonprofit Apache Software Foundation to act as a legal and financial umbrella organization for supporting continued development of the Apache open source projects.

Apache became known for both its robust behavior in response to the varied demands of an Internet service and for its rigorous implementation of the HTTP protocol standards. I served as the "protocol cop" within the Apache Group, writing code for the core HTTP parsing functions, supporting the efforts of others by explaining the standards, and acting as an advocate for the Apache developers' views of "the right way to implement HTTP" within the standards forums. Many of the lessons described in this chapter were learned as a result of creating and testing various implementations of HTTP within the Apache project, and subjecting the theories behind the protocol to the Apache Group's critical review.

Apache httpd is widely regarded as one of the most successful software projects, and one of the first open-source software products to dominate a market in which there exists significant commercial competition. The July 2000 Net craft survey of public Internet websites found over 20 million sites based on the Apache software, representing over 65% of all sites surveyed [http://www.netcraft.com/survey/]. Apache was the first major server to support the HTTP/1.1 protocol and is generally considered the reference implementation against which all client software is tested. The Apache Group received the 1999 ACM Software System Award as recognition of our impact on the standards for the Web architecture.

15.4.3 Deployment of URI and HTTP/1.1-compliant Software

In addition to Apache, many other projects, both commercial and open-source in nature, have adopted and deployed software products based on the protocols of the modern Web architecture. Though it may be only a coincidence, Microsoft Internet Explorer surpassed Netscape Navigator in the Web browser market share shortly after they were the first major browsers to implement the HTTP/1.1 client standard. In addition, many of the individual HTTP extensions that were defined during the standardization process, such as the Host header field, have now reached universal deployment.

The REST architectural style succeeded in guiding the design and deployment of the modern Web architecture. To date, there have been no significant problems caused by the introduction of the new standards, even though they have been subject to gradual and fragmented deployment alongside legacy Web applications. Furthermore, the new standards have had a positive effect on the robustness of the Web and enabled new methods for improving user-perceived performance through caching hierarchies and content distribution networks.

15.5 Architectural Lessons

There are a number of general architectural lessons to be learned from the modern Web architecture and the problems identified by REST.

15.5.1 Advantages of a Network-based API

What distinguishes the modern Web from other middleware is the way in which it uses HTTP as a network-based Application Programming Interface (API). This was not always the case. The early Web design made use of a library package, CERN libwww, as the single implementation library for all clients and servers. CERN libwww provided a library-based API for building interoperable Web components.

A library-based API provides a set of code entry points and associated symbol/parameter sets so that a programmer can use someone else's code to do the dirty work of maintaining the actual interface between like systems, provided that the programmer obeys the architectural and language restrictions that come with that code. The assumption is that all sides of the communication use the same API, and therefore the internals of the interface are only important to the API developer and not the application developer.

The single library approach ended in 1993 because it did not match the social dynamics of the organizations involved in developing the Web. When the team at NCSA increased the pace of Web development with a much larger development team than had ever been present at CERN, the libwww source was "forked" (split into separately maintained code bases) so that the folks at NCSA would not have to wait for CERN to catch-up with their improvements. At the same time, independent developers such as myself began developing protocol libraries for languages and platforms not yet supported by the CERN code. The design of the Web had to shift from the development of a reference protocol library to the development of a network-based API, extending the desired semantics of the Web across multiple platforms and implementations.

A network-based API is an on-the-wire syntax, with defined semantics, for application interactions. A network-based API does not place any restrictions on the application code aside from the need to read/write to the network, but does place restrictions on the set of semantics that can be effectively communicated across the interface. On the plus side, performance is only bounded by the protocol design and not by any particular implementation of that design.

A library-based API does a lot more for the programmer, but in doing so creates a great deal more complexity and baggage than is needed by any one system, is less portable in a heterogeneous network, and always results in generality being preferred over performance. As a side effect, it also leads to lazy development (blaming the API code for everything) and failure to account for non-cooperative behavior by other parties in the communication.

However, it is important to keep in mind that there are various layers involved in any architecture, including that of the modern Web. Systems like the Web use one library API (sockets) in order to access several network-based APIs (e.g., HTTP and FTP), but the socket API itself is below the application-layer. Likewise, libwww is an interesting cross-breed in that it has evolved into a library-based API for accessing a network-based API, and thus provides reusable code without assuming other communicating applications are using libwww as well.

This is in contrast to middleware like CORBA. Since CORBA only allows communication via an ORB, its transfer protocol, IIOP, assumes too much about what the parties are communicating. HTTP request messages include standardized application semantics, whereas IIOP messages do not. The "Request" token in IIOP only supplies directionality so that the ORB can route it according to whether the ORB itself is supposed to reply (e.g., "Locate Request") or if an object will interpret it. The semantics are expressed by the combination of an object key and operation, which are object-specific rather than standardized across all objects.

An independent developer can generate the same bits as an IIOP request without using the same ORB, but the bits themselves are defined by the CORBA API and its Interface Definition Language (IDL). They need a UUID generated by an IDL compiler, a structured binary content that mirrors that IDL operation's signature, and the definition of the reply data type(s) according to the IDL specification. The semantics are thus not defined by the network interface (IIOP), but by the object's IDL spec. Whether this is a good thing or not depends on the application -- for distributed objects it is a necessity, for the Web it isn't.

Why is this important? Because it differentiates a system where network intermediaries can be effective agents from a system where they can be, at most, routers.

This kind of difference is also seen in the interpretation of a message as a unit or as a stream. HTTP allows the recipient or the sender to decide that on their own. CORBA IDL doesn't even allow streams (yet), but even when it does get extended to support streams, both sides of the communication will be tied to the same API, rather than being free to use whatever is most appropriate for their type of application.

15.5.2 HTTP is not RPC

People often mistakenly refer to HTTP as a remote procedure call (RPC) mechanism simply because it involves requests and responses. What distinguishes RPC from other forms of network-based application communication is the notion of invoking a procedure on the remote machine, wherein the protocol identifies the procedure and passes it a fixed set of parameters, and then waits for the answer to be supplied within a return message using the same interface. Remote method invocation (RMI) is similar, except that the procedure is identified as an {object, method} tuple rather than a service procedure. Brokered RMI adds name service indirection and a few other tricks, but the interface is basically the same.

What distinguishes HTTP from RPC isn't the syntax. It isn't even the different characteristics gained from using a stream as a parameter, though that helps to explain why existing RPC mechanisms were not usable for the Web. What makes HTTP significantly different from RPC is that the requests are directed to resources using a generic interface with standard semantics that can be interpreted by intermediaries almost as well as by the machines that originate services. The result is an application that allows for layers of transformation and indirection that are independent of the information origin, which is very useful for an Internet-scale, multi-organization, anarchically scalable information system. RPC mechanisms, in contrast, are defined in terms of language APIs, not network-based applications.

15.5.3 HTTP is not a Transport Protocol

HTTP is not designed to be a transport protocol. It is a transfer protocol in which the messages reflect the semantics of the Web architecture by performing actions on resources through the transfer and manipulation of representations of those resources. It is possible to achieve a wide range of functionality using this very simple interface, but following the interface is required in order for HTTP semantics to remain visible to intermediaries.

That is why HTTP goes through firewalls. Most of the recently proposed extensions to HTTP, aside from WebDAV, have merely used HTTP as a way to move other application protocols through a firewall, which is a fundamentally misguided idea. Not only does it defeat the purpose of having a firewall, but also it won't work for the long term because firewall vendors will simply have to perform additional protocol filtering. It therefore makes no sense to do those extensions on top of HTTP, since the only thing HTTP accomplishes in that situation is to add overhead from legacy syntax. A true application of HTTP maps the protocol user's actions to something that can be expressed using HTTP semantics, thus creating a network-based API to services, which can be understood by agents and intermediaries without any knowledge of the application.

15.5.4 Design of Media Types

One aspect of REST that is unusual for an architectural style is the degree to which it influences the definition of data elements within the Web architecture.

15.5.4.1 Application State in a Network-based System

REST defines a model of expected application behavior, which supports simple and robust applications that are largely immune from the partial failure conditions that beset most network-based applications. However, that doesn't stop application developers from introducing features, which violate the model. The most frequent violations are in regard to the constraints on application state and stateless interaction.

Architectural mismatches due to misplaced application state are not limited to HTTP cookies. The introduction of "frames" to the Hypertext Markup Language (HTML) caused similar confusion. Frames allow a browser window to be partitioned into sub windows, each with its own navigational state. Link selections within a sub window are indistinguishable from normal transitions, but the resulting response representation is rendered within the sub window instead of the full browser application workspace. This is fine provided that no link exits the realm of information that is intended for sub window treatment, but when it does occur the user finds them self-viewing one application wedged within the sub context of another application.

For both frames and cookies, the failure was in providing indirect application state that could not be managed or interpreted by the user agent. A design that placed this information within a primary representation, thereby informing the user agent on how to manage the hypermedia workspace for a specified realm of resources, could have accomplished the same tasks without violating the REST constraints, while leading to a better user interface and less interference with caching.

15.5.4.2 Incremental Processing

By including latency reduction as an architectural goal, REST can differentiate media types (the data format of representations) according to their user-perceived performance. Size, structure, and capacity for incremental rendering all have an impact on the latency encountered transferring, rendering, and manipulating representation media types, and thus can significantly impact system performance.

HTML is an example of a media type that, for the most part, has good latency characteristics. Information within early HTML could be rendered as it was received, because all of the rendering information was available early -- within the standardized definitions of the small set of mark-up tags that made up HTML. However, there are aspects of HTML that were not designed well for latency. Examples include: placement of embedded metadata within the HEAD of a document, resulting in optional information needing to be transferred and processed before the rendering engine can read the parts that display something useful to the user; embedded images without rendering size hints, requiring that the first few bytes of the image (the part that contains the layout size) be received before the rest of the surrounding HTML can be displayed; dynamically sized table columns, requiring that the rendered read and determine sizes for the entire table before it can start displaying the top; and, lazy rules regarding the parsing of malformed mark-up syntax, often requiring that the rendering engine parse through an entire file before it can determine that one key mark-up character is missing.

15.5.4.3 Java versus JavaScript

REST can also be used to gain insight into why some media types have had greater adoption within the Web architecture than others, even when the balance of developer opinion is not in their favor. The case of Java applets versus JavaScript is one example.

Java TM is a popular programming language that was originally developed for applications within television set-top boxes, but first gained notoriety when it was introduced to the Web as a means for implementing code-on-demand functionality. Although the language received a tremendous amount of press support from its owner, Sun Microsystems, Inc., and rave reviews from software developers seeking an alternative to the C++ language, it has failed to be widely adopted by application developers for code-on-demand within the Web.

Shortly after Java's introduction, developers at Netscape Communications Corporation created a separate language for embedded code-on-demand, originally called Live Script, but later changed to the name JavaScript for marketing reasons (the two languages have relatively little in common other than that). Although initially derided for being embedded with HTML and yet not compatible with proper HTML syntax, JavaScript usage has steadily increased ever since its introduction.

The question is: why is JavaScript more successful on the Web than Java? It certainly isn't because of its technical quality as a language, since both its syntax and execution environment are considered poor when compared to Java. It also isn't because of marketing: Sun far outspent Netscape in that regard, and continues to do so. It isn't because of any intrinsic characteristics of the languages either, since Java has been more successful than JavaScript within all other programming areas (stand-alone applications, servlets, etc.). In order to better understand the reasons for this discrepancy, we need to evaluate Java in terms of its characteristics as a representation media type within REST.

JavaScript better fits the deployment model of Web technology. It has a much lower entry-barrier, both in terms of its overall complexity as a language and the amount of initial effort required by a novice programmer to put together their first piece of working code. JavaScript also has less impact on the visibility of interactions. Independent organizations can read, verify, and copy the JavaScript source code in the same way that they could copy HTML. Java, in contrast, is downloaded as binary packaged archives -- the user is therefore left to trust the security restrictions within the Java execution environment. Likewise, Java has many more features that are considered questionable to allow within a secure environment, including the ability to send RMI requests back to the origin server. RMI does not support visibility for intermediaries.

Perhaps the most important distinction between the two, however, is that JavaScript causes less user-perceived latency. JavaScript is usually downloaded as part of the primary representation, whereas Java applets require a separate request. Java code, once converted to the byte code format, is much larger than typical JavaScript. Finally, whereas JavaScript can be executed while the rest of the HTML page is downloading, Java requires that the complete package of class files be downloaded and installed before the application can begin. Java, therefore, does not support incremental rendering.

Once the characteristics of the languages are laid out along the same lines as the rationale behind REST's constraints, it becomes much easier to evaluate the technologies in terms of their behavior within the modern Web architecture.

15.6 Summary

This chapter described the experiences and lessons learned from applying REST while authoring the Internet standards for the Hypertext Transfer Protocol (HTTP) and Uniform Resource Identifiers (URI). These two specifications define the generic interface used by all component interactions on the Web. In addition, we have described the experiences and lessons learned from the deployment of these technologies in the form of the libwww-perl client library, the Apache HTTP Server Project, and other implementations of the protocol standards.

Each one of us has, somewhere in his heart, the dream to make a living world, a universe. Those of us who have been trained as architects have this desire perhaps at the very center of our lives: that one day, somewhere, somehow, we shall build one building which is wonderful, beautiful, breathtaking, a place where people can walk and dream for centuries.

At the beginning of our efforts within the Internet Engineering Taskforce to define the existing Hypertext Transfer Protocol (HTTP/1.0) and design the extensions for the new standards of HTTP/1.1 and Uniform Resource Identifiers (URI), I recognized the need for a model of how the World Wide Web should work. This idealized model of the interactions within an overall Web application, referred to as the Representational State Transfer (REST) architectural style, became the foundation for the modern Web architecture, providing the guiding principles by which flaws in the preexisting architecture could be identified and extensions validated prior to deployment.

REST is a coordinated set of architectural constraints that attempts to minimize latency and network communication while at the same time maximizing the independence and scalability of component implementations. This is achieved by placing constraints on connector semantics where other styles have focused on component semantics. REST enables the caching and reuse of interactions, dynamic substitutability of components, and processing of actions by intermediaries, thereby meeting the needs of an Internet-scale distributed hypermedia system.

The following contributions to the field of Information and Computer Science have been made as part of this dissertation:

- a framework for understanding software architecture through architectural styles, including a consistent set of terminology for describing software architecture;
- a classification of architectural styles for network-based application software by the architectural properties they would induce when applied to the architecture for a distributed hypermedia system;
- REST, a novel architectural style for distributed hypermedia systems; and,
- Application and evaluation of the REST architectural style in the design and deployment of the architecture for the modern World Wide Web.

The modern Web is one instance of REST-style architecture. Although Web-based applications can include access to other styles of interaction, the central focus of its protocol and performance concerns is distributed hypermedia. REST elaborates only those portions of the architecture that are considered essential for Internet-scale distributed hypermedia interaction. Areas for improvement of the Web architecture can be seen where existing protocols fail to express all of the potential semantics for component interaction, and where the details of syntax can be replaced with more efficient forms without changing the architecture capabilities. Likewise, proposed extensions can be compared to REST to see if they fit within the architecture; if not, it is more efficient to redirect that functionality to a system running in parallel with a more applicable architectural style.

In an ideal world, the implementation of a software system would exactly match its design. Some features of the modern Web architecture do correspond exactly to their design criteria in REST, such as the use of URI as resource identifiers and the use of Internet media types to identify representation data formats. However, there are also some aspects of the modern Web protocols that exist in spite of the architectural design, due to legacy experiments that failed (but must be retained for backwards compatibility) and extensions deployed by developers unaware of the architectural style. REST provides a model not only for the development and evaluation of new features, but also for the identification and understanding of broken features.

The World Wide Web is arguably the world's largest distributed application. Understanding the key architectural principles underlying the Web can help explain its technical success and may lead to improvements in other distributed applications, particularly those that are amenable to the same or similar methods of interaction. REST contributes both the rationale behind the modern Web's software architecture and a significant lesson in how software engineering principles can be systematically applied in the design and evaluation of a real software system.

For network-based applications, system performance is dominated by network communication. For a distributed hypermedia system, component interactions consist of large-grain data transfers rather than computation-intensive tasks. The REST style was developed in response to those needs. Its focus upon the generic connector interface of resources and representations has enabled intermediate processing, caching, and substitutability of components, which in turn has allowed Web-based applications to scale from 100,000 requests/day in 1994 to 600,000,000 requests/day in 1999.

The REST architectural style has been validated through six years of development of the HTTP/1.0 and HTTP/1.1 standards, elaboration of the URI and relative URL standards, and successful deployment of several dozen independently developed, commercial-grade software systems within the modern Web architecture. It has served as both a model for design guidance and as an acid test for architectural extensions to the Web protocols.

Future work will focus on extending the architectural guidance toward the development of a replacement for the HTTP/1.x protocol family, using a more efficient tokenized syntax, but without losing the desirable properties identified by REST. The needs of wireless devices, which have many characteristics in common with the principles behind REST, will motivate further enhancements for application-level protocol design and architectures involving active intermediaries. There has also been some interest in extending REST to consider variable request priorities, differentiated quality-of-service, and representations consisting of continuous data streams, such as those generated by broadcast audio and video sources.

15.7 Review Questions

1. Discuss the following
    - Redefinition of Resource
    - Manipulating Shadows
    - Remote Authoring
    - Binding Semantics to URI
    - REST Mismatches in URI
    - REST Applied to HTTP
    - Extensibility
    - Self-descriptive Messages
    - Performance
2. Explain the REST Mismatches in HTTP Matching Responses to Requests.